The
BOOK OF
INVESTING WISDOM

ALSO AVAILABLE IN THE WISDOM SERIES

The Book of Business Wisdom

Offers 54 essays from such legends of commerce and industry as John D. Rockefeller, Jack Welch, Sam Walton, P. T. Barnum, J. Paul Getty, Andrew Grove, and Henry Ford.

Topics include: the essentials of good management, how to get ahead, and maintaining individuality in the corporate world.

The Book of Leadership Wisdom

Offers 52 essays from such legendary leaders as Andrew Carnegie, David Packard, Bill Gates, Michael Eisner, H. Ross Perot, Katharine Graham, Akio Morita, and T. Coleman Du Pont.

Topics include: leading revolution, dealing with adversity, and corporate culture.

COMING IN THE FALL OF 1999:

The Book of Entrepreneurial Wisdom

Offers 50 essays from such entrepreneurs as Lillian Vernon, Michael Dell, Ben Franklin, Howard Schultz, Colonel Sanders, and Warren Avis.

Topics include: the gunslinging attitude and other necessary characteristics, the start-up, and entrepreneurial management.

The
BOOK OF
INVESTING
WISDOM

Classic Writings by
Great Stock-Pickers and Legends of Wall Street

Edited by Peter Krass

John Wiley & Sons, Inc.

New York • Chichester • Weinheim • Brisbane • Singapore • Toronto

Copyright © 1999 by Peter Krass. All rights reserved.

Published by John Wiley & Sons, Inc.

Published simultaneously in Canada.

The Book of Investing Wisdom™ is a trademark of John Wiley & Sons, Inc.

This publication is designed to provide accurate and authoritative
information in regard to the subject matter covered. It is sold with the
understanding that the publisher is not engaged in rendering legal,
accounting, or other professional services. If legal advice or other
expert assistance is required, the services of a competent professional
person should be sought.

Library of Congress Cataloging-in-Publication Data:

The book of investing wisdom : classic writings by great stock-pickers
   and legends of Wall Street / edited by Peter Krass.
         p.   cm.
   Includes bibliographical references and index.
   ISBN 0-471-29454-3 (cloth : alk. paper)
     1. Investment analysis.   2. Securities.   I. Krass, Peter.
   HG4529.B66   1999
   332.6—dc21   98-54153
                                                            CIP

Printed in the United States of America.

10 9 8 7 6 5 4 3 2 1

Contents

Contents

Contents

Contents

Introduction

*W*all *Street.* The phrase alone conjures up a spectrum of words and images, from wise investing to reckless gambling, from power deals to pots of gold, from venerable legends like Warren Buffett to infamous traders like Michael Milken. But legends and allure aside, most of us, in some way, are connected to Wall Street and the phrenetic world of investing. Whether we be professional money managers, do-it-yourself investors, or simply are vested in a 401(k) plan, a chunk of our personal money is in securities. That's why even amateurs must be not only Wall Street literate, but savvy as to what they have invested in and why. The need to be a superb student extends to the pros, too—just ask Warren Buffett, who studied religiously under Benjamin Graham.

But why do we need such an edge? Because, ever since the day the French aristocracy first started trading forward contracts for commodities in the twelfth century, every broker, trader, and investor has looked for that advantage to buy cheap and sell dear—and sometimes that means blindsiding the sucker. As the notorious stock manipulator Daniel Drew allegedly said, "To speckilate as an outsider is like trying to drive black pigs in the dark." Not that insiders are guaranteed success, according to Peter Lynch, who wrote in *One Up on Wall Street* that "professional investing" is an oxymoron on a par with "military intelligence." So where does that leave the pro as well as the amateur? In need of recruiting a panel of the greatest stock-pickers and market gurus, past and present, to instruct on the art of investing. Where can we find such a panel? Here in *The Book of Investing Wisdom*.

Wall Street. From its historical beginnings, it has been an epicenter for epic battles, financial and otherwise. One large step backward in time is necessary to give full meaning to Wall Street. Its roots lay in 1624, when the Dutch founded and settled New Amsterdam on the southern tip of Manhattan, reportedly buying it from the native Americans for about $24 worth of trinkets (a deal Donald Trump, who concludes this collection, must certainly admire). Unfortunately for the Dutch, the British also had their eyes on this upscale piece of property, and the residents of New Amsterdam were forced to build a 12-foot-high wooden stockade to protect themselves from repeated attacks. Not to be stymied, in 1664 the British simply sailed their cannon-laden warships into the harbor, and the Dutch surrendered. In 1685, the British built a road along the line of the stockade, which had been torn down, and named it Wall Street. Little did they know that on this same spot the financing would be raised to pay for the war that would expel them from the United States.

While the French had been trading paper since the twelfth century and the English had established securities markets by 1720, the United States did not witness any securities trading until the Revolutionary War, when a smattering of bonds were issued to raise fighting money. However, the first major issue of U.S. securities did not come until 1790, when the Federal Government issued $80 million in bonds to refinance all war debt. And so, the national debt was birthed. At that time New York City was the nation's capital, so it immediately took center stage in American finance, and public securities auctions were held there twice daily in 1791 and 1792. The first step toward a more formal stock exchange came in 1792, when 24 prominent brokers gathered under a buttonwood tree on Wall Street and signed the "Buttonwood Agreement," which established a bond of trust between them and—more important—set minimum commission rates. The New York Stock Exchange traces its roots to that historic day. Of course, as the market flourished, it wasn't long before those once-trusting brokers entered into skirmishes against each other; their fights, however, were a bit more civilized than those that took place there between the Dutch and the British.

The ensuing battles along Wall Street involved more slick financial skills than weapons, although Jim Fisk, stock manipulator extraordinaire and major player in the infamous gold corner of 1869, was shot to death by a jealous rival— both men were courting the same woman. The financial skulduggery of Fisk and his cronies, like Daniel Drew (see Part VI, "Lessons from Notorious Characters"), were important to Wall Street, as they actually served as catalysts for stock exchange reform. They were operating in the mid-1800s, when railroads ruled the country, both powering economic development and controlling the flow of goods. The first railroad stock was listed in 1830, when there were only 73 miles of track. Ten years later there would be 3,328 miles of track and 13 railroad stocks listed, providing ample opportunity for manipulating prices and stock watering. One result: In 1866, the New York Stock Exchange began requiring companies to provide financial reports to help prevent deceptive practices.

Other major reforms also followed scandal or financial disasters. As a result of the 1907 panic (see Frank Vanderlip), the Federal Reserve System was established in 1913; after the 1929 crash (see Edwin Lefèvre), the Securities Exchange Commission was established in 1934; after the 1987 crash (see George Soros), the SEC instituted measures to control the extreme price movements that resulted from the growth of computer-generated trades. Since the mid-1800s, technical innovations have helped modernize the various exchanges. In 1844 the telegraph was invented, paving the way for brokers to operate effectively in every American city—they could receive timely news for making decisions and were able to execute trades immediately. In 1867 the first practical ticker was introduced, which also aided the dissemination of information in real time. These technological innovations made the stock exchanges more accessible to the population.

By the early 1900s, the stock market was a pop phenomenon, with songs such as "Bulls and Bears March and Two Step" hitting the street circa 1901, and with Stock Market Cigars being manufactured by an Ohio company circa 1903. American culture and the stock market became intertwined forever, a subject tackled by Robert Prechter, whose essay, "Elvis, Frankenstein and Andy Warhol," appears in Part IV. One of the results of the rising popularity of the stock market in the early 1900s was rampant speculation by the small investor. Meanwhile, a new school of thought was formulating in the mind of one Benjamin Graham, who began his Wall Street career in 1914 and quickly recognized the need to cut through all this speculative nonsense that had taken hold of America.

In his memoirs, Graham recalled that a burgeoning financial services industry, which included pioneers John Moody and Roger W. Babson, was providing huge quantities of information ripe for analysis. "But in 1914," Graham wrote, "this mass of financial information was largely going to waste in the area of common stock analysis. The figures were not ignored, but they were studied superficially and with little interest. . . . To a large degree, therefore, I found Wall Street virgin territory for examination by a genuine, penetrating analysis of security values." The ultimate result was his seminal 1934 book, *Security Analysis*, coauthored by David Dodd, which is now regarded as the investor's bible. Graham sought to discover the true value of a company and return expectations through diligent analysis, not through inside information, rumors, tips, and flights of fancy.

The importance of securities analysis cannot be ignored or treated lightly, which is why *The Book of Investing Wisdom* begins with "The Nuts and Bolts of Analysis," and who better to lead off the section than Warren Buffett, who worked and studied under Graham. As with the prior two collections in this series, *The Book of Business Wisdom* and *The Book of Leadership Wisdom,* this anthology is organized into eight thematic parts to address different aspects of investing and to provide insight into the various nuances of the exchanges. Each section is introduced with a few lines to summarize its purpose and to pull out some of the dominant themes. For example, Part II focuses on the attitude the investor needs to bring to the table, and one of the themes is skepticism—John Bogle, founder of The Vanguard Group, warns the investor about "past performance syndrome," which is a money manager's propensity to promote past successes when you should be focusing on the present. In another example, Part V provides the opportunity to look at investing from the professional's perspective. In this section, hedge-fund manager Michael Steinhardt writes that "short selling is psychologically unnerving and takes a greater degree of discipline than that needed in buying stocks." He goes on to admit that he is not sure the trading volume and portfolio turnover they generate is justified.

Not all of the authors are great stock-pickers; for example, B. C. Forbes was William Randolph Hearst's top finance columnist before founding *Forbes* magazine, and Edwin Lefèvre was a prolific financial journalist who wrote the investment classic, *Reminiscences of a Stock Operator.* Regardless, these astute observers of Wall Street have a wealth of information to share. Regrettably, for a variety of reasons a few prominent names are missing from the collection. The primary reason: The right stuff for this kind of collection wasn't available. Some prudent investment gurus are not going to share their secrets, except for the occasional sound bite. In other cases, a particular essay might be too constrained to the time when it was written or might even be too technical and dry.

The ultimate purpose of *The Book of Investing Wisdom* is to help you make money. Whether you are an amateur or a professional investor, you'll find practical advice, strategic wisdom, and intriguing history in *The Book of Investing Wisdom*. Investing doesn't have to be like a throw of the dice at the craps table or a wild roller coaster ride at the amusement park. Taking the gambling out of investing requires diligent study. Who better to learn from and be inspired by than the panel of investor laureates assembled here?

PART I

The Nuts and Bolts of Analysis

First and foremost, all investors must do their homework—only doing this homework well doesn't mean getting a gold star from the teacher. The stakes are higher—it makes the difference between winning and losing fortunes. In the opening essay, Warren Buffett declares that facts about a company and its track record rule whether to invest. Having the facts right makes you right, and what others say, whether they are company spokespeople or the media, must be ignored. In addition to studying a company's financials, reading up on economic and political issues can be crucial. As Jim Rogers, who was once George Soros' partner, warns: "The smart investor learns to listen to the popular press with an ear tuned for panic extremes." The essays in Part I make it clear that analysis goes beyond looking at P/E ratios and book values.

WARREN E. BUFFETT
1930–

As a youngster, the billionaire investor was said to have discovered money like "Mozart discovered music." Warren Buffett
operated two paper routes, retrieved golf balls and resold them,
and then later graduated to managing pinball machines in the
local barbershops, among other endeavors. Born and raised in
Omaha, he has chosen to remain there even after all the success.
A colleague once pointed out the advantage: "Warren's kept his
perspective clear by living in Omaha, away from it all, and looking at what's important rather than what's urgent or fashionable."
His well-grounded philosophy is the result of having worked as
an analyst under the conservative Benjamin Graham, the undis-
puted father of modern securities analysis.

After a two-year apprenticeship with Graham, Buffett returned
to Omaha and set up his own investment partnership with
$100,000. Some 30 years later, Omaha was reputed to have 52
"Buffett millionaires." For all his conservatism, Buffett did something radical in 1969: He simply dissolved the partnership in the
midst of a bull market. He believed that the entire market was
overpriced, and no stock winners could be found or held. At that
time, he also admitted, "My idea quota used to be like Niagra
Falls—I'd have many more than I could use. Now it's as though
someone had damned up the water and was letting it flow with
an eyedropper." The investor's version of writer's block.

Not to worry, Buffett went on to become one of the richest
people in the United States by taking aggressive stock positions
in companies like Coca-Cola, Geico, and the Washington Post
Company. One firm he came to control virtually by accident was
Berkshire Hathaway, Inc. It was a down-and-out textile company
when he ran across it in 1962. Its stock was trading below $8,
but he realized it had $16.50 per share of working capital alone.
The rest is history. One of the key elements that goes into Buffett's analysis is the company's past performance and managerial
competence, which he discusses in *Track Record Is Everything*.
To make his point, Buffett indulges in a smattering of both
serious and hilarious anecdotes that include allusions to Albert
Einstein, Saint Peter, and the Kentucky Derby.

Track Record Is Everything
Warren E. Buffett

I've often felt there might be more to be gained by studying business failures than business successes. In my business, we try to study where people go astray, and why things don't work. We try to avoid mistakes. If my job was to pick a group of 10 stocks in the Dow Jones average that would outperform the average itself, I would probably not start by trying to pick the 10 best. Instead, I would try to pick the 10 or 15 worst performers and take them out of the sample, and work with the residual. It's an inversion process. Albert Einstein said, "Invert, always invert, in mathematics and physics," and it's a very good idea in busines, too. Start out with failure, and then engineer its removal.

---

*Unfortunately . . . what happens in business
and investments [is that] people know better,
but when they hear a rumor—particularly
when they hear it from a high place—they just
can't resist the temptation to go along.*

In Berkshire Hathaway Inc.'s 1989 annual report, I wrote about something I called the "institutional imperative." I didn't learn about it in business school, but it tends to have an enormous impact on how businesses are actually run. One of its main tenets is a copycat mechanism that decrees that any craving of a leader, however foolish, will be quickly supported by detailed rate-of-return and strategic studies prepared by his troops.

For example, every time it becomes fashionable to expand into some new line of business, some companies will expand into it. Then they get out of it about five years later, licking their wounds. It's very human; people do the same thing with their stocks.

I've often felt there might be more to be gained by studying business failures than business successes.

To illustrate, let me tell you the story of the oil prospector who met St. Peter at the Pearly Gates. When told his occupation, St. Peter said, "Oh, I'm really sorry. You seem to meet all the tests to get into heaven. But we've got a terrible problem. See that pen over there? That's where we keep the oil prospectors waiting to get into heaven. And it's filled—we haven't got room for even one more." The oil prospector thought for a minute and said, "Would you mind if I just said four words to those folks?" "I can't see any harm in that," said St. Pete. So the old-timer cupped his hands and yelled out, "Oil discovered in hell!" Immediately, the oil prospectors wrenched the lock off the door of the pen and out they flew, flapping their wings as hard as they could for the lower regions. "You know, that's a pretty good trick," St. Pete said. "Move in. The place is yours. You've got plenty of room." The old fellow scratched his head and said, "No. If you don't mind, I think I'll go along with the rest of 'em. There may be some truth to that rumor after all."

That, unfortunately, is what happens in business and investments. People know better, but when they hear a rumor — particularly when they hear it from a high place — they just can't resist the temptation to go along.

It happens on Wall Street periodically, where you get what are, in effect, manias. Looking back no one can quite understand how everyone could have gotten so swept up in the moment. A group of lemmings looks like a pack of individualists compared with Wall Street when it gets a concept in its teeth.

When I was a graduate student at Columbia University, I got a piece of advice from Ben Graham, the founding father of security analysis, that I've never forgotten: You're neither right nor wrong because other people agree with you. You're right because your facts are right and your reasoning is right — and that's the only thing that makes you right.

A group of lemmings looks like a pack of individualists compared with Wall Street when it gets a concept in its teeth.

And if your facts and reasoning are right, you don't have to worry about anybody else. Watch that track record. The best judgment we can make about managerial competence does not depend on what people say, but simply what the record shows. At Berkshire Hathaway, when we buy a business we usually keep whoever has been running it, so we already have a batting average. Take the case of Mrs. B, who ran our Furniture Mart. Over a 50-year period, we'd seen her take $500 and turn it into a business that made $18 million pretax. So we knew she was competent. She's also 97 years old. In fact, now she's competing with us; she started a new business two years ago. Who would think you'd have to get a noncompete agreement with a 95-year-old? Clearly, the lesson here is that the past record is the best single guide.

Then you run into the problem of the 14-year-old horse. Let's say you buy The Daily Racing Form and it shows that the horse won the Kentucky Derby as a four-year-old. Based on past performance, you know this was one hell of a horse. But now he's 14 and can barely move. So you have to ask yourself, "Is there anything about the past record that makes it a poor guideline as a forecaster of the future?"

The situation may also arise in which there is no clear past record. Let's say that when you left college they gave you a little bonus: You got to pick out anybody in your class and you'd get 10 percent of his or her future earnings. All of a sudden you look at the whole group in a different way. You've seen them in class; you know their grades and their leadership capabilities. Taking these factors into account, you ask yourself, "Who do I pick?" But how good a choice do you think you could make? It would be a lot easier if you could make that decision at your tenth class reunion, after you've seen their actual business performance, wouldn't it?

These are the judgments that Berkshire Hathaway makes about management all the time. We try to find businesses that we really feel good about owning. What a company's stock sells for today, tomorrow, next week, or next year doesn't matter. What counts is how the company does over a five- or 10-year period. It has nothing to do with charts or numbers. It has to do with businesses and management.

What a company's stock sells for today, tomorrow, next week, or next year doesn't matter. What counts is how the company does over a five- or 10-year period.

Another thing I learned in business school was that it doesn't help to be smarter than even your dumbest competitor. The trick is to have no competitors. That means having a product that truly differentiates itself.

Say a customer goes into a drugstore and asks for a Hershey's bar. The clerk says, "We don't have any, but why don't you take this other chocolate bar instead; it's a nickel cheaper." And the customer says, "I'll go across the street." It's when the customer will go across the street that you've got a great business.

PHILIP FISHER

Warren Buffett calls Philip Fisher a "giant" of investing. "From him," Buffett says, "I learned the value of the 'scuttlebutt' approach: Go out and talk to competitors, suppliers, customers to find out how an industry or company really operates." Instead of analyzing balance sheets, San Francisco–based Fisher prefers to study people and organizations—his pioneering contribution to securities analysis. "I have stressed management, but even so, I haven't stressed it enough. It is the most important ingredient." He looks for leaders who are on the cutting edge, welcome dissent, and promote innovation. One management practice he disdains is the wholesale firing of people in the name of cost-cutting.

Fisher, whose father was a doctor and personally educated him, entered college at 15, then attended Stanford Business School for a year. There, he learned about talking to company management teams by tagging along with a professor who did consultant work. After school, his first job was with a San Francisco bank, performing securities analysis. He then went on to a stock exchange firm, only to have the 1929 crash derail his career. It was for the best as he started his own firm in 1931, Fisher & Co., with two great advantages working for him: Most Depression-era executives had little to do and were willing to talk to him about their businesses, and most potential clients were pretty unhappy with their current advisors. At the age of 89 he was still managing money for a handful of clients.

One of his winning strategies that came out of the Depression was to look to the long term. "The companies I invest in have enough momentum to keep going three to five years," he says. In fact, he'll hold on to stocks for decades; for example, he held Food Machinery Corporation, one of his first buys back in 1931, into the 1960s, when he finally sold some shares. Other multidecade holds include Texas Instruments and Motorola. In general, however, if a stock hasn't met his expectations after three years, he sells. Fisher uses Motorola as a case study in *The People Factor,* in which he discusses the importance of a company's management when making investment decisions.

The People Factor
Philip Fisher

B riefly summarized, the first dimension of a conservative investment consists of outstanding managerial competence in the basic areas of production, marketing, research, and financial controls. This first dimension describes a business as it is today, being essentially a matter of results. The second dimension deals with what produced these results and, more importantly, will continue to produce them in the future. The force that causes such things to happen, that creates one company in an industry that is an outstanding investment vehicle and another that is average, mediocre, or worse, is essentially *people*.

Edward H. Heller, a pioneer venture capitalist whose comments during his business life greatly influenced some of the ideas expressed in this book, used the term "vivid spirit" to describe the type of individual to whom he was ready to give significant financial backing. He said that behind every unusually successful corporation was this kind of determined entrepreneurial personality with the drive, the original ideas, and the skill to make such a company a truly worthwhile investment.

Within the area of very small companies that grew into considerably larger and quite prosperous ones (the field of his greatest interest and where he scored his most spectacular successes), Ed Heller was undoubtedly right. But as these smaller companies grow larger on the way to becoming suitable for conservative investment, Ed Heller's view might be tempered by that of another brilliant businessman who expressed serious doubts about the wisdom of investing in a company whose president was his close personal friend. This man's reason for lack of enthusiasm: "My friend is one of the most brilliant men I've ever known. He always has to be right. In a small company this may be fine. But as you grow, your men have to be right sometimes, too."

The first dimension of a conservative investment consists of outstanding managerial competence . . .

Here is an indication of the heart of the second dimension of a truly conservative investment: a corporate chief executive dedicated to long-range growth who has surrounded himself with and delegated considerable authority to an extremely competent team in charge of the various divisions and functions of the company. These people must be engaged not in an endless internal struggle for power but instead should be working together toward clearly outlined corporate goals. One of these goals, which is absolutely essential if an investment is to be a truly successful one, is that top management take the time to identify and train qualified and motivated juniors to succeed senior management whenever a replacement is necessary. In turn, at each level down through the chain of command, detailed attention should be paid to whether those at this level are doing the same thing for those one level below them.

Does this mean that a company that qualifies for truly conservative investing should promote only from within and should never recruit from the outside except at the lowest levels or for those just starting their careers? A company growing at a very rapid rate may have such need for additional people that there just isn't time to train from within for all positions. Furthermore, even the best-run company will at times need an individual with a highly specialized skill so far removed from the general activities of the company that such a specialty simply cannot be found internally. Someone with expertise in a particular subdivision of the law, insurance, or a scientific discipline well removed from the company's main line of activity would be a case in point. In addition, occasional hiring from the outside has one advantage: It can bring a new viewpoint into corporate councils, an injection of fresh ideas to challenge the accepted way as the best way.

In general, however, the company with real investment merit is the company that usually promotes from within. This is because all companies of the highest investment order (these do not necessarily have to be the biggest and best-known companies) have developed a set of policies and ways of doing things peculiar to their own needs. If these special ways are truly worthwhile, it is always difficult and frequently impossible to retrain those long accustomed to them to different ways of getting things done. The higher up in an organization the newcomer may be, the more costly the indoctrination can be. While I can quote no statistics to prove the point, it is my observation that in better-run companies a surprising number of executives brought in close to the top tend to disappear after a few years.

Of one thing the investor can be certain: A large company's need to bring in a new chief executive from the outside is a damning sign of something basically wrong with the existing management—no matter how good the surface signs may have been as indicated by the most recent earnings statement. It may well be that the new president will do

a magnificent job and in time will build a genuine management team around him so that such a jolt to the existing organization will never again become necessary. Consequently,
in time such a stock may become one worthy of a wise
investor. But such rebuilding can be so long and risky a
process that, if an investor finds this sort of thing happening
in one of his holdings, he will do well to review all his investment activities to determine whether his past actions have
really been proceeding from a sound base.

---

*The company with real investment merit is the
company that usually promotes from within.*

A worthwhile clue is available to all investors as to
whether a management is predominantly one man or a
smoothly working team (this clue throws no light, however,
on how good that team may be). The annual salaries of top
management of all publicly owned companies are made public in the proxy statements. If the salary of the number-one
man is very much larger than that of the next two or three, a
warning flag is flying. If the compensation scale goes down
rather gradually, it isn't.

For optimum results for the investor it is not enough that
management personnel work together as a team and be
capable of filling vacancies above them. There should also be
present the greatest possible number of those "vivid spirits"
of Ed Heller's—people with the ingenuity and determination
not to leave things just at their present, possibly quite satisfactory, state but to build significant further improvements
upon them. Such people are not easy to find. Motorola, Inc.
has for some time been conducting an activity that the financial community has paid little or no attention to that indicates it is possible to accomplish dramatically more in this
area than is generally considered possible.

In 1967 Motorola management recognized that the rapid rate of growth anticipated in the years ahead would inevitably require steady expansion in the upper layers of management. It was decided to meet the problem head on. In that year Motorola opened its Executive Institute at Oracle, Arizona. It was designed so that, in an atmosphere remote from the daily details of the company's offices and plants, two things would happen: Motorola personnel of apparent unusual promise would be trained in matters beyond the scope of their immediate activities in order to be able to take on more important jobs; top management would be furnished significant further evidence as to the degree of promotability of these same people.

A large company's need to bring in a new chief executive from the outside is a damning sign of something basically wrong with the existing management . . .

At the time of the Executive Institute's founding, skeptics within the management questioned whether the effort would be worth the cost. This was largely because of their belief that fewer than a hundred people would be found in the whole Motorola organization with sufficient talent to make it worthwhile from the company's standpoint to provide them with this special training. Events have proven these skeptics spectacularly wrong. The Institute handles five to six classes a year, with fourteen in each class. By mid-1974 about 400 Motorola people had gone through the school; and a significant number, including some present vice-presidents, were found to have capabilities vastly greater than anything contemplated at the time they were approved for admission. Furthermore, those involved in this work feel that, from the company's standpoint, results in the more recent classes are even more favorable than in the earlier ones. It now appears that, as total employment at Motorola continues to expand with the company's growth, enough promising Motorola people can be found to maintain this activity indefinitely. All of this shows, from the investor's standpoint, that if enough ingenuity is used, even the companies with well-above-average growth rates can also "grow" the needed unusual people from within so as to maintain competitive superiority without running the high risk of friction and failure that so often occurs when a rapidly growing company must go to the outside for more than a very small part of its outstanding talent.

Everyone has a personality—a combination of character traits that sets him or her apart from every other individual. Similarly, every corporation has its own ways of doing things—some formalized into well-articulated policies, others not—that are at least slightly different from those of other corporations. The more successful the corporation, the more likely it is to be unique in some of its policies. This is particularly true of companies that have been successful for a considerable period of time. In contrast to individuals, whose fundamental character traits change but little once they reach maturity, the ways of companies are influenced not only by outside events but by the reactions to those events of a whole series of different personalities who, as time goes on, follow one another in the top posts within the organization.

However much policies may differ among companies, there are three elements that must always be present if a company's shares are to be worthy of holding for conservative, long-range investment.

1. The company must recognize that the world in which it is operating is changing at an ever-increasing rate.
All corporate thinking and planning must be attuned to challenge what is now being done—to challenge it not occasion-

ally but again and again. Every accepted way of doing things must be examined and re-examined to be as sure as is permitted by human fallibility that this way is really the best way. Some risks must be accepted in substituting new methods to meet changing conditions. No matter how comfortable it may seem to do so, ways of doing things cannot be maintained just because they worked well in the past and are hallowed by tradition. The company that is rigid in its actions and is not constantly challenging itself has only one way to go, and that way is down. In contrast, certain managements of large companies that have deliberately endeavored to structure themselves so as to be able to change have been those producing some of the most striking rewards for their shareholders. An example of this is the Dow Chemical Company, with a record of achievements over the last ten years that is frequently considered to surpass that of any other major chemical company in this country, if not in the entire world. Possibly Dow's most significant departure from past ways was to break its management into five separate managements on geographical lines (Dow USA, Dow Europe, Dow Canada, etc.). It was believed that only in this way could local problems be handled quickly as best suited local conditions and without suffering from the bureaucratic inefficiencies that so often accompany bigness. The net effect of this as told by the president of Dow Europe: "The results that today challenge us are being made by our sister [Dow] companies throughout the world. They, not our direct competitors, are turning in the gains that push us to be first." From the investor's standpoint perhaps the most important feature of this change was not that it was made but that it was made when Dow still had a total sales volume much smaller than many other multinational companies that were operating successfully in the established way. In other words, change and improvement arose from innovative thinking to make a workable system better—not from a forced reaction to a crisis.

This is but one of the many ways this pioneering company has broken with the past to attain its striking competitive record. Another was the unprecedented step for an industrial company of starting from scratch to make a success of a wholly owned bank in Switzerland so as to help finance the needs of its customers in the export market. Here again the management did not hesitate to break with the past in ways that engendered some risk in the early stages but that ended up by enhancing the intrinsic strength of the company.

Many other examples could be cited from the record of this company. However, just one more will be mentioned merely to show the extreme variety of areas such actions may cover. Far earlier than most other companies, Dow not only recognized the need to spend sizable sums to avoid pollution but concluded that, if major results were to be attained, something more was needed than just exhortations from top management. It was necessary to obtain the consistent cooperation of middle-level managers. It was decided that the surest way of doing this was to appeal to the profit motives of those most directly involved. They were encouraged to find profitable methods of converting the polluting materials to salable products. The rest is now business history. With the full power of top management, plant management, and highly skilled chemical engineers behind these projects, Dow has achieved a series of firsts in eliminating pollution that has won them the praise of many environmental groups that are usually quite antibusiness in their viewpoints. Possibly more important, they have avoided hostility in most, although not all, of the communities where their plants are located. They have done this at very little over-all dollar cost and in some cases at an operating profit.

2. *There must always be a conscious and continuous effort, based on fact, not propaganda, to have employees at every level, from the most newly hired blue-collar or white-collar worker to the highest*

levels of management, feel that their company is a good place to work.

This is a world that requires most of us to put in a substantial number of hours each week doing what is asked of us by others in order to receive a paycheck even though we might prefer to spend those hours on our own amusement or recreation. Most people recognize the necessity for this. When a management can instill a belief, not just among a few top people but generally among the employees, that it is doing everything reasonably to be expected to create a good working environment and take care of its employees' interests, the rewards the company receives in greater productivity and lower costs can vastly outweigh the costs of such a policy.

The first step in this policy is seeing (not just talking about it but actually assuring) that every employee is treated with reasonable dignity and consideration. A year or so ago I read in the press that a union official claimed that one of the nation's largest companies was compelling its production-line employees to eat lunch with grease-stained hands because there was not sufficient time, with the number of washroom facilities available, for most of them to be able to wash before lunch. The stock of this company was of no investment interest to me for quite different reasons. Therefore, I have no knowledge of whether the charge was based on fact or was made in the heat of an emotional battle over wage negotiations. However, if true, this condition alone would, in my opinion, make the shares of this company unsuitable for holding by careful investors.

Besides treating employees with dignity and decency, the routes to obtaining genuine employee loyalty are many and varied. Pension and profit-sharing plans can play a significant part. So can good communication to and from all levels of employees. Concerning matters of general interest, letting everyone know not only exactly what is being done but why frequently eliminates friction that might otherwise occur. Actually knowing what people in various levels of the company are thinking, particularly when that view is adverse, can be even more important. A feeling throughout the company that people can express their grievances to superiors without fear of reprisal can be beneficial, although this open-door policy is not always simple to maintain because of the time wasted by cranks and nuts. When grievances occur, decisions on what to do about them should be made quickly. It is the long-smoldering grievance that usually proves the most costly.

A striking example of the benefits that may be attained through creating a unity of purpose with employees is the "people-effectiveness" program of Texas Instruments. The history of this program is an excellent example of how brilliant management perseveres with and perfects policies of this sort even when new outside influences force some redirection of these policies. From the early days of this company, top management held a deep conviction that everyone would gain if a system could be set up whereby all employees participated in managerial-type decisions to improve performance but that, to sustain interest on the part of employees, all participants must genuinely benefit from the results of their contributions. In the 1950s semiconductor production was largely a matter of hand assembly, offering many opportunities for employees to make brilliant individual suggestions for improving performance. Meetings, even formal classes, were held in which production workers were shown how they could as individuals or groups show the way to improving operations. At the same time, through both profit-sharing plans and awards and honors, those participating benefited both financially and by feeling they were part of the picture. Then mechanization of these former manual operations started to appear. As this trend grew, there was somewhat less opportunity for certain types of individual contributions, as in certain ways the machines controlled what would be done. A few foremen within the organization began feeling that there was no longer a place for lower-level contributions to management-type participation. Top management took quite the opposite viewpoint: People-participation would play a greater role than ever before. Now, however, it would be a group or team effort with the workers as a group estimating what could be done and setting their own goals for performance.

A feeling throughout the company that people can express their grievances to superiors without fear of reprisal can be beneficial, although this open-door policy is not always simple to maintain because of the time wasted by cranks and nuts.

Because workers started feeling that they (1) were genuinely participating in decisions, not just being told what to do, and (2) were being rewarded both financially and in honors and recognition, the results have been spectacular. In instance after instance, teams of workers have set for themselves goals quite considerably higher than anything management would have considered suggesting. At times when it appeared that targeted goals might not be met or when inter-team competition was producing rivalry, the workers proposed and voluntarily voted such unheard-of things (for this day and age) as cutting down on coffee breaks or shortening lunch periods to get the work out. The pressure of peer groups on the tardy or lazy worker who threatens the goals the group has set for itself dwarfs any amount of discipline that might be exerted from above through conventional management methods. Nor are these results confined to U.S. workers with their lifelong background in political democracy. They appear to be equally effective and mutually beneficial to people, regardless of the color of their skin and their origins from countries of quite different economic backgrounds. Though the performance-goal plan was first initiated in the United States, equally striking results have appeared not just in Texas Instruments plants in the so-called developed industrial nations such as France and Japan but also in Singapore, with its native Asian employees, and in Curaçao, where those on the payroll are overwhelmingly black. In all countries the morale effects appear striking when worker teams not only report directly to top management levels but also know their reports will be heeded and their accomplishments recognized and acknowledged.

For the conservative investor, the test of all such actions is whether management is truly building up the long-range profits of the business rather than just seeming to.

What all this has meant to investors was spelled out when company president Mark Shepherd, Jr., addressed stockholders at the 1974 annual meeting. He stated that a people-effectiveness index had been established consisting of the net sales billed divided by the total payroll. Since semiconductors, the company's largest product line, are one of the very few products in today's inflationary world that consistently decline in unit price and since wages have been rising at the company's plants at rates from 7 percent a year in the United States to 20 percent in Italy and Japan, it would be logical to expect, in spite of improvements in people-effectiveness, this index to decline. Instead it rose from about 2.25 percent in 1969 to 2.5 percent by the end of 1973. Furthermore, with definite plans for additional improvement and with further increases in profit-sharing funds tied into such improvement, it was announced that it was the company's goal to bring the index up to 3.1 percent by 1980—a goal that, if attained, would make the company a dramatically profitable place to work. Over the years Texas Instruments has frequently publicized some rather ambitious long-range goals and to date has rather consistently accomplished them.

From the investment standpoint, there are some extremely important similarities in the three examples of people-oriented programs that were chosen to illustrate aspects of the second dimension of a conservative investment. It is a relatively simple matter to mention and give a general description of Motorola's institute for selecting and training unusual talent to handle the growing needs of the company. It is an equally simple affair to mention that Dow found a means to stimulate people to work together to master environmental problems and to make them profitable for the company, or to state a few facts about the remarkable people-effectiveness program at Texas Instruments. However, if another company decided to start programs like these from scratch, the problems that could arise might be infinitely more complicated than merely persuading a board of directors to approve the necessary appropriation. Programs of this kind are easy to formulate, but their implementation is a quite different matter. Mistakes can be very costly. It is not hard to imagine what might happen if a training school such as Motorola's selected the wrong people for promotion, with the result that the best junior talent quit the company in disgust. Similarly, suppose a company tried to follow, in general, a people-effectiveness plan but either failed to create an atmosphere where workers genuinely felt themselves involved or failed to compensate their employees adequately, with the result that they became disillusioned. The misapplication of such a program could literally wreck a company. Meanwhile, companies that do perfect advantageous people-oriented policies and techniques usually find more and more ways to benefit from them. For these companies, such policies and techniques—these special ways of approaching problems and of solving them—are in a sense *proprietary*. For this reason they are of great importance to long-range investors.

3. Management must be willing to submit itself to the disciplines required for sound growth.

It has already been pointed out that in this rapidly changing world companies cannot stand still. They must either get better or worse, improve or go downhill. The true investment objective of growth is not just to make gains but to avoid loss. There are very few companies whose managements will not make claims to being growth companies. However, a management that talks about being growth-oriented is not necessarily actually so oriented. Many companies seem to have an irresistible urge to show the greatest possible profits at the end of each accounting period—to bring every possible cent down to the bottom line. This a true growth-oriented company can never do. Its focus must be on earning sufficient current profits to finance the costs of expanding the business. When adjustment for earning the required additional financial strength has been made, the company worthy of farsighted investment will give priority to curtailing maximum immediate profits when there are genuine worthwhile opportunities for developing new products or processes or for starting new product lines or for any one of the hundred and one more mundane actions whereby a dollar spent today may mean many dollars earned in the future. Such actions can vary all the way from hiring and training new personnel that will be needed as the business grows to forgoing the greatest possible profit on a customer's order to build up his permanent loyalty by rushing something to him when he needs it badly. For the conservative investor, the test of all such actions is whether management is truly building up the long-range profits of the business rather than just seeming to. No matter how well known, the company with a policy that only gives lip service to these disciplines is not likely to prove a happy vehicle for investment funds. Neither is one that tries to follow these disciplines but falls down in executing them, as, for example, a company that makes large research expenditures but so mishandles its efforts as to gain little from them.

HENRY CLEWS
1834–1923

Like many other successful investors, Henry Clews was known for his flamboyance. For example, he advertised that he would conduct stock and bond trades for his clients at one-half the cost of other firms (discount brokerage services long before Fidelity or Charles Schwab), which was considered outrageous for the time. "This was such a bombshell in the camp of these old fogies," he wrote, "that they were almost paralyzed." But Clews had to do what was considered radical for his time to break into the old-boy network. The materialistic world of Wall Street was a far cry from the career his parents had desired for him—the ministry. That prospect fell by the side when Clews, who was born in England, visited New York in 1850 and was seduced by the American lifestyle.

Clews started out as a clerk for a large importer before moving over to the financial side of the business. Ever ambitious, Clews and several of his friends opened a private bank on Wall Street. Next he set his sights on joining the New York Stock Exchange, which he joined shortly after the panic of 1857, during which prices fell about 50 percent. "This crisis sounded the death knell of old fogyism in the 'street,'" Clews wrote. "A younger race of financiers arose and filled the places of the old conservative leaders." For all his flamboyance, Clews was a value investor. He understood that "at the bottom of all this turbulent mass of facts there are natural laws at work which, if we study them in relation to the objects which they control, will be found to be as sure in their operation as sunrise."

In 1908, Clews published *Fifty Years in Wall Street*, which has proved indispensible for anyone studying both history and the markets. After all, Clews rubbed shoulders with the great financiers such as J. P. Morgan and the notorious robber barons such as Cornelius Vanderbilt, and he took the time to record history and his own thoughts, including what it takes to succeed on Wall Street. One of the problems investors face, he said, is their unwillingness "to act on conclusions that conflict with their desires . . ." In *The Study of the Stock Market,* Clews provides a list of characteristics that every investor must embrace.

The Study of the Stock Market
Henry Clews

Anything that is worth doing is worth doing well. In order to do anything well, one must study the subject thoroughly, not necessarily in books, because books are, except as to the laying down of principles, rather unsatisfactory teachers.

The stock market is a most fruitful and fascinating field of study. It attracts more influential and well-to-do men than any other arena of activity in American life, and of course a great deal of study is bestowed upon it. The reasons why the results of so much study are not always commensurate with the labor and time employed are numerous. Some of them are substantially as follows: —

People have preconceived notions. They are not willing to clear their minds of existing theories and bring themselves down to close dealing with facts. They are apt to base their conclusions on the opinions of others. Now, opinions as to the value of anything are sure to differ, and opinions as to future values differ still more widely, just as the spokes of a wheel are wider apart as you travel away from the hub. When you reach out into the future, you are getting away from the hub of the present. People are usually unwilling to act on conclusions that conflict with their desires, and that involve the acceptance of immediate losses. They resemble the wounded man who refuses to let the surgeon cut off his leg when he is told that amputation will probably save his life. They are apt to study in a superficial manner, without thoroughness, using scraps and smatterings of knowledge when even the most exact information is hardly sufficient.

Other reasons could be adduced, but they might be needless. A certain king excused the municipality of a town that neglected to fire a salute in his honor on their giving him the first one of fifty good reasons, — that they had no powder. The other forty-nine were suffered to remain undivulged. Enough reasons have been given here to explain why so many people fail to study the stock market successfully.

But while it is very easy to pick to pieces the various systems that are sure to win on the stock exchange, and to criticise the methods of study of the prejudiced, it is most difficult to lay down absolute rules for the successful study of the share market. One invariable rule there is, but it requires large capital and patience to practise it. It is this: Buy only what you can pay for; buy when cheap and sell when dear. The veriest financial infants can see the force of this.

Yet even this precept has its weak points. For instance, how is a person to be absolutely certain that a given stock is cheap or dear at a given time? You say, by comparison? But if he compares the price with what it was at any past period, he must also be able to state all the facts that existed, at that period having any bearing on this stock, and since these facts may run into the thousands as to number, and into all parts of the country as to place, our learner has a heavy contract on hand. Then, too, he must bring to bear a clear judgment, and a resolution such as soldiers exercise when they charge batteries, and he must be prepared next day to find out that he was wrong. After a careful and exhaustive search into all the materials at hand, he buys shares at, say, 60 per cent. of par, as being cheap at the price, and really worth more money, and next day they may be offered at 50. He then has really lost $10 on each share; but if he holds the purchase, and it ultimately advances to par, he has gained $40 per share.

And suppose he sells on any given day at par, and a week after that the shares sell at 110, he then loses $10 per share. So that this "safe" road to success has its stumbling blocks as well as others, although they are not so dangerous. In such a road there are no deadly pitfalls. The men who travel it are not tempted to defalcations and suicides.

People have preconceived notions. They are not willing to clear their minds of existing theories and bring themselves down to close dealing with facts.

Horace Greeley once said that the way to resume specie payments was to resume; and it might also be said that the way to study the stock market is to study it. One distinguished and generally-successful stock operator of the period is credited with being in daily receipt of numerous pieces of information from various parts of the country as to the condition of crops, weather, freights, passenger traffic, in short, all facts that go to make up the status of railroad enterprises. These private bits of information are not open to the general public—they cost too much, and call for too much machinery; but the bureaus of public information are continually sending out intelligence, and it is mostly trustworthy. This class of facts must be distinguished from mere rumors.

Rumor is, as a rule, uncertain and untrustworthy. It has been compared to an animated thing that begins its career by being small and compact, but as it stalks along it becomes larger and less definite as to form, until at last it is like a monstrous cloud that has neither shape nor consistency, and finally disappears, no one knows how or where. But to study facts leads to generally accurate conclusions; and accurate conclusions are apt to lead to wise transactions.

Thus, the fact of large harvests in the year 1891 in the United States, coupled with the fact of poor harvests in Europe in the same year, led to the conclusion that our grain would be in demand for foreign shipment, and that the earnings of our railroads would be increased. The conclusions were sound and the earnings were increased, and judicious students of the market bought stocks for a rise. Then the fact that stocks rose and kept on rising, coupled with the fact that the general public were buyers, and with the additional fact that the public prefer to be buyers and to buy at high prices, and not to buy at all unless prices are high, led these same judicious students to sell the same stocks during the prevalence of high prices, — both the stocks which they owned and large amounts which they did not own. Again, the study of facts led to wise conclusions, and these ended in successful results. Both as bulls and as bears the wise students have fared well. The careless and superficial public, coming in too late as bulls, found themselves at last compelled to become unwilling sellers at greater or less losses, in some cases so severe as to shatter households and drive citizens to ruin.

Thus the person who studies real values must not be content with that alone. He must also study the facts that in times of stress and storm make real values fluctuate as wildly in manner, if not in amount, as those of the most fanciful securities, and he must learn that no operation on margin is really safe unless the margin is large beyond the ordinary run, and is backed by equally large reserves. Some financial teachers lay it down that your risks should not exceed 25 per cent. of your capital. This is excessive prudence; but the man who keeps half a mile away from the edge of a cliff will never fall from it. One who has studied the share market carefully has eventually found that if he is able to pay one half the market price of his holdings, he need have little fear as to the other half; that is, on judicious selections of properties.

No mention is made here of shares that sell in December at 72 and in March at 30. Whoever buys such goods should pay for them and put them away, and let them incubate with such patience as is attributed to the hopeful setting hen.

The student of the stock market has at certain periods no easy task before him. Imports are sometimes large, and exports small. We sell to foreigners a million per week of cotton, and buy from them two millions per week of coffee, the cotton yielding us a small profit, the coffee yielding foreigners an immense profit. Other nations at times do not seem to prefer our grains to those of Russia and the East, despite those foreign markets of bewildering extent and good prices which exist, I fear, only in the imagination of free-traders. Then, too, the indebtedness of corporations and individuals acts as a constant menace to the natural tendency of loose capital to be lent out to useful enterprises.

Some financial teachers lay it down that your risks should not exceed 25 per cent. of your capital. This is excessive prudence; but the man who keeps half a mile away from the edge of a cliff will never fall from it.

Yet, at the bottom of all this turbulent mass of facts there are natural laws at work which, if we study them in relation to the objects which they control, will be found to be as sure in their operation as sunrise. The collapse of the iniquitous coal combination, as cruel as one to raise the price of water or air, was the result of natural law, and the same laws are busy to-day, and the facts are always with us. It is the business of the diligent to find them and to profit thereby.

Long before Arnold Bernhard founded Value Line, Inc., the Williams College graduate was a reporter, reviewing plays, movies and nightclubs. The stock market craze in the 1920s, however, soon attracted his attention and he took a job in the office of Jesse Livermore, a renowned speculator. (Livermore was the model for Edwin Lefèvre's classic, *Reminiscences of a Stock Operator.*) After his short stint with Livermore, he moved on to Moody's Investors Service, first as an analyst and then as an account executive. In 1931, he lost his job, but immediately founded Arnold Bernhard & Company.

The first issue of the *Value Line Investment Survey,* which ranks stocks for their projected market performance, came out in 1936. Like so many other great investors, Bernhard wanted to do away with emotionalism—a lesson learned in 1929 when emotions were running high. He watched helplessly as his mother lost all of the insurance money left to her by her deceased husband. She simply refused to let go even though one of her stocks, Cities Service, fell from $50 to $2 a share. "If all the deviltry of all the crooked stock market riggers of all time were raised to the hundredth power," Bernhard wrote, "it would count as nothing compared to the desolation wrought by deluded crowds whose imagination knows no discipline."

Bernhard admitted, "even if we concede that the value of a stock is just a matter of psychology, or, as Lord Keynes once said, 'the average man's opinion of what the average man's opinion will be,' we still must recognize that they are influences that shape the psychology of the average man over a period of time. Something makes the psychology." For Bernhard, it was a matter of finding the right buttons or statistics that drives the value of a stock and the market. Two of those buttons are the company's past performance, which is based on the growth trend of earnings and dividends and their stability, and the other is what he calls "appreciation potentiality," which is based on forecasting earnings and dividends on a three- to five-year horizon. Bernhard develops these ideas and rejects some classical methods for determining the value of a stock in *The Valuation of Listed Stocks.*

The Valuation of Listed Stocks
Arnold Bernhard

At the moment of writing [1949], the Dow Jones Industrial Average stands at 165. Stock prices, as reflected in this Average, are lower in the writer's opinion than values. The reader may agree that stocks are undervalued now, but it is obvious that most investors do not think so, because, if they did, their buying would force prices up to the point where stocks would no longer be undervalued. That raises the question whether it is possible to determine objectively, and in conflict with prevailing opinion, how different the price of a stock ought to be from what it is. More and more one hears the expression: "This or that stock is undervalued and overvalued or fully valued." When an analyst or an investor speaks in such terms, he implies that he has a standard of value in mind, whether he defines that standard or not.

VALUE DIFFERS FROM PRICE

Value often differs from price. Charles H. Dow, whose theory of price trends has had enormous influence in Wall Street, insisted that every student of the market should "first of all know value."

31

Another famous authority on stock prices, Baron Roth-schild, said that the way to succeed in the stock market was to "buy stocks when they are cheap and sell them when they are dear." He too implied a standard of value, though he did not define it. One cannot buy something cheap or sell something dear unless he knows what cheap is and what dear is. Those are relative terms, and they must be related to some kind of a standard.

Value is something that exists in the mind. It is, therefore, as difficult to define as life itself. In all economic history there has never been a definition of pure economic value that has won universal acceptance. All the great economists have attempted to define value — Aristotle, Adam Smith, Ricardo, Bohm-Bawerk, Jevons, Clark, Pareto — but there is no definition of value in the economic sense that has been accorded universal acceptance.

One cannot say that a stock's value is the equivalent of its price. If that were so, it would be a waste of time to discuss value at all. Value would be price and price value, and that is all one would need to know.

One cannot buy something cheap or sell something dear unless he knows what cheap is and what dear is. Those are relative terms . . .

The classical definition of the value of a common stock is the one that holds the value of a common stock to be equal to the sum of all the dividends it will pay in the future, discounted to the prevailing interest rate. It is difficult to see how any one could take exception to this theory of value. The only trouble with it is that it is unusable. It is unusable because nobody knows what the sum of all the future dividends will be. If one could determine in advance what the sum of dividends would be over a 20-year span, or whatever life expectancy the company is determined to have, common stocks would not be issued. Capital, instead of being asked to assume a partnership risk, would be granted a contract, specifying the return to be paid on the investment over a period of time and the date when the capital would be returned out of the depreciation reserve. There would be little or no need for common stocks.

The very reason for the existence of common stocks is that nobody knows or is expected to know what the dividends will total in the future. To define the value of a stock, therefore, as the sum of its future dividends, discounted to the interest rate, boils down to this: that the value of a common stock is a mystery.

It is not necessary to give up the search, however, even if no perfectly satisfactory definition of value is available, for it may be found possible to determine value within certain limits.

One cannot say that a stock's value is the equivalent of its price. If that were so, it would be a waste of time to discuss value at all.

Up to this point it has been reasoned that value is something different from price and that it cannot be defined. Value is something that exists in the minds of people. But, since the common conception of value is expressed in price at a given moment, we seem to be forced back to the premise that price and value are the same thing, since they are both the expression of value as it exists in the minds of the buyers and sellers who participate in a free market.

The reasoning is not perfectly circular though. There is a break in the circle which offers an opportunity for evolving a practical standard of value. That break lies in this fact: that people—the very same people—do not put the same price tag on a stock at all times. If the market price of General Motors is 30 in March of 1938 and 30 is its value, in the opinion of all buyers and sellers who participate in a free market, and if the price of General Motors should be 50 in October of 1938, also in the opinion of all buyers and sellers, can we find, in this price variation, the clue to those factors that determine value and, through value, price? Admitted that, since value cannot be defined, the verdict of the market as to what value is must be accepted. That does not mean that the verdict of the market must be accepted at every moment. Obviously, the market changes its mind. What causes it to do so?

CLASSICAL DEFINITION IMPRACTICABLE

We reject the theory that the value of a stock is the total of the dividends it will pay during its life, not because this is theoretically incorrect, but because it is impracticable. However, common sense tells us that dividends in some way or other have a bearing on the price at which a stock will sell and, therefore, on its value.

It is known too that dividends can only be paid from profits and that profits are not always the same as dividends. Profits are often reinvested in the business and not paid out in dividends. Although dividends may be said to be a function of profits, they are not the equivalent. Therefore, it may be assumed that profits in their own right have some bearing on what the market will think the price of a stock should be.

Assets also have some weight. Many court tests reveal that book values are given weight in reorganization proceedings in an effort to determine the amount of equity available for apportionment to various claimants.

There is reason also to believe that habit of mind has something to do with price determination. If United States Steel sells for $100 a share during a given year, that figure will influence the thinking of buyers and sellers of United

States Steel in the following year, even though other factors significantly related to value have changed.

To repeat the argument to this point: Value and price are not necessarily the same thing. Yet the only determinant of value, which is something that cannot be defined, is price. We find a break in the circle of reasoning in the fact that prices are not the same at all times and that changes in certain variables, such as earnings, dividends, and assets, are related to the corresponding changes in prices. If it can be found that a certain relationship between prices on the one hand and the variables of earnings and dividends and assets on the other has been maintained for a long period of time, it might then rightly be concluded that at such moments, or even in such years, as the market deviates from this long held relationship, the distortion is a measure of disparity between price and value. It can be said that, at such times when a given level of earnings, assets, and dividends fails to command the price that has been placed on it most of the time in the past, that is a time of overvaluation or undervaluation. And we can logically use this measure, not as a definition of value, but as a description of it, and as a method for determining the direction in which the market price will probably move by way of readjustment. It is the virtue of a normal relationship that it can be expected to prevail most of the time. What we wish to know is what will be the opinion, expressed in price, of all the buyers and sellers participating in a free market, most of the time.

Value is something that exists in the minds of people.

One cannot be perfectly sure that the variables of earnings and dividends and assets and habit of mind will actually determine the opinion of buyers and sellers. But one can make certain assumptions and then test them mathematically, to see whether or not a correlation exists between changes in the variables of earnings, dividends, and assets, and habit of mind on the one hand, and prices on the other, and, if such correlation is found to exist, whether the coefficient is so high as to be beyond the possibility of explanation by pure chance.

If a statistician were to correlate earnings, dividends, assets, and last year's average price of a given stock (last year's average price is the specific way of expressing "habit of mind"), he could do so through a computation known as a multiple variable correlation analysis. The Value Line rating, about which the reader may have heard, is a single line which expresses that correlation. In that line is expressed the price that the market over a 20-year span has placed on earnings, assets, and dividends at the various levels of experience, most of the time.

What we wish to know is what will be the opinion, expressed in price, of all the buyers and sellers participating in a free market, most of the time.

If through such a correlation over a period of 20 years the market can determine the specific weights to be assigned to each variable, then one could with reason determine what the future value of a stock will be in terms of market price, provided only that the future earnings and dividends and assets of that stock could be forecast with reasonable accuracy. It cannot be said with certainty that the future price will accord with the normal capitalization of earnings and assets as determined by the 20-year experience. But it can be said that the probability that the future price will conform to the long term sense of value is so high as to justify the effort and to provide a basis for a rational investment program.

To summarize: In the absence of a commonly accepted definition of value, we must, to be practical, go on the assumption that value is in the long run the equivalent of price. But we may also proceed on the assumption that price at any given time is not always the same as value, because there is such a thing as a long term price appraisal which may differ from the current price appraisal. We find that the changes in price that occur from year to year can be ascribed in significantly high degree to corresponding changes in such variables as assets, earnings, and dividends, and habit of mind (price lag). We conclude, therefore, that the evolution of a standard of value, based on a correlation between changes in price and changes in factors of value, when found, should enable us to project the probable future of a stock, not with certainty, but with a sufficiently high degree of probability to validate the premise that such a projection is a practical standard by which to identify areas of undervaluation or overvaluation, not only in the stock market as a whole, but in the prices of individual stocks as well.

It is recognized that the practicality of such a rating depends on ability to forecast the future level of earnings and dividends with reasonable accuracy. Although space does not permit a discussion of the methods by which this can be done, there is evidence to prove that it can be and has been done. At the very least, the analysis proves that the normal capitalization of a given level of earnings and assets can be determined in advance and that, because the capitalization is normal, it will probably be realized. The inescapable hazard of projecting future earnings and dividends remains, of course. But the price that the market will probably place on a given level of earnings and dividends need no longer remain in the realm of pure guess.

If this method of evaluation is sound, then it follows that the stocks that are most deeply undervalued according to this standard should give the best account of themselves in the open market during a period of 6 months to 18 months, regardless of the trend of the market as a whole. This, as a matter of fact, is a result that has been proved in experience. That is to say, the stocks most deeply undervalued and therefore most strongly to be recommended have, as a class, outperformed in the market the stocks that, as a class, merit a lower recommendation, and those that merit the second best recommendation have outperformed as a class those that merited the third class recommendation, and so on. In short, it is possible by this method to separate the sheep from the goats in the market, according to value. This is not to say that every stock that merits the strongest recommendation will outperform every stock that deserves the second strongest recommendation, but it is to say that, taken as a group, the most strongly recommended stocks outperform, in a practical market sense, the stocks that are in a less favorable position relative to an objective mathematical standard of value, and this happens consistently, as audited records prove.

The writer is of the opinion that the differences between actual market price and the standard of value expressed in the Value Line rating can be very largely explained in terms of market sentiment. One good measure of market sentiment is the ratio of stock yields to bond yields. If such an average ratio be inserted into the equation as a fifth independent variable, the correlations emerge as almost perfect. (Coefficients of determination as high as 0.96 are not infrequent, and nearly all stock equations have an R^2 of over 0.85.) All this seems to mean, at first blush, is that, if one can predict where the stock market averages and the interest rate will be next year, he can forecast pretty accurately where the price of a particular stock will be too, if he can forecast its earnings and dividends. Actually, though, the exercise is more promising than at first appears, because, for one thing, the stock-bond yield ratio lends itself to forecast better than the stock market averages alone, and, second, even if not forecastable, a stock-bond yield ratio, inserted into a multiple variable correlation analysis, gives a truer weighting to the other variables of earnings, assets, dividends, and price lag. The nonpredictable variable (stock-bond yield ratio) can then be held constant, and a projection of the predictable variables in the equation can be made with greater assurance that they will reveal the true value of the stock, ex sentiment.

PAUL F. MILLER, JR.

Paul Miller surprised Wall Street when he decided to leave his high-profile position as CEO of Drexel Harriman Ripley, an investment banking firm, and start one of the first "boutique" money management firms, Miller, Anderson & Sherrerd. That pioneering effort and his phenomenal investment record make him more than worthy of reading. In 1969 they had not one customer and they were asking for a minimum investment of $20 million. Ten years later they had about $1 billion in assets that then mushroomed to $12 billion seven short years later. What amazed him was that so few of his clients ever requested an interview; they made decisions based on Miller's past track record alone, which happened to include a recent streak of amazing gains. A realistic Miller said of himself and other money managers, "You have no remote idea how well they're going to do in the future. You know how many five-year records have been blown apart?"

The success can partly be attributed to the firm's culture; Miller liked to encourage independent and creative thinking without destructive inoffice competition. "I've seen a lot of organizations that are just blown apart by incentive systems that pit one investment manager versus another," he said. As for his style: "When you go back and analyze our successes, so often they were the result of strategic decisions rather than deciding to invest a bundle of money in some hot stock." What makes a great investor? "First of all," Miller said, "many of these people use a valuation model of some kind, so they never tie their judgment on a stock's price to intuition or light bulbs flashing. And they're never frantic—purchases are made for the long term."

Miller ultimately believes in the "perfect-market hypothesis", although he knows the overall market performance can be beaten. As he surveyed Wall Street in the late 1980s, he commented, "In some ways, the old days were better. I really believe that never have so many people made so much money for contributing so little to the world as Wall Street is today." However, in his essay, *The Dangers of Retrospective Myopia,* he questions traditional thought when it comes to predicting stock prices.

The Dangers of Retrospective Myopia
Paul F. Miller, Jr.

Peter Drucker has said that capital formation in the United States is shifting from the entrepreneur who invests in the future to the pension trustee who invests in the past. While Drucker is correct that pension funds are non-entrepreneurial and are increasingly directing the flow of savings, he is wrong if he is implying that pension trustees are basically different from portfolio investors of past eras. Indeed, the history of portfolio investment is a series of responses to the past, some of them clothed in sophisticated terms and unrecognized as being retrospective.

Human behavior relative to the making and losing of money from the purchase and sale of assets is the most reliable, most consistent factor in the investment world. Recognition of this is the most crucial step toward the maturity of any investor. For this reason, I have always told newcomers to the investment business that a study of financial history is at least as important as Modern Portfolio Theory. A reading of Charles Mackay's *Extraordinary Popular Delusions and the Madness of Crowds* written in 1841, is worth every bit as much as the studies of Sharpe, Blume, Friend, and Malkiel. Of more recent vintage, a search of the files for reports by First-Team, All-American analysts of the late 1960's and early

1970's, which rationalized P/E's of 40–80, is as valuable as the various discussions of risk adjusted returns. In fact, a study of the history of portfolio management concepts has only one objective, that of reinforcing the idea that there really is no answer except that of recognizing, through common sense, the infrequent extremes of human fear and greed, and keeping in mind that there is such a thing as a sensible price for a business.

As Aldous Huxley once put it, "How can we have a brave new world with all the same old people in it?" The quest for investment success is unending. The "answers" that are always being "discovered" are inevitably based upon relatively recent history either empirically or in terms of a subconscious psychology. What worked well in the past is presented as a prescription for the future. In fact, such prescriptions may work for a while and gain a large "fan club" which ultimately carries some specific concept to an extreme and then to its downfall, as demonstrated dramatically by the so-called "growth stocks" of the 1960's. Currently, the questioning of equities as inflation hedges is probably a skepticism based on recent history which will ultimately have its demise. Often the successful life span of such historically based prescriptions is quite short. Let's take a look at a few of the more striking examples:

FIXED TRUSTS

In case the current proponents of "passive cores" for portfolios have not discovered their ancestors, the early 1930's provide an example of passive investing *in extremis* in the form of the fixed trust.

The bankers, investment bankers, and industrialists who had become heroes to investors of the 1920's by using leverage and alleged inside information to create outstanding results for their investment trusts had, by 1930 and 1931, fallen into disrepute. These trusts had sold at huge premiums over net asset values in the mania of 1927–29. The subsequent rapid switch from the worship of investment management to complete disillusionment left Wall Street looking for something to merchandise to the public that could exploit the new skepticism. Consequently, fixed trusts, which had been around in specialized forms for many years, were designed in a diversified form. The idea was simple. Why bother with investment management at all if it was worthless? Just select a list of good quality stocks and leave it undisturbed unless—and it was the "unless" that did in the fixed trust—a dividend was passed.

The history of portfolio investment is a series of responses to the past, some of them clothed in sophisticated terms and unrecognized as being retrospective.

Obviously, the 1930's were not auspicious dividend years, and the fixed trusts' portfolios were decimated by dividend cuts and omissions that occurred after the prices of the stocks had declined in anticipation thereof. Fixed trusts died quietly in the mid-1930's.

FORMULA TIMING

In the late 1930's and during the early postwar-World War II years, a glance at a chart of stock market history made it apparent that most market fluctuations in this century had been contained within a pair of parallel lines that were rising at a long-term trend rate of about 3.0%. (see Chart I) Major violations of this band occurred in the late 1920's—and then in the early 1930's. Within the band, however, major market moves had occurred frequently, and it seemed logical to assume that, the further up or down the market moved within the band, the greater the probability was that the direction of movement would change. With the known difficulties of "buying low and selling high," it seemed sensible to reduce common stock positions as prices rose and increase them as prices fell. The next step was to divide the long-term band into "zones" that would operate so as to change the equity ratio gradually to a fully invested position by the time stocks had fallen to the bottom limits of the band, and to reduce a portfolio to negligible stock holdings by the time stocks hit the upper limits.

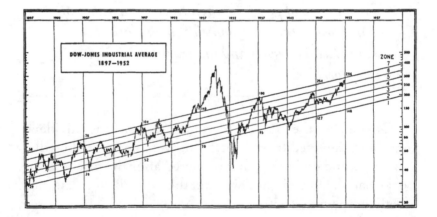

Some critics called this idea a compromise, because it was admitting that investors couldn't discern market bottoms and tops and was a substitution of a mechanical tool for sound judgment. As it turned out, that wasn't the important point. Rather, the fatal assumption was that the long-term band within which stock prices had been confined most of the time for 40 years was something more than historical accident. As can be seen from Chart II, the National Formula Plan had portfolios down to 25% in stocks by 1951, only two years into what was ultimately to be a 20-year bull market. Adding to the woe, this Plan had the investor 75% in bonds just as interest rates were unpegged and the 30-year bear market in bonds began.

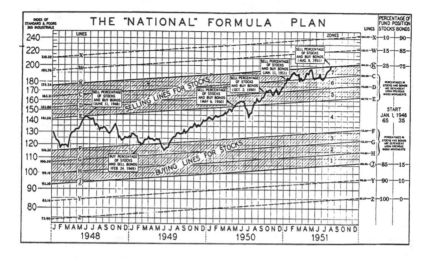

The 1951 edition of Graham and Dodd's *Security Analysis* commented on formula timing plans as follows:

> They are especially popular with the finance committees of colleges, philanthropic institutions, and the like, where the trustees are justifiably anxious to mitigate the responsibilities of common stock investment with the aid of reasonable appearing impersonal devices.

All of which sounds remarkably like today's approach toward passive cores and indexing.

Another glance at Chart I used by Keystone Custodian Funds as the basis for a formula timing approach, shows the Dow Jones Industrials at 350; and near the upper limit of the band. The Dow was just about to soar beyond the limits of the bands over the next ten years by rising by 100%; after 1954, it would remain in Zone 7 until this day. So much for another investment "answer"!

Sound Value

In 1953, when I first began practical security analysis, Robert D. Hedberg and I, using an approach based on depression psychosis, constructed models of a declining economy, and then tested the earning power of companies under these pessimistic assumptions. As I recall, we assumed a 10% drop in GNP, came up with earnings figures, applied a normal P/E, and came up with a "sound value" price. Buy and sell points were 20% above and below sound value. Needless to say, not only were the assumptions pessimistic, but we also missed the whole point, i.e., that the economy's stability would be the basis for a spectacular rise in P/E's.

By whatever name, most investors of the late 1940's and early 1950's were doing essentially the same thing, letting the previous 20 years be the basis for their investment approach. The focus was on economic instability when it should have been on just the opposite. Fortunately, we had time to change and not miss the whole ball game, but the opportunity costs of the first several years were high.

Compound Annual Growth Rates

By the time of the 1957–58 recession, the U.S. economy had satisfied the backlog of demands that had accumulated during the depression and the war. National defense considerations, arising from the cold war and the Korean conflict, had led to the granting of fast writeoffs of expenditures for new capacity in basic industries under certificates of necessity. Not surprisingly, therefore, the raw and intermediate materials sectors had excess capacity. Yet, these were the very industries which had led the boom and had become investor favorites. By 1960, it became clear that earnings of these companies were in a cyclical pattern.

In contrast, the dull stocks that had been thought of as the widow and orphan variety had, by then, compiled a record of extraordinary consistency. It began to dawn on investors that a 10% per year growth in, say, General Foods or Florida Power and Light was more attractive than the volatile earnings patterns of steel, aluminum, paper, or chemicals. The growth had greater stability and could be expressed in compound terms. Thus, compound annual growth rates were discovered and the mathematical magic of compounding was seized upon as the basis for a great speculative boomlet in the stock market. The boomlet was eagerly fed by underwriters who discovered that all the public needed was a five-year earnings record of consistent gains that could be used for speculative extrapolation of a compound annual growth rate. The new issue boom was wild and undiscerning. Past growth rates dominated valuations without regard to the quality or size of the enterprise.

Even though the speculation of 1960–62 fell of its own weight, the concepts it engendered, and the outstanding investment results compiled by certain nontraditional institutional investors, had considerable durability. Compound growth rates, derived largely from past records, became *de rigueur*, formed the basis of the "one-decision" stock speculation of 1971–73, and remain with us today as the mainstay of most valuation procedures for stocks, even in the aftermath of the collapse of growth stocks. The usefulness of growth rates depends upon a stable economy, for without a high degree of economic stability they are a useless concept, difficult to forecast with any confidence, and requiring the use of a normalized earnings approach.

All of which raises the important question of the effect of inflation upon the usefulness of compound growth rates. With only modest exaggeration it can be said that inflation has turned every company into a growth company, at least in terms of reported earnings. While there has been some good work done that attempts to remove general price level inflation, underdepreciation, and inventory profits from reported earnings, there is little attention being paid to the effect of specific inflation (by product line) on the bottom line. For example, what is the effect of inflation upon Texas Instruments as compared with, say, Procter & Gamble? Texas Instruments' major product line is declining in price while Procter & Gamble's is not. But are semiconductors, microprocessors, minicomputers, and calculators declining less in price than would be the case with lower inflation rates? How much less?

Inflation has turned every company into a growth company, at least in terms of reported earnings.

I was fortunate to have Professor Julius Grodinsky of the Wharton School as my first teacher in security analysis. He maintained that it is relatively simple to identify growing and declining industries by examining the price trends of their products. True growth industries, he maintained, are those that can produce growing earnings as a *result* of lower real prices for their products. Lower product prices widen markets and the wider markets produce lower unit costs of production. Industries that have matured need stable real prices while declining industries are constantly fighting for higher real prices. In my opinion, this is still a valid concept that needs to be used more by analysts in discerning growth from inflationary benefits and seeking to answer the question of whether there really is an inherent compound growth rate for a company or an industry or whether the past growth rate is an economic accident.

TOTAL RETURN-PERFORMANCE INVESTING

With the Merrill Lynch-University of Chicago study of the mid-1960's, it became fashionable to rationalize equity investing on the basis of long-term returns expressed as a compound annual rate of total return. This study, together with the spectacular returns compiled by the early starters in the performance race in the years 1954–64, were the foundation stones for the total return-performance revolution of the mid-1960's.

True growth industries . . . are those that can produce growing earnings as a result *of lower real prices for their products.*

There was nothing complicated about the rationale. If unmanaged equities had provided a 9% return over a long period that included boom, depression, and war, what wonders might be wrought by a group of well-educated, expert, professional portfolio managers? The answer was there for all to see: certain aggressive mutual fund portfolios had compiled five-year records that were far superior to the diversified, blue chip portfolios that had been the typical province of banks and traditional investment advisors. It's hard to believe now, but managers did not provide and clients did not demand performance statistics in those days prior to 1965. The main reason for this indifference to relative performance, I suppose, was that absolute returns were high enough to be satisfying in themselves. Traditional portfolios, however, began to look a bit pale as the postwar boom faded and the service economy began to be the dominant growth sector. The technological impetus from the Soviet launching of Sputnik also gave rise to hundreds of previously nonexistent or unknown but now booming companies that exploited the flow of Federal dollars to the space and missile programs.

Whole new industries were discovered, labeled, generously brought to market for the first time by their owners and the investment bankers, and greedily devoured by investors, both directly and through mutual funds. Leisure time, textbooks, specialty retailing, home builders, land developers, direct mail insurance, lodging, semiconductors, and many other industries made their initial appearances.

Heroes in Wall Street were commonplace, led by the enigmatic Gerald Tsai, whose Manhattan Fund garnered some $200 million in its public offering. Oh, random walk, perfect market, where were you then? The "Go-Go-Era" was in full swing, and it was fun.

It was a gigantic speculative boom that attracted a widening list of adherents. Pension funds became players, as did endowments and foundations. The convention of the Financial Analysts Federation gave way to the Institutional Investor Conference, where the heroes were worshiped at the altar of performance, complete with lavish entertainment by brokerage houses financed by swollen commissions under fixed rates.

By the late 1960's, only the Vietnam War stood between investors and Nirvana. Investors, looking back in their typical fashion, had seized upon the experience of the previous decade as the basis for constructing portfolios. Inflation had been creeping upward, but it was thought to be largely the result of the war, and faith existed that public policy could deal with it effectively. Total return investing was the only legitimate goal, and yields were unimportant. In retrospect, it seems clear that the concept of total return as it was applied then was nothing more than an unconscious rationalization of low yields and high valuations by investment managers and of higher spending rates by institutional investors. Today, when valuation levels are depressed, the concept of total return is being increasingly questioned, just when its applicability is most relevant.

Once again, the use of recent history as a prescription for the future failed miserably. There was an abundance of studies showing the historical superiority of "growth stocks." The new brand of economic uncertainty, born out of inflation, price controls, and the harsh, unfamiliar environment reinforced the attraction of past, sure, old reliable earnings growth of a select group of quality companies. "One-decision stocks," the stocks that had really done the job, became the rallying cry that took these issues to what was the most speculative extreme in our generation involving really big money. My friend, John Neff, one of the best investors of our time, shook his head in disbelief, saying, "There has to be more to this game than buying a list of growth stocks and then spending the next 20 years on the golf course." This ridiculous institutional speculation, participated in by many of the greatest names in the financial community, came home to roost in 1973–74.

HISTORICALLY BASED PROBABILITIES AND SIMULATIONS

The use of historical probabilities for simulations of future portfolio returns, so much in fashion now, is the epitome of reliance on past experience as a tool. The problem with this approach is not so much that the future will be unlike the past, as assured as that is. Rather, these probabilities are used without regard to the starting point. It's obviously ludicrous to suggest that future returns and the probability of achieving them are the same from beginning levels of valuations that are significantly different. Such an approach would suggest that the future holds the same probabilities of given levels of return over, say, five or ten years, from today's valuation levels for stocks as it did in 1972. To say that optimum portfolios can be constructed using historically derived probabilities just has to be nonsense, unless we recompute the probabilities from various valuation levels for equities, or unless one is using time periods that are so long as to be meaningless in the investment lifetimes or careers of individuals. Long before history has had time to prove itself, there will be new people with new prescriptions making the decisions.

MPT, Index Funds, Etc.

The latest in the parade of history's answers is Modern Port-folio Theory.

Actually, all that MPT does is provide some quantitative measuring devices for certain portfolio characteristics that experienced investors have known about for generations. Stripped of its fine points, MPT says:

Some stocks rise and fall more in bull and bear markets than others.

Portfolios that fluctuate more violently should be expected to provide higher returns than more stable portfo-lios.

Most of a portfolio's fluctuations reflect general market fluctuations.

Diversification lessens risk. Non-market risk can be diver-sified away and probably should be.

Thus, we may be able to control variability of returns although not the returns themselves.

Transaction and investment management costs are signifi-cant penalties to returns.

That choice of asset mix is the most important influence on future returns and future risk.

Although these are all valuable investment concepts, many users of MPT seem to see an implied precision in their quantitative machinations and gain a comfort therefrom that may be dangerous. This danger arises primarily because it diverts too much attention from the big question of whether to own stocks or bonds at all, and in what relative amounts. I'm not speaking here of market timing decisions or deci-sions regarding the theoretically optimum long-term asset mix, but a much bigger question of whether or not we are in one of those crucial decision periods that occur only rarely in an investment lifetime.

Looking back on my career of about 30 years, there have been three such decision periods. The first was in the late 1940's and early 1950's, when equity valuations were low because of the postwar depression psychosis, while at the same time, interest rates were being artificially supported. The second was in the late 1950's and early 1960's, the end of the postwar and postdepression catch-up, when it became necessary to recognize the rise of a new generation of investments in secondary and tertiary industries that were far different from the primary industries that spearheaded the postwar boom. The third was in the late 1960's and early 1970's, when it was crucial to recognize that equity valuation levels were in generally high ground and that the investor's insulation from disappointment regarding growth and/or economic stability was nonexistent. In each of these cases there was a period of three–five years during which correct decisions could be made, decisions that have dominated the longer term return levels of portfolios.

We know, of course, that only a few investors make these decisions well. The reason for this is simply that most let the experience of the previous period dominate their thinking. This is exactly what is occurring now. The poor returns generated by equities, combined with the parade of economic, monetary, social, and political discontinuities of the past decade, are responsible for the substantial reductions of equity ratios, diversion of pension fund cash flow from equities, and the resultant depressed valuation levels of equities. True to historical form, investors have rationalized these valuation levels with sophisticated valuation approaches, incorporating current levels of interest rates and historical risk premiums. In the process, they avoid the big question of whether or not we are in a period of general and substantial undervaluation of stocks that will prove to have offered a very, very big opportunity, or whether we are entering a period of severe economic decline and chaos that will turn the apparent undervaluation into overvaluation.

Index funds, "yield tilt" funds, passive portfolios, or the inclusion of foreign securities in domestic portfolios, all of which are based one way or the other on historical experience, are not the answer to optimizing future returns. For this purpose, nothing strikes me as wrong as an indexed portfolio, which could turn out to be every bit as wrong as formula timing was in 1951.

I say this for two reasons. First, it does nothing to help you escape the ultimate asset allocation decision—do you want to be in the market or don't you? If the market goes into a tailspin, the investor holding an index fund will gain small comfort by matching the market's decline or by knowing that many other investors are doing even worse. Then the risk is that such discouraged investors will convert their funds to cash at the very bottom, which is just further proof that indexing does not help you out over the asset allocation problem.

Only a few investors make ... decisions well. The reason for this is simply that most let the experience of the previous period dominate their thinking.

Second, it obviously does nothing to guarantee that you will do better than the market on the way up. The investor in index funds would fall short in a period in which the stocks of the large companies that dominate the index were substantially underperforming the smaller companies or newer industries that are either not yet in the index or carry a low weight in it. As we know from the decade of 1958–68, such a period can last for five or ten years or longer.

Will the statistics on "risk adjusted return" be any consolation or will the indexing decision be abandoned after a period of low returns relative to the many success stories of other investors? One may think one can remain objective, rational, and true only to long-term objectives when the short-term results become frustrating, but to quote Aldous Huxley again, "the only completely consistent people are the dead." Unmanaged, indexed portfolios will assuredly turn out to be client-managed portfolios, that is, the client will decide he can do better, or in the case of the collapse of stocks, that only cash will do.

MPT AND RISK

One of the problems that MPT addresses is that of defining risk. The quantification of risk has been eluding investors for generations. The definition of risk was never fully formalized even though investors understood that it really meant the possibility of a permanent loss of value in a stock or portfolio in either nominal or real terms. Risk exists because businesses can go bad and/or because investors can pay too much for a specifically or generally assumed future.

The use of historical variability leads to the odd conclusion that stocks are riskier today at the 850 Dow Jones level than they were at 1050 . . .

The concept of investment quality was used (and is still used by many investors) as a proxy for risk. It is an obviously inadequate proxy, because it deals only with the riskiness of a company's business or its finances, which in turn may be linked only weakly with the riskiness of the stock.

Largely because it is easily quantifiable now that we have computers, the riskiness of a stock has become defined as relative price volatility, most of which is associated with the volatility of the market, the remainder being associated with other factors. For an entire portfolio, risk is defined as variability of return. While the concept of variability is undoubtedly an important element of risk, the use of historical variability as a risk measurement can in itself be ludicrous. Over the past ten years, the stock market has been more volatile and provided more variability of return than in the previous 20 years. Not only have returns been more variable, but they have also been disappointly low as a result of a rather constant erosion in the valuation of earnings, assets, and dividends.

The use of historical variability leads to the odd conclusion that stocks are riskier today at the 850 Dow Jones level than they were at 1050, i.e., riskier at 7 times earnings than they were at 20 times earnings. The same holds true for individual issues. A stock that declined in a jagged price pattern from 200% of book value while the stock market was stable or rising would show a high independent volatility. Does this mean that it is riskier after the decline than before? Or, take the case of two stocks with predicted future returns that are equal, say 15%, which have high financial quality and an equal history of price volatility. Yet, one of these stocks sells at 17 times earnings and the other at 6 times earnings. Are they equal in risk? The validity of such questions assures me that a satisfactory quantification of risk, except in hindsight, remains elusive.

FOREIGN EQUITIES

Recently, foreign equities have been advocated for inclusion in U.S. portfolios because they have had historically low covariance with U.S. stocks and have provided a higher return. Thus, foreign equities seem to offer a portfolio with both lower variability and higher returns. But shouldn't we remember that foreign industrialized economies started from a depressed level because of World War II, and were stimulated by U.S. policies of direct aid as well as other policies to offset the dollar shortage? How about the aftereffect of an erosion of the dollar (following the overachievement of success of U.S. policies) and the contribution of that erosion to the high returns on foreign stocks?

These conditions that contributed to the happy result of foreign investing no longer exist. Foreign economies are on their own now, are heavily reliant on U.S. technology, and do not even approach the natural advantages of the U.S. economy or, in most cases, the political stability of the U.S.

REAL ESTATE

As everyone knows, real estate investments generally have been far superior to common stocks over the last 15 years. In fact, just about every kind of asset has been superior to common stocks.

After an extended period of massive credit infusions that have served to stimulate the real estate inflation, many large portfolios are now concluding that that is where they ought to be. It seems likely that those portfolios are making the same mistakes that were made in 1972 by assuming that growth stocks were the only place to be after price/earnings ratios had tripled and quadrupled.

FIXED-INCOME SECURITIES

Fixed-income securities are deemed useful to dampen variability of return, in other words, to lessen "risk." While I would acknowledge that long-term fixed-income returns are heavily dependent on the interest rate on the reinvestment of interest income, which in turn may give the investor a shot at matching inflation, this concept has no validity for many investors such as endowments, foundations, and individuals who must spend rather than reinvest their income. Such investors assure themselves of a permanent loss of value from inflation by owning long-term fixed-income securities.

Indeed, investors are today, rightly or wrongly, assuming that inflation is the biggest economic problem they face. At the same time, they assume that cash equivalents will continue to be superior to other securities just because they have been superior up to now. How they can be so inconsistent as to *assure* themselves of doing no better than inflation, and probably worse, if inflation stays high, is beyond me.

Doesn't risk avoidance argue that a portfolio should at least have a chance of maintaining its real value? Isn't the purpose of investing to *increase* real value? If investors are not to be schizophrenic, shouldn't they look upon a bond as a hedge against *deflation* rather than merely as a variability dampener?

FINAL OBSERVATIONS

Perhaps I am too firm in my conviction that history's major lesson is that there really is no answer and that most mistakes are the result of using historical evidence to design strategies for the future. I have not meant to put down those who are doing serious research in the field of portfolio management even if it is heavily reliant on historic data. Indeed, they have taught us a great deal. The active practitioners of Modern Portfolio Theory have constructed ways to limit their narrowly defined risk and have enabled all of us to dissect our portfolios in new ways and increase our understanding of portfolio dynamics. Inevitably, however, the ways in which MPT is being applied today are heavily influenced by the experience of the past decade, during which time risk-free assets earned higher returns than stocks.

Poor performance in the 1950's was the result of the influence of the experience of the 1930's and the post World

War I period. Poor performance in the 1960's was the result of staying with the "smokestack" companies that did so well in the 1950's. Poor performance in the 1970's was the result of a philosophical commitment to the growth concepts that had worked in the 1960's, as well as overconfidence concerning the ability of public policy to deal with economic and price stability. Poor performance in the 1980's will be the result of myopia borne out of the experience of the 1970's.

Specifically, investors should question the set of widely accepted assumptions that now dominate the psyche of investors. A few of the more obvious of these are:

— Inflation is bad for stocks
— Inflation will be the major economic problem of the next decade
— Worldwide depression is highly unlikely
— Stock prices and bond prices move together
— The energy problem is a growth inhibitor
— Risk and variability of return are synonymous
— Highly diversified portfolios are desirable as a protection against risk

Answers to such questions don't come easily. Nevertheless, a recognition that there are no absolute truths in this business requires that they be asked, for we are almost assuredly in one of those rare and crucial decision periods, the aftermath of which will dominate the investment records of portfolios for years to come.

Jim Rogers made millions as George Soros' first partner and then on his own. He grew up in the small, isolated Alabama town of Demopolis, where at age five he first started making money by picking up bottles after baseball games. While a capitalist at heart, he was unsure of what he wanted to do with his life; so, after graduating from Yale in 1964, he decided to take a summer job with a securities firm and then go to Oxford in the fall to study economics, philosophy, and politics. After Oxford and a stint in the Army he returned to investing. As he once said, "What I liked about it was not so much investing money, because at that time I didn't have any, but that if you were smart, used your wits, and paid attention to the world it was all you had to do."

Rogers, who has made his mark as an international investor, likes to wager not on a few stocks, but on whole countries that he feels are better off than most others realize. For example, he started investing in Portugal in the mid-1980s right after the communist government was overthrown—against the advice of a Portugese investment firm. Rogers bought all 24 stocks on the Lisbon exchange and made a killing. Part of his success is simply finding ways to invest in a country that has few or no financial institutions catering to investors. When Rogers was interested in putting money in Brazil, a stock exchange official there told him the only way for foreigners to do so was through the black market. Rogers asked where the black market was, and the official replied, he was it.

In 1990, Rogers and his girlfriend set out to travel the world by motorcycle. Over the next 22 months, they traveled 65,067 miles, a record. When he arrived back, people asked Rogers how the United States looked to him. His response: "I hate to say it, because this is my home, but I see America as an obvious short." He believes we're still too isolated from the world and are unwilling to address our economic problems. In *Get Smart . . . and Make a Fortune,* Rogers explains why it's important to not turn a blind eye and to listen to what others are saying, especially in the media, when determining the optimal time to buy and sell securities.

Get Smart . . . and Make a Fortune
Jim Rogers

I
n 1980, the price of a barrel of oil had risen alarmingly, and long lines of frustrated motorists sat fuming at every petrol pump in the United States. Newspaper articles appeared daily that bemoaned the permanent shortages in non-renewable fuels, and every learned expert on Wall Street and in academia was certain that oil had to rise from $40 to $100.

Interest rates had risen alarmingly and investors were in a panic over high inflation and labour unrest. There was a sense that the US was slipping as a world power and that shortages in all sorts of goods were permanent; indeed, that the world was running out of everything.

It is learning to listen to the gloom and doom at bottoms and question it, and to the exultation at tops and question this as well, that makes a sharp investor.

True, the supply of oil *was* smaller than the demand for a while in the 1970s. But with the rise in prices had come the inevitable rise in production. There were more drilling rigs, more money pouring into holes in the ground in the Gulf of Mexico, the North Sea and South America, and more young people deciding to study geology as a career. By the mid-1980s, though, the bottom had dropped out of the oil market and prices collapsed.

The smart investor learns to listen to the popular press with an ear tuned for panic extremes. At market tops, the tune will run: "This time it's different from all other times. . . . This is an investment you put money in and forget."

Even in 1980, the iron law of supply and demand still held, as common sense suggests it must. If there is more of an item for sale than there are buyers, the price goes down; if there is less, the price goes up. There may be time lags, but it always works like this.

The smart investor learns to listen to the popular press with an ear tuned for panic extremes. At market tops, the tune will run: "This time it's different from all other times. Trees will continue to grow and grow and grow. Buy yourself a tree and watch it reach 50ft, 100ft, 1,000ft. This is an investment you put money in and forget."

At bottoms, the song will become a dirge. Prices are severely depressed. Every company with any sense is getting out of this market. It has only a marginal future. Words such as "disaster" and "doomed" and "dead" will be used to describe such a market, and the alert investor will hear them clearly without a newsletter to advise him or a call from his stockbroker.

It is an old story. Today, news articles trumpet the stock market as the ideal place to increase assets over the long term. Indeed, the Dow Jones index just now is over 6,000. But, 15 to 20 years ago when it was under 1,000, *Business Week* ran a cover declaring: "Stocks are dead."

(Some investors claim they are able to profit by following the opposite tack from *Business Week*'s covers: they sell when the magazine declares something is a good investment, and buy on the something-is-dead covers.)

In all markets, supply and demand are rising and falling constantly, hurtling from one extreme to the other. To an investor with the right ear and eye, fortunes are waiting to be made.

Is it easy? No. Does it take work? Yes.

How, then, can you time when to buy and when to sell? It is difficult. Note, however, that all large bottoms are alike, whether they be in the wheat, stock or property markets, and that the same is true for tops.

It does not take esoteric knowledge or an MBA degree or some mystical skill. Read the newspapers, watch the television news — and think.

Pick any previous top or bottom, anywhere, any time, from the beginning of time until now. When you study it, the conviction of certainty of all the participants — at the extreme top and the extreme bottom — will be startling.

As well, watch who is going into, and who is getting out of, a business. At bottoms, many who have been in the business for a long, long time will be leaving in droves or "diversifying".

At tops, those who have little or no experience will crowd in.

As a classic example, US Steel bought Marathon Oil at the top of the oil boom in order to diversify. But it should have stuck to the business it knew and bought mini-mills, which turned out to be solidly profitable even as oil fell.

As another example: remember all the farmers and labourers who ran west in the gold rush? Often, in earlier stock market tops, many doctors and dentists gave up their practices to enter the financial community.

At the top of the 1980s' hotel-building boom in China, professors fled the security of the university to work as bell-boys. The pay in tourism was so much better and the future so much rosier.

It is learning to listen to the gloom and doom at bottoms and question it, and to the exultation at tops and question this as well, that makes a sharp investor. It does not take esoteric knowledge or an MBA degree or some mystical skill.

The smart investor . . . learns to buy fear and panic and to sell greed and hysteria.

Read the newspapers, watch the television news—and think. It did not take a financial genius to see that when US farmers were going broke in the 1980s, and singer Willie Nelson was conducting Farm Aid concerts to raise money for them, that some sort of bottom was establishing itself.

It helps to have a sense of the history of the public markets, too, and the library is full of books about their rise and fall, something which is driven by mob psychology. That is, tops and bottoms are creatures of extremes. They rise above all rational expectation and hang there, and they fall farther than common sense suggests.

The smart investor — the one who does not consider himself a financial genius but trains himself to analyse the newspapers and television and to pick tops and bottoms by the extremes in the public's attitudes — learns to buy fear and panic and to sell greed and hysteria.

PETER LYNCH
1944–

The *Wall Street Journal* named Peter Lynch one of the greatest investors of all time for his remarkable performance as manager of Fidelity's renowned Magellan Fund. When Lynch took it over in 1977, the fund was comprised of some 45 stocks worth about $20 million. By the time he retired from active duty at Fidelity in 1990 to spend more time with his family, the fund had diversified into more than 1,200 businesses and was worth almost $13 billion. By visiting more than 500 companies a year and talking to dozens of executives each week, Lynch brought back an astounding return. An investor who plunked down $10,000 with him in 1977 would have walked away with $280,000 in 1990. Not all investments were based on meticulous research; for example, he bought into Taco Bell after trying one of their burritos on a road trip.

Lynch, who grew up in a Boston suburb, first started learning about investing as an 11-year-old caddy at the local country club, where he listened to the big shot executive members talk money. The job was thrust upon him; his father died when he was 10 and he had to help with the family finances. He went to Boston College on a caddy scholarship, then to Wharton for an MBA, before being hired by Fidelity in 1969. He started as a research analyst, specializing in the metals industry. In 1974 he was promoted to research director, and three years later he was picked to run Magellan.

His investment philosophy is simple: "Go for a business that any idiot can run—because sooner or later any idiot probably is going to run it." In the 1980s Lynch disdained the merger mania that swept the country, preferring to invest in more pedestrian opportunities like a chain of funeral homes—something everyone would eventually need. Another favorite maxim: "Know what you own and be able to explain it to a twelve-year-old in a minute." To find those stocks, he advises looking close to home, where you come into contact with companies everyday. In *Stalking the Tenbagger,* he illustrates how one of those backyard companies might just turn into the exalted tenbagger, a company whose stock has the potential to increase tenfold.

Stalking the Tenbagger
Peter Lynch

T he best place to begin look-
ing for the tenbagger is close to home — if not in the backyard
then down at the shopping mall, and especially wherever you
happen to work. With most of the tenbaggers . . . — Dunkin'
Donuts, The Limited, Subaru, Dreyfus, McDonald's, Tam-
brands, and Pep Boys — the first signs of success were apparent at hundreds of locations across the country. The fireman
in New England, the customers in central Ohio where Kentucky Fried Chicken first opened up, the mob down at Pic
'N' Save, all had a chance to say, "This is great; I wonder
about the stock," long before Wall Street got its original clue.

The average person comes across a likely prospect two
or three times a year — sometimes more. Executives at Pep
Boys, clerks at Pep Boys, lawyers and accountants, suppliers
of Pep Boys, the firm that did the advertising, sign painters,
building contractors for the new stores, and even the people
who washed the floors all must have observed Pep Boys'
success. Thousands of potential investors got this "tip," and
that doesn't even count the hundreds of thousands of customers.

At the same time, the Pep Boys employee who buys
insurance for the company could have noticed that insurance
prices were going up — which is a good sign that the insur-

ance industry is about to turn around—and so maybe he'd consider investing in the insurance suppliers. Or maybe the Pep Boys building contractors noticed that cement prices had firmed, which is good news for the companies that supply cement.

You don't have to be a vice president at Exxon to sense the growing prosperity in that company . . . You can be a roustabout, a geologist, a driller, a supplier, a gas-station owner, a grease monkey, or even a client at the gas pumps.

All along the retail and wholesale chains, people who make things, sell things, clean things, or analyze things encounter numerous stockpicking opportunities. In my own business—the mutual-fund industry—the salesmen, clerks, secretaries, analysts, accountants, telephone operators, and computer installers, all could scarcely have overlooked the great boom of the early 1980s that sent mutual-fund stocks soaring.

You don't have to be a vice president at Exxon to sense the growing prosperity in that company, or a turnaround in oil prices. You can be a roustabout, a geologist, a driller, a supplier, a gas-station owner, a grease monkey, or even a client at the gas pumps.

You don't have to work in Kodak's main office to learn that the new generation of inexpensive, easy-to-use, high-quality 35mm cameras from Japan is reviving the photo industry, and that film sales are up. You could be a film salesman, the owner of a camera store, or a clerk in a camera store. You could also be the local wedding photographer who notices that five or six relatives are taking unofficial pictures at weddings and making it harder for you to get good shots.

You don't have to be Steven Spielberg to know that some new blockbuster, or string of blockbusters, is going to give a significant boost to the earnings of Paramount or Orion Pictures. You could be an actor, an extra, a director, a stuntman, a lawyer, a gaffer, the makeup person, or the usher at a local cinema, where the standing-room-only crowds six weeks in a row inspire you to investigate the pros and cons of investing in Orion's stock.

Maybe you're a teacher and the school board chooses your school to test a new gizmo that takes attendance, saving the teachers thousands of wasted hours counting heads. "Who makes this gizmo?" is the first question I'd ask.

How about Automatic Data Processing, which processes nine million paychecks a week for 180,000 small and medium-sized companies? This has been one of the all-time great opportunities: The company went public in 1961 and has increased earnings every year without a lapse. The worst it ever did was to earn 11 percent more than the previous year, and that was during the 1982–83 recession when many companies reported losses.

So often we struggle to pick a winning stock, when all the while a winning stock has been struggling to pick us.

Automatic Data Processing sounds like the sort of high-tech enterprise I try to avoid, but in reality it's not a computer company. It uses computers to process paychecks, and users of technology are the biggest beneficiaries of high-tech. As competition drives down the price of computers, a firm such as Automatic Data can buy the cheaper equipment, so its costs are continually reduced. This only adds to profits.

Without fanfare, this mundane enterprise that came public at six cents a share (adjusted for splits) now sells for

$40—a 600-bagger long-term. It got as high as $54 before the October stumble. The company has twice as much cash as debt and shows no sign of slowing down.

The officers and employees of 180,000 client firms could certainly have known about the success of Automatic Data Processing, and since many of Automatic Data's biggest and best customers are major brokerage houses, so could half of Wall Street.

So often we struggle to pick a winning stock, when all the while a winning stock has been struggling to pick us.

THE TENBAGGER IN ULCERS

Can't think of any such opportunity in your own life? What if you're retired, live ten miles from the nearest traffic light, grow your own food, and don't have a television set? Well, maybe one day you have to go to a doctor. The rural existence has given you ulcers, which is the perfect introduction to SmithKline Beckman.

A great patient's drug is one that cures an affliction once and for all, but a great investor's drug is one that the patient has to keep buying.

Hundreds of doctors, thousands of patients, and millions of friends and relatives of patients heard about the wonder drug Tagamet, which came on the market in 1976. So did the pharmacist who dispensed the pills and the delivery boy who spent half his workday delivering them. Tagamet was a boon for the afflicted, and a bonanza for investors.

A great patients' drug is one that cures an affliction once and for all, but a great investor's drug is one that the patient has to keep buying. Tagamet was one of the latter. It provided fantastic relief from the suffering from ulcers, and the direct beneficiaries had to keep taking it again and again, making indirect beneficiaries out of the shareholders of SmithKline Beckman, the makers of Tagamet. Thanks largely to Tagamet, the stock rose from $7½ a share in 1977 to $72 a share at the 1987 high.

These users and prescribers had a big lead on the Wall Street talent. No doubt some of the oxymorons suffered from ulcers themselves—this is an anxious business—but SmithKline must not have been included on their buy lists, because it was a year before the stock began its ascent. During the testing period for the drug, 1974–76, the price climbed from around $4 to $7, and when the government approved Tagamet in 1977, the stock sold for $11. From there it shot up to $72.*

Then if you missed Tagamet, you had a second chance with Glaxo and its own wonder drug for ulcers—Zantac. Zantac went through testing in the early eighties and got its U.S. approval in 1983. Zantac was just as well-received as Tagamet, and just as profitable to Glaxo. In mid-1983 Glaxo's stock sold for $7.50 and moved up to $30 in 1987.

Did the doctors who prescribed Tagamet and Zantac buy shares in SmithKline and Glaxo? Somehow I doubt that many did. It's more likely that the doctors were fully invested in oil stocks. Perhaps they heard that Union Oil of California was a takeover candidate. Meanwhile, the Union Oil executives were probably buying drug stocks, especially

---

* Throughout the day I'm constantly referring to stock charts. I keep a long-term chart book close to my side at the office, and another one at home, to remind me of momentous and humbling occurrences.

What most people get out of family photo albums, I get out of these wonderful publications. If my life were to flash before my eyes, I bet I'd see the chart of Flying Tiger, my first tenbagger; of Apple Computer, a stock I rediscovered thanks in part to my family; and Polaroid, which makes me remember the new camera that my wife and I took on our honeymoon. That was back in a more primitive era, when we had to let the film develop for sixty seconds before we could see the picture. Since neither of us had a watch, Carolyn used her physiology training and counted out the seconds with her pulse.

the hot issues like American Surgery Centers, which sold for $18.50 in 1982 and fell to 5 cents.

In general, if you polled all the doctors, I'd bet only a small percentage would turn out to be invested in medical stocks, and more would be invested in oil; and if you polled the shoe-store owners, more would be invested in aerospace than in shoes, while the aerospace engineers are more likely to dabble in shoe stocks. Why it is that stock certificates, like grasses, are always greener in somebody else's pasture I'm not sure.

Perhaps a winning investment seems so unlikely in the first place that people can best imagine it happening as far away as possible, somewhere off in the Great Beyond, just as we all imagine that perfect behavior takes place in heaven and not on earth. Therefore the doctor who understands the ethical drug business inside out is more comfortable investing in Schlumberger, an oil-service company about which he knows nothing; while the managers of Schlumberger are likely to own Johnson & Johnson or American Home Products.

Though people who buy stocks about which they are ignorant may get lucky and enjoy great rewards, it seems to me they are competing under unnecessary handicaps . . .

True, true. You don't necessarily have to know anything about a company for its stock to go up. But the important point is that (1) the oil experts, on average, are in a better position than doctors to decide when to buy or to sell Schlumberger; and (2) the doctors, on average, know better than oil experts when to invest in a successful drug. The person with the edge is always in a position to outguess the person without an edge — who after all will be the last to learn of important changes in a given industry.

The oilman who invests in SmithKline because his broker suggests it won't realize that patients have abandoned

Tagamet and switched to a rival ulcer drug until the stock is down 40 percent and the bad news has been fully "discounted" in the price. "Discounting" is a Wall Street euphemism for pretending to have anticipated surprising developments.

On the other hand, the oilman will be among the earliest to observe the telltale signs of revival in the oil patch, a revival that will inspire Schlumberger's eventual comeback.

Though people who buy stocks about which they are ignorant may get lucky and enjoy great rewards, it seems to me they are competing under unnecessary handicaps, just like the marathon runner who decides to stake his reputation on a bobsled race.

THE DOUBLE EDGE

Here we've been talking about the oil executive and his knowledge, and lumping him and it together in the same chapter with the knowledge of the customers in the checkout line at Pep Boys. Of course it's absurd to contend that the one is equal to the other. One is a professional's understanding of the workings of an industry; the other is a consumer's awareness of a likable product. Both are useful in picking stocks, but in different ways.

The professional's edge is especially helpful in knowing when and when not to buy shares in companies that have been around awhile, especially those in the so-called cyclical industries. If you work in the chemical industry, then you'll be among the first to realize that demand for polyvinyl chloride is going up, prices are going up, and excess inventories are going down. You'll be in a position to know that no new competitors have entered the market and no new plants are under construction, and that it takes two to three years to build one. All this means higher profits for existing companies that make the product.

Or if you own a Goodyear tire store and suddenly after three years of sluggish sales you notice that you can't keep up with new orders, you've just received a strong signal that Goodyear may be on the rise. You already know that Goodyear's new high-performance tire is the best. You call up your broker and ask for the latest background information on the tire company, instead of waiting for the broker to call to tell you about Wang Laboratories.

Unless you work in some job that's related to computers, what good is a Wang tip to you? What could you possibly know that thousands of other people don't know a lot better? If the answer is "nada," then you haven't got an edge in Wang. But if you sell tires, make tires, or distribute tires, you've got an edge in Goodyear. All along the supply lines of the manufacturing industry, people who make things and sell things encounter numerous stockpicking opportunities.

It might be a service industry, the property-casualty insurance business, or even the book business where you can spot a turnaround. Buyers and sellers of any product notice shortages and gluts, price changes and shifts in demand. Such information isn't very valuable in the auto industry, since car sales are reported every ten days. Wall Street is obsessed with cars. But in most other endeavors the grass-roots observer can spot a turnaround six to twelve months ahead of the regular financial analysts. This gives an incredible head start in anticipating an improvement in earnings — and earnings, as you'll see, make stock prices go higher.

It doesn't have to be a turnaround in sales that gets your attention. It may be that companies you know about have incredible hidden assets that don't show up on the balance sheet. If you work in real estate, maybe you know that a department store chain owns four city blocks in downtown Atlanta, carried on the books at pre–Civil War prices. This is a definite hidden asset, and similar opportunities might be found in gold, oil, timberland, and TV stations.

You're looking for a situation where the value of the assets per share exceeds the price per share of the stock. In such delightful instances you can truly buy a great deal of something for nothing. I've done it myself numerous times.

You can develop your own stock detection system outside the normal channels of Wall Street, where you'll always get the news late.

Thousands of employees of Storer Communications and its affiliates, plus countless others who work in cable TV or network TV, could have figured out that Storer's TV and cable properties were valued at $100 per share, while the stock was selling for $30. Executives knew this, programmers could have known it, cameramen could have known it, and even the people who come around to hook up the cable to the house could have known it. All any of them had to do was buy Storer at $30 or $35 or $40 or $50 and wait for the Wall Street experts to figure it out. Sure enough, Storer was taken private in late 1985 at $93.50 a share—which by 1988 turned out to have been a bargain price.

I could go on for the rest of the book about the edge that being in a business gives the average stockpicker. On top of that, there's the consumer's edge that's helpful in picking out the winners from the newer and smaller fast-growing companies, especially in the retail trades. Whichever edge applies, the exciting part is that you can develop your own stock detection system outside the normal channels of Wall Street, where you'll always get the news late.

MY WONDERFUL EDGE

Who could have had a greater advantage than yours truly, sitting in an office at Fidelity during the boom in financial services and in the mutual funds? This was my chance to make up for missing Pebble Beach. Perhaps I can be forgiven for that incredible asset play. Golf and sailing are my summer hobbies, but mutual funds are my regular business.

I'd been coming to work here for nearly two decades. I know half the officers in the major financial-service companies, I follow the daily ups and downs, and I could notice important trends months before the analysts on Wall Street. You couldn't have been more strategically placed to cash in on the bonanza of the early 1980s.

The people who print prospectuses must have seen it—they could hardly keep up with all the new shareholders in the mutual funds. The sales force must have seen it as they crisscrossed the country in their Winnebagos and returned with billions in new assets. The maintenance services must have seen the expansion in the offices at Federated, Franklin, Dreyfus, and Fidelity. The companies that sold mutual funds prospered as never before in their history. The mad rush was on.

Fidelity isn't a public company, so you couldn't invest in the rush here. But what about Dreyfus? Want to see a chart that doesn't stop? The stock sold for 40 cents a share in 1977, then nearly $40 a share in 1986, a 100-bagger in nine years, and much of that during a lousy stock market. Franklin was a 138-bagger, and Federated was up 50-fold before it was bought out by Aetna. I was right on top of all of them. I knew the Dreyfus story, the Franklin story, and the Federated story from beginning to end. Everything was right, earnings were up, the momentum was obvious.

How much did I make from all this? Zippo. I didn't buy a single share of any of the financial services companies: not Dreyfus, not Federated, not Franklin. I missed the whole deal and didn't realize it until it was too late. I guess I was too busy thinking about Union Oil of California, just like the doctors.

PART II

Attitude and Philosophy

"Stocks and sentiment do not mix," concludes Ellen Williamson, who survived the 1929 crash and became a notable author on investing. After deciding to invest, bringing the right temperament to the table is crucial. Can a psychological test predetermine success, as Adam Smith playfully suggests? Maybe, but John Moody makes it clear that you must be a venturesome dreamer, imaginative, and foresightful. To that list, John C. Bogle, founder of The Vanguard Group, adds skepticism to penetrate various marketing ploys and the hype generated by brokerage houses. Realistic expectations come as a result of purging emotion from decision making and help one avoid the graveyard depicted by Fred Schwed, renowned author of *Where Are the Customer's Yachts?* That graveyard is reserved for the investing fools who take to crystal-ball gazing. The right attitude goes a long way toward achieving success and avoiding the pitfalls of investing.

ADAM SMITH
1930–

Adam Smith, or George J. W. Goodman as his mother called him, made a huge impression on Wall Street with his 1968 best-seller, *The Money Game,* which takes a hard but funny look at the emotional investor and the irrational crowd. One thing he learned: "Even people on Wall Street are playing a game; they're concerned about what they make, what the other guy makes, but the money *as* money doesn't mean anything." Thus, *The Money Game.* The psuedonym was the result of his own game. For an article on securities analysts, he signed his name *Procrustes.* An anonymous editor changed it to *Adam Smith,* and an icon was reborn. For two years his true identity remained hidden, and then a fellow reporter let the cat out of the bag. Regardless, Goodman was still using the name 20 years later as host of public television's *Adam Smith's Money World.*

After graduating from Harvard University in 1952 and spending several years at Oxford University as a Rhodes scholar, Goodman embarked on his writing career in 1956 as a reporter for *Collier's.* The next year was spent at *Barron's,* and then on to *Time* and *Fortune.* During those early years he wrote three novels satirizing the upper class, all of which were well received. In 1960, he shifted his focus and became a portfolio manager for the Lincoln Fund. "I think," he said, "I'm a person who likes to learn things. . . . The only reason I know anything about Wall Street is that I was curious to know why some people make money and others don't." Over the years, Goodman has discovered that of all the people who want to make money on Wall Street, few want to put in the effort. But for those who do, he thinks the rewards are more than just money. "It is daily theatre," he says, "and it's a way of looking at the world and following the world."

As for what makes a great investor, he actually believes that those with an athletic background excell, because sports has made them more competitive. Knowing economics, business cycles, and security analysis does not guarantee success, Goodman says, because there is this troubling factor known as mass psychology. In *Can Ink Blots Tell You . . . ,* he provides a humorous, yet insightful, psychological test for would-be investors.

Can Ink Blots Tell You Whether You Are the Type Who Will Make a Lot of Money in the Market?
Adam Smith

The social scientists may be too busy reconstructing Vietnamese society along their own lines to pursue the elusive *Australopithecus* of a market animal, but one psychologist of my acquaintance has at least begun to ask some questions and to make the first hypotheses. The hypotheses are not on mass psychology but on individual psychology, so we will have to come back to the crowd. . . . Some of my Boston fund-managing friends put me onto Dr. Charles McArthur at Harvard, since their funds were using him as a consultant to scout out prospective security analysts. Usually Dr. McArthur sits in the splendid Jose Maria Sert building testing Harvard students, and then a couple of the Bostonians figured that if you could spot a dropout with multiple choices and ink blots, maybe the same thing would work for money men. One thing led to another, and now Dr. McArthur spends part of his time firing ink blots at guys who think they can manage a hundred million dollars.

That is how I found myself slicing into the horse steak at lunches at the Harvard Faculty Club. If the President ever appoints you liaison to the intelligentsia or if you find yourself at the Harvard Faculty Club for any other reason, you will be well advised to order the horse steak. That shows you are one of us. The horse steak has been on the menu since the

World War II meat shortages, and the Harvard cognoscenti, always alert for new taste thrills, found it gamier and more interesting than plain old cow steak, especially when washed down with an amusing little Australian Pinot Chardonnay. So it stays on the menu, a permanent fixture. Horse steak is the symbol of the open, questing mind, which is how Harvard likes to think of itself.

Anyway, Dr. McArthur is slicing his way through his own horse steak, modestly pointing out that his samples are too small to be sure. That means if he published this as a scholarly paper with a colon in the middle of the title, the academic psychologists and social scientists might jump all over him. They would probably jump all over him anyway for the very idea of searching for anything so sordid as the type of personality that makes money. Money is anathema in the groves of Academe unless it comes from foundations or the Government, especially the Government.

One thing Dr. McArthur's probings outline is that there is a personality difference between the people who are good at finding stocks and the people who call the shots on the timing and manage the whole portfolio. Security analysts dog down information and come up with an idea about what should be bought or sold, but they do not necessarily make good conductors for the whole orchestra. If they are woodwind players to start, they tend to hear the whole orchestra as woodwinds, and it takes another type to keep the woodwinds and brasses and strings in line.

How is a good security analyst spotted? The first thing the testers give you—and the potential conductor too—is a Strong test, named after the Stanford psychologist who devised it. Somewhere along the line you have already taken a vocational preference test, so this one will be familiar to you. It is designed to tell you what you like, just in case you have been conning yourself. The questions are multiple choice, like this:

Tomorrow is a holiday, and you can do anything you want. Would you rather

a) fly an airplane
b) read a book
c) catch up on some sleep
d) go down to your neighborhood tavern and mix
    it up with the boys
e) work in your garden cutting flowers

That's the kind of thing. When the test gets going, you can really get involved.

An expedition is announced to explore the dangerous upper reaches of the Amazon, where piranha fish rule in the water and vicious headhunters on land. Would you rather
a) lead the expedition
b) raise the money for this scientific endeavor
c) go along and write up the story when you get
    back
d) just as soon not go

You see yourself leading an expedition up the Amazon? That may seem pretty glamorous, but maybe you have dangerous fantasies and almost certainly you are going to get an itchy bottom sitting at a desk reading stock market reports. If you pick *c*, we might let you write our weekly stock market letter, but you had better be able to do some other things, too.

You are coming home from a party, and you are having a fight with your wife. The fight is about
a) what time you finally got her to leave
b) how much she (you) had to drink
c) what she was (you were) doing with that fellow
    (lady) on the couch
d) money
e) the children

In this fight, it is more efficient to
a) say nothing and let her talk herself out
b) make sure she understands your point of view,
for her own good
c) establish who runs things, quickly and firmly
d) keep peace any way you can

If you wanted to leave before your wife did, if she had more to drink than is good for her, if the fight was about money and the children, you are right along with 81.1 percent of all our testees, and welcome to our organization. You do know better than your wife and you want to be sure she understands that and we like that attitude here.

Portfolio managers used to have the same sort of profile as a CPA, because portfolio managers were usually trust officers, safe, sound Prudent Men who wore green eye-shades, sleeve garters, and said "My good man."

Preference tests have been given for years and by now they have revealed patterns—on punched cards, at that—which group various occupations together. Analysts end up in Groups V and IX on the Strong test. Group V is social services, telling people what to do for their own good. Group IX is sales, extroverted, common sensical, and "people-centered atheoretical." It won't do you any good to dig up the good idea if you can't put it across.

The portfolio manager is another animal, currently in the process of escaping from Group VIII, office detail. Portfolio managers used to have the same sort of profile as a CPA, because portfolio managers were usually trust officers, safe, sound Prudent Men who wore green eye-shades, sleeve garters, and said "My good man." But the really swinging man-

agers, portfolio as personality, out running super-aggressive
funds, have profiles much more like the entrepreneurs who like
to get an idea, round up people, and start a business or a project. The trust officer portfolio manager tolerates detail; the
aggressive fund manager can barely stand it. All portfolio managers are supposed to be physically vigorous, but the aggressive
portfolio managers play squash, tennis, and row, so that they
don't have to be on anybody's team. Presumably the CPA-type
manager would run best on a relay team or play soccer, or do
something where the whole team would be in on the scoring.
(The new, itchy, aggressive manager is a breed lately arrived.
We do not have much of a dossier on him. . . .)

Other tests with pen and pencil peel away other veils.
John has four apples, Mary has three oranges, and they both
get on a train that is going forty miles an hour which left the
station at 2:10. When the train arrives, John has two apples
and Mary has six oranges. What time is it?

---

*If you really know what's going on, you don't
even have to know what's going on to know
what's going on.*

The analyst is inductive. He will break the problem into
its components and work away at each, building up to the
answer. The old portfolio manager will settle happily into the
problem; he loves it. The aggressive portfolio manager says,
"What the hell kind of stupid question is that, and how is
that going to make me any money?" and goes into the same
kind of rage he did when his wife wouldn't leave the party.
He has to get the Concept in one fell swoop or he is very
restless.

While the analysts can do the problems, they make a lot
of arithmetic errors, unlike the accountants, who get everything right to the decimal point. But good analysts have high
aptitude with both words and numbers. They shine best in

Vocabulary. It is when the functioning gets abstract, both numerically and verbally, that they begin to fade.

Everybody in the whole field is very smart. The bottom IQ is 130, so if you're dumb, better stop right here—all the other people are too bright. The range is from bright to near-genius. Are you ready for the blot? A sample blot is shown below.

What do you see in the blot? How many things did you see? Is it the whole blot, or only part of the blot? How quickly did you see it?

If it will make you feel any better, a lot of other people have seen those bugs, animal hides, and outstretched hands. But you have to do better than that, since you are only seeing what everybody else sees. You had better find something of your own within the first twenty seconds.

The point of the blots is not what you see in the blots, but your response pattern to them. How high is your evidence demand? That is, how much do you have to see before you will commit yourself?

The analyst really wants to be right, his ego needs the pleasure of being right, and he would almost rather be right than make money.

Again the analyst is building inductively, but the real gunslinger of a portfolio manager can't stand second thoughts. He bounces with the stimulus, is enthusiastic, almost overresponds. The analyst really wants to be right, his ego needs the pleasure of being right, and he would almost rather be right than make money. The aggressive portfolio manager doesn't really care about being right on each judgment, as long as he wins when you tot up the score. He has to be right more than wrong, naturally, but he tends to go in white-hot streaks and hope that his decisions add up more right—and so weighted—than wrong. What he is really doing is testing—quickly and unconsciously—each stimulus against the "apperceptive mass" of his own intuition, his intuition including all the "cognitive perception" he has used for years.

This portrait of an aggressive portfolio manager is not one that will make ancient trustees in paneled board rooms feel secure. But, as we have said, there are not many such; the portrait is really of a handful of hedge fund and mutual-fund managers, not that of trust officers or the managers of large institutions.

These performance-oriented managers are new enough that their game is still on trial, but they have already weathered some of the bumps. What distinguishes this kind of investing—the quick reaction to the information—from that of the small investor who hears a tip and rushes out and buys? The small investor has the reaction without the knowledge. He has no "aperceptive mass" behind the reaction; the portfolio manager, quite simply, can remember the profit margins of a hundred companies, how the stocks react to a variety of situations, and where in the spectrum of managers he himself fits. If he knows these things, he can be away from the market and still know where its rhythm and his are meshing. In short, if you really know what's going on, you don't even have to know what's going on to know what's going on. All you need is a hell of an aperceptive mass, an IQ of 150, and a dollop of ESP, and you can ignore the headlines, because you anticipated them months ago.

There is one requirement that is absolute in money managing, and you have already learned it with the first Irregular Rule: If you don't know who you are, this is an expensive place to find out. The requirement is emotional maturity.

"You have to use your emotions in a useful way," says Dr. McArthur. "Your emotions must support the goal you're after. You can't have any conflict about what you're after, and your emotional needs must be gratified by succeeding at what you're doing. In short, you have to be able to handle any situation without losing your cool, or letting your emotions take over. You must operate without anxiety."

There is one requirement that is absolute in money managing . . . If you don't know who you are, this is an expensive place to find out.

The psychological tests can't really tell you whether you are going to be an ace at making money; they are descriptions of existing groups, some of them followed up with later tests for incumbency (how long in the job), contentment, and success. You may be out of the patterns and still succeed, or the world may change to the point where these are not the successful patterns. But given the world as it is, this is the way the Game goes. Some analysts should not manage their own money, some portfolio managers should be running funds with other characteristics, and some investors should be cutting flowers in their garden and letting smart people run the money.

Some analysts should not manage their own money, some portfolio managers should be running funds with other characteristics, and some investors should be cutting flowers in their garden and letting smart people run the money.

You may even come out a fine fellow on tests, but the real test is how you behave when the crowd is roaring the other way. We know a little about some individual types, but the crowd, the elusive *Australopithecus,* is still largely an unknown, an exercise in mass psychology still not accomplished.

Iowa native Ellen Wiliamson wrote the well-received *Wall Street Made Easy—An Unconventional Guide to Profitable Investing.* While she admitted she wasn't a famous tycoon, nor a Harvard professor, nor a former president of the New York Stock Exchange (all aparently prerequisites for penning investment books), she felt she had two traits going for her: (1) she had been playing the market since 1927 and was still solvent; and (2) she hated the dry and jargon-filled books currently on the market. In fact, her reason for writing the book, she said, was to give the reader a practical guide that wasn't compromised by cryptic language and an overabundance of charts and graphs.

Williamson, who graduated from Vassar College in 1927, was certainly brash and honest; consider her thoughts on mutual funds: "Mutual funds are perfect for the people who don't give a fig for high finance, or who can't make decisions, or who are just plain lazy." Her 1965 investment book was based on experience; she was a trainee at the Guaranty Trust Company's bond school and later was a director of Hazeltine & Perkins, a pharmaceutical company, for 26 years. One of her strategies in picking stocks was to bounce ideas off four or five more experienced friends.

But ultimately, Williamson believed you had to have faith in yourself, and she snubbed Wall Street firms, especially when leadership was needed. Whether banking or investment institutions, she did not believe they acted as "steadying forces" in the face of crises or panics. "And why is this? Because these institutions are managed by individuals who worry like regular folks. . . ." She also believed there was only so much an individual could do to control their own future. Regardless of how much attention you pay to various market indexes, Williamson warned, "In conclusion, don't forget that nothing but nothing can foretell what's going to happen in the future; also it's hard to find a substitute for good judgment . . ." Like other successful investors, she understood that temperament was critical, and in *Do-It-Yourself Investing* she explains why you can't be a muffin, a snowflake, or an impatient Griseldo.

Do-It-Yourself Investing
Ellen Douglas Williamson

So you don't like bankers and brokers and bullish-and-bearish advisors and being pushed around by investment counsel men who act as if it were their money? So you'd rather live with your own mistakes? Frankly, so would I.

It's the same as when you paint the living room a clear lemon yellow and all the guests look as if they were getting over hepatitis, it's better to have it your own whimsical decision than to have to look at it every day and get madder and madder at that two-headed interior decorator. If it's your fault, it's an interesting experiment; if the decorator did it, you run the risk of a complete collapse from pure rage.

Now, if you buy yourself 100 shares of the Little Daisy Window Washing Company at 20 and it sinks promptly to 10 and you have only yourself to blame, at least you can chalk it up to experience or bad timing or poor health. But if someone else talked you into buying it—well! It's almost too difficult to live with your own infuriation—how *could* that so-and-so pick up such a stinker of a stock—if he'd been an alchemist he couldn't have made it go down faster—he gets his tips from his grandmother's ouija board, that's what he does.

So you decide to invest for yourself. But first, are you the type who can? Temperamentally? Some people can't, you know:

MUFFIN THE MODEL

For example, I helped a young model friend with her investments several years ago. Her name was Muffin Richardson when she lived in Iowa, but on her arrival in New York it became Flicka Stark.

Her hands often appeared in television commercials, daintily shaving a slim leg with a fancy little electric razor, or spilling ink on a pillow treated with something miraculous.

So you decide to invest for yourself. But first, are you the type who can? Temperamentally? Some people can't, you know . . .

Sometimes, only her feet did commercials, and they too were popular and highly paid. When she appeared in total, slim and laughing, perhaps smoking a cigarette on her way to a picnic, or ecstatically waving a hair spray over her shining blond tresses, she received $3000 or $4000 at the time the commercial was released, and half of that sum for its second appearance, and half of that amount for the third appearance (residuals), etc., etc. The girl was coining money, and was smart enough to realize that her luck and her feet weren't going to last forever, and sensible enough to invest most of it as fast as the checks appeared in her mailbox.

Muffin didn't know any more about stocks than the Flopsy Bunnies, but at my suggestion she obediently purchased 100 shares of each of the following:

Standard Oil of New Jersey
Sears, Roebuck & Company
Central and Southwest Corporation
New York Chicago & St. Louis Railroad
Thompson Ramo Wooldridge

By the time these were all bought, over a period of six months, and locked up in her safe-deposit box, she was an avid *aficionada* of the second section of the New York *Times,* where the market quotations are listed, and, as her holdings grew, she took to telephoning me at the queerest hours.

"Dolling," she would coo in her best semi-British accent, "what's wrong with Jehsey Standard? It's ecting *owfly* queah, down a half point today, down three eights yestahday. It's rilly *veddy* odd—what's wrong?"

One evening I was paged in the Hotel Plaza's Oak Room. I was sure that my husband's plane had crashed or that my daughter had been expelled from college, and was most relieved and soon most exasperated to find that it was only Muffin.

"Do you think that my Nickel Plate is *rilly* safe?" Her voice came to me dimly above the clatter of dishes. "I've just been to a cocktail potty and met a man theah who says that railroads are a veddy risky investment—honestly, dolling, I'm just teddibly worried."

And later on that week: "Dolling, I'm calling from the Stork. Have you *seen* what's happening to Seahs? It's too *ghastly!*"

This sort of thing went on intermittently until President Eisenhower's heart attack. That day the Dow-Jones averages declined 31.89 points from 487.45 to 455.56. Muffin telephoned from Hollywood. She was hysterical.

"I'm ruined," she sobbed. "Everything is lost. I can't *stand* it."

I tried to reassure her but it didn't work at all. She was beside herself.

"It's all your fault," she interrupted. "Again I am poverty stricken and it's all your fault."

Two months later, after the stock market had recovered from its scare and the Dow-Jones averages were back to 485.26, Muffin, or I mean Flicka, flew in from the West Coast, all smiles and chuckles. She brought me an expensive beach bag encrusted with pearls and magenta flowers, and insisted on buying champagne cocktails for the two of us in a small dark highly air-conditioned bar.

It took over an hour and a lot of champagne, but I finally did it. I persuaded her to sell all of her stocks, and to put the money into plain old stodgy government bonds.

Today she seems emotionally stable and well adjusted, has quite a pile of governments, and by way of sublimation owns two temperamental poodles and a finicky Alfa Romeo. I no longer see her proclaiming the glories of a new detergent on television but she has a good steady job modeling Butterfly Frocks or some such name, and often when I open my bill from Bloomingdale's her smiling face and her trim figure will catch my eye as I throw the little brochure of drip-dry dresses into the wastebasket.

MISS ELDERLY SNOWFLAKE

More recently I briefly helped a second-cousin-once-removed with her securities, and she also turned out to be the kind who should stick to the dullest and most uninteresting bonds possible.

This lady was fresh from a Nevada divorce, was forty-odd and crazy about the boys. She had jet-black hair (due to a rinse), a creamy white skin (due to a layer of make-up), and a penchant for wearing floaty chiffon dresses and high-heeled, very pointed shoes. If she ever kicked anyone it would be worse than being gored by a bull. She had with her a huge alimony settlement, and asked me to help her invest it properly.

Flattered to pieces, I went to a lot of trouble. I asked counsel from my investment counselors, and went to several other sagacious men of finance. I spent hours over what stocks to buy in the industries that seemed best for her, what percentages of her stocks to go into what industries, and so on.

She thanked me sweetly for the neatly typewritten investment program, asked a few pertinent questions about it, wrote down the name of my broker, and departed. It turned out that she didn't buy anything that I recommended.

For example, I had suggested the purchase of two oil stocks: Royal Dutch and Kerr-McGee. The broker became alarmed when she told him that I was advising her to buy Zapata Off Shore and Ambassador Oil. He thought I'd gone daft and telephoned to say so. I called Miss Elderly Snowflake (never mind about her real name) and found that on leaving me she had taken a taxi straight to her astrologist. It seems that the stars weren't sitting quite right for Royal Dutch Oil, and Kerr-McGee was no good for her *ever*—for some reason that had to do with Libra.

Furthermore, she hadn't bought any Litton Industries because she didn't like the name Litton, and she couldn't buy any Eli Lilly stock as lilies are associated with funerals and are therefore bad luck. I hung up, and every time I think of her I feel cross.

And to make me feel more cross, she now lives in Rapallo in a beautiful remodeled *castello* or *palazzo* looking down on the blue Mediterranean, and they say it has more bathrooms than any other villa south of Rome.

Maybe there is something to this astrology after all.

IMPATIENT GRISELDO

There is another quality essential to investing for yourself: Patience. In 1932, when the depression was at its lowest ebb, a friend of mine came to New York as a young man, found himself a good job in the radio business, and was making money. He felt sure that stocks were underpriced (the understatement of the year), and so did his broker. But he never made any money, he was so busy buying and selling and buying and selling.

There is another quality essential to investing for yourself: Patience.

For example, he bought some United Fruit at 11 (down from a high of 146) and some Libbey-Owens-Ford at 22, and soon after sold them at 12½ and 24. Then he was switched in and out of Bendix and Union Pacific the same way—making a small profit in each, then bought and sold Electric Auto-Lite and Fairbanks, Morse, and then back into United Fruit and Libbey-Owens-Ford, which by now had each gone up several more points, and so on and so on. The broker made money from all the commissions, but impatient Griseldo almost went broke making a profit—something no man is ever supposed to do.

NO TIME FOR HEARTS AND FLOWERS

There is one other type who should stay away from the investment world and that is the person who is Fraught with Sentiment.

"Oh, I just couldn't *bear* to part with my Florida Dehydrated Power," she will say with a beseeching look. "It belonged to my great-grand-daddy Atkins. I don't know what I'd do without it, we've had it in the family for so long."

"Sell my Mrs. MacBeth Spot Remover Common? Never!" another will shriek. "It was very good to me for all

those years, and now even when it's not paying any dividends I'll be good to *it.*"

---

*There is one other type who should stay away
from the investment world and that is the
person who is Fraught with Sentiment.*

Or: "I'd kinda hate to have you sell General Pushing and
Shoving—you see, Ellsworth gave it to me as a present on
my fortieth birthday. I'll never forget what a wonderful day
it was. . . ."

Moral: Stocks and sentiment do not mix.

John Moody would be proud to know that his firm's ratings are still highly valued and can make or break both company and government. Born in Jersey City, New Jersey, he started his career as a 'stamp licker and errand boy' for a banking house at 21. There he stayed for 10 years, working his way up through the bookkeeping department and then the selling side, where he was eventually put in charge. During that time, Moody also organized a statistical department. Finally, in 1898, he struck out on his own. His goal was to compile statistics about existing securities and the rapidly growing number of stocks and bonds being issued as the number of public companies mushroomed. There was only one problem: He had no capital for startup. So Moody worked on his statistics at night and pounded the pavement during the day, looking for customers to subscribe.

Fortunately, enough subscriptions were pledged to keep him going, and his manuals were a popular hit when they were introduced in 1900. Unfortunately, the 1907 panic forced him to surrender his business to creditors. However, the 1907 panic also inspired him to start analyzing and rating securities, in addition to providing the raw statistics. From such dire moments arose Moody's philosophical outlook on the market: "The saying that you never can tell is one that applies strictly to Wall Street. The professional traders make their money, not by escaping losses, but by making their profits outbalance their losses. A quick readiness to take a loss is one of their indispensible characteristics."

Moody was concerned with more than just numbers and felt strongly that speculation should be left to the professional speculators. "In one sense of the word," he said, "speculation is practically identical with gambling. In another sense not. . . . They [speculators] are men with broad vision, keen powers of calculation, patient natures, cool judgment, and remarkable power of quick and decisive action." Moody likened the amateur stock player to the ignorant gambler who steps up to the roulette table. As for defining what is investment versus what is speculation, Moody takes on this deceptively difficult task in *Investment versus Speculation*.

Investment versus Speculation
John Moody

Both the word "investment" and the word "speculation" are much misused terms. There are perhaps no two words in the English language which are less clearly defined or understood. This fact is not only true in a general sense, but it is particularly true in what we might term a "Wall Street" sense. There are many out-and-out speculators who call themselves investors and who honestly think they are investors. On the other hand, we constantly meet people who are really trying to follow sound investment methods and yet consider themselves speculators.

The main reason why there is so much confusion regarding the meaning of these terms, especially in connection with the security markets, is that investment and speculation so lap over each other and are so closely related that it is extremely difficult to draw any distinct line of demarcation between them. The vast majority of security investments carry some element of a speculative character; whereas a respectable percentage of securities which are inherently in a speculative class always embrace elements of stability and genuineness which give them an investment tinge. . . .

If we look over the entire security field of America we will find that investments and speculations could be subdivided, in the matter of degree, into hundreds of different classes. Starting with the highest and most secure type of investment known (United States bonds), we can follow the divisions down to some arbitrary line of demarcation where the investment groups, so-called, practically end with securities in which real investment elements slightly overbalance speculative elements. And from then on down through the various degrees of speculative propositions, from the so-called speculative-investment or good speculation until we reach the low grade or almost worthless speculative scheme.

No outstanding or clear-cut line of demarcation can be determined between that large group of securities which can be fairly classed as investments and that even larger group which we would define as speculations. One great group tends to blend into the other. There is always a sort of twilight zone between them. . . .

For many years I have expressed the view that in the long run more money is probably lost by people who attempt to invest their money conservatively and sanely, but ignorantly, than is lost by those who enter into frank speculations. The loss of a high percentage of investment capital is due to the fact that proper consideration is not given to the broad, fundamental influences which are often so far-reaching and so permanent in their effects.

Any one who wishes to become a successful investor must first of all familiarize himself with broad economic conditions and tendencies as they exist in our modern industrial society. He must know something about modern finance and must understand the significance of general trends and of structural changes which are constantly at work everywhere.

The man who a dozen years ago gave thought to the fact that slowly but surely the world's interest rate was rising and the average cost of living and cost of production increasing, need not have been caught with investments in enterprises like street railways and other franchise corporations whose revenue is fixed or limited by law but whose producing or operating costs must necessarily increase with the trend of the times. Such a man would not have bought or held Interborough Rapid Transit 5s which were then selling above 95.

Many people cherish the notion that investment in partially developed activities or relatively new undertakings is always more speculative than investment in old and tried and seasoned securities. But this theory does not hold in many cases. As a matter of fact, the old and seasoned security, unless purchased at the proper level and at the proper time (assuming, of course, that it is not merely a short term obligation) often proves to be the poorest thing to buy.

More money is probably lost by people who attempt to invest their money conservatively and sanely, but ignorantly, than is lost by those who enter into frank speculations.

Men like John D. Rockefeller, Andrew Carnegie, and Henry Ford are constantly mentioned as persons who in their early days were venturesome dreamers and daring speculators in their particular fields. Of course, these men did many speculative things, took chances, and had many narrow escapes from disaster. But the real thing that gave them success, as compared with thousands of others of equal ability, courage and general intelligence, was their special understanding of certain fundamental facts which were in the making in their early days. John D. Rockefeller had imagination enough to recognize the far-reaching possibilities in the development of the petroleum industry. The question as to whether he could currently make money in a small oil-producing concern and compete with many others was not the big idea with him. The secret of his success was his recognition of the revolution which would be wrought in modern society by the newly discovered uses for petroleum. Herein was his investment sense demonstrated.

Andrew Carnegie had imagination enough to foresee the inevitable revolution which would be brought about by the development of Bessemer steel. Carnegie may have been a great speculator when he capitalized his companies and sold them for a fabulous sum to the Morgan syndicate, but in his early days he was a shrewd investor.

Henry Ford many years ago foresaw the revolution which would inevitably be brought about by the development of the automobile. He had imagination enough to understand that the most far-reaching change would be the adoption of the motor car by the millions rather than by the few. He therefore chose to serve the millions and has consequently become one of the most successful business men in the world.

The speculator is almost invariably one who is looking for quick profits.

The point to be emphasized in these illustrations is that these men gave full thought to the big underlying facts which were developing before their eyes, but which the mass of mankind did not see at all.

Finally, to draw a distinction between intelligent investment and speculation, it should again be emphasized that successful investing involves far more attention to the meaning of fundamental trends and general economic conditions than does the ordinary speculation. The person who intentionally places his capital to work for income and genuine stability of principal should be more concerned with possible changes in general conditions and with the broad underlying currents of trade and finance than the man who frankly goes into a speculative proposition for the purpose of quickly increasing his capital. The speculator is almost invariably one who is looking for quick profits. Ordinarily he does not expect or intend to keep his capital in any given thing for any great period of time. Underlying influences affect his position, of course, but if his speculation is a wise one, its strength may be so great as to offset general adverse influences should such come along.

The investor, theoretically at least, is placing his capital to work more or less permanently. He does not expect to change his holdings of securities with every month or every year. If he buys bonds or stocks for investment at a certain yield, his intention is to hold such bonds and stocks. He may change frequently to other issues without becoming a frank speculator. But if, unexpectedly, his investment promptly shows him a large profit and he sells out, he has simply cashed in on a speculative development which he did not foresee.

This situation, of course, exists in thousands of cases and this is why there is no clear-cut distinction between the great investor group and the great speculator group. Many a man is both an investor and speculator at the same time. Many are investors for a period and then become speculators for a period. In fact, every investor who does not give proper consideration to the broad, underlying fundamentals is in danger of unknowingly becoming a speculator at any time. He may buy what he thinks is a high-grade investment, but the time may quickly come when to his surprise he finds himself the holder of a speculation.

The investor, theoretically at least, is placing his capital to work more or less permanently.

To sum up, the investor pure and simple is the person who, when placing his capital at work, gives as full thought and consideration to general and fundamental factors underlying our modern civilization as he does to the specific questions of security, management, past records, financial stability, and earning power of the proposition itself. He may often be in error and exercise unsound judgment. He may be misled or misinformed and his knowledge may be superficial. If he does not look at the whole picture and acts only on a section of it, he will, sooner or later, come to grief.

JOHN C. BOGLE
1929–

Until his heart transplant in 1996, John C. Bogle ran a mutual fund company whose total assets were second only to Fidelity's. Bogle founded The Vanguard Group, Inc., in 1974. Its assets grew to over $100 billion in the next 20 years and were well over $200 billion in 1998. Keeping down costs was one of the keys to Bogle's success. For example, the cost of the average Vanguard fund has been less than one-third of the industry average. One reason is that Bogle and his company espouse index funds, which they have successfully run at about one-fifth of the average cost. Besides relying heavily on computers to handle analysis and transactions, Bogle has kept costs low in other ways. The office lights are controlled by motion detectors, there are no fancy amenities like private dining rooms, and no one is allowed to fly first class.

Bogle, whose grandfather had founded American Can, learned thriftiness by watching his less-than-disciplined father lose the family fortune in the Great Depression. Fortunately, he was able to attend Princeton University on a scholarship; he wrote his senior thesis on mutual funds. After college, Bogle went straight to work for Willington Management, where he convinced his employer to start the Windsor Fund. He pulled an all-nighter and wrote the prospectus in 24 hours. Hard work took its toll, and Bogle had a heart attack at the age of 30, but against doctor's orders he kept right on working.

Bogle started promoting index funds because he believes in market efficiency—half of the market's investors will lose relative to the market's overall performance and the other half will win—so he decided that if you can't beat the market, join it. In 1976 he put together the Index Trust 500 fund, which was modeled on the S&P 500, and for the next 15 years his returns beat 85 percent of all diversified stock funds. While Bogle admits that there are select money managers who can beat index funds, the problem for the investor is finding them ahead of time. Bogle devoutly believes in watching out for the investor, and in *A Mandate for Fund Shareholders* he develops his four rules: (1) be canny, (2) be thrifty, (3) be active, and (4) be skeptical.

A Mandate for Fund Shareholders
John C. Bogle

"**T**he fault, dear Brutus, is not in our stars, but in ourselves." So said the protagonist in Shakespeare's play *Julius Caesar*. ... [T]he mutual fund industry ... can be greatly improved and can provide far better opportunities for investors. Positive change will take place, however, only if we lay the responsibility for the industry's shortcomings not in our stars but in ourselves as shareholders. If enough investors demand a better mutual fund industry, we will have a better mutual fund industry. All you need to do is stand up for your rights as investors.

It may seem difficult for a shareholder with a relatively small investment to advance change. After all, the average investor owns perhaps a $10,000 holding in a $500 million mutual fund, or a voting interest of something like 2/1000ths of 1%. But if you believe, as I do, that even one person can make a difference, any change that enough mutual fund shareholders demand will surely come to pass. I am not suggesting that mutual fund shareholders must act in concert with each other. That proposition would take organization, tedium, and patience. Rather, I am suggesting that if all shareholders merely act independently in concert with their own financial needs and best interests, the mutual fund industry will soon improve.

In considering exactly what is in your best interests as a mutual fund investor, I suggest that you abide by these four elementary rules: (1) be canny, (2) be thrifty, (3) be active, and (4) be skeptical. In the following pages I will review these rules as if they were mutually exclusive, but intelligent investors will want to incorporate all four into their investment programs.

THE CANNY INVESTOR

It seems almost naive to suggest that if investors are canny—wise enough to rely on their own common sense and good judgment—the mutual fund industry will be an even better investment medium. Nonetheless, I believe it to be true. As an industry, it is exceptionally responsive to investors' needs and demands. Through modern, sophisticated direct marketing techniques and energetic, highly motivated sales forces, the industry responds to consumer demands as quickly as any financial services business I have ever observed. The problem is that investors have largely demanded the *wrong* things and have for the most part ignored the right things. So any industry improvement depends first on a change in investors' attitudes—acting wisely and carefully in the selection and ownership of mutual fund shares.

In considering exactly what is in your best interests as a mutual fund investor . . .
(1) be canny, (2) be thrifty, (3) be active, and (4) be skeptical.

While it seems trivial to suggest that the canny investor begin by reading fund prospectuses, that is where it really *does* begin. Which prospectuses should you read? Surely not those of all of the funds in the industry, nor even the 1,000 or so funds that might be covered in the leading statistical services, nor even the hundreds that might be involved if you decided on, say, a common stock fund. Perhaps a selection of prospectuses from among a dozen stock funds, half as many bond funds, and half that many money market funds, would be appropriate. That gives you just over 20 prospectuses to wade through and review the important points. It is a worthwhile investment of your time.

Where do you begin the process of selecting sample prospectuses? The most logical starting point is to review the prospectuses of some of the funds that comprise the better-known mutual fund complexes. Most fund complexes have been in business for 50 years or more, which suggests that they are doing *something* right. But do not exclude smaller funds or fund families that you may have learned about through mutual fund evaluation services and financial publications. The advice of friends who are experienced investors is often helpful, as are suggestions from your lawyer or accountant. For investors who need more professional advice, reputable financial planners and stockbrokers can provide a useful service at an additional cost.

While it seems trivial to suggest that the canny investor begin by reading fund prospectuses, that is where it really does *begin.*

How should the canny investor read the prospectus? It would be unrealistic to suggest that you read the entire document from cover to cover. For the long-term investor, knowing the fund's objectives, investment policies, returns, risks, and total costs (sales charges, annual expenses, redemption fees, etc.) is probably sufficient. The shorter-term active investor should also know the fund's key transaction policies, such as how to redeem shares, how to exchange shares to another fund, and any transaction limitations such as redemption fees or limits on the frequency of fund exchanges.

Once you have narrowed down the field, turn to the supplemental information provided by the fund's sponsor, including a precise description of the fund, performance statistics, and financial information. After giving appropriate, but not excessive, weight to the fund's past performance—including both capital return and income return—and following the selection criteria . . . you'll be ready to make your fund selections. The canny investor will look through this information and make sure that all or at least most of it has been provided. If it has not, there are lots of fish in the sea, and there are many similar funds from which to choose.

For the long-term investor, knowing the fund's objectives, investment policies, returns, risks, and total costs . . . is probably sufficient.

What is required is that you do your homework and demand useful information, including the fund's compound rate of return over an extended period, the comparative standards used to evaluate this record, a clear statement of risk, and a thorough presentation of cost factors. If enough investors follow this process of selecting funds on the basis of the substance, breadth, and fairness of the information they provide, only those funds that make adequate information available to investors will ultimately remain in business.

THE THRIFTY INVESTOR

If mutual fund investors become more cognizant of the costs they are paying in the form of sales loads, management fees, and other fund expenses, and then act on this awareness, these costs will surely decline. It is as simple as that. If you purchase only the shares of the lower-cost funds (perhaps even by redeeming your investments in the higher-cost funds), mutual fund sponsors will quickly get the message. They'll learn that reducing their costs to investors will help them to increase the level of assets that they manage; failing to do so will lead to an unremitting capital outflow.

This is not a utopian concept. To some degree, this scenario is already unfolding in the mutual fund industry. Consider the money market funds. In a broad sense, the lower the level of a money market fund's expense ratio, the larger the amount of assets it attracts. All of the largest funds have expense ratios that are at or below the industry norm. As far as I am concerned, the jury is now in on the fee waiver issue that I discussed earlier: temporary fee waivers *do* draw in assets. But when the fund sponsor ceases to absorb the expenses of the fund it is promoting and the expense ratio rises to its "normal" level, much of the money that was enticed into the fund by cut-rate costs is enticed out, as it were, by other funds with durable low costs and high yields. That this reversal in cash flow takes place despite the sponsor's failure to notify its shareholders about any fee increases suggests that, at least in the money market arena, investors are not only thrifty but keenly aware of the yields that they earn. In fact, when the first money market funds were formed, several carried sales loads; however, this expense was simply too much baggage for the marketplace to accept, and the practice soon vanished.

In the bond fund arena, the importance of being thrifty appears not to have been fully recognized. It is as if profligacy, not thrift, were the central theme. It is remarkable to me that so many bond mutual funds with assets upward of $1 billion incur annual expenses in excess of 1.25%. At this cost, and assuming a gross yield of 7.0%, expenses consume something like 18% of a fund's income, reducing the fund's dividend distribution to its shareholders by that same 18%.

It is astonishing to see that more than half of all bond funds are actually sold with sales charges. The net result is that investors earn their net income (assuming a 5% load) on only 95% of their assets. If you hold a bond fund for five years, the result is an annual sacrifice of 1% each year in yield. At a 1.25% expense ratio, the fund's combined annual costs and sales charges over a five-year period are 2.25%, consuming nearly *one-third* of the fund's 7% gross yield.

If mutual fund investors become more cognizant of the costs they are paying in the form of sales loads, management fees, and other fund expenses, and then act on this awareness, these costs will surely decline.

As I noted earlier, the ability of any bond fund manager to earn excess returns sufficient to offset these prodigious costs is quite limited. Thus, it is contrary to expectations that nearly 70% of bond fund assets are held by load funds and only about 30% are held by no-load funds. There are hints that these percentages are converging, but a major shift can transpire only when bond fund investors act on their thrifty impulses.

In the stock fund arena, the presales-charge records of load and no-load funds are generally comparable. After adjusting for sales charges, no-load funds carry a distinct advantage. The marketplace seems to see this difference, and nearly 40% of the assets of all stock funds are represented by no-load funds. Most equity funds with very high operating expense ratios (say, over 2.5%) have attracted limited amounts of assets. It is difficult to determine, however, just where the link among high expenses, low performance, and a small asset base begins. Nonetheless, it seems clear to me that two trends will develop in the years ahead: (1) all equity funds — particularly the mainstream funds — will feel the cost pressure as price competition in the marketplace increases and (2) assuming that index funds "work," those that attract the most assets will be the ones that do not charge sales loads and have the lowest operating costs.

THE ACTIVE INVESTOR

Once you own shares of a mutual fund, you gain "certain inalienable rights." Among them are the right to vote proxies, the right to express your opinions to management, and finally the ultimate right, the right to "vote with your feet" and redeem your investment in the fund. This final option frightens fund sponsors greatly. Not only does it suggest that they have somehow failed the investor, but it reduces the fees they receive from managing the fund.

The right to vote proxies is significant, since management fee increases must be approved by mutual fund shareholders. (Curiously enough, so must the almost unheard-of proposals to reduce fees.) It follows that, since investors — after reading the fund's prospectus — tacitly approved the management fee when they purchased their shares, they will want to examine carefully any proposal to change the terms of the contract. Each shareholder *must* vote, and vote intelligently.

To do so, you will need complete and candid information on why a fee increase is being requested. If the proxy does not provide it, a no vote should be automatic. Many proxies, sadly, fall far short of adequate disclosure. Begin with the cover page. It often calls attention to "a vote to amend the fund's investment advisory agreement." Rarely, if ever, does it state "a vote to increase the fees you pay to the fund's investment manager by 25%." So careful examination of the details of the proxy is a must.

Fair reasons for a management to increase its fee rates might be "the need to have the resources to hire additional investment professionals," or "to expand the range of services provided to shareholders." Very few proxies, however, state that these are the reasons. Most suggest that, after long consideration, the fund's directors have approved the fee increase requested by the management company, since the fund's fee rates were below industry norms.

The right to vote proxies is significant, since management fee increases must be approved by mutual fund shareholders . . . Each shareholder must vote, and vote intelligently.

This reason seems more like a rationalization. (Must not half of the funds in the industry always have below-average fees and half always have above-average fees?) The real reason for most fee *rate* increases is to improve the profitability of the management company. Remember that the *dollar* amount of the fee has automatically increased—often enormously—with the increase in fund assets, although in many cases the fee rate is scaled down moderately as fund assets increase. While higher profits for fund managers are not necessarily wrong in the abstract, shareholders are entitled not only to a candid statement of that profit objective but a clear financial tabulation showing the revenues that the adviser receives from the fund both before and after the fee increase, the nature and extent of the fund's expenses, and the margin of profit it realizes on operating the fund.

If an adviser expends $0.50 out of each $1.00 of fee revenue to operate the fund, the pretax profit margin is 50%. If this margin is to go to 75%—an astonishing increase, but hardly unprecedented—let it be so stated. While huge compared to most industries, a 50% profit margin has not been uncommon among the larger mutual fund complexes. In order to merit your favorable vote, the management company should provide these profit margin figures (not only for the fund at issue but for the funds in the complex in the aggregate) and address their reasonableness.

Fund shareholders seem to ignore the issues presented in proxies, even when the fund provides reasonable disclosure. Shareholders of one investment company recently voted to approve a 31% fee increase to a manager who was already making a pretax profit equal to 85% of its gross revenues. Table 1 shows the figures, as published in the proxy. The fee paid to the manager rises by some $1.6 million, to more than $7 million. Since the manager's expenses remain at about $800,000, the manager's profit, too, rises by $1.6 million, a 40% increase. As a result, the profit margin on this particular fund rises from 85% to 88%, a level that is surely amazing.

Management Company Profit Margins

	Before *fee increase*	*After* *fee increase*
Management fees	$5,369,000	$7,055,000
Operating expenses	823,000	823,000
Operating profit	$4,546,000	$6,232,000
Profit margin	85%	88%

A second issue that demands that shareholders vote is the 12b-1 distribution plan. . . . Sadly, since more than half of all funds already have such plans, the remaining opportunities to vote to approve or disapprove new plans are likely to be few. And, given the increasingly controversial nature of 12b-1 plans, the likelihood of any funds having the temerity to propose to increase such distribution fees seems remote in the extreme. Suffice it to say that if the fund plans to spend any of the assets that you as a shareholder have entrusted to it simply to bring additional assets into the fund, the justification for the expenditure should be clearly articulated, both in understandable conceptual terms and in detailed financial terms. Otherwise, "just vote no."

Freedom of speech to fund management is another inalienable right of fund shareholders. Few investors are aware that the management of any enlightened mutual fund is interested in the opinions of the fund's shareholders. In my experience, shareholders are rarely heard from except in matters relating to performance and the accurate processing of their accounts. One major area in which shareholders should make their opinions known is the quality of the communications they receive from their fund. Many annual reports are superficial and incomplete. Any annual report worth its salt should meet the standards I suggested. . . .

Many funds fall short of providing all — or indeed *any* — of this information to their shareholders. In fact, these sins of omission are more the industry norm than the exception. Most funds seem to believe that performance comparisons are odious and, implicitly at least, that "there is no fair standard against which we may be measured." One assumes the fund's independent directors themselves receive some comparison and evaluation of the fund's performance. An obvious solution is to make that information available to the actual *owners* of the fund — the shareholders. There is nothing wrong with presenting an imperfect comparison and then describing its limitations. But every fund simply *must* give its investors appropriate and enlightening information in its annual report. The active investor should demand no less.

In April 1993 the SEC, presumably frustrated by the industry's recalcitrance, adopted a requirement that mutual funds provide comparisons of their performance relative to an appropriate index along with a narrative discussion of strategies and factors that materially affected the fund's performance during the year, along with a ten-year comparative chart. While this requirement is a welcome step forward, funds have been given the option of providing the information either in their annual reports or in their prospectuses. Which alternative funds will choose remains to be seen. But it is ironic that many fund sponsors, whose portfolio managers rely on full disclosure from corporations, must be required by a federal agency to provide full disclosure to the shareholders of the funds they manage.

One major area in which shareholders should make their opinions known is the quality of the communications they receive from their fund.

While it is more difficult to articulate, shareholders have the right not only to hold the fund to comparative standards that are consistently applied from year to year but also to a candid evaluation of these returns by the fund's chief executive officer. (In the typical case, the fund's CEO—responsible for *appraising* the results—is also the CEO of the investment adviser—responsible for *generating* the results. As a result, reporting to shareholders with candor is no mean challenge.) The active investor should demand fund reports that begin with something like, "last year, your fund's performance was inferior both absolutely and relative to fair competitive standards," rather than, for example, "the year's most important event was the expansion of IRA eligibility," or "your fund's assets increased by $100 million during the past year."

But the issue does not end with fair presentation of the facts and figures of the mutual fund's performance results and at least some perspective on what they mean. Overall, what is involved is a spirit of candor, in which a fund's failures receive at least as much attention as its successes, and its problems as much emphasis as its opportunities. If even 50 active investors would place this demand for candor before the fund's chairman (copies to the fund's independent directors), I believe many funds would respond affirmatively, for two reasons. First, the fund's management may not have previously considered the issue all that important and may now realize that investors care. Second, the fund's management will ultimately act with an enlightened sense of the fund's (and the adviser's) long-run self-interest.

If the demand for candor is not met even when you let your opinions be known, you can take an even more forceful action. The ultimate nightmare of fund managers is that you vote with your feet, redeem your shares, and walk away from the fund. Of course, many investors redeem their shares under the most normal of circumstances. Reallocating your assets in order to increase or reduce your common stock exposure is one obvious reason. Achieving your original financial goals *demands* redemption (e.g., sooner or later your accumulated education fund will be spent on college tuition bills). Unfortunately, leaving a fund because the fund has let you down may involve otherwise unnecessary penalties. The most obvious are (1) the cost of the sales commission you originally may have paid, especially onerous after a short period of time (i.e., a 5% sales commission reduces a fund's one-year return by −5%, but a five-year return by "only" −1% per year); and (2) the taxes payable on any capital gains you would realize if the net asset value of your shares has increased. Nonetheless, redemption of shares is the ultimate weapon of the active investor.

THE SKEPTICAL INVESTOR

Unlike the active investors, skeptical investors do not yet own a particular fund. They are looking at the information presented to them and deciding whether or not to invest their assets. In this age of aggressive fund marketing and promotional hype, the industry has earned their skepticism. Three areas come quickly to mind: in advertising, the exaggeration of the importance of a fund's past performance; in calculating yields, the inadequate disclosure of low credit quality or substantial use of risky derivative instruments to obtain exaggerated yields; and in promotion, the development of new fund concepts that are based on unproven or untested principles.

114

All investors want funds that provide good performance. And all funds seek to provide it. But despite overpowering evidence to the contrary, investors seem to believe that past performance is the precursor to future performance. Fund sponsors—good businessmen all—respond to investors' predispositions by exploiting a fund's past performance as if there were some link, however tenuous, between past and future returns.

The most blatant manifestation of this "past performance syndrome" is in mutual fund advertising, especially advertising that proclaims a fund #1, even as the small print reveals that the fund is first only in some limited group, of some limited size, over some limited period. Given the large number of these limited universes, literally hundreds of funds can lay claim to #1 status at any time. And when a particular fund inevitably regresses to the mean, it can be replaced in the advertising by another fund with #1 credentials offered by the same sponsor. If the sponsor operates many highly specialized aggressive funds, this option is always available.

Despite overpowering evidence to the contrary, investors seem to believe that past performance is the precursor to future performance.

What is important about this issue is something that the sponsors must know but do not say: the chance that a #1 fund in, say, the *past* ten years will repeat as #1 in the *next* ten years is essentially zero. The skepticism of the investor who pays little heed to such claims will be well rewarded.

The future founder of a publishing empire was one of 10 children born to a tailor in Scotland. To help support the family, B. C. Forbes started working at the age of 14, when he unfortunately agreed to a 7-year apprenticeship as a compositor for a newspaper for 75 cents a week (he thought he was being hired to be a writer as in composition). "I soon discovered" he recalled, "that what I had agreed to become meant that I was to stand in front of cases of type, day after day, month after month for seven years, doing nothing but pick up one metallic letter at a time . . . I felt as if I had been sentenced to seven years penal servitude." Not one to give up, Forbes decided he would "make them want to make me a reporter." At night he took a course in shorthand, a prerequisite for reporters, and he did indeed get a job writing.

It took a woman to break his spirit. After the object of his affection decided to marry someone else, Forbes left Scotland. "I shook the dust of Scotland off my feet," he said, "and sailed for the remotest corner of the world I could think of, South Africa, then in the close of the Boer War, where I figured I could find enough excitement to assuage my black, black woe." After two years in South Africa, he came to the United States. In New York City he started writing for a number of papers, covering business from the money market to the foreign exchange. When William Randolph Hearst decided he wanted better financial pages in his *New York American* newspaper, he recruited Forbes, who consequently became Hearst's best-known financial columnist.

Forbes founded his namesake magazine in 1917. He was going to call it *Doers and Doings,* but friends convinced him to change his mind; they believed his name alone was a great marketing tool. Even after Forbes founded his magazine, Hearst asked him to write a syndicated financial column. The astute observer of Wall Street happenings agreed. Forbes was not afraid to attack such infamous Wall Street men as Jay Gould, whom he criticized for "his narrowness of vision, his unreasoning jealousy, his chronic suspicions, etc." Drawing on his experiences with both scoundrels and heroes, he offers his view of the typical Wall Street operator in *Wall Street Millionaires.*

Wall Street Millionaires
B. C. Forbes

"What sort of men are your Wall Street millionaires?" I was asked the other day.

"How long is a railroad journey?" I felt like replying, but didn't. Instead, I merely said: "Very much like other people."

"But aren't they horribly uncouth? I always thought they were terribly uncultured—and worse."

"Not at all," I replied in defense of a much-maligned class. "Some of them are among the finest men in America."

"You surely do not mean that? Do they really possess a full measure of the virtues?"

I assured the questioner that, taking them as a class, they did.

"Wall Street millionaires" are not all a pack of wolves seeking whom they may devour.

The term "Wall Street" is more elastic than a rubber band. It embraces anything—in the popular imagination—from the get-rich-thievishly fraternity, who never see Wall Street, to the strongest of our financiers and banking institutions. "Wall Street millionaires" include alike the spectacular speculators who have made fortunes in sheer gambling and the most conservative of our bankers and local capitalists.

How many men have made—and retained—millions SOLELY through stock speculation. Not many.

Men like John W. Gates—a typical Wall Street millionaire of the fiction writer's brand—had to be more than gamblers and had to do more than buy and sell stocks in order to
get where they did. Before he blew into Wall Street Gates
had earned the reputation of being the best salesman in the
United States. He knew how to make nails and pull wire—
the genuine article—better than any expert in the business.
And having made supplies he knew how to sell them. He was
thus no nonentity, no brainless cipher. But his famous offer
to "bet you a million" was remembered, while his real
achievements in the field of industry were quickly forgotten—if they were ever known—by the public.

---

*The term "Wall Street" . . . embraces
anything . . . from the get-rich-thievishly
fraternity . . . to the strongest of our financiers
and banking institutions.*

Not one "Wall Street millionaire" of the most criticised
pattern will be found devoid of special ability in some direction or other. The self-made ones who stay millionaires are
not fools. Few of them are knaves, either.

The trouble is that the crazy exploits of the few besmirch
the reputation of the many. And of course when a Wall
Street plutocrat runs amuck it makes a spicy front-page
story.

In one hour at a Monte Carlo table Charles M. Schwab
earned more unpleasant notoriety than years of amazing
achievement in steel making could combat. It drove him, in a
sense, from the presidency of the greatest industrial organization in the world, the billion-dollar Steel Corporation.
Since then he has done bigger things than any other steel
worker in the United States, but nine people in ten would,
on hearing Schwab's name mentioned, recall the Monte
Carlo incident and let the rest pass.

118

I have never met a more generous, a larger-hearted set than "Wall Street millionaires." Even the worst of them have the redeeming virtues of generosity and charity. They practise these virtues, too, on a scale the public can not imagine.

On the other hand, there are a few black sheep in the "Wall Street millionaire" fold. The most rapid-fire swearer and blasphemer I have ever encountered is one of our very prominent traction magnates. And his vocabulary betrays him as being what he really is. Then others admittedly could not write Greek poetry nor rival Caesar or Cicero as Latin writers.

But that is their misfortune rather than their fault. Quite a few of them do their best to make up for what they missed. They try hard to develop a taste for and an appreciation of art and music. They spend lavishly in encouraging and cultivating the refinements of life. They may know more about Reading than about Rembrandts, but when they get away from the one they do often try to become acquainted with the other.

The trouble is that the crazy exploits of the few besmirch the reputation of the many. . . . when a Wall Street plutocrat runs amuck it makes a spicy front-page story.

Then there is another and more numerous class of "Wall Street millionaires." Men of the Morgan, Speyer, Seligman, Kahn, Barton Hepburn calibre need no apologist on the score of culture. Not a few of the finest intellects in the country find their sphere of activity in "Wall Street."

Mixing the good with the bad, the resulting composite "Wall Street millionaire" is not such a worthless, disreputable, dishonest character as is too often misrepresented.

FRED SCHWED, JR.
1901–1966

Fred Schwed's 1940 book, *Where Are the Customer's Yachts?*, is considered an investment classic. The title comes from a once-popular Wall Street joke: The guide for a visitor to New York's financial district points to some beautiful boats anchored offshore. "Look," the guide says, "those are the bankers' and brokers' yachts." To which the naive visitor says, "Where are the customers' yachts?" Schwed's book, which is based on his own experience, takes a satirical look at Wall Street in the spirit of Mark Twain. It also provides some poignant philosophy, such as: "Investment and speculation are said to be two different things, and the prudent man is advised to engage in the one and avoid the other. This is something like explaining to the troubled adolescent that Love and Passion are two different things."

Born in New York City, his exposure to Wall Street shenanigans came early—his father was a member of the New York Curb Exchange. Schwed went to Princeton but was thrown out in his senior year for having a girl in his dorm room past the bewitching hour. He finished his degree at Columbia University. After graduation, he was a reporter for *The New York Times,* then *The Wall Street Journal,* before moving on to become an account representative for a stock brokerage firm. Apparently he didn't think highly of the job, considering what he said about mutual fund salesmen: "They can properly compare to life-insurance salesmen. You remember the life-insurance guy: first he was a minor nuisance, then he became loathsome, then he pushed a policy down your throat."

Schwed also dabbled in trading, but claimed he never got rich as a trader because he listened to a cynical Irish coworker: " 'What were securities created for in the first place?' The Irishman said. 'They were created to be sold, so sell them.' " That cynicism is certainly on display in *The Wall Street Dream Market,* for Schwed pokes fun at the Wall Streeter who considers himself a prophet, a scholar, and a magician with money.

The Wall Street Dream Market
Fred Schwed, Jr.

"**W**all Street," reads the sinister old gag, "is a street with a river at one end and a graveyard at the other."

This is pretty neat, but, if only there were a kindergarten located in the middle, it would be even neater.

For over ten years I have been viewing the activities of this street each working day, mostly from the vantage point of a trading desk. We have access, in this business, to every form of communication except the heliograph. What we are constantly exchanging over an incredible network of wires are quotations, orders, bluffs, fibs, lies, and nonsense. The first four are the necessary agenda of doing brokerage in securities. The downright lies are rather exceptional and in the long run prove to be unprofitable business practice. What I am interested in examining here is the nonsense — a commodity which keeps sluicing in through the weeks and years with the irresistible constancy of the waters of the rolling Mississippi.

Over these many wires it is my job to talk constantly with order clerks, traders, partners, and speculators. The first part of their conversation is usually sensible and competent and sometimes verges on the brilliant. This is the part concerned with the quotes and the fibs. Then, however, if the occasion and mood seem to call for it, comes the time when, still under the impression that they are doing an important day's work, they present their Thoughts. These may be on a particular stock, on The Market in general, or on the destiny of the nation.

What we are constantly exchanging over an incredible network of wires are quotations, orders, bluffs, fibs, lies, and nonsense.

Let us consider two highly typical Thoughts.

Thought Number One is: "Looks there might be a little rally after lunch." This is proffered by young Mr. Joseph Wisenheimer, who had two years at Central High. At the time of his inspiration he is chewing gum and watching the ticker tape. He accompanies his pronouncement with a look so knowing it scarcely misses being a leer.

Thought Number Two is presented by Mr. S. Hugo Bigshot, and goes out on all wires. Let me skip down to its conclusion:

> It therefore becomes clear that over the period of the next fifteen years the investment demand for sound convertible issues bearing a low coupon but carrying an attractive conversion feature will find such a deserved popularity with the long-sighted investor as to cause the more classic forms of indenture to look to their laurels.

Now the question is: Which of those two statements is the sillier? Either of them, you understand, might be correct. And both of them (or statements much like them) have sold billions of dollars' worth of securities.

Perhaps you veer toward Thought Two, because onomatopoeically it has a sillier sound.

This I hardly think is fair. Young Joe doesn't know so many long words. But he claims that he is saying something that has some meaning and he claims it just as definitely as Mr. Bigshot. The latter, having been to business college and also having taken courses in English literature, can make his statement *sound* sillier. But, since neither of them has any factual or intellectual basis for saying either of these things, I claim the honors are even.

Now it should be said right here that neither of these men is a liar or even a faker.

If you ask Joe why there will be a little rally after lunch, he will tell you in no uncertain terms. He will say that he observes that the volume is decreasing on the down side, that he can see that steels are strongly pegged just above the last previous lows, and that "they" (whoever "they" are) are beginning to accumulate the second-grade carriers. "But it won't go very far," he may add (proving that at heart he is no wild-eyed optimist—more the old-line banker type): "they wouldn't want to see this market run away."

It is a marvelous thing, the way this lingo is universally used in board rooms, not just in New York but from coast to coast. It is as though someone had invented an Esperanto for saying absolutely nothing in a variety of ways.

DREAM STREET

And, if you ask the other chap, the educated one, on what he predicates his fifteen-year opinion, he will give you so many reasons that you will wish you had not asked. But he ought to know better. If he should ever lift his nose out of the minutiae of his fascinating business and view it and its history whole, he would be forced to admit the sad truth that pitifully few financial "experts" have ever known for three years (much less fifteen) what was going to happen to any class of securities—and that the majority are usually spectacularly wrong in a much shorter time than that.

Still, he is not a liar; nor is our other friend. They are both subject to the wishful delusions of the child, who cannot bear to believe anything that is too unpleasant. But we expect a child to grow up and learn what is reality, as opposed to what are merely his passionate hopes.

This, however, is asking too much of your romantic Wall Streeter—and they are all romantics or they would never have chosen this business, which is a business of dreams. They continue to dream of conquest, coups, and power, for themselves and for the people they advise.

Some Wall Street men manage to shed these, given sufficient years. But the ultimate dream they almost never shed: that there is a secret, with meaning, in the rise and fall of financial enterprises—that a "close study" of this and that will prove something; that it will tell the initiate when there will be a rally or give the speculator a better than even chance of making a killing or guarantee for an estate a safe 4 per cent for a few generations. All these things are demonstrably unpredictable, but the truth is too bitter to look at with open eyes.

No Wall Streeter is willing to be just a croupier. He insists that he is also a prophet, a scholar, and a magician with money.

If this business is a meaningless business, what is going to become of these men who are in it?

I am not speaking of just their livelihood, which is probably at its lowest ebb right now. (There *I* go.) For the tongues of neither men nor angels can keep the public out of Wall Street, once prices are up and booming.

The real menace is to their self-respect. If a man cannot be an authority on his own trade, on what *is* he going to be an authority?

The croupier at the roulette table does not claim that he knows something about the order in which the numbers will come up. He just sees to it that the bets are properly paid off and that the house isn't gypped—which is a job requiring competence.

But no Wall Streeter is willing to be just a croupier. He insists that he is also a prophet, a scholar, and a magician with money.

THE BANKERS AND THE THINKERS

Let us start at the top and work down—a not unusual Wall Street method of pursuing a career. Let us consider the cream of the crop—the truly conservative banker.

This man is an impressive specimen, diffusing the healthy glow which comes of moderation in eating, living, and thinking. He sits enthroned behind a mahogany desk and says, with varying inflections and varying contexts, "No." He is at the top or close to the top of one of those financial empires whose destinies have been guided with such prudence, shrewdness, and soundness that today the Great House has darn near as much money as it had in 1900.

Let us consider the cream of the crop—the truly conservative banker. . . . He sits enthroned behind a mahogany desk and says, with varying inflections and varying contexts, "No."

At that, I believe this fellow does the best job of the lot. Years have gone by, and he hasn't been indicted—there have not even been any scandals; some of the accounts haven't lost anything, and the rest have at least lost their money gradually and respectably. When the great man is asked for investment advice, he immediately picks out something triple-A which can't possibly make the buyer any money and has only a small chance of losing any. He cannot be stampeded into unwary speculation by the hysteria of a boom. He reminds me of what I once heard one doctor say of another: "He doesn't know enough medicine to do a patient any harm."

He sits tight through '26, '27, and '28. Unfortunately, he begins to come in cautiously in '29. (Watching these young whippersnappers make fortunes for three long years does something to the sturdiest characters.) But he pulls out again, and, while a nice piece of money is lost, no one is ruined. He apologizes to himself for having had a human moment and resumes his thirty-year-old policy of listening attentively and saying no.

Way back, generations ago, when it was smart to be tough, the original hundred millions were gathered together in some more realistic business—say, selling firewater to the Indians. And these present grandsons of fortune, sitting up there in a courteous trance, are perhaps not so dumb as they look. I just suspect that they think the buying and selling of securities is a worse occupation than I think it is. But they don't write articles about it; they just avoid it as much as they can without losing the franchise.

We next come to partners, customers' men, heads of trading departments, and statisticians. These gentlemen think steadily and rapidly for five and a half days a week, and when they start losing people's money they really lose it. Their own, too.

Partners as a rule are more impressive than customers' men, because they usually have small private offices, sometimes paneled in oak, in which to have their Thoughts, while the customers' men have to spawn theirs in public out in the board room. The type of customer who habitually sits in a board room is frequently just a gent who loves to chat in masculine company but who doesn't belong to a club. This makes the board room a difficult place for profound thinking.

Nevertheless, the customers' men manage to come to the same tragic conclusions as the partners.

The statisticians are housed way down the hall in scholarly quiet. No noisy tickers or loquacious customers are allowed to intrude, and the Thinkers are surrounded by tomes of reference and the latest news flashes from everywhere. They all carry slide rules, which as everyone knows are more scientific than divining rods. They make exhaustive studies of many a "special situation" and eventually get to know absolutely everything about the affairs of a certain corporation, except perhaps one detail, which is that shortly after the inception of the ensuing fiscal year the corporation is going into 77b.

The type of customer who habitually sits in a board room is frequently just a gent who loves to chat in masculine company but who doesn't belong to a club.

Secluded as they are, the statisticians, too, manage to come to the same general conclusions as do the partners and the customers' men. If these conclusions can be generalized, the underlying principle may be loosely stated thus: Buy them when they are up and sell them when the margin clerk insists that you do so.

It is obviously impossible for the thinking Wall Streeter to avoid acting on that principle.

He certainly can't buy them when they are down, because when they are down "conditions" are terrible. You can't ask an experienced Wall Street man to buy stocks when car loadings have just hit a new low and unemployment is at a peak and steel capacity is less than half of normal and a very big man ("of course I can't tell you his name") has just informed him in confidence that one of the big underwriting houses in the Middle West is in really serious trouble.

Unfortunately for everyone concerned, these are the only times when stocks are down.

When "conditions" are good, the forward-looking investor buys. But, when "conditions" are good, stocks are high. Then, by golly, "conditions" get bad, and stocks go down, and the margin clerk sends him a telegram containing the only piece of financial advice he will ever get from Wall Street which has no *ifs* or *buts* in it.

OCCULT SCIENCE

I know of no more interesting people down below Chambers Street than the Chart Readers, a small but passionate sect.

Your properly consecrated chart reader pays no attention to "conditions" at all — neither flood, famine, pestilence nor war. He arms himself with a chart (the simplest sort of graph) which depicts the ups and downs in price of the market as a whole or of a certain class of stocks or of a commodity. This he studies, well away from the news ticker. It is his claim that he can discern in this jagged line a pattern of behavior which reproduces itself and that certain of the wobbles tell him when it is about to do it again. His technical jargon contains such phrases as "head-and-shoulders formation," "double tops," "double bottoms," and "breakaway gaps."

Your properly consecrated chart reader pays no attention to "conditions" at all — neither flood, famine, pestilence nor war.

There has always been a considerable number of pathetic dopes who busy themselves examining the last thousand numbers which have appeared on a roulette wheel, in search of such a repeating pattern. Sadly enough, they have usually found it.

I am not the man to explain to you the secrets of the charts, although I have had the subject explained to me a number of times. Perhaps I do not understand their true inwardness. As a science, I should say that chart reading shares a pedestal with astrology; but most chart readers have far too much education and mental discipline to consider astrology seriously.

I once suggested to one of the disciples of the Chart that I wasn't a customer and that he should slip me the wink on this tripe. He was as much offended as if I had said something gross about his religious faith.

All I was ever able to conclude from my studies was that chart reading is a complex way of arriving at a simple theorem, to wit: When they have gone up for a considerable time, they will continue to go up for a considerable time; and the same holds true for going down.

There has always been a considerable number of pathetic dopes who busy themselves examining the last thousand numbers which have appeared on a roulette wheel, in search of such a repeating pattern.

This is simple, but it does not happen to be so. The briefest glance at any chart will show you that it is not.

It is the popular feeling in Wall Street that chart readers are pretty occult professors but that most of them are broke. A busted chart reader, however, is never apologetic about his method—he is, if anything, more enthusiastic than the solvent devotee you may occasionally run across. If you have the bad taste to ask him how it happens that he is broke, he tells you quite ingenuously that he made the all too human error of not believing his own charts.

INVESTMENT TRUSTS

This explanation, magnificent in its simplicity, must be the envy of investment-trust presidents. Once each year, except in boom years, these poor fellows have to explain in dignified prose How It All Happened. They have about as much chance of producing an effective apology as a firebug.

It is the popular feeling in Wall Street that chart readers are pretty occult professors but that most of them are broke.

The financial statement of an investment trust is so naked! Not only widows but also orphans can understand it. The trust bought them for so much, and now (after deducting expenses) they are worth only *so* much. Even as you and I.

The president of any other sort of corporation has a comparatively easy time. Not only is his balance sheet Greek to most of his stockholders, but he easily explains his losses as due to the Administration, the drought, the war scare, the Administration, prohibitive costs, and the Administration. But this does not come well from the officers of an investment trust, because they were placed in their high offices on account of their ability to foresee the effects of the Administration, prohibitive costs, the Administration, etc., etc.

The principle of "managed" investment trusts is absolutely sound, granted only one premise. (I am not taking up the subject of "fixed" trusts, because I always wind up losing my temper over them.) The premise is that there are somewhere people of such experience and insight that they can predict with some sort of accuracy the future behavior of securities.

The financial statement of an investment trust is so naked! Not only widows but also orphans can understand it.

So a lot of us who clearly are not magicians pool our money together and hire a set of men to do the guessing. They may not be quite magicians but they have everything that should be necessary—experience, reputation, trained staffs, inside information, and limitless resources for research. Since the amount we pool together is in the neighborhood of a hundred million dollars, we can afford to pay them fortunes for their ability. Paying them fortunes will be a bargain for us, provided only that they come across with the ability.

It is as simple as this: If you wanted to win the class-B golf championship at your country club and the rules permitted you to hire Gene Sarazen, at a reasonable fee, to make your shots for you, what an egotistical fool you would be to play the shots yourself! Well, your money is, no doubt, more important to you than your golf score—but you follow the thought.

The catch is, I am afraid, that there is demonstrable skill involved in playing golf but little evidence that there is any in managing portfolios.

In the terrible fall of 1929 there was an emergency meeting of the board of a certain investment trust. White-faced and irresolute, these men faced each other around the huge mahogany table and tried to avoid each other's eyes. All their convictions were being shattered.

Suddenly one of them spoke, quietly and firmly. "There is no telling how far this thing is going to go," he said. "Such and Such [naming one of the great blue-chip stocks of the day] is down close to two hundred from three hundred and fifty, where it was selling only two months ago. It may sound fantastic, but I believe there is a chance it may yet touch a hundred and fifty. If we could buy ten thousand shares at a hundred and fifty, don't you all think that it would be the sort of bargain which may never be seen again? It probably will never happen, but shouldn't we be prepared, if the opportunity comes?"

At this forceful suggestion, courage ran about the room like a licking flame. Vigorous assents were given, and color came into wan cheeks.

"Put that down," said someone to the young order clerk who was present. "Buy ten thousand Such and Such at a hundred and fifty, open order."

The kid who was addressed obediently leaned forward to write, but as he did so he puckered his lips a little. Very low—but audibly—he gave that distinctive, rubbery sound of contempt which is vulgarly known as "the bird."

Immediately everyone felt less confident. Somehow or other the discussion was reopened, and after a time the suggestion was abandoned.

My informant on this matter has estimated that that little noise saved the trust a matter of three quarters of a million dollars. But no one ever thanked the boy, because no one ever dared admit that he had had anything to do with the decision to cancel that ruinous order.

Once upon a time there was an investment trust of the stuff dreams are made on. It was everything that other trusts are not. Its guiding genius was a young fellow who was everything I have said a Wall Street man could not be. Its stated principle (I quote from memory) was something to this effect:

It is the belief of the management of this corporation that a well-diversified list of carefully selected securities, held over a period of time, will *not* increase in value.

The young man's performance was even more startling than his principles. At his untimely death in 1931 his investment trust had a large position in only one stock—a "blue chip." And that was on the short side!*

When he died, it was wisely decided to wind up the affairs of the corporation. But the surviving officers could not wind it up quickly enough to avoid making an additional fortune with each week's delay.

IT WASN'T STOLEN—YOU LOST IT!

I am aware that for the last quarter-hour someone in the gallery has been—well, let us say verging on rudeness. You, sir—yes you, the gentleman who has been flourishing the umbrella—will you take the floor and tell us your objections so that we all can hear? . . .

Er, well, ah, hrmph. Yes, I should have taken up that subject earlier. Your point, which is expressed so vigorously, is that Wall Street men are not such dunces at all; that they are crooks and thieves and very clever ones to boot; that they sell for millions what they know is worthless; that, in short, they are villains, not children.

That is certainly a widespread point of view. People would rather believe that they have been robbed than that they have been fools on the advice of fools.

I am even tempted to think that Wall Street men themselves encourage this idea. Faced with explaining the huge losses "investors" have suffered, they subconsciously feel that it is better to be regarded as a Machiavelli than as one who has spent his adult life engaged in mumbo-jumbo.

I defer to no man on a knowledge of how money is stolen in Wall Street. If the popular demand is sufficient, I shall explain in my next lecture how to steal an eighth ($12.50) and also a million dollars (two points on the underwriting of

---

* Nearly all investment trusts forbid themselves ever to take a short position, but this was a brilliant exception. It had a comparatively small number of stockholders.

fifty million dollars' worth of bonds that never should have been underwritten); but this sort of thing, no more prevalent in Wall Street than in any other highly competitive business, is not what has caused you to lose your money. A little of it perhaps—but not your whole patrimony. (I can tell that is what you have blown by the sincerity of your indignation.)

If this seems an extreme statement, consider the history of the last two years or so, when the Securities and Exchange Commission has been functioning like a swarm of watchdogs.

Don't think that the SEC has not been tremendously effective. While its representatives cannot be everywhere, the fear of them literally is everywhere, and it has been a long time since I have seen an honest broker steal his customary eighth.

Faced with explaining the huge losses "investors" have suffered, they subconsciously feel that it is better to be regarded as a Machiavelli than as one who has spent his adult life engaged in mumbo-jumbo.

But a great many new securities were launched in '36 and '37. Before they were issued, they were scrutinized by the SEC (and everyone else in an official capacity except Sistie and Buzzie Dall). It all worked splendidly for a year, because there was a boom on. During a boom, securities issued by villains go very satisfactorily, exactly, in fact, as satisfactorily as all other securities. But, as soon as the recession started, down they went, just as though they had never been sprinkled with holy water. Toward the end of the bull market, some of the approved new securities set modest records for the amount of money an investor can lose within three weeks after his securities have been issued.

Wall Street needed the SEC just as baseball after 1919 needed Commissioner Landis. But people who are interested in baseball are more realistic than people interested in Wall Street. No fan expected that Judge Landis would do more for the game than keep it reasonably honest. They did not expect him to improve the quality of the fielding and hitting. Nevertheless, a considerable part of the public seems to be hoping that the SEC will make speculation safer.

These credulous individuals are reminiscent of the timid soul who said at the beginning of the poker game, "Now boys, if we all play carefully we can all win a little."

WHAT TO DO WITH MONEY

. . . Someone has just had the effrontery to ask me what an investor should do with his excess money.

Obviously I haven't the dizziest idea. But I once had such a plan outlined to me and I never forgot it, because it had a certain originality.

I was discussing the broad history of bonds (a depressing subject) with a man I considered a sensible fellow. He had spent the last twenty-five years trading bonds with other people's money. His own money he had always carefully spent.

I finally said: "What a hopeless game! Tell me, Mac, what would you do if you had, today, two hundred and fifty thousand dollars of your own?"

He answered with such promptness that I could see he had given a good deal of thought to this improbability.

"I would put it into twenty-five envelopes, in cash, of ten thousand dollars each. At the beginning of each year I would take out an envelope and I would risk not living more than twenty-five years longer. That would give me two hundred dollars a week. But, since a man has got to be doing something and I like gambling, I would live on a hundred a week and with the other hundred I would play the horse races.

That would give me a real interest in life. Most weeks I'd live at the rate of a hundred—but occasionally at the rate of a thousand."

"But the percentage against you on the horses is certainly as bad as in the market," I reminded him.

"Worse," he said cheerfully, "but playing the horses is at least fun."

Perhaps we have time for one more question before Professor Jones takes over this room for his discussion of "Rationalistic Fallacies of Primitive Peoples." . . .

Yes, I'm glad you brought that up. You want to know, if Wall Street is the sort of hit-or-miss place I have described, why it shouldn't be legislated out of existence.

Well, it shouldn't, and I am not being sarcastic. Why not? Well, tell me, what is your business? . . .

You are a plumber? Well then, for your sake—as well as for the sake of countless other persons.

I can name you offhand, sir, a dozen corporations whose products you use in your business, and all those corporations need at least a few million dollars apiece for the kind of plants they run. None of their stuff can be produced by some fellow and his uncle in the back of a garage. Now it may be just unfortunate, but the only successful way so far devised for getting such sums out of the public, for enterprises good or bad, is a system similar to the devious mechanisms of Wall Street. And the system has always included all of the nonsense. (Money has occasionally been raised from the public by smacking the citizens with the broad side of a saber, but the results of this were always less than satisfactory.)

In conclusion, I must remind you that I work in Wall Street and assure you that my organization is quite different from anything I have described here. If you have any knotty investment problems, just stop in at my office and let us recommend a program. I will see to it personally that your inquiries are referred to the head of our crystal-gazing department.

PART III

Strategy

After making the decision to invest, a comprehensive strategy is needed. Should a contrarian approach be taken, as Edward Johnson, founder of Fidelity, espouses? Following the crowd can be dangerous, he says; crowds "tend to commit suicide." Should you think long term or short term? Peter Bernstein assesses the time factor, weighing the importance of volatility, liquidity, and the need for income. Timing is a critical element in formulating a strategy because, as Gerald Loeb, long-time vice-chairman of E. F. Hutton, states, more errors are made in deciding when to sell, not when to buy. That's when most opportunities are lost. Other considerations include diversification, buying on margin, and Mario Gabelli's mysterious "catalysts." In a strategic case study, Gabelli describes how finding "catalysts" can boost your net worth. Sticking to a strategy, while periodically assessing it, takes the gambling out of investing.

Edward C. Johnson, II founded the Fidelity Management and Research Company in 1946 and ran the firm until relinquishing the reins to his son in 1974. That year the company had 14 funds and was managing about $2 billion. Today it is the largest mutual fund company. He began his investment career in the 1920s, and in all those years, he relied primarily on intuition, not science. "I have been absorbed and immersed since 1924," he said, "and I know this is no science. It is an art. Now we have computers and all sorts of statistics, but the market is still the same and understanding the market is still no easier."

Johnson was mostly concerned with satisfying his customers and always putting them first. He actually felt a twinge of guilt if he believed the firm made too much money. Take one year in the mid-1960s, when Fidelity made $5.5 million: "A company like ours should never make this much money," he said. He felt that way because Fidelity didn't manufacture anything; it was "just a business of ideas." Johnson made two points when it came to investing: "First . . . make only the investment decisions about which you have a reasonably high level of conviction. It is a simple, but often overlooked lesson: you cannot turn a profit if you are always second-guessing yourself. . . . Second, cut your losses and cut them fast; do not listen to reason or emotion, just say good-bye."

According to his son, Edward III, Johnson always espoused unorthodox thinking. "He believed that being too secure led to trouble. From the firm's earliest years, he encouraged us to oppose orthodox thinking." But you also had to respect the forces at work. "My father had given me a healthy respect for the market—a respect that came from his own experience watching a whole generation lose money in the late 1920s and 1930s." Johnson's key to success was being a contrarian; he tuned into the market forces, and when people were timid, he was bold, and vice versa. In *Contrary Opinion in Stock Market Techniques,* he explains why you have to pay attention to the "tuning fork" inside your own body.

Contrary Opinion in Stock Market Techniques
Edward C. Johnson, II

W e approach the problem of investment first and foremost from a money-making point of view. We are not interested in fancy ideas and theories; we are interested in things that work. You might call us empirical pragmatists. Those are almost too heavy words for anyone to swallow, but I hope they convey a picture. Our almost religion is that we believe strongly in analysis of the present. The past is dead. We can learn from it, trying not to indulge in the "backward" successes we might have made. The future is a dream. That may be as may be. If you come to think of it, the present (I talk like a Zen Buddhist now) the present is really the only thing that anybody can actually use. So many people spend their lives thinking about the future ahead that they are hardly conscious of the present. Now there is not much you can do with the future. You can't love it, you can't taste it, you can only dream about it. This is our actual approach; we don't try to forecast. We can't buy or sell securities a month from now; we can only do it today. So what do we do today? That is enough for us to know.

The present we try to use, however, is not a static affair. It is dynamic, full of motion. It is the analysis of these dynamics and motion that is completely vital. To analyze correctly in this way the present . . . is to take advantage of the future without the desperate chances inherent in successful forecasting.

We approach the practical investing problem from two angles. First is so-called fundamental research. Let's now look at Contrary Opinion itself. I got to considering it last night. I began to wonder what made Contrary Opinion useful and what was the kind of Contrary Opinion we were interested in. For example: The sun rises tomorrow. I suppose that the general opinion is that the sun will rise tomorrow and it is obvious that here is not an opinion that we wish to be contrary to. Same way with opinions about the weather. Why? Because the opinion itself has no effect on the fact. The general opinion that the sun is going to rise, of course, has no effect on the sun rising, nor has the opinion on the state of the weather any effect on the weather. So may we not say that the test for usefulness of Contrary Opinion is the extent to which the opinion affects the fact under consideration. For example, in contrast to the sun and weather let us look at the stock market. Obviously the general opinion on whether the stock market is going up or down has a profound effect on the action of the market itself. The more unanimous the opinion, the greater the what might be called inverse effect on prices will be.

We approach the problem of investment first and foremost from a money-making point of view. We are not interested in fancy ideas and theories; we are interested in things that work. . . . Our almost religion is that we believe strongly in analysis of the present. The past is dead.

All right, let's take that rule; let's look at so-called fundamental research. What do we do? We send men out all over the country and they talk to company officials and others, and with competitors particularly. Now so far as fundamental research is concerned I can't see that Contrary Opinion is too important. What people think IBM is going to do in the way of earnings and dividends has probably relatively little effect on what IBM does accomplish—yes, some effect—because if people have a good opinion of you maybe you are apt to do things that you wouldn't do so well if they had a poor opinion of you. But it is not a large factor. Again, one thing we do in particular; our men go around to competitors which is the first place you go to find out about a given company. We get the general opinion that a particular company is able, well run, and so forth and so on. We don't go contrary to that; we use it in [reaching] our conclusions. So Contrary Opinion probably wouldn't be useful there, either.

Next I'd like to discuss a rather subtle application of the principle of Contrary Opinion. Let us look at a certain kind of what might be called emotional involvement. Emotional involvement is a very broad thing—it comes up constantly in many forms. For example, an analyst gets emotionally involved with a company he goes to see, a psychiatrist gets emotionally involved with his patient, and the sexes get emotionally involved with each other (to put it mildly). This is something we have to allow for. When we find an analyst is getting that way—and you can tell almost by the tone of his voice and the way he looks when he talks about a company that this is happening—we cannot afford to satisfy the deep human instinct of faithfulness and trust which underlie emotional involvement. Because of the very nature of our business we have to follow the "love 'em and leave 'em" principle.

When troubles loom ahead for a company, what is one's natural instinct? You want to take off your coat and get out with management to tackle and solve the difficulties. But unfortunately that isn't our business, which is to keep investment dollars working in the most productive media. The men running the company involved of course stay with it through thick and thin, but our question always has to be whether other pastures may not be greener. We have the ability to change businesses which the ordinary man in a particular business does not. This is one of the things that makes our business so unnatural, but also, strangely, very satisfying too. So fascinating is our business that we have difficulty holding very good men because a man who can fairly consistently on balance make substantial money in securities is rare and he is coveted by the whole world. One of the things that may hold him, I think, is the fascination of the business of investing and the universality of it. The stock market represents everything that anybody has ever hoped, feared, hated, or loved. It is all of life. You leave that and you go to the XYZ Bottling Co. and the rest of your life is bottles.

Crowds, when they carry often sound ideas to foolish extremes, tend to commit suicide.

Now, this emotional involvement is, I think, one of the things we combat by being contrary. This is, we go contrary to the deep instinct in everybody which wants to stand by the ship and fight through to the finish, so to speak. To paraphrase a famous statesman talking about nations, we have no loyalties or friends, only interests. Maybe this contrary element in our business contributes to its fascination, and it's often tough on the families at home because we in the business love it so much that we are apt to work unreasonably long hours.

Back to Contrary Opinion: Why does it pay to be contrary? Let's take the 1920's as an extreme example of how it works in the stock market. In 1929 nearly everybody who could had bought all the stocks he and his borrowing power could absorb, and in those days there were lots of 5% margins around. You had probably a very extreme example of a universal opinion that stocks were going up. Therefore, you had a nation jammed with potential sellers. The buying had all for the moment been done and way overdone. The panic

of 1929 was a natural result. Again that shows how Contrary
Opinion works. Crowds, when they carry often sound ideas
to foolish extremes, tend to commit suicide. Ideally stock
market prices should express average opinion of a fair estimate of probabilities and generally this is so. In other words,
every price in itself is a healthy exercise of a kind of Contrary Opinion. I am referring to that part of the stock
exchange transactions which you might call voluntary, not
the necessity kind. Every transaction represents an opinion
by the buyer that the price is wrong, it ought to be or become
higher. And by the seller that the price is wrong, it ought to
be or become lower. You go on beyond that and you get
opinions of stock by the general public and you get a new
element coming in. The crowd tends to suck others in its
train so that A thinks thus because B does and B because C
and so on. A body of general opinion tends to work on itself
and create other similar opinions like a thunderstorm creating its own wind. A mass opinion tends to grow on itself, and
here I believe is the heart and soul of the Contrary Opinion
doctrine. It is this artificially engendered superheated general opinion that it pays to "copper" because it isn't really an
opinion at all—it's a crowd psychology phenomenon. Now,
all of us have inside of us a part of the crowd. I have always
wondered about Humphrey and just how he gets his dope on
what general opinions are. I never have to go outside the
confines of my own room. Every one of us has a tuning fork
inside of himself that vibrates to a greater or lesser extent
along with the crowd. It works so uniformly that when
sometimes I talk to salesmen of mutual funds I give them a
rule, which is this: That the more it hurts them and the more
they have to fight themselves to make a sale, the better it will
be for the customer and also for the salesman himself. And
that just means going contra to his inborn crowd segment.

That is the thing you get in the kind of area where you
have superheated opinions—where the thing builds itself up.
Another analogy is the chain letter effect. Are there any of
you who are old enough to remember the chain letter? They

were a great, great fad. There was a little fellow named Ponzi down my way who went on the same principle. In other words, the idea of the game is fine so long as you get new suckers to keep coming and bail the old ones out. The later Imrie deVegh called it the Bigger Fool Theory. You buy at a foolish price, but you hope you will get a bigger fool to pay you a bigger price later on. Dickson Watts was a famous cotton speculator, I think, and he laid down some principles for trading. He put it this way: "Against the crowd act boldly. With the crowd act cautiously. It may at any time turn and rend you." I think in very few words he has expressed in another way the principle involved in this kind of thing.

The stock market represents everything that anybody has ever hoped, feared, hated, or loved. It is all of life.

Actually, operation in securities is not mainly a matter of reasoning at all. The talented operators I know don't really reason things out (although they often pretend to). They just do it instinctively by experience. As a man plays golf or rides a horse. Our nation is a remarkable phenomenon, for we Americans are a very interesting group of people as seen in the light of history. We are essentially men of action. Do something about it! We are also men of science—tremendous men of science. But when we turn to art we find that it is not reasoning and not scientific; it is basically a matter of individual emotion and feeling for universality, channeled into a particular mode of expression such as painting, music, or philosophy as the latter involves understanding of the human soul. It is really an instinctive sense of things that exist but are too complicated to reason out. Here Americans appear deficient, somewhat as the Romans were. Thus you take a psychiatrist today—here you have an example of the attempt to apply the scientific method to the human mind.

And it just plain doesn't work, because the conscious and subconscious human mind is so vast—the stock market, by the way, is just a bunch of minds—that there is no science, no IBM machine, no anything of that sort, that can tame it. What this means to us in practical affairs is that if we are able to do the thing that Americans find very hard to do— that is, understand ourselves (and consequently others) to some degree—we have really a chance of becoming effective stock operators. That is a hard thing and a rare thing.

Now coming down from these theoretical heights, let's look at the so-called technical aspect of markets. I suppose that word is a good one. The technical side of the stock market is an attempt to understand the demand-supply situation in securities as distinct from the fundamental which, of course, is the thing I was telling you about: going to see companies and checking industries and facts. There are a great number of "technical indicators." There is nothing secret about any of them (that are worth using). There is nothing very complicated. You can't get complicated anywhere in this business without being lost; each complication begets ten others, and so on.

Operation in securities is not mainly a matter of reasoning at all. The talented operators I know don't really reason things out (although they often pretend to).

You have these various tools: We have a number of test tubes that we experiment with and look at—such as the simplest of all, moving averages of stock prices. Take for example, say, a 12-month moving average of [the] Dow Jones Industrial Average. If any one of you people wanted to close your mind to everything else—never mind about all the forecasts— just the moving average, and use a few simple techniques, that moving average would get you into all big bull markets and would keep you out of all big bear markets. It would be far from perfect, but workable. Did you ever hear of anyone who ever did this in practical operation? I never did.

For light here let's look at the ancient Greeks. The Greeks were always great favorites of mine and, as you know, they used to have many gods and goddesses; and it was a trick to know which god or goddess to back. You remember Paris had a choice to make, for he had a golden apple to be given to the fairest goddess, and here were three leading goddesses standing in front of him — to whom should he give the apple? Foolishly he gave it to Venus. If he had given it to Athene or even Hera it would have been far better for everyone, including himself, because he already had a devoted girl friend who was far from ugly or ill favored. But he chose Venus and so destroyed his whole family and his whole city and nation because of it. You see, any choosing among gods or goddesses isn't easy. To choose one was to antagonize another. The Hebrews, on the other hand, looked to a single God, just one, and that did make life simpler at the cost of what one may learn or gain or lose through choosing for himself.

There's no one god in the investment world, so how are you going to decide which one of these indicators you are going to pick? . . . I wonder if, in the realm of art, too much thinking may not often be more responsible for trouble than too little thinking. If you will make the thinking that you do so simple as to choose some one "god" among all these technical things — then you have a chance. Remember the words: "Your God is a jealous God," and that is especially true in this kind of work. Various services put much stress on looking at many indicators and [g]oing along with a weighted majority. I submit to you that there's no mathematical way of averaging or weighing your indicators for practical stock market operation.

A violin to me is just wood and a bunch of strings. It takes an artist to play on it. These technical things are nothing but tools — nothing but the violin. They are no good without the player. Now this means that we don't want an orthodox investment approach. [A]n orthodox investment approach, handling as it does stupendous amounts of investment funds, more or less has to obtain average investment results. There isn't any other way of doing it. Unusual results in securities, as I say, have to be looked for in the basically artistic camp, which is relatively small in number as are all artistic groups.

PETER L. BERNSTEIN

Peter Bernstein has both written best-selling books and made millions of dollars for his clients as an investment adviser. He has also taught at colleges and universities; he started his own consulting company, Peter L. Bernstein, Inc.; and he founded the *Journal of Portfolio Management* in 1974. By bridging real-world investing and the world of academics, Bernstein created a certain synergy. "The *Journal* has kept me younger than anything else," he said, "because the learning process has been so intense. When you have to read all that stuff—read it, not skim it, and the bad as well as the good—you just can't help learning from it." His education started in New York City, where he went to a private school, graduating in 1936. His next stops were Harvard and then the Air Force during World War II.

When his father—who cofounded Bernstein-Macaulay, a family-oriented investment counseling firm, in 1934—died unexpectedly in 1951, Bernstein joined the company. That year he made a mere $7,500. Back then, Bernstein recalls, everyone was very conservative because they still remembered the 1929 stock market crash. In those early years, even Bernstein advised clients to stick with blue chips and bonds. "Our one big adventure," he said, "was in identifying the puberty boom early on and taking big positions in Gillette and Tampax; the latter was barely mentionable in polite conversation at that time." Not until the 1960s, when "those old guys began to die off," did he notice a change in the willingness to take on more risk.

When his wife died in 1971, and with the United States in turmoil, protesting Vietnam and promoting social revolution, Bernstein decided it was time for him to make some changes, too. In 1973 he started his own consultant firm, mostly advising institutional investors. Another change in the investing world that he has witnessed has been the loss of balanced money managers. "The sylish cafeteria of specialized managers that we see today leads to a mishmash of risks and covariances that most clients fail to understand," he said. Risk and volatility are two topics he addresses in *Is Investing for the Long Term Theory or Just Mumbo-Jumbo?*

Is Investing For the Long Term Theory or Just Mumbo-Jumbo?

Peter L. Bernstein

What do we mean by "investing for the long term"? The aim of this paper is to demonstrate that "long term" is in the eye of the beholder.

For those investors infested with quarterly measurements, a year can be the long run and five years is just about the outer limit. For enthusiasts of the Dividend Discount model, the long run is the indefinite future. Most of us fall somewhere in between. Yet each of us will define the long run with a different time span in mind, which means that yours will be appropriate for me only by coincidence. But no matter how we figure it, there is more to the long run than shutting your eyes and hoping that some great tidal force will bring your ships home safe, sound, and laden with just the right merchandise for the occasion.

I am going to approach the issue from two different viewpoints. First, we shall explore whether there really is such a thing as long run. Second, assuming that we can identify and define the long run, I shall try to demonstrate that moving from the short run to the long run transforms the investment process in ways that are far more profound than most people realize.

How Long Is the Long Run?

When people talk about the long run, they are really saying that they can distinguish between the signal and the noise. Yet the world is a terribly noisy place. Discriminating between the main force and the perpetual swarm of peripheral events is one of the most baffling tasks that human beings must confront—and can never duck.

For those investors infested with quarterly measurements, a year can be the long run and five years is just about the outer limit.

Do two unusually warm winters in a row signify the onset of global warming, or are they a normal variation, to be succeeded by bitterly cold winters in the years following? When the championship baseball team loses three games in a row, is that the beginning of the end of their league dominance, or a brief interruption in their string of victories? When the stock market drops 10 percent, is that the start of a new bear market or just a correction in the ongoing bull market? Was October 1987 the beginning of the end, or the end of the beginning?

Those long-run investors who believe that they can distinguish signal from noise scorn the traders who are so busy chasing the wiggles and the ripples that they run the risk of losing the main trend. The watchwords of the true long-run investor are "regression to the mean." In the long run, everything will even out; main trends are identifiable; main trends dominate. This concept rules much active investment management. The very idea of "undervaluation" or "overvaluation" implies some identifiable norm to which values will

150

revert. Other investors may choose to succumb to fads and whims and rumors, but investors who hang in there will win out in the long run.

Or will they? The lesson of history is that norms are never normal forever. Paradigm shifts belie blind faith in regression to the mean. This is precisely the problem with which Alan Greenspan is now wrestling: Has the long and reliable relationship between M2 and nominal GNP finally crumbled, or is the current disturbance just an anomaly? Here is another: For 170 years, the highest-quality long-term bonds in the United States yielded an average of 4.2 percent within a standard deviation of only a percentage point. In 1970, yields broke through the old upper limits and started heading for 7 percent. Investors stared: How could they decide whether this was a blip or a new era? And then there was the moment in the late 1950s when the dividend yield on stocks slipped below bond yields. Again, investors back then had no handy rules to tell them whether this totally unexpected development was a fundamental shift in market structure or just a temporary aberration that would soon correct itself, with the "normal" spread of stocks yields over bond yields reestablishing itself.

When people talk about the long run, they are really saying that they can distinguish between the signal and the noise. Yet the world is a terribly noisy place.

John Maynard Keynes, who knew a few things about investing, probability, and economics, took a dim view of the idea that you can look through the noise to find the signal. In a famous passage, he declared that:

The long run is a misleading guide to current affairs.
In the long run, we are all dead. Economists set themselves too easy, too useless a task if in the tempestuous
seasons they can only tell us that when the storm is
long past the ocean will be flat.

Keynes is suggesting that the tempestuous seasons are the
norm. The ocean will never be flat soon enough to matter. In
Keynes' philosophy, equilibrium and central values are
myths, not the foundations on which we build our structures. We cannot escape the short run.

---

*Those long-run investors who believe that they
can distinguish signal from noise scorn the
traders who are so busy chasing the wiggles
and the ripples that they run the risk of losing
the main trend.*

These considerations explain why I asserted at the outset
that the long run is in the eye of the beholder. The way you
feel about the long run and the way you define it are ultimately gut issues. These issues are resolved more by the
nature of your basic philosophy of life, or even how you feel
when you get up each morning, than by rigorous intellectual
analysis.

Those who believe in the permanence of tempestuous
seasons will view life as a succession of short runs, where
noise dominates signals and the frailty of the basic parameters makes normal too elusive a concept to worry about.
These people are pessimists who see nothing in the future
but clouds of uncertainty. They make decisions based only
on the short distance ahead that they can see.

Those who live by regression to the mean spend their time entirely differently. They expect the storm to pass, so that one day the ocean will be flat. On that assumption, they can make the decision to ride out the storm. They are optimists who see the signals by which they will steer their ships toward that happy day when the sun shines through.

My own view of the matter is a mixture of these two approaches. Hard experience has taught me that chasing noise leads me to miss the main trend too often. At the same time, having lived through the bond yield/stock yield shift of the late 1950s and the breakthrough of bond yields into the stratosphere beyond 6 percent in the late 1960s—just to mention two such shattering events out of many—I look with suspicion at all main trends and all those means to which variables are supposed to regress. To me, the primary task in investing is to test and then retest some more the parameters and paradigms that appear to govern daily events. Betting against them is dangerous when they look solid, but accepting them without question is the most dangerous step of all.

THE IMPACT OF THE LONG RUN ON INVESTMENT MANAGEMENT

It is a truism that investing for the long run is different from short-term trading. But I would argue that time is such a critical variable in the investment process that the differences between short- and long-term investing are far more profound than most people realize. The long-term game is so unlike the short-term game that you need a whole new set of rules when you are playing it. I shall mention three areas where this requirement applies.

1. *Volatility*

The first difference is in the impact of volatility. Volatility is noise. The short-term trader bets on the noise; the long-term investor listens to the signal. But the long-term investor who thinks that the main trend will even out volatility over time is in for a shock. Volatility is the central concern of all investors, but it matters more in the long run than in the short run.

The long run is in the eye of the beholder. The way you feel about the long run and the way you define it are ultimately gut issues.

Volatility matters, because it defines the uncertainty of the price at which an asset will be liquidated. The Ibbotson Associates data tell us that the expected total return on the S&P 500 for a one-year holding period is about 12.5 percent, but you should not be surprised if you come out somewhere between −8 percent and +32 percent, a spread of 400 basis points. The range for individual stocks is much wider. So volatility appears to matter a lot if you are going to hold for only a year.

Stretch your holding period out from one year to ten years, and the range of the expected return narrows to between about +5 percent to +15 percent a year, a spread of only 100 basis points and implying very little chance of loss over the ten-year period. Although volatility now seems much less troublesome than it did in the one-year horizon, and although the odds on losing money when you liquidate are now greatly reduced, do not be lulled by that relatively narrow range of annual rates of return. What matters is not the annual rate of return but the final liquidating value at the end of ten years. A dollar invested for ten years at 5 percent compounds to $1.63; at 15 percent, it compounds to $4.05. As a dollar invested for one year is likely to end up at the end of the year between $0.92 and $1.28, the spread in liquidating value over one year is far narrower than the probable outcomes over a ten-year holding period, despite the greater standard deviation of returns. So where is the uncertainty greater—in the short run or the long run? Talk about the ocean being flat! It could be very flat indeed.

2. Liquidity

When you buy something to make a few points, or even ten or twenty, eighths and quarters matter. Good execution counts for a lot. When you buy to hold for the long run, for years, even a few points on the price will not matter a great deal. Liquidity is a concern of the short-term investor and a minor matter for the long-term investor.

Volatility is noise. The short-term trader bets on the noise; the long-term investor listens to the signal.

The point is obvious, but it receives too little attention. How much does pricing matter for assets that are not about to be liquidated? If you are a multibillion-dollar investment management organization that has no choice but to acquire and hold indefinitely Exxon and IBM and other major high-cap companies, what difference does the daily price fluctuation make? Why bother to watch their daily action? Throughout our financial system, many more assets are marked to market than is necessary, creating serious distortions as to the soundness of the institutions involved. Assets held for the long pull are simply not the same thing as assets that are to be liquidated in a matter of weeks or months.

155

3. Income

Investment income is a critically important link between the short and the long run. Income is also a dramatic illustration of the important principle of Hegelian dialectics that changes in quantity ultimately become changes in quality.

For the short-term trader, the dividend on a stock is a gauge to valuation, but the actual money income from the dividend is irrelevant. The trader's return will be dominated by price change, because prices tend to move in ranges that far exceed one year's income receipt. Now expand the time horizon. Income payments pile up over time, altering the character of the return structure. Investors who are able to reinvest income now begin to have the opposite desire from short-term traders: traders want prices to rise so they can sell, while investors reinvesting income are buyers and must want prices to fall while the buying process is going on.

In the case of bonds, this story is obvious. Current coupons being what they are, interest and interest-on-interest soon prevail over price change and, for long-maturity bonds, account for an overwhelming share of the total return.

The story in the stock market is similar in character, but few people take notice of it. If you had put a dollar in the stock market at the end of 1925 and just let it appreciate, spending all the income you received over those 66 years, you would have $30 today. If you ignored the price appreciation and simply piled up the sixty-five years' worth of dividends, without any reinvestment income, you would have a pile equal to $20. Not bad. In fact, given the starting period in 1925 and the intervening stock market crash of 1929 to 1932, your growing pile of dividends would have exceeded the market value of your portfolio for thirty-five years from 1930 to about 1965; the dividend pile fell behind the portfolio value by a meaningful amount only after 1982 — fifty-seven years after your original purchase.

Let me go back to the end of 1925 for a moment, to give you the full flavor of what I am talking about. According to the Ibbotson Associates data, a dollar invested in the stock market at the end of 1925, with all dividends reinvested and no taxes and brokerage paid, would have grown to about $600 today, far above the $30 from appreciation alone. The difference of $570 comes from the receipt and reinvestment of that pile of income, swelling the total to the magnificent sum of $600. An investor who came into the market at the top in 1929 would have had to wait until 1953 before stock prices would have returned to what they cost to purchase. Yet, with income reinvested, break-even would have arrived in 1944, nine years sooner.

Therefore, the role of price in determining total return diminishes steadily in importance as we move from the short run to the long run. The mean annual income return since 1925 has been 4.7 percent a year with a standard deviation of only 1.2 percentage points. The annual appreciation return has averaged 7.1 percent, but with a standard deviation of twenty percentage points. These facts explain why the income turtle puts up such a good race against the appreciation hare. But they also help to explain why the standard deviation of returns tends to shrink with the passage of time.

The long run is a complex, ambiguous, even elusive concept, better in theory than it often is in practice.

Quite aside from the demonstration that volatility matters a lot more in the long run than conventional wisdom would lead us to believe, there is an additional and overwhelmingly important lesson here for investors. Do not simulate equity portfolio returns with the familiar long-term

Ibbotson figure of 10 percent to 12 percent a year unless the portfolio can accumulate and reinvest all the income that it earns.

Investors who must pay taxes on their income or, even worse, are not in a position to accumulate and reinvest every penny of dividend income they receive cannot rely on the long run to bail them out of the inherent volatility of equity investments. There have been fifty-six ten-year rolling holding periods beginning with 1925–35. In nine of those cases — of which only three were in the 1930s — stock prices ended up below where they started. In another twelve cases, the increase in stock prices over ten years lagged the rise in the cost of living, so that the portfolio lost real value. This means that the market's price performance was negative one-third of the time in these ten-year holding periods even though, over the whole span of sixty-six years, prices rose thirtyfold, or 5.1 percent a year. Those are scary numbers without the precious support and smoothing of income accumulation. Equity investing is risky business, even in the long run.

NOISES, SIGNALS, AND TEMPESTUOUS SEASONS

The long run in the popular view is a process that smooths the bumps, that cuts through the clutter, that captures the main trend. But if there is a moral to the story I have related here, it is that the long run is a complex, ambiguous, even elusive concept, better in theory than it often is in practice. We cannot escape those difficulties. They are part of life.

Despite the complexity, ambiguity, and elusiveness of the long run, there is another moral, and a useful one. Time matters. Quantitative changes become qualitative changes, and fundamental transformations take place as the time period lengthens. Although I am not sure where the short run ends and the long run begins, I do know that the character of my expected investment results are dependent on the length of the holding period. That, at least, is a beginning to wisdom.

As far back as the 1950s, long before global investing became fashionable, Sir John Templeton was searching the world for opportunity. By the mid-1960s, the Templeton Funds were investing in Japan. At that time Japanese stocks were trading at 4 times earnings, while U.S. stocks were at 16 times earnings. "People are always asking me where is the outlook good," he said, "but that's the wrong question. The right question is: Where is the outlook most miserable?" The purpose is to find the most depressed prices. It's about risk/reward ratios, and the risky international strategy paid off—a $10,000 investment with him in 1954 was worth $2.3 million 40 years later, which works out to a compound rate of 17 percent per year.

Growing up in rural Tennessee, Templeton was intrigued by the stories that visiting Christian missionaries told of foreign countries, and he decided to join them. However, after attending Yale and then going to Oxford as a Rhodes scholar, he realized he wasn't cut out to be a missionary. "But I also realized," he said, "that I was more talented with money than they were. So I decided to devote myself to helping the missionaries financially." His first major investment was in 1939, when he bought $100 worth of every stock on every exchange that was trading at less than $1 (the money to do so was borrowed). After holding onto them for an average of four years, he netted over $40,000. Shortly thereafter, Templeton found an investment counselor who wanted to sell his business, which he bought for $5,000.

One of his habits over the years, was leading the Templeton Growth Fund directors in prayer—praying to make the right investment decisions. For Templeton, who became a British citizen and was knighted in 1987, it was not blasphemous. "I think all careers are more successful and satisfying if you use spiritual principles," he said. Templeton believes that spiritual research and progress is just as important as that in science. In 1994, for example, he donated over $10 million to religious causes. Prayers aside, Templeton had a well-defined strategy for investing, which he boils down to the essentials in *The Time-Tested Maxims of the Templeton Touch.*

The Time-Tested Maxims
of the Templeton Touch
Sir John Templeton

1. For all long-term investors, there is only one objective — "maximum total real return after taxes."
2. Achieving a good record takes much study and work, and is a lot harder than most people think.
3. It is impossible to produce a superior performance unless you do something different from the majority.
4. The time of maximum pessimism is the best time to buy, and the time of maximum optimism is the best time to sell.
5. To put "Maxim 4" in somewhat different terms, in the stock market the only way to get a bargain is to buy what most investors are selling.
6. To buy when others are despondently selling and to sell when others are greedily buying requires the greatest fortitude, even while offering the greatest reward.
7. Bear markets have always been temporary. Share prices turn upward from one to twelve months before the bottom of the business cycle.
8. If a particular industry or type of security becomes popular with investors, that popularity will always prove temporary and, when lost, won't return for many years.

9. In the long run, the stock market indexes fluctuate around the long-term upward trend of earnings per share.

10. In free-enterprise nations, the earnings on stock market indexes fluctuate around the replacement book value of the shares of the index.

11. If you buy the same securities as other people, you will have the same results as other people.

It is impossible to produce a superior performance unless you do something different from the majority.

---

12. The time to buy a stock is when the short-term owners have finished their selling, and the time to sell a stock is often when short-term owners have finished their buying.

13. Share prices fluctuate much more widely than values. Therefore, index funds will never produce the best total return performance.

14. Too many investors focus on "outlook" and "trends." Therefore, more profit is made by focusing on value.

15. If you search worldwide, you will find more bargains and better bargains than by studying only one nation. Also, you gain the safety of diversification.

16. The fluctuation of share prices is roughly proportional to the square root of the price.

17. The time to sell an asset is when you have found a much better bargain to replace it.

18. When any method for selecting stocks becomes popular, then switch to unpopular methods. As has been suggested in "Maxim 3," too many investors can spoil any share-selection method or any market-timing formula.

19. Never adopt permanently any type of asset or any selection method. Try to stay flexible, open-minded and skeptical. Long-term top results are achieved only by changing from popular to unpopular the types of securities you favor and your methods of selection.

20. The skill factor in selection is largest for the common-stock part of your investments.

21. The best performance is produced by a person, not a committee.

22. If you begin with prayer, you can think more clearly and make fewer stupid mistakes.

Mario Gabelli, who likens himself to a jet fighter pilot, has built a financial empire that includes an institutional brokerage firm, a mutual fund management company, and a money management business that advises institutions and private investors. Astounding success and personal energy have earned him the moniker "Super Mario." Like Peter Lynch and some other top stock pickers, Gabelli, who grew up in the Bronx, first became interested in the stock market while caddying for executives. After attending Fordham University on a scholarship, he received an MBA from Columbia University, where he was most influenced by a professor who taught security analysis in the spirit of the meticulous and conservative Benjamin Graham.

In 1967, he embarked on his Wall Street career as an auto parts analyst for Loeb Rhoades, then moved on to William D. Witter. In 1977, he founded Gabelli Asset Management. Over the years he has added a couple of twists to Graham's approach to fundamental analysis. One is to introduce the idea of "private market value" into the mix—that is, what a public company would be worth if it were taken private. He likes to back out such expenses as taxes, depreciation, and interest to get truer net income and asset numbers. Another concept he introduced is to look for what Gabelli calls a "catalyst," an event that will boost a company's stock, such as a merger or a change in government regulation.

Gabelli, who reads annual reports the way others read novels, has earned the reputation of being a tireless worker as he has built a firm that manages over $10 billion in assets. "This is not my job," he says. "This is my passion. Some people collect art or ride horses or play in castles in Ireland. I like to pick stocks." Toward that end, there are plenty of 5 A.M. to 9 P.M. days, and even the occasional Sunday afternoon staff meeting. While hardworking, Gabelli has a lighter side, which is reflected in the name of a fund that focuses on global entertainment and media companies—the Gabelli Global Interactive Couch Potato Fund. As for his investment style, he elaborates on finding "catalysts," among other strategies, in *Grand Slam Hitting.*

Grand Slam Hitting
Mario Gabelli

T he ancient Greek dramatist
Euripides said, "The best of seers is he who guesses well."
Each year since 1980, *Barron's* has given me the opportunity
to sit down with a distinguished group of good guessers at
the annual Roundtable and divine what the economy, the
markets and some individual stocks would do in the year
ahead. Now, in honor of *Barron's* 75th Anniversary, I've been
invited to stick my neck out even further and discuss several
investment themes that will theoretically enrich readers over
the next five years. Fair enough.

I will begin with the confession that over the past 20
years, our annual macroeconomic and market forecasts
haven't always been right. Fortunately for our clients and
Barron's readers, our investment methodology is not built
upon accurately predicting interest-rate trends or timing the
market, but rather on picking stocks, and many of our picks
have fared quite well.

One reason is that we've had a good batting average iden-
tifying trends—we call them catalysts—that have unlocked
value in selected industry groups. A catalyst can be a change
in regulatory standards such as the original cable television
deregulation bill of 1984 that led us to lucrative investments
in cable stocks. It can be consolidation within an industry.

The scramble for filmed entertainment assets engendered by expanding distribution systems throughout the 1980s and early 1990s inspired us to take substantial and ultimately quite profitable positions in Warner Communications, MCA and Paramount prior to their acquisitions by Time Inc., Matsushita and Viacom, respectively.

Our investment methodology is not built upon accurately predicting interest-rate trends or timing the market, but rather on picking stocks, and many of our picks have fared quite well.

Catalysts can also be corporate restructurings. The recent trend to help realize shareholder value through the sale or spinoff of businesses has helped us earn good returns from "Humpty Dumpty" companies as all the king's horses and all the king's men help break conglomerates into pieces again. Among them have been Tenneco, American Brands, American Express, ITT and, now, AT&T.

Over the next five years, the most powerful trend we see is the explosive growth of the international marketplace for American goods and services. This traces its roots to two major catalysts: the rejuvenation of American industry spawned by a declining cost of capital and enormous productivity gains, and the victory of global capitalism symbolized best by the crumbling of the Berlin Wall. Good old-fashioned Yankee ingenuity has made us more than competitive with Japan and Germany. We are now in a terrific position to conquer new international economic frontiers.

With free-market economies evolving in China and the former Soviet bloc, and the middle classes rapidly expanding in developing nations in Latin America and the Pacific Rim, there will be 2.5 billion to three billion new consumers by the turn of the century. How is this emerging international middle class going to spend its money? If past is prologue—and we can learn something by looking back at the economic evolution of the great American middle class—the new international middle class will upgrade their food consumption habits; if it is made available, they will buy telephone service; they will spend money on entertainment, and they will travel.

Investors of our persuasion—stockpickers, if you will—can't talk about investment trends without naming some names. Unlike the Roundtable, where we are constantly prodded both by *Barron's* and our colleagues to fill in the fundamental blanks on individual stock selections, I won't be providing hard data on the companies I mention in this article. Nor will I make predictions about short-term earnings and cash flow. That said, consistent with our Graham-and-Dodd-oriented value philosophy, we would like to own the businesses named here for the long term.

IT'S NOT CHICKENFEED

Let's start in, of all places, Iowa. The American grains farmer is the most productive in the world. Iowa is agriculturally state-of-the-art. Let me give you a hypothetical example. There are seven ounces of grain needed to produce one ounce of meat at market. If chicken or pork consumption in China were to increase by one ounce per capita, and Iowa were to produce all the grain used to fatten these Chinese chickens and hogs, on a gross national product basis, Iowa would be among the richest countries in the world. This may be perceived as a silly example. But its purpose is to call attention to the tremendous upside potential for American grain farmers and vendors to those farmers. Agricultural equipment manufacturers like John Deere, companies that move grains in shipping centers, like Archer-Daniels-Midland, and irrigation-equipment makers like Lindsay Manufacturing should all be long-term beneficiaries of the increased role the American farmer will play in feeding the world.

DIALING FOR DOLLARS

Once the new international consumer puts some more meat on the table, what else would make his or her life better? Being able to call friends and family on the telephone would be a big step forward. In fact, you could argue that telecommunications is both the engine and the caboose in the emergence of the international middle class. To compete on the global stage, businesses in developing countries need healthy stock markets to attract global capital. Modern telecommunications systems are a prerequisite. As efficient telecommunications systems further enhance economic growth and expand the middle class, the demand for more universal telephone service increases. Here, we need to tip our hat to Craig McCaw's evolutionary theory of time and space, which effectively jump-started the cellular telephone industry. And when it comes to developing countries, it is wireless service that will help bring telecommunications services at reasonable prices.

Arguably, telecommunications is the No. 1 global growth industry for the next decade or more. Consequently, long-term investors will not have to be terribly discriminating to earn pretty good returns in this sector. But rather than take a scattershot approach, investors might maximize their returns by focusing on those segments of the industry that will grow the fastest and the dominant players therein. The big three U.S. long distance companies, AT&T, MCI and Sprint, are rapidly developing the strategic alliances with national and local carriers around the world that should allow them to dominate the international long-distance market. Telecommunications equipment manufacturers like Lucent, the spin-off from AT&T, and Northern Telecom will play a big role in wiring the world. Suppliers of advanced cable equipment like Scientific Atlanta also have terrific international growth prospects. On the wireless side, cellular-phone makers like Motorola and Nokia should thrive. A special mention should go to AirTouch, which has done a terrific job winning joint-venture cellular-telephone franchises throughout Europe. Two other cellular investments worth considering are 360 Communications, which is the domestic cellular spinoff from Sprint, and Britain's Vodafone.

If you favor a more focused "special situation" approach, the Canadian telephone giant BCE should benefit when it sells off its substantial investment in Northern Telecom and as Canadian deregulation catches up to the rest of the world. On a per capita basis, the Vancouver metropolitan area has the highest concentration of expatriate Chinese in North America. This could prove to be a great "gateway to China."

Telecommunications is the No. 1 global growth industry for the next decade or more. Consequently, long-term investors will not have to be terribly discriminating to earn pretty good returns in this sector.

GLOBAL EYEBALLS

No American products travel better than filmed entertainment and pre-recorded music. Several years ago, the investor relations people at Time Warner were kind enough to give us a tape of Warner cartoon characters, providing a global geography lesson dubbed in a dozen foreign languages. We've used this tape at our annual client meeting to illustrate the global reach of the American entertainment industry. There is simply no place you can go in the world without American film being a staple of cinematics, cable TV or broadcast entertainment. The same goes for music. Just look at the convergence of the computer, telephone and cable television industries in the U.S. Overseas opportunities beckon as well. In the past five years alone, the number of satellite dishes in India has gone from 400,000 to 10 million. As the distribution channels expand worldwide, the value of entertainment will continue to increase.

With the consolidation we've already experienced in the filmed entertainment industry, there are fewer ways to participate. Time Warner is a dominant global company in both filmed entertainment and pre-recorded music. Assuming the marriage with Turner Broadcasting is consummated, Time could become an international cable TV powerhouse as well. The stock price has been restrained by concerns about Time's debt, the unwinding of what has become an acrimonious relationship with US West, and the uncertain prospects for Time Warner's huge cable television operations. Investors are currently blind to the forest through the trees on this one. In the long run, however, we are confident the market will recognize Time Warner's pre-eminent global position in entertainment software.

Other beneficiaries of this favorable long-term trend for entertainment software producers and packagers also include Viacom — the world wants its MTV; Seagram, the new owner of MCA, and Liberty Media, John Malone's combination of Tele-Communications Inc.'s cable network investments.

UP, UP AND AWAY

Air traffic is tremendously sensitive to increases in personal income. The new international middle class will be taking to the friendly skies. They will fly for business, and they will fly for pleasure. Over the next five years, you could probably make a lot of money investing in international airline stocks. But it will be less complicated and perhaps just as profitable investing in Boeing, which along with Europe's Airbus consortium will build the foreign fleets to accommodate increasing air traffic abroad.

We are almost right at the bottom of a five-year down cycle in the aircraft industry. Industry studies indicate that in the next 20 years, there will be 12,000 new aircraft built to satisfy incremental global demand and 4,000 to replace aircraft that will be retired because they are too old or fuel-inefficient or don't meet new noise-control requirements. That's 16,000 new airplanes to be built over the next two decades. Boeing, which is a technological leader, will get the lion's share of orders.

Over the next five years, you could probably make a lot of money investing in international airline stocks.

Another option is to invest in vendors to Boeing. There are very few pure plays in this arena, but companies deriving a material volume of revenues from commercial aerospace include Ametek, Precision Castparts, Moog, Crane, SPS Technologies, Honeywell and Curtiss-Wright. Sequa Corp., whose Chromalloy division is a leader in jet engine maintenance and repair, would be a good "aging of the existing fleet" play.

THE DEAL

Another global dynamic that isn't new, but is far from finished, is strategic merger-and-acquisition activity. At the 1995 Roundtable, I said there would be a ton of deals done in the year ahead. It worked out to be $158 billion in deals in the U.S. and $866 billion globally. I don't know that we will see that kind of record volume this year, but you will see some big numbers. Why? The world is awash in liquidity, rising equity markets make stock a more valuable currency and, most importantly, it is still cheaper to buy businesses on global stock markets than it is to build them from scratch.

Another global dynamic that isn't new, but is far from finished, is strategic merger-and-acquisition activity. . . . It is still cheaper to buy businesses on global stock markets than it is to build them from scratch.

How do you take advantage of this long-term trend? I am going to unabashedly preach for my own church here. As Benjamin Graham and his successor at Columbia, Roger Murray, instructed us, and as Warren Buffett has put so profitably into practice, you approach stocks as if they were pieces of a business you want to buy at a discount to what Graham called intrinsic value, others call economic value, and what years ago was termed "private market value."

How do you go about quantifying value? We believe free cash flow, defined as earnings before interest, taxes and depreciation (EBITD), or a slight variation, EBITDA, both minus the capital expenditures necessary to grow the business, is the best barometer of a company's value. Most corporate merger-and-acquisition people look at the very same thing. When the informed industrialist is evaluating a business for purchase, he or she is not going to put a lot of weight on stated book value. That's for accountants, not for savvy buyers of businesses. They probably don't care much about net earnings. Clever corporate managements can be creative in booking earnings. What that informed industrialist wants to know is: How much cash is this business throwing off today and how much is he going to have to invest in this business to sustain or grow this stream of cash in the future.

There are other factors in determining a stock's private market value. Cost of capital always affects a company's values. That's why stocks tend to be valued lower when interest rates rise. Cash flow growth rates will alter values, too. Just as growth-stock investors will pay a higher price-to-earnings ratio for higher earnings growth, private-market-value investors will pay a higher multiple of cash flow for faster cash-flow growth. Finally, sophisticated business buyers will look beyond the balance sheet for hidden assets—valuable land on the books at original cost or an overfunded pension plan—as well as hidden liabilities, like unfunded health-care responsibilities or potentially costly environmental problems.

By doing this kind of analysis of income statements and balance sheets, and checking out all those little footnotes attached, and keeping an eye on the prices businesses are being bought and sold at every day out there in the real world, you can quantify the value of a business or group of businesses. You can usually find fundamental bargains—stocks selling at substantial discounts to private market value. Then you have to ask the subjective questions: Who might want to own this company? Would management be receptive to a takeover proposal? Are the target company's assets so unique that someone might pay well above fair value?

You approach stocks as if they were pieces of a business you want to buy at a discount . . .

If you can come up with some positive answers to questions like these, you may well have found yourself a terrific takeover candidate.

DON'T EXPECT TOO MUCH

Lastly, some comments on the longer-term prospects for equities. I'm not talking about what is going to happen to the market over the next quarter or even the next several years. However, I do think investors should have some perspective on what they can expect. The average annualized return on equities over the last 15 years, as measured by the S&P 500, is 14.8%. That's almost 50% above the historical return on stocks on an annualized basis. When you compound this out 10 years, the differential is staggering. Will we see the same kind of returns from stocks over the next 15 years? I wouldn't bet the ranch on it. Sooner or later, this roaring bull market will end, either with a substantial correction or a bear market or preferably, an extended period of much more modest returns.

How should today's investor prepare for this? I would start by adjusting expectations. When making financial planning assumptions, use conservative return figures for equities, and save and invest accordingly. In other words, if you are putting a given amount of dollars into equities and assuming that it will compound at 15% a year over the next 10–20 years, you will likely find your children's college fund or your retirement nest egg more than a little short.

Secondly, you might want to look at alternative investment strategies. Market-neutral disciplines like risk arbitrage, which is capable of delivering low- to mid-double-digit annualized returns regardless of the direction of the broad equities market should be considered. This will be particularly rewarding if what we have characterized as the third great wave of mergers continues as long as we expect it to.

Finally, although one can play many global trends from the relative comfort of the New York Stock Exchange, investors should internationalize their portfolios. Twenty-five years ago, U.S. equities represented 66% of the capitalization of the total global equities market. Today it is 38%. Twenty years ago, only the most adventurous Americans would invest in places like Spain or Italy. Today, there are billions of American dollars in emerging markets in Latin America and the Pacific Rim. It has always been my inclination to challenge the conventional wisdom. But I do think there is some legitimacy to the idea that many foreign economies will grow faster than the U.S. and that returns from foreign equities markets will trend higher than our own.

Gerald Loeb made a name for himself as a premier marketer of investments, and *Forbes* magazine once called him "the most quoted man on Wall Street." His 1935 book, *The Battle for Investment Survival,* is considered a classic, and the first edition sold over 250,000 copies. One reason for its success was that it was written in zippy, accessible language that didn't require the intellectual capacity that Benjamin Graham's 1934 book, *Security Analysis,* did. Loeb's forte was mass marketing, reaching your average Joe Investor. Consider the following metaphor aimed at the novice investor: "One must confine one's first efforts at cooking to boiling eggs; one does not begin with Baked Alaska, no matter how fine a desert the latter may be."

Loeb, whose father, a French wine merchant, lost his business in the 1906 San Francisco earthquake, struck out on an investment career in 1921. His first job was as a bond salesman, and he was known for refusing to sell any security he didn't trust. Within a few years he found himself in New York City with E. F. Hutton & Co., where he was made a partner at the young age of 30. Like a few other lucky ones, Loeb foresaw the 1929 crash, and he sold all of his and his clients' holdings before it hit. That year he was also named vice-chairman, a position he held until he retired in 1965. In the 1930s and later, he excelled as a savvy marketer for a battered and bruised industry, and he wrote several more books, as well as a national newspaper column under the title, "Loeb on Wall Street."

Although he worked for a brokerage house, Loeb forthrightly said, "People expect too much of investment. They think, incorrectly, that they must always keep their money 'working.' " Those who saved and were able to limit their losses to inflation were doing just fine, according to Loeb. While his writings have been criticized for lacking technical instruction, he makes up for it with practical advice, such as: "Travel is a wonderful education and education is a wonderful hedge these days to those who can capitalize on it." In *Importance of Correct Timing,* Loeb offers some pragmatic insight into why an investor's mindset makes selling more difficult than buying.

Importance of Correct Timing
Gerald M. Loeb

As soon as a security is purchased, the buyer loses the power to avoid a decision. It becomes necessary for him to decide whether to hold or sell. As an inexorable consequence, the percentage of correct conclusions must be lowered. Therefore, intelligent investors expect to make a great many more errors in closing transactions than in opening them.

When nothing but cash is held, no decision need be made at all unless conditions are completely satisfactory. Either a suitable opportunity may be present, so that a purchase can sensibly be made, or the pros and cons may be so balanced that nothing is done.

Losses must always be "cut." They must be cut quickly, long before they become of any financial consequence.

The worst that can happen if the latter decision is reached is that an opportunity will be missed through caution, which is an inconsequential misadventure. Other opportunities always come in due time, and if one's attitude towards speculation and investment is shaped along the lines described . . . nothing will be lost in either eventual profits or peace of mind.

Another reason why selling at the right time is more difficult than buying is that the development of a frame of mind in which only real bargains are sought carries with it a tendency to lose confidence too early. Periods of overvaluation and public overconfidence are, naturally enough, likely to follow periods of depression, and often do. Likewise, very good general business conditions will normally succeed very bad conditions. In such active periods, stocks will sell at excessive valuations, so that their price advances will often outrun the most optimistic expectations of those who bought very early and very low. The latter will begin to feel uncomfortably unsure of their position as soon as normal valuations are restored, or when the indications of overvaluation are first to be seen.

As soon as a security is purchased, the buyer loses the power to avoid a decision. It becomes necessary for him to decide whether to hold or sell. . . . intelligent investors expect to make a great many more errors in closing transactions than in opening them.

For these reasons, the background for intelligent liquidation cannot be described simply as a reversal of the factors that make for a real buying opportunity. Such would be more nearly the case if we were discussing the proper time to make short sales. But what we are concerned with here is not initiating a position but unwinding one already held.

Scores of stocks are unsatisfactory long holdings without being clear-cut short sales.

Other situations may make it necessary to consider selling. The favorable developments which were expected when the security was bought may fall short of original anticipations. Or the holder may face a loss if he sells.

In this one instance it is possible to state a mechanical rule to be followed. Naturally the exercise of good sense and logic and the possession of accurate information, rather than adherence to any formula or system, constitute the basis of all successful investment. But it is sound policy to get out of long positions which begin to prove themselves wrong by declining in price. This is the one automatic proceeding in handling securities, the only proceeding in which no judgment is needed.

Human likes and dislikes will wreck any investment program. Only logic, reason, information and experience can be listened to if failure is to be avoided.

Losses must always be "cut." They must be cut quickly, long before they become of any financial consequence. After the elimination of a stock in this manner, the transaction must be, in a sense, forgotten. It must be left out of future consideration so completely that there is no sentimental bar to reinstating the position at higher level, either very soon or at any later date, if the purchase again seems strongly advisable.

Cutting losses is the one and only *rule* of the markets that can be taught with the assurance that it is always the correct thing to do. As a matter of arithmetic, any grammar school boy can learn the formula. But, as a matter of actual application, it requires a completeness of detachment from human frailties which is very rarely achieved. People like to take profits and don't like to take losses. They also hate to repurchase something at a price higher than they sold it. Human likes and dislikes will wreck any investment program. Only logic, reason, information and experience can be listened to if failure is to be avoided.

Little of a definite nature can be outlined as the proper procedure when the question is whether or not to take profits. A sound practice is to realize a 100% gain with at least part of a large commitment. Such a profit is equivalent to dividends for sixteen years on a straight 6% basis, not compounded and without adjustment for taxes. If a doubling of one's investment can be achieved within six months to a year, the investor can then comfortably enter a long period in which cash is held idle (until the next opportunity presents itself) without diminishing final results to anything nearly as poor as the general average—frequently a net loss—which is obtained through continuous full investment.

It is advisable always to keep uninvested reserve funds on hand in order to take advantage of unexpected opportunities. The need for buying power in such cases may in itself be a factor dictating the sale of securities already held.

Cutting losses is the one and only rule of the markets that can be taught with the assurance that it is always the correct thing to do.

Perhaps the best way to describe when to sell is to review handling of a commitment from its beginning. Belief that a stock is in a buying range justifies a small initial purchase. If the stock declines, it should be sold at a small and quick loss. But if it advances and the indications which supported the original purchase continue favorable,

180

additional purchases can be made at prices which the buyer still considers abnormally low. But once the price has risen into estimated normal or overvaluation areas, the amount held should be reduced steadily as quotations advance.

This is as near as it is possible to come in describing proper selling policies.

"If there ever was a hall of fame for investment advisers," said Warren Buffett, "he'd be among the first ten in it." Philip Carret founded one of the first mutual funds, the Pioneer Fund, in 1928, and he managed it until he sold it in 1963. That same year, he founded Carret and Co., a money management firm. More than 30 years later, at the age of 101, he was still going to the office. Yet, it took him a while to find his calling. After earning a chemistry degree from Harvard and then training as an aviator (World War I ended before he saw action), he wandered around the United States. Carret eventually found a job selling bonds in Seattle, then in Boston, before quitting to become a reporter for *Barron's.* While working for the paper he came up with the idea of pooling money for investment, so in 1927 he left the paper to manage $25,000 contributed by friends and family.

Carret's investment style was to find value and hold it for the long term. As for those fund managers looking for quick scores who hold stocks only for days or weeks, he called their strategy "the pinnacle of stupidity." He advised looking around your immediate environment for investment ideas. For example, he happened to use Neutrogena soap, liked it, and started buying the company's stock. Johnson & Johnson eventually bought the company for $33 a share—Carret had paid $1.

Unlike Philip Fisher, who scrutinizes a company's management, Carret never felt the need to know the management of all the companies in which he had invested, but he did like the executives to own a good chunk of stock. And he hated overly optimistic letters in the annual report, preferring them to be mildly pessimistic. Carret also looked for companies that were leaders in their industry and that reinvested their money wisely. "Management has only so much cash at its disposal," he said. "If it pays dividends, I see it as a confession of failure. The company is saying, *We don't know where to invest the money so we'll give it to you, the stockholders.*" In *When Speculation Becomes Investment,* he provides "Twelve Commandments for Speculators," including: "Be quick to take losses, reluctant to take profits."

When Speculation Becomes Investment

Philip Carret

"**Y**our articles* deal with speculative investment rather than with speculation," said an astute observer of both fields of activity. . . . To this charge the writer was forced to plead guilty. After all it is by no means easy to draw the line between investment and speculation, between speculation and gambling. If one is to discuss the topic of speculation and perhaps thereby induce some readers to attempt it who might otherwise have left speculation alone, it is much more helpful to the average reader, much less dangerous to the reader who might misinterpret what he reads, to discuss that sort of speculation which is on the borderland of investment than the more dangerous and less useful type of speculation which borders on gambling.

Perhaps the best sort of speculation . . . is that which regards it as the business management of a fund.

---

* Philip Carret's *Art of Speculation,* from which this essay is excerpted, originally appeared in serial form.

FANTASTIC POSSIBILITIES

Probably the average man who opens a margin account with $1000 has at least subconsciously the idea that if he doesn't double his money in a year he will be disappointed. If he could really do this consistently and kept his profits in his operations, he would be richer than any man now alive in less than twenty-five years. Stated in this way the thing is an absurdity. In real life the man who starts speculating with a thousand dollars will either be unsuccessful or he will make something more than pure interest on his money and gradually accumulate a moderate fortune. As he grows older his natural tendency probably will be to take fewer and smaller risks, to become more an investor than a speculator.

BUSINESS MANAGEMENT

Perhaps the best sort of speculation, and the kind that is most likely to be successful, is that which regards it as the business management of a fund. With the modern tendency of business to become concentrated in larger units there is less likelihood that an ambitious individual will become sole owner and autocratic manager of a great business enterprise. There are still and always will be opportunities for a business genius to exploit a new idea of business management or a new product with phenomenal success, to duplicate in another field the success of Henry Ford with motors or F. W. Woolworth with merchandising. Comparatively few businesses can expand entirely out of earnings so that even the business genius is likely to find himself sooner or later the employee of a large group of stockholders. Anyone possessed of talent of a lesser order is almost sure to find himself in a salaried executive position, subject to a greater or less degree of control by others. In the management of his personal funds, however, any individual can give his business judgment and initiative free reign.

If the speculator detects evidences of incompetent management in a given corporation . . . he can give silent evidence of his disapproval by selling the corporation's securities . . .

MEN, MATERIALS, MONEY

What does the manager of a business do? He controls men, materials and money, seeking to handle them in such a way that the business will produce a profit. If the business is to be more than a fleeting success, he must in so doing render some real public service either in transforming the materials into a form more useful to the ultimate consumer or in rendering them more readily available. Conceiving the speculator as manager of a business it will be seen that he also controls men, materials and money. The money is the starting point of his business, the materials are the securities which he buys and sells, the men are the directors and managers of the companies in whose securities he invests. His materials are not, to be sure, transformed in his hands, but his very activities in buying and selling tend to make them more or less readily available to the conservative investor. In the same way he exerts an indirect influence over the men who serve him. The compensation and the tenure of office of the directors and executives of even the largest corporations depend in the long run upon the satisfaction that their services give to the intelligent speculators and investors interested in their securities. If the speculator detects evidences of incompetent management in a given corporation, he cannot "fire" the offending management, but he can give silent evidence of his disapproval by selling the corporation's securities or by leaving them alone.

Twelve Commandments for Speculators

As in any business there are standards of management which cannot be disregarded by the business man, so in speculative investment it is possible to formulate certain rules which must be followed intelligently if success is to be attained. The speculator will never be a success if he attempts to follow any set of rules blindly. There will always be exceptions, he must apply his intelligence keenly in any given situation. Nevertheless, so far as the technical details . . . may be summarized in a few paragraphs, it may be useful to do so.

Never hold fewer than ten different securities covering five different fields of business.

Twelve precepts for the speculative investor may be stated as follows:

(1) Never hold fewer than ten different securities covering five different fields of business.
(2) At least once in six months reappraise every security held.
(3) Keep at least half the total fund in income-producing securities.
(4) Consider yield the least important factor in analyzing any stock.

(5) Be quick to take losses, reluctant to take profits.

(6) Never put more than 25% of a given fund into securities about which detailed information is not readily and regularly available.

(7) Avoid "inside information" as you would the plague.

(8) Seek facts diligently, advice never.

(9) Ignore mechanical formulas for valuing securities.

(10) When stocks are high, money rates rising, business prosperous, at least half a given fund should be placed in short-term bonds.

(11) Borrow money sparingly and only when stocks are low, money rates low or falling, and business depressed.

(12) Set aside a moderate proportion of available funds for the purchase of long-term options on stocks of promising companies whenever available.

Ignore mechanical formulas for valuing securities.

MINIMIZING CHANCE

The first rule given suggests a minimum standard of diversification. It is just as important in speculation as in investment that a given fund be divided among several baskets. Diversification accomplishes three important results for the speculator. It minimizes the factor of chance, allows for an occasional error of judgment and minimizes the importance of the unknown factor. As in every other field of human activity, chance plays its part in speculation. An earthquake or some other unforeseeable "act of God" may make a mockery of the best-laid plans. No such accident will affect all securities equally, however, and diversification affords the best possible protection against the effects of accidental factors. Errors of judgment are likewise inescapable. Even the most astute speculator is likely to arrive at wrong conclusions from the data in hand 20% to 25% of the time. If he stakes his entire fund on one security about which his conclusion is wrong, he will suffer heavy loss. On the other hand, a 25% margin of error in judgment will not seriously affect the speculator who has scattered his commitments among ten different securities.

Avoid "inside information" as you would the plague.

The most important factor affecting the value of any single security at any given moment is the unknown factor. Not even the president of a company knows all the facts affecting the intrinsic value of its securities. The speculator must allow a considerable margin for the unknown, even in the case of companies which make frequent reports of their condition and make an honest attempt to keep their stockholders and the public fully informed regarding their affairs. By sufficient diversification these unknown factors affecting individual securities cancel each other. The loss which is due to the unknown factor in one case will be counterbalanced by an unexpectedly large profit in another.

A PSYCHOLOGICAL DIFFICULTY

It is conventional advice to the investor that he should go over his holdings in search of weak spots at least annually. The speculator will naturally watch his holdings much more closely. The second rule means something more than a mere scanning of his list of commitments and calculation of the paper profit or loss that they show. It means that the speculator should seek so far as possible to re-analyze each commitment from a detached standpoint. Psychologically this is a very difficult thing to do, to consider dispassionately a venture in which he has already risked his funds. Nevertheless, the speculator should make a determined effort to do just this. If he has 100 shares of a given stock, for example, which is selling at 90, he should disregard entirely the price that he paid for it and ask himself this question: "If I had $9000 cash today with which to purchase some security, would I choose that stock in preference to every one of the thousands of other securities available to me?" If the answer is strongly in the negative, he should sell the stock. It should make not the slightest difference in this connection whether the stock cost 50 or 130. That is a fact which is entirely beside the point, though the average individual will give it considerable weight.

PATIENCE ESSENTIAL

It is not suggested that the speculator undertake this process of re-analysis much more frequently than once in six months. If he tries to do it oftener, he is likely to fall into the evil and usually fatal habit of frequently switching his commitments. One of the essential qualifications of the successful speculator is patience. It may take years for the market in a given stock to reflect in any large degree the values which are being accumulated behind it. Twenty years of plowing earnings back into property were followed in the case of the Southern Railway by an advance in its common stock from 25 to 120 within two years. Careful analysis may detect values far in excess of market price behind a given stock. The market may not reflect these values until the combination of a bull market and a change in dividend policy supplies the necessary impetus. Even in a bull market a sound stock may lag behind the procession in a discouraging manner for weeks or months. The trader who is always looking for "action" in the market will usually jump from one stock to another during the course of a bull movement only to find at the end that he has made far less money than he would have made by putting his money in ten or a dozen carefully chosen issues at the beginning and holding them. . . .

IMPORTANCE OF INFORMATION

Rule No. 6 lays further stress on the importance of the "unknown" factor in analyzing a security. So far as he is dealing with the unknown the speculator is gambling. He must seek by every means to reduce the element of gambling to a minimum. To do this he must confine his transactions for the most part to securities about which he may obtain at fairly frequent intervals and with a minimum of trouble adequate information. There are many good stocks about which adequate information is not available and money is often to be made in them. Where the information which is forthcoming is favorable or where sufficient information may be obtained by taking some trouble it may be advisable to purchase such a stock, but it is sound policy not to place too great a proportion of a given fund in an issue of this type.

It is sometimes worth while to go to some trouble to obtain sound information. For example, a certain moderate-sized manufacturing company publishes only a condensed annual balance sheet by way of informing its shareholders regarding its operations. For some years this balance sheet showed an item of accounts receivable entirely too large for the size of the business. This fact suggested that the stock might not be a bargain after all at a price equal to half the net quick assets behind it despite a good record of earnings and dividends. A reporter who was also a stockholder attended the 1926 annual meeting. He and one other stockholder outside the management who took the trouble to attend were permitted to see a detailed balance sheet showing that over two-thirds of the accounts receivable item as of December 31, 1925, consisted of United States Treasury notes. Here was a stock genuinely undervalued, though the company's statements, so far as they were readily available, themselves suggested serious doubt as to the values behind it.

WHERE CYNICISM PAYS

Cynics are likely to have few friends, but the cynical attitude depicted in Rule No. 7 will save any trader many losses. Wall Street is thronged with credulous individuals who give ready ear to the wildest rumors. When a certain amusement stock doubled in price in the spring of 1930, earnings estimates 50% in excess of the rate shown in the official statement for the previous six months were glibly quoted on every hand. Following a decline equally spectacular in the following four months, board-room devotees were fully as ready to believe that the company was only one jump ahead of the sheriff.

Vanity plays a great part in the willingness with which traders fall victim to supposed "straight tips" regarding pool operations, mergers, discoveries of secret processes, impending financing and other business secrets. To be the recipient of such confidential information sets him apart from the ignorant herd in the average trader's own estimation. If, however, he will have the humility to believe that he may be the thousandth rather than the first or second to hear the bullish story, this lack of self-pride will probably be well rewarded.

There is one exception to the rule. It is likely that the unknown author of a bearish rumor heard in a strong market may be a genuine philanthropist. Such tips are rare, far

191

more worthy of credence than the bullish propaganda which is widely circulated at the peak of a market movement.

EACH TO HIS OWN DECISION

No one ever attained a fortune by seeking the advice of others. This is the basis for the eighth rule. An efficiency expert may point the way to technical improvements in the conduct of a business, but he can do no more. The responsibility for the success or failure of the business must rest in the final analysis on the energy, character, ability and force of decision of one man. The Fords, Rockefellers, Morgans have not dominated their chosen fields by seeking the advice of "experts," but by following their own judgment, though it may have meant on occasion flying in the face of precedent.

Vanity plays a great part in the willingness with which traders fall victim to supposed "straight tips" ... To be the recipient of such confidential information sets him apart from the ignorant herd ...

The venerable Chauncey M. Depew once gave an interview to an inquiring reporter who wanted to know what had been the greatest mistakes of his life. In reply Mr. Depew detailed three. Financially his greatest error was his failure to purchase a sixth interest in the infant which later became the American Telephone & Telegraph Co. for $10,000. Strongly attracted to the venture Mr. Depew yet deferred action until he had consulted expert advice. To this end he approached a personal friend, the president of the Western Union Telegraph Co., doubtless the best qualified expert available to anyone. In all sincerity he was told that the telephone was impracticable and that in any event Western Union owned patents giving it a better claim to the invention. Mr. Depew lived to see Western Union a subsidiary of American Telephone.

No one ever attained a fortune by seeking the advice of others.

The lesson is clear. Let him who would succeed in speculation seek all the facts diligently, for with inadequate or erroneous information even the most intelligent speculator may reach a wrong conclusion; but let him remember that in the end he must decide for himself what and when to buy and to sell.

PART IV

Market Cycles

For investors looking to time the market or at least understand its behavior, Part IV is essential. The Dow Jones Industrial Average has been a primary barometer for measuring booms and busts since Charles Dow introduced it in 1884, so who better to diagnose market cycles than he? Investor confidence plays a pivotal role, Dow says, and it can be dramatically influenced by any number of events, from presidential elections to public scandals. If cycles are powered by investor sentiment, can they be foretold? William Peter Hamilton, Dow's successor as editor of the *Wall Street Journal*, begins to diagnose primary and secondary movements in the market and discusses how to forecast them. In a more whimsical light, Robert Prechter connects stock market movements to popular culture trends in music, movies and fashion. Whether they are economics, the weather, or social trends, understanding the driving forces behind market cycles helps the investor make strategic decisions.

CHARLES H. DOW
1851–1902

Charles Dow, the cofounder of the *Wall Street Journal* and creator of the Dow Jones Industrial Average, was the serious half of the partnership with the flamboyant Eddie Jones. Dow, who was born in rural Connecticut, and whose father died when Charles was just six, spent his entire life in the newspaper business. At 16 he started working for a local weekly paper as an apprentice printer and reporter. His next job was with a daily in Springfield, Massachusetts, before becoming the New York correspondent for a daily in Providence, Rhode Island. Rather than being a reporter at large, Dow preferred research and analysis, so he next took a job covering mining company stocks for the *New York Mail and Express.* His financial editorials were reportedly the first in the daily press.

About 1880, Dow joined a news reporting service, where he convinced the management to hire his old friend Eddie Jones, who had shown up in New York and confided to Dow that he had both debt and wife problems. Jones started covering the New York Stock Exchange. Finally, in 1882, Dow and Jones decided to start their own news reporting firm, to focus on the stock market and use messenger boys to deliver the news. Their first office was beneath a soda-water establishment in the basement of 15 Wall Street. They spent much of their day visiting bankers, financiers, and members of the Exchange.

To follow the stock market's ebb and flow, Dow alone created the Dow Jones Averages, which first appeared on July 3, 1884, and used 11 representative stocks. Later he increased the number to 20, and then to 30 in 1887. Dow's second great legacy was founded in the summer of 1889—the *Wall Street Journal,* which originally cost two cents a copy and had an initial distribution of about 1,500. In 1899, Dow started a column called "Review and Outlook," which was designed to educate the general reader. As one of Dow's close associates said, "Mr. Dow could make more out of a single sentence or a single fact than anyone I knew." *Booms and Busts* is a medley of three editorials, in which he diagnoses market movements and explains why investor confidence is a "tender plant."

Booms and Busts
Charles H. Dow

April 24, 1899

There is a pronounced difference between bull markets that are made by manipulation and those that are made by the public. The former represent[s] the effort of a small number of persons; the latter reflects the sense of the country on values. It is possible to create a limited public sentiment by manipulation, but the sentiment that endures and sweeps away the strongest interests which oppose it is invariably founded upon general conditions which are sufficiently universal and sufficiently potent to affect the opinions of practically everybody.

The growth of public opinion in regard to values is necessarily slow. The low point in the stock market is generally reached at a time when commodities are well down to the cost of production, when manufacturing interests are depressed, when railroad earnings are small, and when general business is unprofitable. People have sold their investments because the proceeds were needed in their lines of business or for living purposes. Everybody buys from hand to mouth because the experience of the years preceding has been that everything grew cheaper.

At such a time, some one industry begins to improve. Others gradually follow. There are usually some great causes like unusually high prices for crops, which exert an influence. People find themselves to be making money instead of losing it, and that the raw materials or half-finished products which they consume are advancing in price. Merchants and manufacturers begin to increase stocks. People who have money begin to make investments. During this period of advance everybody makes money and grows confident that whatever is undertaken will prove successful. A man who would hardly dare to put in his winter stock of coal one year will be found two years later quite willing to buy a coal mine, with a view of supplying the wants of the community. It takes two or three years for this change to occur, because millions of people have to experience in their own fortunes the change of conditions before they are willing to accept them as genuine.

The effect of a change on the part of a nation of 75,000,000 of people from feeling discouraged and doubtful to being confident and enterprising, is stupendous in its results upon all lines of business, including the stock market. It shows clearly how irresistible such a force becomes when it is focused upon speculative markets. It shows, too, why bull and bear markets persist as they do.

When the public mind has a well-defined tendency, either bullish or bearish, it is not easily changed. Scores or hundreds of people may change, but the mass press on in the same direction. The public mind, when it, as at present, favors the long side of the market, is not likely to alter that opinion until one of several things have occurred. The public may lose its confidence in stocks as the result of some national calamity which arrests attention and creates alarm. It may change on account of such a wave of selling of newly created stocks as prevents advance in prices and creates so many losses or permits so few profits as to tire out the public buyer. It may be checked by such an exhaustion of the supply of money as makes the carrying cost of stocks excessive, and thereby discourages trading.

The public interest in the market of 1872 was checked partly by dear money and partly by apprehensions that the policy of contracting the greenbacks would make a great scarcity of funds throughout the country. This apprehension was well founded, as the panic of 1873 was essentially a money panic. The bull market of 1879 was checked largely by the creation of new railway securities growing out of the expansion in that period of western and southwestern roads. Money was a factor in the case, but it was not the main one. The bull period in 1890 was checked by the selling of American securities from London and was due especially to the Baring panic.

It seems reasonably certain that the present bull market will be checked, when the time comes, by the creation of a greater supply of industrial stocks than the public will be able to absorb. Vast as the surplus fund is, it is no match for the printing presses of the country. We think, however, that while the character of the end of the bull market is tolerably clear, the time is, at least, a year away. It may be considerably more than that.

When the public mind has a well-defined tendency, either bullish or bearish, it is not easily changed. Scores or hundreds of people may change, but the mass press on in the same direction.

The evidence on this point is that to which we have frequently referred. The creation of new securities has not been very large until this year. There has not been time to get them distributed. The public hardly knows the names of many of the new industrials. Before the public will absorb these stocks, there must be a period during which they are made popular and profitable. The public must see them quoted and must learn more or less about them before it will buy. To assume that the bull market is to end this spring is to assume that many of the ablest financiers in the country are going to be left with large lines of new stocks on their hands. Somebody will undoubtedly be left with more stocks than are wanted, but the fact that bankers and syndicates are still willing to take the new stocks of industrial enterprises is evidence that they believe the tide of public interest in securities to be flowing with unabated force.

JUNE 8, 1901

There is always a disposition in people's minds to think that existing conditions will be permanent. When the market is down and dull, it is hard to make people believe that this is the prelude to a period of activity and advance. When prices are up and the country is prosperous, it is always said that while preceding booms have not lasted, there are circumstances connected with this one which make it unlike its predecessors and give assurance of permanency.

The one fact pertaining to all conditions is that they will change. This change follows modifications of the law of supply and demand. The cycle of trade is well known. Beginning with a period of depression, the small dealer finds himself unable to buy the amount of goods required for hand-to-mouth trading quite as cheaply as when the previous purchase was made. He, therefore, buys a little more. The aggregate of this buying increases the business of the jobber, and this swells the output of the manufacturer, who is enabled to employ more labor, resulting in larger purchases by labor of manufactured goods and agricultural products, which brings the circle round to the producer.

At each step in the proceedings, rising prices bring increased purchases and increased confidence, until the retailer buys without hesitation many times the amount of goods which he would have dared to take at the beginning of the cycle of improving trade. This multiplied by millions makes the demand which at times seems inexhaustible, which supplies the railroads with tonnage, and which in its ramifications creates the investment fund which finally seeks employment in Wall Street.

There is always a disposition in people's minds to think that existing conditions will be permanent.

The declining period is accompanied by steady reversal of these varied transactions. When the retailer and the jobber find that goods cost less than before, they shrink purchases. When purchases in advance of requirements bring loss and not profit, they bring also loss of confidence and curtailment of demand. As the process of shrinkage goes on, it touches all points of trade. It is a kind of flame which creates the fuel which is burned.

Experience has shown that it takes about five years for one of these cycles to complete itself. It takes approximately five years for the country bare of stocks to become the country filled with stocks, and it takes about five years more for the overstocked markets of the country or of the world to become practically bare.

As the stock market is always an effect and never a cause, it must respond to these conditions. As, however, the stock market, while an effect, is also a discounted effect, the decline in prices of stocks usually anticipates decline in commodities, because operators for a fall sell in anticipation of the changes which they foresee in business conditions.

The cause of the next depression in stocks will be a falling off in general trade. It will be distinguished by reduced clearings, decreased railroad earnings, a smaller demand for stable goods, smaller exchanges at the clearing house, an increased amount of idle money and smaller additions to the country's wealth.

Experience has shown that it takes about five years for one of these cycles to complete itself.

There are local causes likely to be influential. One will be the effects of commitments by existing corporations. It will be found in some cases that railroad earnings for the future have been overestimated and that the decrease in net will cut seriously into the dividend fund. The probability of decreased or passed dividends will have a direct bearing on many stocks. Loss in industrial profits will bring decline in some industrial properties. New railroad building will threaten the stability of some railway properties.

The buying up of existing roads has for its primary object the reduction of competition by centralizing management. This will be effective as far as it goes, and in many cases it will go far. The high valuation which has been placed on stocks purchased for control will, however, be a strong incentive to the building of competing lines. It will be argued that if an existing road is worth par for the common stock for control, a new road in the same general section will be worth something more than the actual cost of construction; hence, can be financed with profit to the builder and then perhaps sold with substantial profit to the owners.

This is sure to become a matter of importance. When it is known that parallel lines are being built from one point to another, the knowledge will have a depressing effect on the securities of existing companies, because it will be said that the new road will either get business and live, in which case it will take business from the old company, or it will have to be bought up, entailing a burden on the old company for the support of mileage not required by the business in that section.

The same thing will be true to an even greater extent in the industrial field. The difficulty of paralleling an industrial is trifling, except in a few cases, compared with the difficulty in paralleling a railroad. Yet the opportunity for profit in this will be so great as to insure such building. It will be feasible in many cases in the next few years to sell short a substantial line of an industrial stock, then build a competing plant and operate it so as to take away the profits of the other company, thereby causing a large decline in the stock, which can then be bought at a profit to the short seller. Then, when the down-cycle is complete and the up-cycle begins, the two establishments can combine, issue new stock to the promoters at nominal prices, and by the development of business and the payment of substantial dividends obtain a market for this stock at high prices two or three years later.

We do not know just when the period of decline will begin, nor what properties will most keenly feel its effects, but the general course of events along the lines outlined can be predicted with as much certainty as could have been any of the cycles of the past.

AUGUST 31, 1901

There is a general similarity in all "booms" and in all periods of depression. The character of these movements is like a snowball running down an inclined plane and gathering snow as it runs. The movement is slow at the start, becoming quicker as progress is made and usually being quickest of all just before it ends.

When the character of the motive power is considered, it is evident why this should be the case. "Booms" are made by the gradual but increasingly rapid growth of confidence among the people. In 1895 and 1896 confidence was at a low ebb in financial and commercial circles in this country. Nobody wanted to take much risk in his business, and nobody planned very far ahead for that reason. Everybody wanted to see his money again as quickly as possible. This condition of affairs reached a climax in the "Bryan campaign" of 1896, when for a short time business men and financiers did the best they could towards suspending business altogether.

The election of McKinley in that year destroyed the principal fear that had so completely shaken people's confidence in the future. Mr. McKinley was elected in November of 1896, but it was not until the summer and fall of 1897 that the growth of confidence became really notable. This growth was very slow and very disappointing to people in Wall Street at that time. During the latter half of 1897, however, and practically all through 1898 confidence grew more and more rapidly, and in the first three months of 1899 it had become well grown. Then came a check to its growth from the "industrial collapse" and later from the "Boer War," and the effect of these had not passed away when the campaign of "1900" had to be faced.

There is a general similarity in all "booms" and in all periods of depression. The character of these movements is like a snowball running down an inclined plane and gathering snow as it runs.

Mr. McKinley's re-election in 1900, however, gave it renewed growth, and in the six months following his election, if the stock market be taken as a fair index, the "boom" made more progress than it had made in the preceding three years. It went on practically without a check till the "Northern Pacific corner" in May. That event resulted in a decline, temporary, it is true, but of a magnitude and severity surpassing anything recorded in the annals of Wall Street.

Some people ask why there should be a reaction from the boom of the last four years, seeing the growing prosperity of the country at this time. Those who believe that such reaction is coming, and in fact has already begun, answer this question by saying that people are shaken somewhat in their confidence as to the future, partly by the events of last May, partly by the corn crop failure, partly by the steel strike, and partly the depression abroad, and that there is in progress a process of contraction of confidence which will closely parallel the process of growth between 1897 and 1901.

It is not an easy thing at any time to weigh and measure confidence very exactly. No one, however, will deny that the stock market furnishes very clear proof that a different state of things exists in this respect than existed last May before the drop in prices arising from the "Northern Pacific corner." Certain it is, moreover, that the loss of the corn crop has materially shaken a good many business men's confidence in the purchasing power of people in many parts of the country where the loss of corn will be most severely felt. The steel strike has beyond doubt effected a considerable disturbance in the iron trade and has made it very difficult for people in that industry to see their way ahead.

Of course, it can also be said with truth that in parts of the country where people are not directly affected by corn, by steel or by Wall Street, there is no loss of confidence. This is true, for example, of the Northwest, where a bountiful wheat crop is assured. Nobody there is worrying about the future as yet. With all due allowance for this, it is yet a significant fact that, whereas three or four months ago all was harmony in commercial and financial circles, there are now some discordant notes that threaten to become louder as time goes on. It is possible that the discord will only be temporary and that confidence will again be restored where it has been shaken, that bountiful crops next year will repair the damage done this year and, in short, that everything will be as it was last winter. History, however, shows that confidence is a tender plant and that when it is most advanced in growth it can least well stand any injury. No one can say that last spring confidence was not well grown.

William Peter Hamilton, the future executive editor of both the *Wall Street Journal* and *Barron's,* was born in Scotland. As a young man he worked as a clerk on the London Stock Exchange and then as a correspondent for the *Pall Mall Gazette.* But like fellow Scotsman B. C. Forbes, Hamilton sought adventure in South Africa, where he served in the British army, acted as a war correspondent, and dabbled in the Johannesburg stock market. In 1899, he came to the United States and joined the *Wall Street Journal* staff. In 1908, Hamilton became editor of the *Wall Street Journal's* editorial page and acting executive editor, and remained so until he died. Hamilton also served as executive editor for *Barron's* from the day it was launched in 1921.

Clarence W. Barron (who was quite a character, standing 5 feet 5 inches and weighing over 300 pounds) bought a controlling interest in Dow Jones & Company in 1902. "He was the most astonishing worker I ever saw," Hamilton wrote. "He would begin a conversation with me while carrying on business with two secretaries and attending to two telephones. Barron's flamboyant character influenced Hamilton, and editorials that were once characterized as "urbane and placid" became more edgy. Hamilton hit his stride as writer in 1922 when he penned *The Stock Market Barometer,* a very well received book that presented his interpretion of the Dow theory.

Before Charles Dow died in 1902, Hamilton had had a number of conversations with him concerning stock market behavior, and in 1929 that influence became evident. On October 15, he warned against the "speculative frenzy" on Wall Street. Then on October 25, just days before Black Tuesday on the 29th, Hamilton declared the bull market over in an editorial entitled "A Turn in the Tide." He wrote, "On the late Charles H. Dow's well-known method of reading the stock market movement from the Dow-Jones averages, the twenty railroad stocks on Wednesday, October 23, confirmed a bearish indication given by the industrials two days before. In *The Dow Theory,* Hamilton takes a critical look at Charles Dow's ideas and how they can be used to take the gambling out of investing.

The Dow Theory
William Peter Hamilton

An English economist whose unaffected humanity always made him remarkably readable, the late William Stanley Jevons, propounded the theory of a connection between commercial panics and spots on the sun. He gave a series of dates from the beginning of the seventeenth century, showing an apparent coincidence between the two phenomena. It is entirely human and likable that he belittled a rather ugly commercial squeeze of two centuries ago because there were not then a justifying number of spots on the sun. Writing in the New York *Times* early in 1905, in comment on the Jevons theory, I said that while Wall Street in its heart believed in a cycle of panic and prosperity, it did not care if there were enough spots on the sun to make a straight flush. Youth is temerarious and irreverent. Perhaps it would have been more polite to say that the accidental periodic association proved nothing, like the exact coincidence of presidential elections with leap years.

Cycles and the Poets

Many teachers of economics, and many business men without pretension even to the more modest title of student, have

207

a profound and reasonable faith in a cycle in the affairs of men. It does not need an understanding of the Einstein theory of relativity to see that the world cannot possibly progress in a straight line in its moral development. The movement would be at least more likely to resemble the journey of our satellite around the sun, which, with all its planetary attendants, is moving toward the constellation of Vega. Certainly the poets believe in the cycle theory. There is a wonderful passage in Byron's "Childe Harold" which, to do it justice, should be read from the preceding apostrophe to Metella's Tower. This was Byron's cycle:

> Here is the moral of all human tales,
> 'Tis but the same rehearsal of the past;
> First freedom and then glory; when that fails
> Wealth, vice, corruption, barbarism at last,
> And history, with all her volumes vast,
> Hath but one page.

There seems to be a cycle of panics and of times of prosperity. Anyone with a working knowledge of modern history could recite our panic dates—1837, 1857, 1866 (Overend-Gurney panic in London), 1873, 1884, 1893, 1907, if he might well hesitate to add the deflation year of 1920. Panics, at least, show a variable interval between them, from ten to fourteen years, with the intervals apparently tending to grow longer. . . .

PERIODICITY

But the pragmatic basis for the theory, a working hypothesis if nothing more, lies in human nature itself. Prosperity will drive men to excess, and repentance for the consequence of those excesses will produce a corresponding depression. Following the dark hour of absolute panic, labor will be thankful for what it can get and will save slowly out of smaller wages, while capital will be content with small profits and quick returns. There will be a period of readjustment like that which saw the reorganization of most of the American railroads after the panic of 1893. Presently we wake up to find that our income is in excess of our expenditure, that money is cheap, that the spirit of adventure is in the air. We proceed from dull or quiet business times to real activity. This gradually develops into extended speculation, with high money rates, inflated wages and other familiar symptoms. After a period of years of good times the strain of the chain is on its weakest link. There is a collapse like that of 1907, a depression foreshadowed in the stock market and in the price of commodities, followed by extensive unemployment, often an actual increase in savings-bank deposits, but a complete absence of money available for adventure.

Panics, at least, show a variable interval between them, from ten to fourteen years, with the intervals apparently tending to grow longer. . . .

NEED FOR A BAROMETER

Read over Byron's lines again and see if the parallel is not suggestive. What would discussion of business be worth if we could not bring at least a little of the poet's imagination into it? But unfortunately crises are brought about by too much imagination. What we need are soulless barometers, price indexes and averages to tell us where we are going and what we may expect. The best, because the most impartial, the most remorseless of these barometers, is the recorded average of prices in the stock exchange. With varying constituents and, in earlier years, with a smaller number of securities, but continuously these have been kept by the Dow-Jones news service for thirty years or more.

There is a method of reading them which has been fruitful of results, although the reading has on occasion displeased both the optimist and the pessimist. A barometer predicts bad weather, without a present cloud in the sky. It is useless to take an axe to it merely because a flood of rain will destroy the crop of cabbages in poor Mrs. Brown's backyard. It has been my lot to discuss these averages in print for many years past, on the tested theory of the late Charles H. Dow, the founder of *The Wall Street Journal.* It might not be becoming to say how constantly helpful the analysis of the price movement proved. But one who ventures on that discussion, who reads that barometer, learns to keep in mind the natural indignation against himself for the destruction of Mrs. Brown's cabbages.

What we need are soulless barometers, price indexes and averages to tell us where we are going and what we may expect.

DOW'S THEORY

Dow's theory is fundamentally simple. He showed that there are, simultaneously, three movements in progress in the stock market. The major is the primary movement, like the bull market which set in with the re-election of McKinley in 1900 and culminated in September, 1902, checked but not stopped by the famous stock market panic consequent on the Northern Pacific corner in 1901; or the primary bear market which developed about October, 1919, culminating June–August, 1921.

It will be shown that this primary movement tends to run over a period of at least a year and is generally much longer. Coincident with it, or in the course of it, is Dow's secondary movement, represented by sharp rallies in a primary bear market and sharp reactions in a primary bull market. A striking example of the latter would be the break in stocks on May 9, 1901. In like secondary movements the industrial group (taken separately from the railroads) may recover much more sharply than the railroads, or the railroads may lead, and it need hardly be said that the twenty active railroad stocks and the twenty industrials, moving together, will not advance point for point with each other even in the primary movement. In the long advance which preceded the bear market beginning October, 1919, the railroads worked lower and were comparatively inactive and neglected, obviously because at that time they were, through government ownership and guaranty, practically out of the speculative field and not exercising a normal influence on the speculative barometer. Under the resumption of private ownership they will tend to regain much of their old significance.

THE THEORY'S IMPLICATIONS

Concurrently with the primary and secondary movement of the market, and constant throughout, there obviously was, as Dow pointed out, the underlying fluctuation from day to day. It must here be said that the average is deceptive for speculation in individual stocks. What would have happened to a speculator who believed that a secondary reaction was due in May, 1901, as foreshadowed by the averages, if of all the stocks to sell short on that belief he had chosen Northern Pacific? Some traders did, and they were lucky if they covered at sixty-five points loss.

Dow's theory in practice develops many implications. One of the best tested of them is that the two averages corroborate each other, and that there is never a primary movement, rarely a secondary movement, where they do not agree. Scrutiny of the average figures will show that there are periods where the fluctuations for a number of weeks are within a narrow range; as, for instance, where the industrials do not sell below seventy or above seventy-four, and the railroads above seventy-seven or below seventy-three. This is technically called "making a line," and experience shows that it indicates a period either of distribution or of accumulation. When the two averages rise above the high point of the line, the indication is strongly bullish. It may mean a secondary rally in a bear market; it meant, in 1921, the inauguration of a primary bull movement, extending into 1922.

The market represents everything everybody knows, hopes, believes, anticipates, with all that knowledge sifted down to . . . the bloodless verdict of the market place.

If, however, the two averages break through the lower level, it is obvious that the market for stocks has reached what meteorologists would call "saturation point." Precipitation follows—a secondary bear movement in a bull market, or the inception of a primary downward movement like that which developed in October, 1919. After the closing of the Stock Exchange, in 1914, the number of industrials chosen for comparison was raised from twelve to twenty and it seemed as if the averages would be upset, especially as spectacular movements in stocks such as General Electric made the fluctuations in the industrials far more impressive than those in the railroads. But students of the averages have carried the twenty chosen stocks back and have found that the fluctuations of the twenty in the previous years, almost from day to day, coincided with the recorded fluctuations of the twelve stocks originally chosen.

DOW-JONES AVERAGES THE STANDARD

The Dow-Jones average is still standard, although it has been extensively imitated. There have been various ways of reading it; but nothing has stood the test which has been applied to Dow's theory. The weakness of every other method is that extraneous matters are taken in, from their tempting relevance. There have been unnecessary attempts to combine the volume of sales and to read the average with reference to commodity index numbers. But it must be obvious that the averages have already taken those things into account, just as the barometer considers everything which affects the weather. The price movement represents the aggregate knowledge of Wall Street and, above all, its aggregate knowledge of coming events.

Nobody in Wall Street knows everything. I have known what used to be called the "Standard Oil crowd," in the days of Henry H. Rogers, consistently wrong on the stock market for years together. It is one thing to have "inside information" and another thing to know how stocks will act upon it. The market represents everything everybody knows, hopes, believes, anticipates, with all that knowledge sifted down to what Senator Dolliver once called, in quoting a *Wall Street Journal* editorial in the United States Senate, the bloodless verdict of the market place.

DOW'S THEORY, APPLIED TO SPECULATION

. . . Dow's theory of the stock-market price movement . . . could be summed up in three sentences. In an editorial published December 19, 1900, he says, in *The Wall Street Journal:*

213

The market is always to be considered as having three movements, all going on at the same time. The first is the narrow movement from day to day. The second is the short swing, running from two weeks to a month or more; the third is the main movement, covering at least four years in its duration.

It has already been shown that his third and main movement may complete itself in much less than Dow's assumed four years, and also how an attempt to divide the ten-year period of the panic cycle theory into a bear and bull market of approximately five years each led to an unconscious exaggeration. That, however, is immaterial. Dow had successfully formulated a theory of the market movements of the highest value, and had synchronized those movements so that those who came after him could construct a business barometer.

THE TRUTH BENEATH SPECULATION

This is the essence of Dow's theory, and it need hardly be said that he did not see, or live to see, all that it implied. He never wrote a single editorial on the theory alone, but returns to it to illustrate his discussions on stock-market speculation, and the underlying facts and truths responsible not only for speculation (using the word in its best and most useful sense) but for the market itself.

It is not surprising that *The Wall Street Journal* received many inquiries as to the assumptions it made on the basis of Dow's major premise. On January 4, 1902, Dow replies to a pertinent question, and any thoughtful reader of these pages should be able to answer it himself. The correspondent asks him, "For some time you have been writing rather bullish on the immediate market, yet a little bearish in a larger sense. How do you make this consistent?" Dow's reply was, of course, that he was bullish after the secondary swing but that he did not think, in view of stock values from earnings of record, that a bull market which had then been operative sixteen months could run much further. It was a curious contraction, incidentally, of his own minimum four-year estimate, but that major upward swing as a matter of fact ran until the following September. It may be said that such a swing always outruns values. In its final stage it is discounting possibilities only.

A Useful Definition

In the same editorial Dow goes on to give a useful definition from which legitimate inferences may drawn. He says:

> It is a bull period as long as the average of one high point exceeds that of previous high points. It is a bear period when the low point becomes lower than the previous low points. It is often difficult to judge whether the end of an advance has come because the movement of prices is that which would occur if the main tendency had changed. Yet, it may only be an unusually pronounced secondary movement.

This passage contains, by implication, both the idea of "double tops" and "double bottoms" (which I frankly confess I have not found essential or greatly useful) and the idea of a "line," as shown in the narrow fluctuation of the averages over a recognized period, necessarily one either of accumulation or distribution. This has been found to be of the greatest service in showing the further persistence of the main movement, or the possible termination of the secondary movement, so apt to be mistaken for the initiation of a new major trend.

SUCCESSFUL FORECAST

In subsequent discussions there will be no difficulty in showing, from the various studies in the price movement since 1902, standing for record in the columns of *The Wall Street Journal,* that the method for a forecast of the main market movement and for a correct discrimination between that and the secondary movement had been provided in Dow's theory, and that it has been used with surprising accuracy. A prophet, especially in Wall Street, takes his life in his hands. If his predictions are always of the rosiest whatever the facts of the situation may be, he will at worst be merely called a fool for his pains. The charge against him will be far more serious if he sees that a boom has overrun itself, and says so. If he is bearish and right he will be accused of unworthy motives. He will even be held contributory to the decline which he foresaw, although his motives may have been of the highest and he may have not a penny of interest in the market either way.

"RECALLING" A PROPHET

Is the American public so ungrateful to its Micaiahs and Cassandras as this? Yes, indeed, and more so. It does not like unpleasant truths. In 1912, when Colonel C. McD. Townsend of the United States Engineers, an army man with a brilliant record then and since, was president of the Mississippi River Commission, he predicted, from the height of the water in the upper rivers, one of the greatest Mississippi floods. He warned the city of New Orleans that the flood might be expected in a month's time, recommending the most vigorous and immediate steps to lessen the calamity. Was New Orleans grateful? Its citizens held an indignation meeting to demand from President Taft the recall of this "calamity howler" and "dangerous alarmist." Mr. Taft characteristically kept his head, and Colonel Townsend was not removed. A good deal of property in the Mississippi Valley was "removed," and it is needless to record that New Orleans did not escape. The railroads and great industrial concerns, where they were likely to be affected, took the warning seriously, with advantage to themselves. The mayor of New Orleans subsequently rescinded the resolution, with an apology. Anyone who knows one of the ablest and least advertised engineers in the United States Army will readily understand that Townsend regarded the mayor and the previous mass meeting with equal indifference.

A prophet, especially in Wall Street, takes his life in his hands.

Synchronizing the Price Movement

It has been said before that Dow's theory is in no sense to be regarded as a gambler's system for beating the game. Any trader would disregard it at his peril, but Dow himself never considered it in that light, as I can testify from many discussions with him. I was writing the stock market paragraphs of the Dow-Jones news service and *The Wall Street Journal* in those days, and it was, of course, essential that I should thoroughly understand so scientific a method of synchronizing the market movement. Many men in Wall Street knew Dow and set their experience at his service. His mind was cautious to a fault, but logical and intellectually honest. I did not always agree with him and he was oftener right than I. When he was wrong it was clearly from lack of accurate data such as is now available. . . .

AN INSTRUCTIVE EDITORIAL

It would be unfair to Dow if the reader were not given the opportunity of extracting for himself some light on Dow's own application of his theory, or at any rate some idea of his method in the series of editorials which, as I have said before, dealt primarily with stock speculation as such and only incidentally with rules for reading the market. Here is an editorial, almost in full, published on July 20, 1901, only ten weeks after the panic which resulted from the Northern Pacific corner. At the time he wrote he did not see clearly that it was not a culmination of a major swing but a peculiarly violent secondary reaction in a primary bull market. He speaks first of individual stocks:

> There is what is called the book method. Prices are set down, giving each change of one point as it occurs, forming thereby lines having a general horizontal direction but running into diagonals as the market moves up and down. There come times when a stock with a good degree of activity will stay within a narrow range of prices, say two points, until there has formed quite a long horizontal line of these figures. The formation of such a line sometimes suggests that stock has been accumulated or distributed, and this leads other people to buy or sell at the same time. Records of this kind kept for the last fifteen years seem to support the theory that the manipulation necessary to acquire stock is oftentimes detected in this way.
>
> Another method is what is called the theory of double tops. Records of trading show that in many cases when a stock reaches top it will have a moderate decline and then go back again to near the highest figures. If after such a move, the price again recedes, it is liable to decline some distance.

Those, however, who attempt to trade on this theory alone find a good many exceptions and a good many times when signals are not given.

Trading on Averages

There are those who trade on the theory of averages. It is true that in a considerable period of time the market has about as many days of advance as it has of decline. If there come a series of days of advance, there will almost surely come the balancing days of decline.

The trouble with this system is that the small swings are always part of the larger swings, and while the tendency of events equally liable to happen is always toward equality, it is also true that every combination possible is liable to occur, and there frequently come long swings, or, in the case of stock trading, an extraordinary number of days of advance or decline which fit properly into the theory when regarded on a long scale, but which are calculated to upset any operations based on the expectation of a series of short swings.

A much more practicable theory is that founded on the law of action and reaction. It seems to be a fact that a primary movement in the market will generally have a secondary movement in the opposite direction of at least three-eighths of the primary movement. If a stock advances ten points, it is very likely to have a relapse of four points or more. The law seems to hold good no matter how far the advance goes. A rise of twenty points will not infrequently bring a decline of eight points or more.

It is impossible to tell in advance the length of any primary movement, but the further it goes, the greater the reaction when it comes, hence the more certainty of being able to trade successfully on that reaction.

A method employed by some operators of large experience is that of responses. The theory involved is this: The market is always under more or less manipulation. A large operator who is seeking to advance the market does not buy everything on the list, but puts up two or three leading stocks either by legitimate buying or by manipulation. He then watches the effect on the other stocks. If sentiment is bullish, and people are disposed to take hold, those who see this rise in two or three stocks immediately begin to buy other stocks and the market rises to a higher level. This is the public response, and is an indication that the leading stocks will be given another lift and that the general market will follow.

It seems to be a fact that a primary movement in the market will generally have a secondary movement in the opposite direction of at least three-eighths of the primary movement.

If, however, leading stocks are advanced and others do not follow, it is evidence that the public is not disposed to buy. As soon as this is clear the attempt to advance prices is generally discontinued. This method is employed more particularly by those who watch the tape. But it can be read at the close of the day in our record of transactions by seeing what stocks were put up within specified hours and whether the general market followed or not. The best way of reading the market is to read from the standpoint of values. The market is not like a balloon plunging hither and thither in the wind. As a whole, it represents a serious, well-considered effort on the part of farsighted and well-informed men to adjust prices to such values as exist or which are expected to exist in the not too remote future. The thought with great operators is not whether a price can be advanced, but whether the value of property which they propose to buy will lead investors and speculators six months hence to take stock at figures from ten to twenty points above present prices.

In reading the market, therefore, the main point is to discover what a stock can be expected to be worth three months hence and then to see whether manipulators or investors are advancing the price of that stock toward those figures. It is often possible to read movements in the market very clearly in this way. To know values is to comprehend the meaning of movements in the market.

There are assumptions here to which modifications might be offered, but there is no need. It would be impossible to show, except by the research of records covering at least half a century, that there are as many days of advance as of decline. The information would be valueless if obtained. It amounts to saying that heads and tails will equalize themselves if a coin is spun a sufficient number of times.

But what may be commended is Dow's clarity and sterling good sense. What he had to say was worth saying and he stopped when he had said it—a rare virtue in editorial writing. His feeling for the essential fact and for the underlying truth, without which the fact is bare and impertinent, will be readily remarked. He dealt with speculation as a fact, and could still show forth its truth without profitless moralizing, or confusing it with gambling. It will be well to imitate his point of view in further discussion, both on his theory and on the immense and useful significance of the stock market generally.

Roger Babson was both one of the first to circulate a market newsletter and a pioneer in statistical analysis. Born in Gloucester, Massachusetts, where his father was a dry goods merchant and his grandfather owned a large farm, Babson was a natural entrepreneur. As a kid, he earned a few pennies carrying buckets of water from the local well to the town's laundryman and for the elephants in P. T. Barnum's circus when it came to town. The circus meant playing hooky, but his father ended the fun and sent him to his grandfather's farm to hoe the fields. To avoid manual labor, Babson excelled at selling his grandfather's vegetables off a wagon. "My eyes were then opened to this fact: Although there is more profit in selling than in producing, yet, best of all, it is well to be in business for oneself."

After high school, he attended MIT, which was considerably less structured then—the young students were completely on their own. "They could have given us some good advice," he said, "as to the dangers of liquor and sexual diseases." In 1898, Babson found work with a bank, first as a clerk, then as a superb bond salesman. Unfortunately, Babson came down with tuberculosis in 1902, so he decided to start a home-based firm built around statistical compilation for tracking various securities and forecasting market movements. Part of his company was eventually bought by Standard & Poors.

While a technician, Babson wrote extensively for the average investor and had his own set of "Ten Commandments." The first three: "1. Keep speculation and investments separate. 2. Don't be fooled by a name. 3. Be wary of new promotions." As for studying market movements, his specialty, Babson based many of his theories on Newton's law of action and reaction. "Our forecast of future events," he said, "is based on the assumption that the law of action and reaction (Newtonian) applies to economics and human relations, en masse, as it applies to mechanics." Part of that theory was his renowned "Babson Chart," which is described in detail in his seminal book, *Business Barometers and Investment*. In *Three Different Stock Market Movements*, Babson explains which movements to ride and which to ignore.

Three Different Stock Market Movements
Roger W. Babson

In the first place there are the daily fluctuations of which the average trader endeavors to take advantage. These fluctuations may be compared to the ripples on the waters of a bay. They cannot be foretold in any way, and they bear no relation to the intrinsic value of the prospective properties or to conditions in general. Any man who endeavors to make a profit from these movements is, in my opinion, simply a gambler.

Secondly, there are the broad breaks and rallies of from five to ten points, extending over a few weeks and caused by the market's becoming overbought or oversold. These broader movements may be compared to the waves caused by the winds blowing over the waters of a bay. How the winds are to blow no one can tell; but knowing how they are blowing, it is comparatively easy to forecast whether the waters will be rough or smooth. If professional traders would let the market alone, the tide would slowly and regularly advance or recede without these waves, changing in accordance with fundamental conditions; but, owing to their impatience and avariciousness, these operators are continually either pushing the natural movement too far, or else retarding it. If the tendency of the market is thought to be downward, all these operators become bearish and sell

223

stocks short until the market becomes "oversold" and is lower than conditions warrant. As soon as it occurs to the operators that they have done this, they all change their position and begin to buy, continuing until the market becomes "overbought," or higher than conditions warrant. The market, therefore, is very seldom at its logical point based on fundamental conditions; but is almost always above or below this point, based upon these technical conditions.

As to what these operators are to do, it is impossible for any one—even themselves—to foretell; but from a painstaking and systematic study of the tape it is often possible to tell what these operators are trying to do, and thus it is often possible to intelligently guess whether a break or a rally is next in order; but at best it can be only a guess. Of course I do not advise any one to study the market's technical condition for the purpose of trading in these movements; but to those who are bound to trade, I strongly recommend that they fortify themselves by a study of these movements and the technical conditions causing them.

Thirdly, there are the long swings extending over one or more years, caused by corresponding changes in fundamental conditions. These long swings may be compared to the movements of the tide. The ripples cannot be foretold in any way; the wave movements can only be guessed at; but the tide movements can be foretold with absolute accuracy. In the same way, students of fundamental conditions can tell whether the market is at high or low tide, or whether the tide is going out or coming in.

STUDY FINANCIAL CYCLES

All financial and industrial history has been divided into distinct cycles, and each cycle has consisted of four distinct periods of from two to four years. There is the period of business prosperity, during which the insiders liquidate and stocks decline in price; the period of business decline, during which stocks drag on the bottom; the period of business depression, when the insiders are accumulating and stocks are increasing in price; and the period of business improvement, at the last end of which stocks reach abnormally high prices. Moreover, by a systematic and thorough study of both business and investment conditions, with their relations to each other, it should be possible to tell with exactness in which of these four periods we are at any given time, and to estimate fairly closely when a change may be expected.

Since it is thus possible to anticipate these long swings, referred to as the third movement, those with money and the courage of their convictions are enabled to make large fortunes. Moreover, unlike almost any other form of speculation, such men as do take advantage of these movements are performing a distinct service to their country by helping to steady conditions. In fact, every additional investor who henceforth endeavors to profit by these long swings causes the future periods of depression to be less severe and the future periods of prosperity to be less reckless.

In view of the above, two statements should be self-evident. The first one is this: There is no sure way of making money in day-to-day speculation, such as is indulged in by the ordinary trader. Ninety-eight per cent of such traders come to grief, losing not only their money, but also their health, reputation, and what is worst of all, their courage and self-respect. The game is absolutely "rigged" against them, as the powers that be own all the paraphernalia and apparatus, and are subject to no laws or regulations. At Monte Carlo one plays simply against luck, and with the exception of about two and a half per cent in favor of the bank, the player has an equal chance with the bank to win, which is not true when he is playing against Wall Street. Not only are the commissions against the speculator—so that if he should win one-half of the time he would still be out his commissions—but almost everything is "rigged" to beat him.

Don't Follow the Crowd

Most market letters urge the public to buy when they should sell, and to sell when they should buy. The banks lower their money rates and make it easy for people to purchase when stocks really should be sold; and, conversely, they call loans and unintentionally do all that is possible to prevent the public from purchasing when stocks are low. Corporations raise their dividends and publish splendid reports, making their stocks look attractive when they are already too high, and they reduce the dividends and show poor earnings when the stocks are really an attractive and safe investment; and so it is all the way down the line. Banks, corporations, leading men, and even many of the brokers themselves, are all consciously or unconsciously combined to get the public in wrong. Consequently, only about two per cent of the traders who enter Wall Street ever succeed in beating this game, though even a larger percentage of those who play at Monte Carlo beat the bank there.

Of course, if one knew that the Wall Street organization would invariably give the wrong advice, one could—if he had extraordinary self-control and independence—beat the game by always doing exactly the opposite of what some of the news sheets, banks, corporation officials and brokers generally advise; but this also is an impossibility, as these interests sometimes advise correctly for the very purpose of still further bewildering investors and the public generally. Therefore, the first point that I wish to impress upon the reader is that only about two per cent of the speculators and room traders ever succeed in retiring from Wall Street with any profit, and that the majority of this small percentage do it largely through luck.

The second statement that I wish to emphasize is as follows: Although the ordinary speculator has a very small chance of profit, and although it is almost an impossibility to make money in stocks along the lines ordinarily practised, yet there is one method by which it may be done. I refer to the method of taking advantage of the long swings, extending over periods of from one to four years, which is possible by a systematic study of fundamental conditions.

As to what the stock market is to do today or tomorrow, or even next week, or possibly next month, no one knows, and only those fully acquainted with the market's technical conditions can make an intelligent guess. Outside of about half a dozen interests in Wall Street, all the rest of those who play the short swing game are simply tools. These six are well known to all and obtain their power simply through their intimate connections with the press, the corporations and the brokers. Moreover, although these men may have their places taken by others, yet their number will never be much greater; for, as the circle extends, they begin to endeavor to beat one another, which keeps the number down. So one cannot reasonably expect to be one of these.

BE A BIG MAN

There is, however, another and much larger circle of men who represent Wall Street in the popular mind and are continually making and retaining great fortunes. These men, however, are not traders and speculators, as are the first mentioned six, although the public does not recognize the difference. The operations of these bigger men are based wholly on fundamental conditions and long swings. When stocks are cheap and they consider that fundamental conditions are becoming sounder each week, they begin and continue to accumulate so long as fundamental conditions continue to improve. This period usually lasts for about eighteen months, although they may do eighty per cent of their buying during the first few months of the period, when the press, the banks and the corporation officials all seem pessimistic and the public is selling.

At the end of this period, and upon the first sign of real prosperity, these men begin to sell, although many of them continue to talk optimistically so that the public will buy. In other words, the distributing process commences, lasting for one or more years, during which time the leaders are all talking optimistically, the banks are loaning money at low rates, and the corporations are raising their dividends. Nevertheless, fundamental conditions are no longer improving, and these men who study fundamental rather than surface conditions are rapidly selling all of their stocks; in fact, even the money received from the sale of these stocks is loaned on the Street to enable the public to buy stocks more easily.

Then, when the public has absorbed all of the stocks possible and surface conditions are so bright that the ordinary speculator is anticipating no trouble — although fundamental conditions are, of course, unsatisfactory — the word is passed around to "pull the plug." Stocks then begin to tumble and almost every one suddenly becomes pessimistic, banks begin to call loans, corporations reduce dividends and everything is done to force the sale of stocks and cause low quotations. This method of depressing the market is continued for one or more years until fundamental conditions begin to improve, when the accumulating process above mentioned is again commenced, although business, so far as surface conditions show, is still very much depressed.

In short, these men, constantly studying fundamental conditions, enter the market once in every few years to buy or sell according to what these fundamental conditions indicate. After purchasing stocks they hold them for a year or so, selling out when the public begins to buy, and loaning money to the public for a year or more thereafter to make said purchasing easier. When they have sold all of their previous holdings and also are heavily short of the market — while banks, merchants and investors are overextended and fundamental conditions are becoming unsound — they suddenly change their attitude, begin to talk pessimistically and do all they can to depress stocks, as above suggested, preparatory to another period of accumulation.

As to what the market does from day to day or from month to month, these men do not care. They do not trade as do ninety-nine per cent of the speculators, but rather play simply for the long swings. Moreover, although I strongly oppose many of the methods that some of these men employ, yet I believe that the ultimate result of their studies is good for the country, by tending to steady conditions as well as being profitable to themselves.

Of course, this means confining all of one's buying to perhaps one month in two or more years and holding said stocks for a while; confining all one's selling to perhaps a month, and then buying only commercial paper for a while. By so doing, however, one may eventually accumulate a great fortune without much risk; especially if he will confine his investments to high-grade standard securities. Nearly all of the honest great fortunes of this country have been made by a study of fundamental conditions, by independent work along the lines above mentioned. Moreover, it is only by studying fundamental conditions that one can align himself with these large interests — which do not trade from day to day or from month to month — and make money as they do.

BERNARD M. BARUCH
1870–1965

As a boy, Bernard Baruch picked cotton to earn money for powder and shot so he could hunt rabbits. In his autobiography, he recalls growing up in rural South Carolina, where whites and blacks clashed constantly in the post–Civil War years. When a close friend died in a duel, Baruch's father moved the family to New York in 1880. In 1884, young Baruch entered City College. After college, Baruch had a chance to go to Mexico to work for the venerable Guggenheim family, but his protective mother vetoed the idea and found him a job as a banker's apprentice. It didn't last long. Bored and looking for adventure, Baruch went to Colorado to find gold, laboring in a mine during the day and gambling at night.

In 1891, Baruch was back in New York working for a member of the New York Stock Exchange, first as a clerk, then as an analyst. Not long after, he struck out on his own, knocking on doors and looking for money to invest. Baruch, who made friends easily (i.e., the Guggenheims and Rockefellers), made millions in the market. He attributed his success to rigorous self-appraisal. "And as I came to know myself," he said, "I acquired a better understanding of other people." For him, Wall Street was "one long course of education in human nature." In general he was very wary of tips. "There is something about inside information," he said, "which seems to paralyze a man's reasoning powers. . . . He will disregard the most evident facts."

Baruch became such a force on Wall Street that the press started tracking his whereabouts. One newspaper reported: "One of the things which made many of the room traders bearish was a rumor that B. M. Baruch was about to go away on a short vacation. . . ." The one-time gambler eventually became an adviser to U.S. presidents. He served as chairman of the War Industries Board in World War I, and his contributions won him a place on the Nazi hit list in World War II. His rising concern with national issues and the economic health of the United States is reflected in *Does a Stock Market Slump Mean a Business Slide-Off?*, in which he discusses why the market is a barometer for business conditions.

Does a Stock Market Slump Mean a Business Slide-Off?

Bernard M. Baruch

While the stock market remains a reflection of the concentrated, critical judgment of the men who do things, since the war it has lost much significance as a barometer of business.

The stock market is none the less a barometer of business, but it must be read in causes rather than effects.

Naturally the average manufacturer, far removed geographically or mentally from all but the printed record of the market's fluctuations, is still apprehensive over a sudden break or encouraged by a determined rise. But in either case, to be correct in his judgment, he must be able to look beneath the cold figures of rise or fall in stocks to the underlying reason. Take, for instance, the market we have just been through. Its rise dates back to the election of Calvin Coolidge and the hopes men had of what the Coolidge administration was going to do for business. Buying became rampant—not of any particular stocks, but of all stocks.

Speculation ran riot over calm judgment. Business was taking counsel of its hopes.

There had to be an end—a reversal. It came in March. Men who had taken counsel of their hopes began to take counsel of their fears.

Stocks in which there was no inherent reason for a rise quickly fell. But how about other stocks? They fell, too— because in some instances men had to sacrifice the good to protect the purely speculative; in others because of a certain reflex action to which the Exchange is generally susceptible.

Do not condemn the bears—theirs is the purging influence! They supply the balance-wheel to haphazard speculation.

What effect, then, did this movement of stocks have on business—and why? Without looking further into the cause of the movement, let us draw a simple parallel.

You decide after careful study of the trend to buy a certain issue of stock. You telephone your broker, taking counsel of your hopes, and place your order for 1,000 shares of this stock. You pay $100 a share for it. It rises, true to your hopes, to $200. You take note of your finances. You have $200,000 where 6 months before you had but half that much. You are worth, you say, $200,000 because you bought that particular stock.

But suddenly there is a bear movement. (Do not condemn the bears—theirs is the purging influence! They supply the balance-wheel to haphazard speculation.) Your stock falls off 50 points. If you believe in the stock, you hold on; if not, you sell.

But beyond all that you take counsel of your fears! You have lost $50,000! You are $50,000 poorer than you were yesterday. You are still $50,000 richer than you were 6 months ago. But it is not human to figure things that way.

You have lost $50,000? Hang on to everything! And you do, and others—hundreds of thousands of others—do likewise. Purchasing is curtailed—ever so slightly perhaps; money becomes a bit tighter—and business is immediately bad in a million minds and on a million tongues!

But is it? Is the stock market the barometer thereof? Has the liquidation of stocks for which there was no inherent reason for their rise undermined the whole business structure?

The stock-market operator—the speculator— is a dealer in realities. . . . He interprets the news into movement, up or down.

It has to some degree—but why? Because men are now taking counsel of their fears rather than their hopes! Their minds are so intent upon the activity of the moment that they fail to take calm counsel of the past with its reasons, or of the future with its possibilities.

That is, most men do not. A few scan the horizon on all sides. A few get to the bottom of things. A few gird their loins and take a suggestive poke at their courage. A few go on! They see what the fall offers, or the early winter, or the spring. And they have so planned their financial pattern that they are able to get ready for another fill-up period—and they go on.

I do not blame less-informed men for pulling in their horns when the bubble bursts. But those who know the broad international currents that influence the ebb and flow of stocks, who appreciate the importance of peace, of good crops, of a demand for labor, of sound currency in the world's markets, need not follow surface trends too closely.

They must weigh the subsoil, however, for the present situation has its "ifs," of course. But it is a more sound situation than we had in March. The first lopping off of speculative issues has been accomplished. Sound issues have recovered somewhat. It is just the natural movement of the pendulum, which swung too far because men were too full of hope.

The stock-market operator—the speculator—is a dealer in realities. When he reads his paper in the morning, he is fitting the trend of world events to sudden sallies or long-swing movements. He interprets the news into movement, up or down.

Business men may well take a lesson from the speculator. Those who, like him, look behind each word and sentence for the reason therefor, or the possible effects thereof, are leaders in their fields.

I took my son to Niagara Falls one day. We looked down into the cataract, and I pointed to the water, flowing back towards the falls.

"See, son," I said. "That water is flowing up hill: That water is defying nature's law seemingly. Why?"

And then we analyzed how the great force of that water hurtling over the falls forced that movement up and down and back, but finally down, as natural law decrees.

I do not blame less-informed men for pulling in their horns when the bubble bursts.

There are many great forces working night and day to undermine our best judgments, to put to the test our most careful deliberations! They are the "ifs": debt settlements, crops, foreign exchange, British labor troubles, and so on! Each has its place and each its possibility.

Everything may be progressing smoothly—upward— when a sudden upheaval in Russia, in France, in Poland, a frost or a drought, breaks the continuity of thought and arrests the progress of the moment.

Then is the time for looking backward, around and ahead. Then is the time for taking counsel of the concentrated, critical judgment of those men who do things. The answer may be found in the stock market, which is a reflection of their thinking, but again it may not. It all depends on what has gone before or what those keenvisioned speculators who do not deal in dreams see for the future.

The stock market is none the less a barometer of business, but it must be read in causes rather than effects. Those who use it as a guide to business movements should look beyond the mere mathematics or rise and fall to the great national or international forces that are primarily responsible therefor.

Abby Cohen has made a name for herself as the top-ranked market analyst and the preeminent bull of Wall Street in the 1990s. In recognition of her skills, Goldman, Sachs & Co. rewarded her by making her a partner in 1998, a promotion many considered overdue. After graduating from a Queens high school in 1969, Cohen enrolled at Cornell University, where she majored in economics and computer science. Her first job out of school was as a junior economist at the Federal Reserve Board in Washington, D.C. While there, she earned a masters in economics at George Washington University. In 1976 she moved on to T. Rowe Price Associates, where she worked as an analyst.

Six years later, she returned to New York as an investment strategist for Drexel Burnham Lambert. There, Cohen developed her method for forecasting, which involves looking at the economy, individual companies, and global issues. She also adapts her models to the changing times, a lesson learned while working for the Fed. "Parts of the economic model the Fed used had stopped working," she says, "because they hadn't been adapted to reflect changes that had taken place in the economy. This was a fabulous lesson to me to be flexible in my analysis and to look beneath the usual rules of thumb to the underlying dynamics."

While others turned bearish in the mid- and late 1990s, she did not because she believes that the economy is now fundamentally different. One of those differences is the changing nature of the business cycle, which she believes has lengthened and is less susceptible to radical swings. In fact, Cohen dubbed the 1990s U.S. economy "the Silly Putty economy" while she and her kids were messing around with Silly Putty. She had pressed some against the image of a standard business cycle and then stretched it apart until the image became more drawn out and muted. She also compares the U.S. economy to a supertanker: "It may not be the fastest ship, but it's hard to knock off course." In *A Fundamental Strength,* written in 1996, Cohen weighs the importance of GDP growth, inflation, and corporate profits, among other factors, in explaining her bullish outlook.

A Fundamental Strength
Abby Joseph Cohen

It took little more than seven weeks for the Dow Jones Industrial Average to reach 6,500 after passing through the psychological 6,000 barrier on October 4. During that time, pessimists have become ever louder in their predictions of an imminent end to Wall Street's bull run, which has now lasted six years.

Yet I believe that recent gains have been well supported by fundamental developments in the US economy and among America's leading companies. Far from representing warnings of the end of the bull market, they look set to continue for some time to come.

US share prices typically move in a staircase pattern. Substantial price increases (and declines) are telescoped into short periods of time and are then followed by an extended trading range in which share price indices are choppy but trendless. Investors sit back to contemplate the market's action and await future news on the economy and corporate performance. There are movements between sectors at such times as investors gradually construct the most likely scenario for the coming months.

I believe the catalysts for future market activity are largely positive. Principal among them will be moderate economic growth which generates profit increases but little upward pressure on inflation.

The most recent upward step in equity prices began in late July when investors recognised that profit increases were continuing despite a slowing in economic growth. In the third quarter which followed, real growth in gross domestic product was 2 per cent, operating profits in the Standard & Poor's 500 companies increased 7 per cent on the previous year and inflation was unchanged. Inflation fears abated, 30-year Treasury bond yields fell from 7.2 per cent to 6.4 per cent and share prices moved higher.

US share prices typically move in a staircase pattern.

This was an appropriate response to favourable news. As for most of the past six years, the rising market has been supported by evidence that the economic expansion is long-lasting and profit-intensive rather than especially vigorous.

The growth in profits has been stretched out like Potty Putty but the cumulative profit gains have been significant—they have doubled since 1991. Profits generated by companies such as those in the S&P 500 continue pleasantly to surprise investors with their durability and quality.

The durability is linked to the extended nature of business expansion and the upward shift in operating margins since the mid-1980s.

The quality is tied to several factors. First, low inflation means the earnings reported by companies are "real", with very little derived from inflation or inventory-related fluff.

Second, changes in accountancy practices made by the Financial Accounting Standards Board in the 1990s have encouraged conservative accounting approaches on several important issues, including employee benefits.

For example, many companies took large charges against earnings and book value for future healthcare expenditure in the early 1990s when double-digit inflation in medical costs was assumed. Healthcare inflation is now less than 5 per cent, suggesting the possibility that some earlier charges might be reversed.

Third, corporate write-offs for past mistakes and corporate restructuring have shrunk and now represent less than 10 per cent of reported earnings, compared with 40 per cent in 1991.

The growth in profits has been stretched out like Potty Putty but the cumulative profit gains have been significant — they have doubled since 1991.

The gap between modest GDP growth and more energetic profit gains from the S&P 500 companies encourages some to believe that the latter cannot continue for long. But the gap can be explained by three factors that will not soon end:

- The S&P 500 is an actively managed index (please pardon the oxymoron). These are among the best companies in America, and are not meant to represent the average.
- Growth in GDP has been muted by the stagnation in government spending this decade. However, private sector GDP growth — which generates private sector profits — has been more vigorous.
- The output of the substantial offshore direct investments made by US companies boosts the GDP of the host countries — but the resulting profits boost US earnings and US share prices.

How much should investors be willing to pay for corporate earnings? Some sceptics maintain US shares are overvalued even if solid fundamental conditions persist.

I readily admit that US shares are not as attractively priced as they were. At Goldman Sachs, we recommend at present that US portfolios allocate 60 per cent of their assets to equities, down from 70–75 per cent in 1995. But a 60 per cent weighting reflects our belief that equities can generate returns at least in line with growth in corporate earnings and cash flow—and thus that equities are not overvalued at present levels.

Valuation approaches vary by market. In some countries, yield-oriented approaches are the most statistically robust. In the US, earnings-related valuation models are the most helpful.

Nominal dividend yield is quite low in the US market at 2.2 per cent for the S&P 500. But this is tied to low inflation and a record low cash payout of 35 per cent of earnings.

Simply stated, dividends are low not because companies cannot afford to raise them but because they have decided against doing so. Most managements would prefer to reinvest in company operations, an apparently sensible action given average returns on equity of 20 per cent.

We recommend at present that US portfolios allocate 60 per cent of their assets to equities, down from 70–75 per cent in 1995.

In addition, share repurchases have been used as a tax-efficient alternative to paying cash dividends which is often preferred by tax-paying investors. Since the late 1950s, the last time dividend yields on equities exceeded bond yields, investors have increasingly depended on equities for earnings growth and capital appreciation rather than income.

The S&P 500 now trades at less than 16 times the Goldman Sachs estimate for operating earnings in 1997, at a time when the consumer price index (CPI) has been rising at an annual rate of about 2.8 per cent. When inflation has been 3.5 per cent or less over the last 45 years, price/earnings ratios ratios have averaged 16.2.

Share repurchases have been used as a tax-efficient alternative to paying cash dividends which is often preferred by tax-paying investors.

However, even this may be to underestimate the extent to which US shares are undervalued. Many economists believe the CPI overstates inflation and that a truer picture may be offered by other measures such as the GDP deflator which currently suggests inflation of 1.8 per cent.

In the past, protracted periods of 2 per cent inflation have been associated with price/earnings ratios of 18 to 20. Our analysis suggests that share prices can rise from present levels — even without price/earnings ratio expansion — based on additional profit gains expected in 1997.

JOSEPH E. GRANVILLE
1923–

Joseph Granville, the most flamboyant of technical analysts, was known at one time to appear at seminars in costume, accompanied by women in bikinis. His mother was certain he was destined for something special long before he became a celebrity, so she invited the renowned mystic Edgar Cayce to their home. In September 1939, Cayce arrived to uncover young Granville's past life and fortell his future. Granville claimed that Cayce said his "activity will be such that he will never be forgotten!" His father was a more staid man, who was once a banker, but unfortunately had lost the family money in the 1929 crash—an experience that would make Granville an overbearing bear.

Granville served in the Navy during World War II, and was stationed in the Marshall Islands when the atomic bombs were dropped on Japan. After the war, he ran a printing press for $90 a week, barely able to support his wife and four children. At the time, his hobby was tracking the stamp collecting market and predicting stamp price movements, which ultimately helped him get a job tracking the stock market. In 1957, Granville started writing a daily stock market letter for E. F. Hutton on a trial basis. He found the corporate atmosphere restrictive, however, and in 1963 he quit to start his own newsletter.

After a couple of brilliant calls on market movements, his reputation became so great, that when he predicted a market drop and advised his clients to sell everything and go short in January 1981, he actually created a major sell-off, with the largest trading volume day to date in New York Stock Exchange history. Upset investors asked the Securities and Exchange Commission to investigate, but Granville had done nothing wrong—his newsletter and seminar business boomed. But then he predicted another serious drop in the market in 1982, while others were bullish. The market kept going up, and he lost his following. Granville has since rehabilitated his image, and his newsletter still rates as one of the best. *Market Movements* offers a glimpse into some of Granville's more unorthodox thinking as he equates natural market movements to several famous music pieces.

Market Movements
Joseph E. Granville

There are very few "acci-
dents" in the stock market. When a stock advances or
declines there is a "reason" behind the move. It is not the primary concern of a market technician to determine what
the reason is, the assumption being that there is always a
reason. The technician is primarily concerned with timing,
when a stock moves rather than *why* it moves. Since there
cannot be any motion without the presence of some kind
of energy, a study of stock price movements prompts an
investigation of some of the forces behind these movements
and this leads us into a brief discussion of simple physics.

---

*Johann Sebastian Bach . . . could have been a
great stock market technician if he were alive
today.*

Stock price movements often show a tendency to adhere
to some physical laws. You have been introduced to some
basic concepts and now it is time to add some refinements,
relating the *breakout,* the *flatbase breakout, support* and *resistance, gaps* and *climactic moves* to the laws of motion. It will be

illustrated that stocks tend to develop their own "rhythm" and back and fill with a tendency to respond to some of the mathematics of melody and music. You will be shown that the effectiveness of great art is as much a matter of timing as it is construction.

BACH, BEETHOVEN AND KOSMA

There is a predictable order in the universe. All motion is governed by *laws* of motion. There are no accidents. All vacuums are filled. Bodies in motion tend to remain in motion. Bodies at rest tend to remain at rest. You have already seen some of these laws at work in reading a stock price chart. An advance follows an upside breakout. A decline follows a downside breakout. A failure to reach a previous peak leads to a decline. All gaps are filled. All these movements are based on universal laws of motion. They not only apply to the stock market but they equally apply to laws of physics, medicine and mathematics as well as to music.

JESU, JOY OF MAN'S DESIRING

Johann Sebastian Bach, who was born in 1685 and died in 1760, could have been a great stock market technician if he were alive today. His great music *followed every technical principle of stock market analysis*. He might be today a stock price chart reader *par excellence*. Of course Bach was remotely removed in terms of time and temperament from the modern day stock market. However, his music consciously or unconsciously *follows the direction forecasted by the very notes themselves*. Bach was inspired and yet his music almost fits a *mathematical* formula.

Below is written the theme of Bach's "Jesu, Joy of Man's Desiring".

Johann Sebastian Bach
Arranged by Bryceson Treharne

Since there are eight notes in the scale (12 in the chromatic scale) the figure 1 will be assigned to the lowest note in the above theme. Putting the notes of the theme in terms of numbers and letting the first note start with the number 4, they read as follows: 4, 5, 6, 8, 7, 7, 9, 8, 8, 11, 10, 11, 8, 6, 4, 5, 6, 7, 8, 9, 8, 7, 6, 5, 6, 4, 3, 4, 5, 1, 3, 5, 7, 6, 5, 6, 4, 5, 6, 8, 7, 7, 9, 8, 8, 11, 10, 11, 8, 6, 4, 5, 6, 2, 8, 7, 6, 5, 4, 1, 4, 3, 4. Now these numbers are plotted on the chart, on page 246.

Checking the numbers against the chart, pretend that each number represents the fluctuating price of a stock and see how the chart follows all the technical chart principles just reviewed.

The first four figures are 4, 5, 6, and 8. This sets up a *gap* and predicts that the gap will be filled. The next two figures are a pair of 7's, thus filling in the gap. The next figure is a 9 and this represents an *upside breakout* above the previous high of 8. The gap from 7 to 9 on that jump is immediately filled in with a pair of 8's. The pair of 8's and the previous pair of 7's represent *rising bottoms* and this, together with the upside breakout to 9, *constitutes a bullish prediction of new highs to come.*

The new highs are then immediately scored with a *climactic* jump to 11. All figures between 4 and 11 have now been recorded with the exception of the number 10. Fulfilling the law of gaps, the figure 10 is then recorded and since

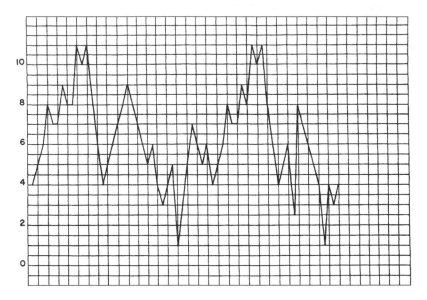

7, 8 and 10 now represent the pattern of rising bottoms the *support* level is at 10 and the *resistance* level is at 11.

The next figure is another 11. This is the resistance level to further advance. *This level fails to be bettered* and the next figure turns out to be an 8. This constitutes a *downside signal,* the first one seen in the chart. *The figure 8 penetrates the support at 10.* This is a technical prediction for lower levels to be reached and the chart immediately obliges. Following the drop to 8, lower levels of 6 and 4 are immediately recorded. The pattern stops declining at 4 because thus far in the chart that level is considered to be the basic *first support* (the lowest figure recorded in the pattern thus far).

Here the chart takes a *phenomenal* twist, considered phenomenal because it is so *utterly logical* from a technical standpoint. In view of the fact that *downside gaps* were created when the decline took place from 11 (11, 8, 6, 4), *these gaps are now filled by a straightline advance from 4 to 9.* In view of the technical fact that the previous supports of 7 and 9 on the way down became resistance levels on the way up, the rise from 4 to 9 cut through the first resistance level at 7 and pro-. vided a technical signal of further rise. The previous figure of 10 has partially filled the gap between 11 and 8 on the way down and thus the technical requirement was only to go to 9 in order to have filled all the gaps from 11 down to 8. In view of the additional fact that a second resistance level on the way back up existed at 9 it was utterly logical that the advance this time *would stop at 9.*

The downturn which now commences at 9 constitutes a *bearish* formation of *declining tops* (the first and higher top at 11). Since the previous rise was a straight-line 4 through 9 advance there is no support on the way down until the previous major support at 4 and thus the figures go down.

The pattern of decline is 9, 8, 7, 6, 5, 6, 4, 3, 4, 5 and 1. Declining tops have been recorded at 11, 9 and now 6. The temporary upturn to 6 set the figure 5 up as temporary support. When the figure 4 immediately followed it meant that the pattern of declining tops and the downside penetration of the support at 5 supplied a *bearish signal* which would not allow the previous basic support at 4 to be maintained this time. Sure enough, the support at 4 was immediately broken with the drop to 3 for the first time. The drop to 3 was another bearish signal for lower figures yet to come but first there was a temporary rise, the figures 4 and 5 following the drop to 3. *The rise had to be temporary for two strong technical reasons.* The drop to 3 had already given a bearish signal and the previous support at 5 on the way down *became the resistance level on the way up.* The pattern then completed itself with a *climactic* decline to 1 (as predicted by the bear signal at 3). Just as the jump from 8 to 11 in the early figures on the way up was climactic on the upside, so was the drop from 5 to 1 climactic on the downside.

Following an upside climax there is a fast retreat. Bach showed this when the initial jump from 8 to 11 was followed by the 8, 6, 4 retreat. *Following a downside climax there is fast advance.* Bach now showed this with the 3, 5, 7 advance after the drop to 1 was recorded. This advance pattern set up gaps at 2, 4, and 6. The gaps at 4 and 6 were then filled by the succeeding figures of 6, 5, 6, 4, 5, 6. The next figure is an 8 and this provides the bull signal for rise, penetrating the previous recovery high of 7. The entire pattern repeats with the remaining variation of filling in the last remaining gap at 2 and providing a balancing upside jump from 2 to 8 with the remaining figures filling in that gap, a masterful piece of music which follows all the directions implied by sound technical stock market analysis.

BEETHOVEN AND THE FIFTH

Ludwig van Beethoven (1770–1827) also subconsciously followed the "technical" line in his music and the opening bars of his immortal fifth symphony provide a good example:

Beethoven
Adapted by John Thompson

Translating these notes into numbers we have the following sequence: 5, 5, 5, 3, 4, 4, 4, 2, 5, 5, 5, 3, 6, 6, 6, 5, 10, 10, 10, 8, 4, 4, 4, 2, 6, 6, 6, 5, 11, 11, 11, 9, 12, 12, 11, 10, 12, 12, 11, 10, 12, 12, 11, 10, 8, 12.

These numbers are now plotted on a chart [following].

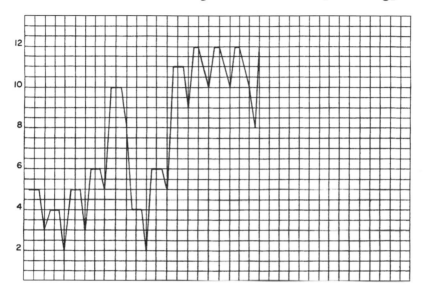

The clear pattern of *rising bottoms* and *rising tops* followed by the *upside breakout* to a *climactic* top is seen followed by a *longer* term *double bottom* which supports the second ascent to a new series of tops. The first seventeen numbers trace out the very bullish pattern of a *rounding bottom* and the upside breakout (at 6) is a key buy signal. This is a pattern which many stock prices follow and it is well to recognize it immediately so as to capitalize on the very bullish upside breakout from this type of rounding bottom.

THE STOCK MARKET REFLECTS
A MIXTURE OF TRUTHS

Technical analysis of the stock market is largely based on many repetitive observations and the truths revealed often can be shown to have parallels in such things as music, medicine, physics, etc. In other words, here and there some natural laws seem to be involved. You have already seen many technical similarities between stock price movements and a piece of music. There is some logic and order in both. There is a strong hint of something which goes beyond just pure chance. Though it is presumptious to say that there is a predictable design, there is enough evidence to more than justify further investigation.

In medicine a disease has certain symptoms which enables the doctor to diagnose correctly. Some diseases have similar symptoms and a less experienced physician may make the wrong diagnosis simply because he overlooks the one symptom which differentiates that disease from many others. There is always a specific set of symptoms which singles out and labels a particular disease correctly. It is the same in the stock market with technical analysis. Each situation in the market has a specific set of technical indicators (symptoms) which correctly labels (diagnoses) the situation for what it is. A less experienced market technician may misread the market simply because he is overlooking perhaps the one indicator which is calling the situation correctly. One cannot expect to become a good market diagnostician overnight anymore than one could become a good doctor without the necessary years of practice and training.

Technical analysis of the stock market is largely based on many repetitive observations and the truths revealed often can be shown to have parallels in such things as music, medicine, physics, etc.

A study of the stock market reveals the workings of many laws of physics and laws of nature. Some of these are:

250

1. A body in motion tends to remain in motion.
2. A body at rest tends to remain at rest.
3. What goes up must come down (gravity).
4. It takes more energy to go up than down (gravity).
5. There are no vacuums in nature.

One cannot expect to become a good market diagnostician overnight anymore than one could become a good doctor without the necessary years of practice and training.

Let us examine these verities and apply them to the market:

1. A Body in Motion Tends to Remain in Motion.
In the market we would call this *price momentum*. If a stock repeatedly failed to move above a price of 30 for a number of years and ultimately did better the 30 level it obviously had a price momentum it did not have in the past. The move above 30 would obviously carry the price still higher. Upside price breakouts through previous price resistance levels have *momentum* and the physical laws of motion can be profitably capitalized upon. This would equally apply when a stock declines below a previous low point. The downside momentum would carry through and a series of new lows would be expected to ensue.

2. A Body at Rest Tends to Remain at Rest.
Right away the *base formation* comes to mind. The stock is doing nothing and the base line may be adhered to for a number of years.... [Y]ou will discover how to differentiate between those stocks in base formations which may sit on their base for a number of additional years and those stocks

in base formations just ready to break out of them on the upside. A stock which is literally doing nothing will tend to continue doing nothing until either accumulation or distribution starts. . . .

3. What Goes Up Must Come Down (Gravity).
There are many refinements of this generalization. If a stock price advances too rapidly then the dangers of retracement on the downside are enhanced. The speed of advance greatly depends on the level it started from. Obviously, if the rapid advance started from a *base formation* then the first physical law has precedence and the price momentum will not be quickly diluted. If the rapid advance occurs after the stock has been advancing in price for some time then this physical law takes precedence and the danger of decline is increased.

It is easier to understand this when it is realized that the price of a stock tends to move in *three phases:* (1) the base formation, (2) the advance from the base formation at about a 30 degree angle and (3) the third phase of maturity where the price is advancing at almost a vertical or 90 degree slant. It is in this latter phase where the danger of sharp decline is the greatest. This is the phase in which the above physical law is most commonly applied.

4. It Takes More Energy to Go Up Than Down (Gravity).
It may take a stock one or two years to rise from 20 to 50 but it could lose half that advance in a period of weeks.

A stock can fall more quickly than it rises by merely the turning off of the faucet of upside energy leaving nothing left except the natural law of gravity to predominate.

The gravity principle shows the downward pull the greatest next to the earth and as we rise above the earth the pull gradually lessens until we gain an easier upside momentum. When enough energy has been expended on the upside then exhaustion wins out and the body returns to earth. It is this way with stocks. This is why a stock will stay in a base area (Phase One) for awhile until enough upside energy (volume buildup) has been generated to overcome the pull of gravity or price inertia. When this takes place the stock moves into the second phase of advance. Upside energy keeps building up until it accelerates the price into the rapid Third Phase and here the *balance* of the upside energy is *expended* and then the stock has nothing left to *fuel* the rise any further and then the laws of gravity once again *predominate*. In other words, it takes energy to overcome gravity. Of course there is nothing new here but these things should be thought of when it comes to stocks.

A stock can fall more quickly than it rises by merely the turning off of the faucet of upside energy leaving nothing left except the natural law of gravity to predominate. It was there all the time but it took constant upside energy exerted to overcome it. Remove it and the price would have to fall of its own accord.

5. There Are No Vacuums in Nature.

Nothing happens without a reason. In nature there is reason and nature wasteth not. Therefore, vacuums are waste and thus there are no vacuums in nature. Being UN-natural, they are thus *filled*. All natural phenomena can be reduced to ENERGY and nature fills vacuums with energy. We have seen the gaps filled between notes in the music of Bach, Beethoven and Kosma and in technical stock analysis we can also say that the *natural* laws of vacuum-filling are fulfilled.

When British native Arthur Crump's *The Theory of Stock Exchange Speculation* reached the shores of the United States in the late 1870s, it was so highly thought of that at least two American publishers put out their own editions. As one editor noted, "Few subjects have been responsible for more printed nonsense than stock speculation. . . . *The Theory of Stock Speculation,* by Mr. Crump, an Englishman, is herewith reprinted as perhaps the sanest consideration of the subject that has been written." Crump, a former bank manager with the Bank of England turned speculator on the London Stock Exchange, wrote a number of books and pamphlets on investing, currencies, and money markets.

Part of Crump's sane advice included striking metaphors—for example, in advising novice investors to seek professional help, he wrote, "A mountain climber who disclaims the aid of a guide, and is subsequently fished out of a crevasse, can expect no other epitaph, even from his friends, than that he has paid the deserved penalty of extreme temerity and folly." But even when seeking help you must be careful, Crump warned, because "People seldom tell of their losses." Crump's warnings were for good reason: In 1870, the Franco-German war threw the London markets into chaos and prices collapsed. On the other hand, the introduction of telegraphic facilities at the exchange in 1872 was a major step forward, making information more accessible. More information meant less swindling and fewer bogus "tips."

For Crump, the foremost requirement for successful investing is to be even-tempered. The investor, he said, must be cool under fire and "should have the power of calling forth emotions which are opposite of those commonly manifested under given circumstances." Taking it a step further, he believed that the investor "must have a concrete hardness of indifference" and must even consider himself somewhat of a bandit who is willing to ambush his adversary without remorse. Of course, the investor must also be a student, which, according to Crump, involves more than financial skills. In *The Importance of Special Knowledge,* he explains why a thorough understanding of the weather is critical to understanding market swings.

The Importance of Special Knowledge
Arthur Crump

If a speculator has not closely studied the special causes that influence the Stock markets at regularly recurring intervals, he has not learned the alphabet of his business. We shall endeavour to pass in review some of these. First of all, there is the temper of the public. Many persons have puzzled over the causes which will at one time combine to produce activity among buyers of stocks, and at another dead stagnation; and it is a very interesting study, albeit somewhat difficult of correct analysis.

There are periods of the year when the temper of investors tends to sulkiness, in sympathy with a fall of the mercury. Dull and disagreeable weather, as a rule, adversely affects the Stock markets more or less, according to the extent of counteracting influences. If we take the beginning of a year, in January investors will usually be found in a conservative frame of mind, with which speculators will sympathise as they perceive it; for it may safely be said that unless the public can be calculated upon to follow their lead, it is useless for professional speculators to stir up the markets. In the first month of the year capitalists are in more or less of a stay-at-home mood; and now so many buyers of securities live on a line of railway, they take as many holidays as they can well find excuse for.

A speculator should have a good aneroid barometer, that has a good big indicator, hung up in his hall, and he would not be very far wrong if he were to buy and sell according to the indications given by this instrument that it was going to be good or bad weather. Most people are like any one you may chance to single out of a crowd, from a physical point of view. The change from fair to foul weather will have the same effect upon a crowd as upon that one man. Foggy, wet, and cheerless weather sends people to their homes with a contented mind, if they feel they can hold their own until the return of sunshine; just as a storm causes navigators to run for a harbour, or seek the nearest shelter from its fury. When buyers keep away from the markets, prices droop with their own weight, and, from the mere absence of any buying at all, will often fall as regards value, out of all proportion to the extent of the sales. Such a period is a very good one to turn round and buy, as there is sure to be a nearly corresponding recovery with a favourable change in the weather.

Unless there are special causes at work, during the first month of the year the Stock markets are usually as hard and inelastic as the frozen earth outside. At Christmas-time people make up their accounts for the year, and most of them, having gained less than the total pictured by their imagination, are more or less out of humour, and disinclined to enter upon commitments outside the limits of their business proper. At such a period, therefore, a speculator may look for fluctuations which as a rule will not occur. As February creeps on, if circumstances are generally favourable for trade, so that the newspapers can dish up their daily fare with sauces that encourage their readers to look on the future with hopefulness, losses that are written off will begin to assume less harrowing proportions, and the old inclination to launch out will come to the front. The professional speculative element in the community sniffs this movement on the part of the public with the accuracy of a pointer that has found his bird, and they commence to draw the credulous by fictitious prices, now and then unloading to be ready when the relapse comes, to commence anew when another favourable opportunity offers. As the spring comes in, with its delights and young verdure, and cheering early sun-rays, which draw the notes of the lark and the linnet, the disposition becomes more general to disregard those strict lines of prudence which the bleak winds of autumn and the shorter days of an aging year, mark out so prominently for observation. At a period of the year when spring is merging in early summer, with all its pleasant prospects of pleasure to come, it is quite natural to suppose that a desire should arise to make money, by which everything could be made smooth and delightful during the most enjoyable part of the year. Then again, as the half-year wears on, there are the dividends to look forward to, which is always an inducement to buyers; the great cities are filling with pleasure seekers, the import and export trade with foreign climes is in full activity after the liberation of whole fleets of vessels which have lain frozen up in northern parts during the winter. The young corn is beginning to clothe the naked furrow, and the various fruits of the earth are appearing, which only to read and hear of is to fill the eye with a sense of plenty that half converts a Tory Stock Exchange operator into an ultra-radical speculator. Under fairly favourable circumstances, the course of general business during the first half of the year is more active than during the second six months. The Parliamentary session is in full swing, and large numbers of people congregate in the capital towns of all European states to transact business, no small part of which is the investment of their surplus profits in public securities. When a new year is fairly on its legs, say in March, if war or such like causes do not interfere with the natural course of events, between that month and the end of June, a speculator for the rise should find, on an average, his greatest opportunities. In the London market more especially is it so, on account of the effect produced on the money market by the collection of the revenue, which always keeps the Bank of England's reserve at a comparatively higher figure during the period named, a circumstance of considerable importance. In the first half of the year also there is more floating capital spread out, and more disposition to extend credit to catch the profits that are to be gathered when the nations of the earth are enticed into activity and movement, both for business and pleasure, by genial weather and long days.

A speculator should have a good aneroid barometer . . . and he would not be very far wrong if he were to buy and sell according to the indications given by this instrument . . .

As regards some stocks, there will be no need to make a special study of causes which affect the dividend; but this is not the case with railway stocks. A speculator in railway stocks must watch the course of trade, the colonial produce, the Manchester and Liverpool markets, and note the character of the business doing in the great staples of Industry. Upon the profitable nature of these trades depend very much the traffic receipts of railways. A speculator devoting his attention especially to railway stocks will, of course, analyze the reports of the various companies, carefully noting the weekly published traffic receipts. Then, again, there are the northern iron and coal districts, the operations in which affect the price of railway stocks in two ways which are obvious. A speculator who operates solely in railway stocks should be posted from hour to hour in such matters, or he will be assuredly "hung up," as the saying is, with stock on which he has made a loss.

Whether there be any more rise or not left in public securities as a body after the turn of the half-year, — we are speaking from a bull point of view, as that is the way in which the public, in ninety-nine cases out of a hundred, operate, — we should always recommend a speculator to pack up his traps and go right away, whether he has won or lost on balance. If he has lost, which will probably be the case, there is all the more reason for not continuing, for he is as certain then as the day dawns, to increase it by going in heavily, or "plunging," as it is termed. If he retires from the scene, and permits his nerves to recover, he will return to be "cleaned" out in a more wholesome frame of mind, which will enable him finally to quit such haunts without probably resorting to such desperate measures as might have been adopted, had his coffers been emptied all at once under a July sun.

At all events, the most methodical and prudent speculator, who manages to amuse himself, and by extreme care, like good whist players, leaves off at the end of six months about even, would not dispute the wisdom of closing his book when all the world was going away for their holidays.

As the first half of the year is favourable for the bull speculator, so the second half is more likely to favour the operations of the bear. When people have had their outing and spent their money, they return to business, and to think of the necessity of prudently providing the comforts needful in the chilly autumn and cold winter. Business begins to slacken in many important branches with the approach of that period of the year when the days and nights come to be of equal length all over the earth, except just under the pole. There may be a good deal of money about at such periods, and yet very little investment business going on in the stock markets. It should be remembered that large extra accumulations of money at the great centres very often mean, in fact, generally, an unprofitable state of trade; and when the foreign shipments leave no profit, from the great merchant princes down through every link in the chain to the labourer at thirty shillings a week, the effect is felt, and there being no profits, there is obviously nothing in the shape of surplus gain to invest. On the contrary, most people wish to sell. In the later months of the year locomotion for nearly all purposes begins to diminish both as regards business and pleasure, which affects the receipts of the railway companies. If there should have been a bountiful harvest, an important favourable influence may thus be exercised; but even as regards this, it has been evident for many years past that the harvest question in England is of comparatively diminishing importance, and there is every prospect that much of the land now under corn will return by degrees to its primitive state, and will pay better as pasture for fattening beasts.

As we spoke of the Bank of England becoming temporarily rich, by the accumulation of revenue early in the year, so it becomes, as a rule, poor in the autumn. People are getting more used to this ebb and flow in Threadneedle Street, and the trouble it caused when Mr. Lowe first begun experimenting is not now experienced to the same extent; but still it is one of the elements which is disadvantageous, and to be kept in view by the speculator as a regularly recurring adverse influence.

It is, of course, of the last importance to keep a watch over the foreign exchanges, as these are affected more or less at certain periods when the imports and exports of special kinds of produce and manufactures are active.

Other influences which occur with machine-like regularity will be referred to as occasion may require, and we now proceed to go more into detail.

We will take activity among buyers:—It is clear that active buying in any market arises from a strong demand from persons who desire to purchase for reasons known to themselves. A strong *bona fide* demand for securities means that the public is making money, as they do not enter the Stock markets as *bona fide* purchasers, unless they have surplus monies which they desire to invest and put by in the form of savings. Now, a speculator who is watching for an opportunity to buy should keep in view one set of circumstances as favourable to his operations in the same way that a seller should watch for an opposite combination of causes as favourable for speculative sales. A bull speculator should know that his great opportunity occurs after securities generally have been driven down in price by a severe commer-

cial crisis, which has compelled holders of stocks upon a
large scale to realize. In other words, when prosperity is
beginning to revive after a prolonged stagnation, and the
prices of stocks are very low, the bull speculator's great
chance occurs. When the great industries of a nation seem to
rise as from the grave, and where lifelessness and inactivity
ruled before the blows of the hammer resound and the blast
furnace roars, a new life springs through the arteries of the
commercial system, and the result is a rise in public securities. The solid rise in the price of stocks is that caused by the
hard money-buying by a public that is well to do. At such a
time the bull speculator should be in the van, for then the
golden harvest prepared for his special sickle invites the
reaper. Every trade gets its turn to a certainty. We will say,
during a period of prosperity, a general recovery of the
sounder stocks to a level at which they yield on the money
invested 4½ per cent. per annum, takes two years from the
time the advance had fairly set in. During that two years is
the bull speculator's opportunity. If he does not make money
then, he never will. Now we come more to the minutiæ: "Any
jackass can take a profit, but it requires a devilish clever fellow to cut a loss," is a well-worn expression in the city of
London, but there never was a truer one. During the two
years of recovery in prices to which we have referred, there
will be a great number of small periods of time when the bull
speculator should be out of the markets altogether. To decide
when those periods are to be is his *pons asinorum*. After he has
once realized the importance of having his accounts open
ready for the periodical waves to carry him in and land his
profit, the difficulty is to get him to realize the importance of
keeping out while the water sweeps back, carrying with it
the greedy speculators, who were not content to take their
profits.

ROBERT R. PRECHTER
1949–

Robert R. Prechter made his name in the 1980s as a premier caller of market movements—at the end of the decade *Financial News Network* named him one of five masters in the world of finance. And to think, at the start of the prior decade, the 1970s, he was a full-time rock musician. For four years he was a drummer in a rock band—in fact, his band originated the song "Some Guys Have All the Luck," which Rod Stewart later made a hit. During that period, he encountered the writings of Ralph N. Elliott, who believed all human behavior follows a pattern. "Using stock market data as his main research tool," Prechter explained, "Elliott isolated 13 patterns, or waves, that recur in markets." He considers Elliott's work as important to social science as Newton's was to physical sciences.

Finally, Prechter made his way to Wall Street, where he first worked for Merrill Lynch as a technical specialist. Still a devout Elliott follower, Prechter left the corporate scene to start publishing the *Elliot Wave Theorist* monthly newsletter in 1979. Although praised, some critics have equated his techniques with numerology. Regardless, he predicted a major bull market in September 1982, stating that the Dow Jones Industrial Average would increase to five times its current level. As the market continued to climb, he found himself a celebrity on *Good Morning America* and *The Today Show.*

As far as Prechter is concerned, a long bull market is not created by a select group of investors. Rather, it's the result of a positive social mood. His degree in psychology (from Yale, 1971) has certainly lent itself to his style of analysis. When contemplating a market movement, he'll even factor in the music being generated and the hemline length on dresses to gauge the public's mood. For example, in 1989 he thought Guns N' Roses' violent hard-rock album *Appetite for Destruction* and Bobby McFerrin's genial *Don't Worry, Be Happy* suggested dissonance in society, a precursor to a down market. In *Elvis, Frankenstein and Andy Warhol,* Prechter takes a historical look at social trends in dress, music, and art, and equates them to stock market performance. Yes, he says, the stock market imitates art.

Elvis, Frankenstein and
Andy Warhol

Robert R. Prechter

Stock market forecasting is an art. But can art also be used to forecast the stock market?

In fact, yes. For the trend in stock prices is a reflection of popular moods within the investment community and, by extension, within society at large. Right now, for example, certain trends in popular culture point to higher share prices. They indicate, indeed, that we may be on a verge of a full-fledged speculative surge.

Stock market forecasting is an art. But can art also be used to forecast the stock market?

Trends in music, movies, fashion, literature, television, popular philosophy, sports, dance, automobile style, mores, sexual identity, family life, campus activities, politics and poetry, all reflect the prevailing mood of the society. But not all in the same way. Television and movies, for example, tend to reveal broader, more gradual change in sentiment. By contrast, shorter swings in the way people feel can be discerned in fashion, since clothes styles can be adopted or discarded quickly, or popular music, where current hit songs rush up and down the sales charts.

The stock market is an excellent place to study mass behavior because it's unique as a place where specific, detailed and voluminous data exist. The main difficulty in assessing indicators of mood other than stock prices is the woeful lack of precise numerical data. Suppose we had trustworthy numbers on sporting-event attendance. On notes and note changes in popular melodies and the lyrical content of popular songs. On the story content in popular books. On hemline lengths, tie widths, heel heights, the prominence of various fashion and pop art colors. On the angularity vs. roundness of automobile styling. On the construction of various architectural styles. Then suppose all of this data were weighted according to volume of sales.

Why, in that case, we could read charts of the public mood in the same way we read charts of aggregate stock prices. The catch, of course, is that such data are not available. So, consider this article not as a systematically developed theory but, rather, the outline of an idea.

The stock market is an excellent place to study mass behavior because it's unique as a place where specific, detailed and voluminous data exist.

Let's look more closely at the various facets of popular culture as indicators of the collective mood. We'll start with fashion. A correlation has long been observed, at least casually, between the trends of hemlines and stock prices. Skirt heights rose to miniskirt brevity in the 'Twenties and 'Sixties, peaking with stock prices both times. Floor-length fashions appeared in the 'Thirties and 'Seventies (the maxi), bottoming with stock prices. It is not unreasonable to hypothesize that a rise in both hemlines and stock prices reflects a general increase in friskiness and daring among the population; a decline in both, a decrease in those qualities.

Because skirt lengths have limits (the floor and the upper thigh, respectively), the reaching of a limit would imply that a maximum of positive or negative mood had been achieved. The same is true of fashion colors. Bright colors have been associated with market tops and dull, dark colors with bottoms. It is no coincidence, then, that the smaller the skirt or swimsuit, the brighter the color(s); floor-length fashions, in turn, are more associated with dull, dark colors such as brown, black and gray.

A correlation has long been observed, at least casually, between the trends of hemlines and stock prices.

All fashion elements reflect the prevailing popular mood. Tie width, heel height, pants leg style, and flamboyance or conservatism in men's fashions vary according to how people feel. And the same variations in feeling that are expressed in fashion determine trends in the stock market.

In popular art, the late 'Sixties produced Peter Max, who specialized in adorning consumer goods with bright, primary colors, and Andy Warhol, who rose to fame turning out colorful trash-art. Art expressing a light, right, positive mood is dominant when stocks are in bull markets and these characteristics go to extremes at market tops; art expressing a heavy, dark negative mood is in vogue when stocks are suffering bear markets and such art reaches extremes at market bottoms.

In a similar way, movies appear to be linked with trends in the stock market. A single example will serve to illustrate the point. In the early 'Thirties, as the Dow Jones Industrials collapsed, horror movies descended upon the American scene. For some 10 years after that, a period stretching slightly past the stock market of 1942, horror films featured Frankenstein monsters, vampires, werewolves and undead mummies.

As the bull market in stocks resumed in the early 'Forties, Hollywood abandoned dark, foreboding themes in the most sure-fire way: by laughing at them. When Abbott and Costello met Frankenstein, horror went out the door.

The next 25 years treated moviegoers to a varied fare as horror themes were muted. All the while, the bull market in stocks rolled on. Immediately following the speculative bull market peak in December 1968, however, the cinematic mood changed.

How far that change had carried did not become fully clear until 1970, when the flesh-eating zombies of *Night of the Living Dead* began packing them into the movie houses. Just look at the chart of the Dow and you'll see the crash in mood which inspired that movie and desire to see it. Then, in 1974, as the dark mood deepened, *The Texas Chainsaw Massacre* premiered and explicit gore was introduced as a horror movie staple.

Art expressing a light, right, positive mood is dominant when stocks are in bull markets . . .

For its part, pop music has been strikingly in tune with the Dow Jones Industrial Average. The ups and downs of the careers of leading youth-oriented pop musicians have eerily paralleled the peaks and troughs in the stock market. At turns in share prices, the dominant popular singers and groups have faded quickly into obscurity, to be replaced by styles that reflected the newly emerging mood.

The 'Twenties bull market featured jazz and ultimately hyper-fast dance music. The 'Thirties bear years brought hard-time laments and mellow ballroom dance music. With the mid-'Thirties bull market came free-wheeling swing music and the lively jitterbug dance style was introduced. The year 1937 ushered in the Andrews Sisters, who enjoyed their greatest success during the 1937–1942 years of stock market correction ("girl groups" were also popular in 1959–1962, another time the stock market underwent a correction).

Movies appear to be linked with trends in the stock market. . . . In the early 'Thirties, as the Dow Jones Industrials collapsed, horror movies descended upon the American scene.

The early to mid-'Forties featured uptempo big band music, which held sway until the market peaked in 1945–46. A late-1940's stock market correction then unfolded, and mellow love-ballad crooners, both male and female, came into style. Even jazz experienced a dramatic slowdown as "cool jazz" took over in 1949, the year of a major low for stocks.

The post-war bull market's initial advance from 1949 through 1953 was accompanied by the mass appearance of new grassroots-style band music on the charts. During that span, 49 Country and Western music titles sold over a million copies each and "race" music sold strongly enough to require its own sales charts in the industry's trade magazines. By 1954, the emerging excitement of an improving public mood, as reflected by the rising stock market, could no longer be contained. The folk band styles of music began to emerge, and high-energy rock 'n' roll exploded on the scene.

Within a few years, the trendsetters were jitterbugging like crazy to work off their collective emotional high. The energetic, positive sentiment proved only a warm-up for the euphoric joy expressed by the melodic, harmonic music of the "British Invasion" and American fun bands. These groups dominated the charts during the final phase of advance in the Dow Jones Industrials from 1962 to 1966.

The 'Thirties bear years brought hard-time laments and mellow ballroom dance music. With the mid-'Thirties bull market came free-wheeling swing music . . .

Suddenly, in 1966, the Rolling Stones outdid the Beatles in Top 10 hits, with themes of drugs, mental breakdown, crying and deaths; the Stones' final hit of the year was in October. Look at the crash in stock prices from January to October 1966 and see how precisely it reflected the new mass mood. By mid-1966, says Philip Norman in *Shout!*, "The latter-day Mersey [i.e., happy-mood English] groups had all gone home to settle down as pork butchers and damp course engineers." The same thing happened to other happy-music bands who failed to change musical direction: their strings of Top 10 hits were snapped abruptly in 1966.

The public was now looking for something else. It found that something else in more "worldly" lyrics and musical accompaniment increasingly involving "distortion," or noise. Coincidentally, the name for rhythmic popular music changed, from "rock and roll" to just plan "rock," a name that correctly suggested the hardness of the new musical style. "Blues" music, which had fallen from popularity in the early 'Fifties, resurfaced as a dominant style.

The mood mixture in popular music between 1966 and 1969 remarkably reflected the bull market/bear market battle that was raging on Wall Street. The secondary indexes were heading for new highs, but the Dow Industrials, which had made their top in January 1966, were already declining. Meanwhile, rock music became consciously artistic, and flowered in terms of innovation, creativity, subtlety and complexity.

The peace-love sentiments of the psychedelic era coincided with the last hurrah in the stock market, which peaked in a speculative frenzy with new all-time highs in such secondary-stock-dominated indexes as the "Value" Line. A string of "Bubble Gum" hits made the charts, a sickly-sweet extreme in trend if ever there was one. At the same time, the pop music groups and stars who had shaped the topping phase abruptly fell from favor.

As the negative mood developed, slow ballad artists began gaining in popularity. The ballad-buyers felt depressed, while the kids felt angry. Background music for the bear market, which dated from 1966 and accelerated in 1969, increasingly was supplied by bands whose accent was on the negative, stressing themes of war (as opposed to peace), hate (as opposed to love), sex (in place of love songs) and the devil. Heavy metal bands, which had originally been satisfied to present merely a noisy, foreboding sound, adopted a calculated theatrical approach to their recordings and performances, and suggested darkness, sexual ambiguity and general nastiness.

The peace-love sentiments of the psychedelic era coincided with the last hurrah in the stock market . . .

The most extreme musical development of the mid-1970's was punk rock. The lyrics of these compositions, as pointed out by Tom Landess, associate editor of The Southern Partisan, resembled T.S. Eliot's classic poem "The Waste Land." The attendant music was anti-"musical" (i.e., non-melodic, relying on one or two chords and two or three melody notes, screaming vocals, little or no vocal harmony, dissonance and noise). Punk musicians made it a point as artists to be non-musical minimalists and to create ugliness. Their reign ended with the bear market in stocks in the early 1980's.

In short, an "I feel good," "I feel bright," or "I love you" sentiment in art, movies, fashion and music parallels a bull market in stocks. At the extreme, an amorphous euphoric "I feel great and I love everybody" sentiment (such as prevailed in the latter half of the 'Sixties) represents a major top in mood, and coincides with a major top in stocks. Conversely, an "I'm depressed," "I feel dark and dull," or "I'll kill you" sentiment in art, movies, fashion and music reflects a bear market. And an amorphous tortured "I'm in agony and I hate *everybody*" sentiment (apparent in the late 'Seventies) indicated a nadir in mood, and coincides with a major bottom in stocks.

In the early 'Eighties, the negative mood manifestations reached extremes that signaled a major bottom, while positive mood manifestations, one by one, began to emerge. The first evidence of the emerging dominance of positive mood forces was the public's stress on physical self-improvement. In 1980, video spread the drive to shape up. Guess what was popular in that very analogous year, 1920—workout *audio*. This same psychology was reflected in the huge popularity of the film, *Rocky*, which expressed the new mood that "you can succeed if you push yourself to the limit."

The 1982–1983 bull market was accompanied by a nostalgia craze. In fashion, the 'Fifties styles in just about everything reappeared, as did tastes for etiquette, the Boy Scouts, baseball, Disney movies, Ray-Ban sunglasses, macho men, westerns, marriage and babies. In music, the love song once more proved an acceptable, if not dominant, theme for pop hits. Several "supergroups" from the negative mood period, such as The Who and Pink Floyd, played their last concerts and disbanded, while the slow-balled singers vanished from the charts. The heavy metal and punk bands began exhausting themselves under the pressure of the new trend, just as the "fun" bands in 1966 and the "art" bands did in 1969.

After the first major stock market advance peaked in 1983, the 'Fifties craze in music began to wane. The 'Fifties styles, while still in evidence, have since yielded largely to those of the early 1960's, specifically the years 1960–1962; in Wall Street, those were years of transition, moving toward the stock market advance of 1962–1966. In dance and music, the new dominant trends in 1984 were "break dancing" (the 'Eighties equivalent of The Twist, which reigned from 1960 to 1962) and girl singers. What may be important for signaling another mood change is that the dominance of women in pop music appears to have reached an extreme this year. Cyndi Lauper graced the March 4 cover of Newsweek, and on May 27, Madonna made the cover of Time.

Meanwhile, the upbeat love song trend, which began in 1980, is again picking up steam. Bands from the early 'Sixties (such as the Beach Boys) have been touring again. From late 1982 to the present, there have been occasional brief expressions of happy pop music. The message of today's popular music is that the uncertain, corrective phase is nearing its end and that a full-fledged speculative bull market in mood is in the offing.

The 1982–1983 bull market was accompanied by a nostalgia craze.

In films, a fascinating event occurred this month, the release of a movie entitled *Return of the Living Dead*, billed as a spoof of the zombie horror movies. In other words, it's Abbott & Costello meet the Zombies. The power of horror is dying, strongly suggesting that "Halloween Part 17" and "Friday the 13th, Part 32" will never be made. The newest trend in movie themes is that science and brains are not nerdy, but cool. Films such as *Weird Science, My Science Project, Real Genius* and computer-oriented adventure stories coincide with a new desire among the young to run computers and manipulate technology, in stark contrast to the values of the late 'Sixties and 'Seventies. These are all hints that better times lie ahead.

271

In popular art, The Wall Street Journal noted last Tuesday that a sculpture entitled "Tilted Arc," created by an artist whom the Journal describes as specializing in "huge, malevolent, steel outdoor structures," may be removed from downtown Manhattan "in response to popular disgust." At the same time, the city fathers of St. Louis are considering a referendum on removal of a similar sculpture from their downtown area. That sort of thing rarely happens unless a positive mood trend is in force.

As with music, movies and art, trends in fashion have changed. Yet, it is still too early to characterize the fashion trends as typical of a major top. Fashion designers keep trying to re-introduce miniskirts, but as yet, the public hasn't rushed to buy them. Two-piece bathing suits are making a comeback, but skimpy bikinis are still worn only by a minority at the beaches. "Daring colors" are being introduced by some fashion designers, while reactionaries are trying to re-introduce the maxi-skirt.

The bright colors and shorter hemlines should win out. And until extreme styles are featured on the covers of Time and Newsweek, and are seen everywhere at the shopping malls, the bull market will have a ways to go.

PART V

Views from the Inside

The view from the gallery at any one of the exchanges is mind boggling; between the paper flying, the shouting, and the mad rushing about, it's amazing that order is maintained. Not much has changed since 1870, when speculator W. W. Fowler described the market as a "roaring maelstrom." Some 120 years later, Laura Pedersen, an options trader who made $1.5 million before turning 24, paints an equally vivid and wild portrait of life on the floor. She likens it to hand-to-hand combat. The purpose of Part V is not only to depict the life of a trader, but to access the exchange's quiet inner sanctums where profound issues are debated. E. H. H. Simmons, president of the New York Stock Exchange from 1926 to 1930, and Otto Kahn, the J. P. Morgan of his day, present their views on sticky issues such as credibility and public opinion, and, in the process, raise more questions. Charles Merrill and E. A. Pierce answer those questions by offering some practical advice on how to win over the public. By understanding the mind-set of the professional broker and trader and looking at investment from their perspective, investors know where they stand.

W. W. FOWLER
1833–1881

W. W. Fowler's insights into the New York Stock Exchange have proved useful to more than one historian, and he is must reading for any student of the Street. As a speculator operating in the mid-1800s, he rubbed shoulders with the likes of Daniel Drew and Cornelius Vanderbilt. "These men," he said, "are the Nimrods, the mighty hunters of the stock market; they are the large pike in a pond peopled by a smaller scaly tribe." Fowler himself operated according to Charles Darwin's theory of survival of the fittest: "In the battle of life, it is the few strong, determined and favored men who win the prizes. Pre-eminently is this true of Wall Street."

Fowler witnessed the rise of the railroads, which, beginning in the 1840s, powered the stock market. At the start of the 1860s the railroads couldn't have been stronger; Wall Street expected a boom, but then the Civil War broke out. Fowler wrote, "The roar of the cannondale at Fort Sumter speedily dispelled these illusions. In three days, thirteen of the leading stocks dropped an average of twenty percent." After the initial panic, Wall Street realized there was money to be made in war and a bull market ensued. "Wars bring forth generals; and revolutions, statesmen" Fowler said. "Times of financial excitement in the stock-market develop skill and ability in that field and bring forth what are termed *Bull-leaders.*" Half the fun of investing, according to Fowler, was watching the bulls and bears go head-to-head as each tried to control the exchange.

Fowler himself had some experience in those battles. Specifically, he and some friends were bearish on pork, and he personally shorted 1,000 barrels. "We thought pork," he said, "talked pork, handled pork, dreamed of pork, and did everything with it except eat it, because it cost too much." On the other side of the battle line was a group determined to corner pork—and they did, keeping the price inflated. Fowler's takeaway: Short selling was no different than gambling—and, in fact, even the great Drew eventually went bankrupt by being a bear once too often. From his many experiences, Fowler paints a vivid picture of those early days in *The Stock Exchange.*

The Stock Exchange
W. W. Fowler

The tide of humanity that pours down Broadway, is dashed against the bulwarks of Wall Street, and whirled to the eastward, between the mighty walls of granite and sandstone, which line that renowned thoroughfare. Through two mouths, New Street and Broad Street, it is sucked into that seething, whirling, roaring maelstrom — the stock-market. Speaking in the language of the common-place, these two streets are merely avenues in the lower part of the city for the passage of men and loaded wains, and for the transaction of business; but these streets also form the environs of the Stock Exchange, which, as from the focus of a gigantic parabolic reflector, throws a light, more or less lurid, over the whole financial community. That lofty façade on Broad Street, builded as of snowy marble of Paros, "of kingliest masonry," sinks into a modest, two-story brick rear on New Street, emblematical of the stately fortunes which enter that stately front, and issue diminished from that diminished rear.

This is our palace of Aladdin. Here may be found that wonderful lamp which gives speedy and fabulous wealth to him who grasps it. Here also is stabled that remarkable horse, which, on being mounted, often flies away and leaves its rider on a certain desolate island, called Ruin.

The edifice is built to defy the powers of the air and fire —
massively, of stone, iron, brick and glass, with thin veneerings
of wooden floorings; its ruins ages hence may for aught we
know be among those which the coming New Zealander may
gaze upon as he sits on a mound of dust which was once old
Trinity and moralizes on the fall of nations.

---

*The environs of the Stock Exchange . . .
throws a light, more or less lurid, over the
whole financial community.*

A dull sound like the murmur of distant waters greets the
ear as we stand before it. Let us enter between the corinthian
columns through the Broad street door. A deep hall with lofty
ceiling supported by fluted iron pillars, covers the length and
breadth of the ground floor in the form of a letter L. Through
the apertures in the thick walls in front and rear and through
opaque plates of glass from above, streams in a dim, though
not a religious light, by which we can hardly recognize the
faces in a roaring screaming, turbulent crowd. This is the
"Long Room," so-called. To the left, as we enter, is a broad
stair-case with solid-set balusters leading to the upper room,
where the members of this Stock Exchange hold their regular
sessions. Directly in front of us is a heavy railing pierced with
a gateway, where sits the Cerberus of this Hades, whose office
it is to see that none pass inside of this barrier except the members of the Board of Brokers and outsiders who have paid one
hundred dollars for a year's privilege of being spectators of the
purchases and sales, and of giving their orders to buy or sell
on the spot to the Brokers whom they employ. Passing inside
this railing we find ourselves on a marble-paved floor fifty by
fifty, beyond which rises an elevated platform, seventy by
fifty, abutting on the west, on the New Street side. The centre
of this platform is scooped into an elliptical pit graded by a
series of steps encircled by an iron railing, and capable of con-

taining several hundred men, when closely packed. Within this enclosure none are allowed except the brokers. Outside the railing, stand they who have secured this privilege by paying an admission due as already described.

This is our palace of Aladdin. Here may be found that wonderful lamp which gives speedy and fabulous wealth to him who grasps it.

It is a field day on 'Change. Stocks which for weeks have been slowly rising, are now jumping upwards ten per cent. in an hour. The Long Room is like Bedlam broke loose. The pit is jammed with buyers and sellers, brandishing their arms, shrieking with every variety of tone, from the booming basso to the shrill tenore. Wall Street is fully represented this morning. The great Banking and Brokerage firms are on the ground executing their orders and reaping a golden harvest of commissions. Files of sharp-looking, smug fellows are rushing in and out, on the double-quick, holding in their hands pads of paper, on which the latest quotations are recorded; while the telegraph with ceaseless click is flashing the prices to every commercial city in the Union. The speculators both inside and outside are all here. The cunning artificers of "rings" and diggers of "pools," are moving about among the crowd watching the effect of their schemes and cheering on their journeymen. Here is the veteran Drew, the silent Shelton, the busy Woodward and the gladiatorial Morrissey; Tobin of the opalescent eye, Stimpson of the fine Roman nose, and Dick Schell, looking like a jolly punchinello, are all here. The benevolent features of Henry Keep are missing, but the jetty beard of Gould and the blonde locks of the unterrified Fiske, are hard by; as for the "Commodore," he has a heavy hand in this game which he is playing in an office not far away, through the medium of wires.

Nearly all the outsiders have a greater or lesser interest in the course of the market. Some of them stand by the railing that surrounds the pit, others watch the battle afar off, standing between the entrance rail and the door. These outside operators have faces strongly marked by the exciting life they lead. Their features often become set into a fixed expression of anxiety. They gaze at the scale of prices with an apparent apathy, disturbed by the pain of loss or lighted up by the pleasure of gain only for an instant. Some of them seem to wear the waxen mask which grows on the faces of gamblers covering every emotion and rarely dropped except when some keener pang or more intense thrill startles them off their guard.

The Long Room is like Bedlam broke loose. The pit is jammed with buyers and sellers, brandishing their arms, shrieking with every variety of tone . . .

The combat between the bulls and bears commences with light skirmishing. As the day wears away, the solid columns move against each other, under a fire of heavy artillery. The bears begin to give ground and their banners wander in disarray. Suddenly a deafening hubbub breaks out from the pit. New York Central has risen ten per cent. in as many minutes. Some great bear is buying stock to cover his contracts, his followers rush after him and the whole army of bears are soon at work buying in or settling up. The bulls have won the day, and after counting the dead, wounded and missing, and reckoning the spoils and losses, respectively, the armies retreat to their camps, and prepare for new campaigns.

The association known as the New York Stock Exchange, was formed early in the present century. It germinated sixty years ago, in a little clique of stock dealers numbering scarcely a round dozen, who were wont to meet under a sycamore tree, which stood in Wall Street, opposite to the present banking house of Brown, Bros. & Co., and job off small lots of governments or stock in the Manhattan Company, and Bank of New York. In 1816, a permanent organization existed, consisting of twenty-eight members. The names of most of the men composing this coterie linger now only in the memory of the old New Yorkers, or are written on the "dull cold marble" which records in the conventional phrase of olden times, the virtues of these men of 'change. Two of them, A. N. Gifford and Warren Lawton, veterans of a hundred campaigns and survivors of fifty years of the sharp vicissitudes of Wall Street, are, or lately were, still wearing out a green old age.

These outside operators have faces strongly marked by the exciting life they lead. Their features often become set into a fixed expression of anxiety.

As early as 1837, the organization had grown to be a power, but a power for evil rather than good, since it stimulated in the community a thirst for speculation. In that year, too, fell the great banking and brokerage firm of J. L. and S. Josephs, agents of the Rothschilds, and rated at $5,000,000, involving multitudes in a wide-spread ruin. The successors and assigns of the twenty-eight brokers of 1816, have, indeed, fed on strong food, and waxed exceeding great. They number, in 1870, between ten and eleven hundred, and own, or control wealth which is counted by the ten million. The old sycamore has decayed, and fallen beneath the storm, and they meet no longer under the "greenwood tree," though there is a poetic fitness in such a place of meeting for the taurine and ursine herd; but in a marble temple dedicated to Mammon, the God of riches, the ponderous iron doors whereof turn like the Miltonic gates of the celestial city on golden hinges.

EDWARD H. H. SIMMONS
1876–1955

The nephew and namesake of robber baron E. H. Harriman had the unfortunate experience of presiding over the New York Stock Exchange in 1929, the year of the Great Crash. Edward Simmons, a New Jersey native, graduated from Columbia University in 1898, and two years later he bought himself a seat on the New York Stock Exchange. Well respected from the start, he became a governor of the exchange in 1909; he was elected vice-president in 1921; and president in 1926, a position he held until 1930. During his term as president, he championed reform. In particular, Simmons despised "bucket shops," which were gambling saloons that used securities and market fluctuations as a basis for laying bets.

In 1925, he said, "If I could reach all the investors of America—and who is not an investor nowadays?—I would try to impress upon them the menace of the bucket-shop keeper and the security swindler." As Simmons pointed out, the swindler does not use violence like common criminals; however, he said, "His career can be traced by broken hearts and ruined lives. He strikes at the foundation of credit upon which the success of individuals, as well as of the country as a whole, is based." Tragically, Simmons himself was swindled by his good friend Richard Whitney, who followed in his shoes as president of the New York Stock Exchange. Whitney stole money from a number of people to cover bad investments.

After the creation of the Securities and Exchange Commission in 1934 and with internal reform inevitable, the board of the stock exchange decided to rewrite its constitution. A committee of three members, with Simmons named chairman, was appointed to draft and recommend changes. Simmons also strengthened the stock exchange by adding to its physical size, increasing the membership by 275 seats. In a historically significant and somewhat ironic 1926 essay, *The Stock Exchange as a Stabilizing Factor in American Business,* he suggests that the market keeps business affairs in the open and everyone on their toes. Ironic because three years later the market would disintegrate into utter chaos, jump-starting the Great Depression.

The Stock Exchange as a Stabilizing Factor in American Business
Edward H. H. Simmons

When we speak of the New York Stock Exchange as a stabilizing factor in American business, it is necessary to consider not only what the Exchange really is, but also in what business stability really consists. Just now the plea to "stabilize business" is heard on every side but all too few of its advocates ever stop to define very exactly what they mean by "stabilization." Some apparently think that stability in prices consists in continually raising them. Most men, in fact, are human enough to show the maximum enthusiasm over programs for stabilizing business under which they themselves will be likely to profit the most in immediate dollars and cents. On the other hand, it should be obvious that if business stability is to be narrowly defined as a complete lack of change, and an endless perpetuation of existing business conditions, all progress and invention must be ruled out as factors in our future economic well-being. It is therefore apparent that the real virtue of stabilizing any given situation in business depends very largely on circumstances, and should not be entered into without due consideration and analysis. When carried to artificial and extreme lengths, programs for stabilizing business invariably run up against economic laws which in the long run prove insuperable. A century ago a noted philosopher exclaimed "Liberty! What crimes are committed in thy name!" The modern day philosopher might be justified in making the same remark about "stabilization," if some of the pseudo-stabilizing schemes so insistently urged for almost all departments of business, were actually and suddenly put into effect.

Despite all the attempted misuses of plans for stabilizing business, however, everyone recognizes that needless, irrational and unjustified changes in business conditions are almost universally harmful and deplorable. As a matter of fact, the effort to stabilize business is profoundly and vitally presupposed by the very processes of all civilization. On its material side, indeed, civilization might be defined as a process of eliminating or at least minimizing the risks and dangers of daily life. Slowly yet none the less steadily, civilization has lessened the individual's daily risk of physical violence. It has none the less strikingly worked to reduce the risks of sickness and disease. It is little wonder, therefore, that in the sphere of business no less than in the political and medical aspects of life, civilization is more and more incessantly demanding a similar cessation of the preventable risks attendant upon the individual in his economic life.

If business stability is to be narrowly defined as a complete lack of change . . . all progress and invention must be ruled out as factors in our future economic well-being.

While undoubtedly the great popularity of the slogan "Stabilize business" is comparatively recent, the roots of the movement extend far back into history. Consciously or unconsciously, the desire for more dependable and steady economic conditions has prompted progressive legislation, and stimulated the development of sound business methods, for many centuries. But it has only been in the last half-century, when the overwhelming risks of war and disease

282

have come to yield step by step to the onward march of civilization, that mankind has been able to spare time from its preoccupation with the struggle for existence to think about the struggle for a standard of living.

It is in his economic capacity that man provides himself with food, clothing, shelter and amusement. In proportion as the risks of war and disease are mitigated by the progress of civilization, the risks attendant upon his economic life become more and more a claim to his attention and his constructive efforts. It is thus quite probable that the present movement to stabilize business and economic affairs will prove one of the greatest problems of the present century. Genuine achievement in the way of reducing the needless risks of business is, therefore, something more than the neat solution of a merely abstract economic problem. It is an indispensable contribution to the better and fuller flowering of civilization, in even its highest and most spiritual aspects. It makes directly for the more intense and satisfying enjoyment of life, liberty and the pursuit of happiness by all the race.

In its risky and uncertain youth, America had more excuse for constant tumult and fickleness in its business affairs than it has today, when the United States has so obviously attained the fuller powers of economic maturity. Many of us here tonight can recall quite clearly the great business crises which occurred in this country in 1907, in 1914, and again in 1920—all within the last twenty years. Certainly none of us would choose to conduct his business through another crisis of the same kind if he could help it. It is a practically universal feeling on the part of American business men that prompts the common present-day question, "Can catastrophes in trade be actually prevented in the future by stabilizing business—and if so, how?"

Certainly in the vigorous cooperative effort which American business has made since the panic of 1907 to prevent another such occurrence in the future, one of the most important and most constructive accomplishments has been a thorough overhauling of the machinery of American business, and the development of new business institutions and new business practices capable of relieving and mitigating undue and dangerous economic conditions of strain in the future. Although human nature changes very little, nevertheless to a considerable extent the business men of this country have themselves grown wiser, and more anxious to exercise in their own operations an intelligent foresight and an enlightened self-restraint. But what is probably still more important—we have in the past twenty years very greatly improved the ordinary methods by which business is carried on in this country, and very considerably expanded and improved those credit institutions upon which the brunt of a business crisis so heavily and invariably falls.

Should American business be seriously menaced in the future, the Stock Exchange will be found fighting shoulder to shoulder with the Federal Reserve system and other constructive institutions of the land to restore, preserve, and to sustain business prosperity.

The most conspicuous example along just this line has undoubtedly been the development of our splendidly staunch and flexible Federal Reserve banking system. In 1920 the business horizon was once again darkened with thunderclouds, but the storm did not fall—as previously it had in 1907—upon thousands of completely separate and isolated banking institutions without a common leadership, a united purpose, or the tremendous strength which comes from nation-wide cooperation. Instead—and for the first time in the history of American finance—the after-war collapse in 1920 was met resolutely, unitedly and intelligently by our American banks under the leadership of the Federal Reserve system. If today—only six years afterwards—the United States finds itself enjoying an unparalleled prosperity from coast to coast, it is well for us all to remember the efficient and courageous work that the Federal Reserve system performed in the very gloomy years of 1920 and 1921, when pessimistic prophets were not backward in assuring us that America's brief heyday of war prosperity was the last that this generation might see. In these days of our prosperity it is only just and fitting to recall the institutions which, in that time of severe depression, came most powerfully and effectively to the assistance of American business.

Although the fact is not so often recognized, the New York Stock Exchange belongs to this same group of institutions which are particularly useful to the entire American business community during periods of pressure and strain. Based on its own past record, I have no hesitation in saying that should American business be seriously menaced in the future, the Stock Exchange will be found fighting shoulder to shoulder with the Federal Reserve system and other constructive institutions of the land to restore, preserve, and to sustain business prosperity. The New York Stock Exchange was not, of course, created in the last twenty years—it was founded over a century ago. Yet within the past twenty years the Stock Exchange has experienced an expansion in its machinery and a perfection in its technique that have been truly remarkable, and that have rendered it the thoroughly national and democratic financial institution which it is today. But it has not been my purpose to come here tonight so much to praise the Stock Exchange and its operations, as to explain them. Accordingly, I wish to call to your attention some of the principal ways in which the Stock Exchange today serves to render all American business a more constant and stable proposition.

One of the greatest services in behalf of business stability which the New York Stock Exchange performs, lies in the important part it plays in directing investment capital into the particular lines of business where it is needed and can be profitably employed, and diverting it from other business activities where additional capital is neither required nor justified. Economists tell us that business depressions are to a large degree due to a disproportion and maladjustment of capital between the many departments of modern business. Today there are over 1,000 separate stock issues and nearly 1,400 separate corporation bond issues listed on the New York Stock Exchange. Thus a vast panorama of American and even foreign commercial and industrial enterprise is set before the countless thousands of modern investors, with current quotations available on the tape or in the newspapers. More and more the stock market tends to rise and fall by groups of securities rather than as a whole. In a given year, steel securities—let us say—may be dull, while railway securities experience an active and rising market. In a general way, such a development would indicate that more investment capital is needed in railroading but not—for the time being at least—in the steel industry. During every so-called "boom" in the stock market, certain groups of securities will lag behind, while during every stock-market depression certain groups will decline very little. It is the Stock Exchange which brings out these inevitable economic tendencies into the light, which makes them evident to the man in the street, and thereby provides the machinery for a swift and intelligent mobilization of public opinion in regard to the proper direction of the nation's investable funds. The consequence of this perfectly normal and therefore frequently overlooked process is, that American industry more and more is able to avoid a glut of capital in one place and a famine of capital in another. The steady and accurate guidance of investment funds into the different departments of American business is a major stabilizing force in prosperity, and the New York Stock Exchange proves each year a principal factor in facilitating it.

But stabilization, as I have already pointed out, should by no means involve inflexible and unchangeable prices. It is because prices on the Stock Exchange are ever changing, that the Exchange is able to increase the efficiency with which the savings of our people are employed in industry. Any artificial and uneconomic stabilization of Stock Exchange prices would consequently vitiate one of its most important services in the larger stabilization of all American commerce and industry.

Perhaps the most serious menace to stability in the American investment markets is the very old and very widespread problem of fraudulent securities.

A second important contribution to the cause of business stability made by the Stock Exchange is the steadily increasing public knowledge regarding corporate affairs which it facilitates. For many years the Exchange has led the fight for wider and more complete corporate publicity. Recently the listing requirements of the Stock Exchange have been again expanded and particularized, to embrace foreign government bonds as well as domestic and foreign corporations. One does not realize how far we have all progressed in the dissemination of current and accurate information regarding our leading business companies, until he examines the business information available to the average investor 50 or 60 years ago. The old prospectuses of railroad securities back in that period are very illuminating and curious to us now. The investor used to be told how large the new issue was to be, how many miles of track the company operated, and a few other scattered and inconclusive scraps of information. There were no balance sheets and income statements regularly published. There was no regular and dependable information regarding dividends. Anyone who purchased securities on this basis — even when the securities represented the largest and most substantial business companies in this country—had to depend on gossip and blind faith rather than upon analysis or sober business judgment.

But we have not yet by any means reached the end of this constantly growing demand for wider corporate publicity, and the Stock Exchange is still doing all it can to further and assist the movement. There can be little stability in general business without stability of investment conditions, and stable investment is completely dependent upon knowledge and upon facts. An important element in the depressions which we are all desirous of minimizing or avoiding in the future, is the tendency of business in prosperous periods to build up large capital structures out of proportion to future earning power. It is questionable whether public law or private example can ever wholly eliminate this perennial enemy of stable business. But it can be checked and—compared at least with former periods—it is being checked by the more complete and accurate information regarding business companies for which the New York Stock Exchange has so long striven.

Panics in this country have not been due so much to any actual poverty or lack of property, as to a sudden illiquidity or unsalability of property.

Perhaps the most serious menace to stability in the American investment markets is the very old and very widespread problem of fraudulent securities. I do not hesitate to assert that the enormous sums which inexperienced American investors are each year persuaded to pour into worthless and crooked business enterprises is not only a serious drain upon the resources of American business but also a prime factor in hampering and limiting the proper stabilization of our national business conditions. In recent years the New

York Stock Exchange has made a persistent and strenuous attempt to warn the investors of this country against security swindlers, and by close cooperation with government and private fraud-fighting bodies and institutions, to render the prosecution of security frauds more certain, more severe and more effective. Not until this most important task of fighting the security swindler and all his works is actively taken up by business men all over this country, can this constant and serious danger to stable business in this country be effectively eliminated.

For securities . . . represent a surplus, and in consequence the New York Stock Exchange represents a market for the national surplus of wealth.

Probably the most obvious service performed by the Stock Exchange in the interest of business stability consists in the high degree of ready marketability which it lends to the enormous aggregate amount of securities listed upon it. The market value of securities listed on the New York Stock Exchange at the present time totals nearly seventy billions of dollars—a sum approximately a quarter to a fifth of our total national wealth. On the whole, the New York Stock Exchange has been remarkably successful for over a century in this work of maintaining a reliable open market for the leading American securities. In connection with stabilizing business, this main function of the Stock Exchange—to render its listed securities always salable and purchasable—is exceedingly important. In the past, the panics in this country have not been due so much to any actual poverty or lack of property, as to a sudden illiquidity or unsalability of property. Due mainly to the New York Stock Exchange, stocks and bonds have proved the most readily salable commodity that we have. Time and again when raw materials, real estate and even staple merchandise have suddenly proven unsalable, business men have been able to tide themselves over with cash derived from the sale of their securities on the Stock Exchange. It is especially important from the standpoint of national business to have a market of this sort where securities can be speedily sold. For securities, as far as their holder is concerned, represent a surplus, and in consequence the New York Stock Exchange represents a market for the national surplus of wealth. Like all other surpluses, it grows in times of prosperity and is drawn upon in days of adversity. In fact, the same economic forces which cause the upward and downward movements in our individual surplus wealth are responsible for the major upward and downward movements in security prices on the Stock Exchange. It is of course desirable that these alternations between increasing and decreasing our surplus should be attended with as little violence or strain as possible—or, to put the matter in a slightly different way, that the movement of the Stock Exchange security prices should be stabilized. But we must realize at the outset that any program for such an extreme stabilization of security prices as would prevent the full usefulness of our surplus, would be a delusion in the first instance and tremendously harmful to all business in the second. As a prominent financier of the preceding generation used to point out, the only reason for maintaining a surplus is to use it. If American business in times of adversity expects to gain stability for itself by dumping its surplus security investments on the Stock Exchange markets, it must not complain if the prices in these markets experience a considerable fluctuation as a result.

It is important to note that the Stock Exchange performs the same stabilizing services in this regard for banks that it does for individual investors. The banks of this country hold very large amounts of government and corporate bonds, and these are mainly liquid assets because so many of them can be instantly sold upon the Stock Exchange. Just as the stability of general business is largely dependent upon the liquidity of our banking system, so the latter is in turn due to an important degree to the smooth and efficient operation of the securities market. But the Stock Exchange market is essentially democratic. It is open to all investors, large or small, on precisely the same terms. A considerable drop in security prices on the Exchange thus arrays almost automatically the buying power of investors all over the United States behind our listed issues. The work which the Stock Exchange has done in thus arraying and mobilizing the buying power of the American investing public, is consequently a major contribution to the cause of general business stability.

OTTO KAHN
1867–1934

German-born Otto Kahn became the J. P. Morgan of his era as the star partner of the powerful Kuhn, Loeb investment banking house. One colleague described him as "the Lorenzo de Medici of his day . . . with an air of detachment from anything as plebian as money." And this was a man who never completed grammar school and who loved to write essays, poems, and stories. His mother, however, advised that he burn his writings. At 16 he embarked on his banking career as an apprentice in a small bank. His first promotion, he said, was "in recognition of the zeal, energy and accurateness with which I had accomplished the functions of stamplicker." In 1890 he convinced his employer, the Deutsche Bank, to transfer him to its London branch. Three years later, he found himself in New York as an arbitrage clerk for Speyer & Co., an international banking house.

Once in New York, Kahn surveyed the banking scene and discovered that J. P. Morgan and Kuhn, Loeb were the two most powerful firms. He then sought employment at the latter. In 1896 he married a partner's daughter, apparently a tradition in the company for men who wanted to join the firm. There, he joined in the fray as Kuhn, Loeb battled J. P. Morgan for the control of major railroads. The money made from the railroads and his own personal investing made Kahn extremely wealthy. He felt it was his duty to give back to society, and in 1903 he joined the board of the Metropolitan Opera, a pet project. Many a time, a partner at the office would see an opera score opened next to a stock exchange report.

The progressive Kahn was never afraid to say publicly that the government needed to regulate business. That forthrightness soon attracted President Theodore Roosevelt, who began to consult Kahn on fiscal issues. Like Charles Merrill, Kahn promoted better self-regulation and shocked Wall Street from time to time with proposals that would make everyone more honest. In *The New York Stock Exchange and Public Opinion,* he addresses some of those sticky issues, such as moral obligations and the public image of Wall Street.

The New York Stock Exchange and Public Opinion
Otto Kahn

A few weeks ago I went to Washington to contradict, as a voluntary witness before a Committee of Congress, under the solemn obligation of my oath, a gross and wanton calumny which, based upon nothing but anonymous and irresponsible gossip, had been uttered regarding my name.

On my way between New York and Washington, thinking that, once on the stand, I might possibly be asked a number of questions more or less within the general scope of the Committee's enquiry, I indulged in a little mental exercise by putting myself through an imaginary examination.

With your permission, I will state a few of these phantom questions and answers:

SHOULD THE EXCHANGE BE "REGULATED?"

Question:
There is a fairly widespread impression that the functions of the Stock Exchange should be circumscribed and controlled by some governmental authority; that it needs reforming from without. What have you to say on that subject?

Answer:

I need not point out to your Committee the necessity of differentiating between the Stock Exchange as such and those who use the Stock Exchange.

Most of the complaints against the Stock Exchange arise from the action of those outside of its organization and over whose conduct it has no control. At times, no doubt, there have been shortcomings and laxity of methods in the administration of the Stock Exchange just as there have been in every other institution administered by human hands and brains. Some things were, if not approved, at least tolerated in the past which are not in accord with the ethical conception of to-day.

The same thing can be said of almost every other institution, even of Congress. Until a few years ago, for instance, the acceptance of campaign contributions from corporations, the acceptance of railroad passes by Congressmen and Senators were regular practices which did not shock the conscience either of the recipients or of the public. Now they are no longer tolerated by public opinion, and have rightly been made illegal.

Most of the complaints against the Stock Exchange arise from the action of those outside of its organization and over whose conduct it has no control.

Ethical conceptions change; the limits of what is morally permissible are drawn tighter. That is the normal process by which civilization moves forward.

The Stock Exchange never has sought to resist the coming of that more exacting standard. On the contrary, in its own sphere it has ever aimed to advance the standard, and it has shown itself ready and willing to introduce better methods whenever experience showed them to be wise or suggestion showed them to be called for.

In its requirements for admission of securities to quotation, in the publicity of its dealings, in the solvency of its members, in its rules regulating their conduct and the enforcement of such rules, the New York Stock Exchange is at least on a par with any other Stock Exchange in the world, and, in fact, more advanced than almost any other.

The outside market "on the curb" could not exist if it were not for the stringency of the requirements in the interest of the public, which the Stock Exchange imposes in respect of the admission of securities to trading within its walls and jurisdiction.

There is no other Stock Exchange in existence in which the public has that control over the execution of orders, which is given to it by the practice — unique to the New York Stock Exchange — of having every single transaction immediately recorded when made and publicly announced on the ticker and on the daily transaction sheet.

I am familiar with the Stock Exchanges of London, Berlin and Paris, and I have no hesitation in saying that, on the whole, the New York Stock Exchange is the most efficient and best conducted organization of its kind in the world.

The recommendations made by the Commission appointed by Governor Hughes some time ago were immediately adopted in toto by the Stock Exchange. Certain abuses which were shown to have crept into its system several years ago were at once rectified. From time to time other failings will become apparent (there may be some in existence at this very moment which have escaped its attention) as failings become apparent in every institution, and will have to be met and corrected.

I am satisfied that in cases where public opinion or the proper authorities call attention to shortcomings which may be found to exist in the Stock Exchange practice, or where such may be discovered by the governing body or the membership of the Exchange, prompt correction can be safely relied upon.

Sometimes and in some respects, it is true, outside observers may have a clearer vision than those who are qualified by many years of experience, practice and routine.

If there be any measures which can be shown clearly to be conducive toward the better fulfillment of those purposes which the Stock Exchange is created and intended to serve, I am certain that the membership would not permit themselves to be led or influenced by hide-bound Bourbonism, but would welcome such measures, from whatever quarter they may originate.

Sometimes and in some respects, it is true, outside observers may have a clearer vision than those who are qualified by many years of experience, practice and routine.

IS THE EXCHANGE MERELY A PRIVATE INSTITUTION?

Question:
Do I understand you to mean, then, that the Stock Exchange is simply a private institution and as such removed from the control of governmental authorities and of no concern to them?

Answer:
I beg your pardon, but that is not the meaning I intended to convey. While the Stock Exchange is in theory a private institution, it fulfills in fact a public function of great national importance. That function is to afford a free and fair, broad and genuine market for securities and particularly for the tokens of the industrial wealth and enterprise of the country, i. e., stocks and bonds of corporations.

Without such a market, without such a trading and distributing centre, wide and active and enterprising, corporate activity could not exist.

If the Stock Exchange were ever to grow unmindful of the public character of its functions and of its national duty, if through inefficiency or for any other reason it should ever become inadequate or untrustworthy to render to the country the services which constitute its raison d'être, it would not only be the right, but the duty of the authorities, State or Federal, to step in.

While the Stock Exchange is in theory a private institution, it fulfils in fact a public function of great national importance.

But thus far, I fail to know of any valid reasons to make such action called for.

SHORT SELLING — IS IT JUSTIFIABLE?

Question:
You have commenced your first answer with the words, "I need not point out to your Committee." That is a complimentary assumption, but I don't mind telling you that we here are very little acquainted with the working of the Stock Exchange or the affairs of you Wall Street men in general. What about short selling?

Answer:
I do not mean to take a "holier than thou" attitude, but personally, I never have sold a share of stock short. Short sellers are born, not made. But if there were not people born who sell short, they would almost have to be invented.

Short selling has a legitimate place in the scheme of things economic. It acts as a check on undue optimism, it tends to counteract the danger of an upward runaway market, it supplies a sustaining force in a heavily declining market at times of unexpected shock or panic. It is a valuable element in preventing extremes of advance and decline.

The short seller contracts to deliver at a certain price a certain quantity of stocks which he does not own at the time, but which he expects the course of the market to permit him to buy at a profit. In its essence that is not very different from what every contractor and merchant does when in the usual course of business he undertakes to complete a job or to deliver goods without having first secured all of the materials entering into the work or the merchandise.

Short selling has a legitimate place in the scheme of things economic.

The practice of short selling has been sanctioned by economists from the first Napoleon's Minister of Finance to Horace White in our day. While at various times laws have been enacted to prohibit that operation, it is a noteworthy fact that in every instance I know of, these laws have been repealed after a short experience of their effects.

I am informed on good authority—though I cannot personally vouch for the correctness of the information—that there is no short selling on one nowadays fairly independent Stock Exchange, that of Tokyo, Japan. You will have seen in the papers that when President Wilson's peace message (or was it the German Chancellor's peace speech?) became known in Tokyo, the Stock Exchange there was thrown into a panic of such violence that it had to close its doors. It attempted to reopen a few days later, but after a short while of trading was again compelled to suspend.

Assuming my information to be correct, we observe here an illuminating instance of cause and effect.

Short selling does become a wrong when and to the extent that the methods and intent of the short seller are wrong. The short seller who goes about like a raging lion (or "bear") seeking whom he may devour; he who deliberately smashes values by dint of manipulation or artificially intensified selling amounting in effect to manipulation, or by causing alarm through spreading untrue reports or unverified rumors of a disturbing character, does wrong and ought to be punished.

Perhaps the Stock Exchange authorities are not always alert enough and thorough enough in running down and punishing deliberate wreckers of values and spreaders of evil omen. Perhaps there is not enough energy and determination in dealing with the grave and dangerous evil of rumor mongering on the Stock Exchange and in brokers' offices. I need hardly add that the practices to which I have referred are quite as wrong and punishable when they aim at and are applied to the artificial boosting of prices as when the object is the artificial depression of prices.

But after all, as the present investigation shows, even Congress, with the machinery of almost unlimited power at its hand, does not always seem to find it quite easy to hunt the wicked rumor-mongers to their lairs and subject them to adequate punishment. Yet the unwarranted assailing of a man's good name is a more grievous and heinous offence than the assailing, by dint even of false reports, of the market prices of his possessions.

Does the Public Get "Fleeced"?

Question:
We hear or read from time to time about the public being fleeced. There is a good deal of smoke. Isn't there some fire?

Answer:

If people do get "fleeced," the fault lies mainly with outside promoters or unscrupulous financiers, over whom the Stock Exchange has no effective control. Some people imagine themselves "fleeced," when the real trouble was their own "get-rich-quick" greed in buying highly speculative or unsound securities, or having gone into the market beyond their depth, or when they have exercised poor judgment as to the time of buying and selling. Against these causes I know of no effective remedy, just as there is no way to prevent a man from overeating or eating what is bad for him.

In saying this, I do not mean to imply that stockbrokers have not a duty in the premises. On the contrary, they have a very distinct and comprehensive duty toward their clients, especially those less familiar with stock market and financial affairs, and toward the public at large. And they have furthermore the duty to abstain from tempting or unduly encouraging people to speculate on margin, especially people of limited means, and from accepting or continuing accounts which are not amply protected by margin.

In respect of the latter requirement, the Stock Exchange rightly increased the stringency of its rules some years ago, and it cannot too sternly set its face against an infringement of those rules or too vigilantly guard against their evasion.

Against unscrupulous promotion and financiering a remedy might be found in a law which should forbid any public dealing in any industrial security (for railroad and public service securities the existing commissions afford ample protection to the public) unless its introduction is accompanied by a prospectus setting forth every material detail about the company concerned and the security offered, such prospectus to be signed by persons who are to be held responsible at law for any willful omission or misstatement therein.

Such a law would be analogous in its purpose and function to the Pure Food Law. If it went beyond that purpose and function it would be apt to overshoot the mark. The Pure Food Law does not pretend to prescribe how much a man should eat, when he should eat or what is good or bad for him to eat, but it does prescribe that the ingredients of what is sold to him as food must be honestly and publicly stated. The same principle should prevail in the matter of the offering and sale of securities.

If people do get "fleeced," the fault lies mainly with outside promoters or unscrupulous financiers, over whom the Stock Exchange has no effective control.

If a drug contains water, the quantity or proportion must be shown on the label, so that a man cannot sell you a bottle filled with water when you think you are buying a tonic. In the same way the proportion of water in a stock issue should be plainly and publicly shown.

The purchaser should not be permitted to be under the impression that he is buying a share in tangible assets when, as a matter of fact, he is buying expectations, earning capacity or goodwill. These may be, and often are, very valuable elements, but the purchaser ought to be enabled to judge as to that with the facts plainly and clearly before him.

The main evil of watered stock lies not in the presence of water, but in the concealment or coloring of that liquid. Notwithstanding the unenviable reputation which the popular view attaches to watered stock, there are distinctly two sides to that question, always provided that the strictest and fullest publicity is given to all pertinent facts concerning the creation and nature of the stock.

Do "Big Men" Put the Market Up or Down?

Question:
Is it not a fact that some of the "big men" get together from time to time and determine to put the market up or down so as to catch profits going and coming?

Answer:
As to "big men" meeting to determine the course of the stock market, that is one of those legends and superstitions hard to kill, inherited from olden days many years ago when conditions were totally different from what they are now, and when the scale of things and morals, too, was different.

The fluctuations of the stock market represent the views, the judgment and the conditions of many thousands of people all over the country, and indeed, in normal times, all over the world.

The current which sends market prices up or down is far stronger than any man or combination of men. It would sweep any man or men aside like driftwood if they stood in its way or attempted to deflect it.

True, men sometimes discern the approach of that current from afar off and back their judgment singly, or a few of them together, as to its time and effect. They may hasten a little the advent of that current, they may a little intensify its effect, but they have not the power to either unloosen it or stop it.

If by the term "big men" you mean bankers, let me add that a genuine banker has very little time and, generally speaking, equally little inclination to speculate, and that his very training and occupation unfit him to be a successful speculator.

The banker's training is to judge intrinsic values, his outlook must be broad and comprehensive, his plans must take account of the longer future. The speculator's business is to discern and take advantage of immediate situations, his outlook is for tomorrow, or anyhow for the early future; he must indeed be able at times to disregard intrinsic values.

The temperamental and mental qualifications of the banker and the speculator are fundamentally conflicting and it hardly ever happens that these qualifications are successfully combined in one and the same person. The banker as a stock market factor is vastly and strangely overestimated, even by the Stock Exchange fraternity itself.

The current which sends market prices up or down is far stronger than any man or combination of men.

May I add that a sharp line of demarcation exists between the speculator and the gambler? The former has a useful and probably a necessary function, the latter is a parasite and a nuisance. He is only tolerated because no means have been found thus far to abolish him without at the same time doing damage to elements the preservation of which is of greater importance than the obliteration of the gambler.

Charles Merrill's lasting legacy is that he brought Wall Street to Main Street, doing for the stock exchange what Henry Ford did for the automobile industry—making it something for the common man. It was, however, a long journey from his birthplace in Florida. Although his father was a prosperous country doctor, Merrill helped pay his tuition at Amherst College in Massachusetts by waiting tables and selling mail-order clothes. After college, he returned to Florida and played semipro baseball. Eventually, he took a job with a New York investment brokerage firm and became the head of its bond department. Merrill founded his own company in 1914, and not long after formed a partnership with Edmund C. Lynch.

As for the individual investor, his advice was simple: "Invest little by little, and not just in stocks—in a house and furniture, too. That way, your investment will grow just as surely as American business has grown." The dream of making Wall Street accessible to the common man was still years away. In the interim, Merrill semiretired in 1929 after the crash, but returned full-time in 1938 with a new partnership, Merrill Lynch Pierce Fenner & Beane (E. A. Pierce had taken over Merrill's brokerage business in 1930). Finally, in 1941, Merrill set out to realize his dream.

To win the public's confidence, he started paying his brokers salaries instead of commissions; he instituted a training program to mold his people into financial advisors, as opposed to fast-talking salespeople; and his firm always made public disclosures about the partner's activities and holdings. Advertising was also key: He wanted to educate the public, and his ads often read like textbook essays. Merrill's partner, E. A. Pierce, shared his vision and was a progressive thinker when it came to reforming Wall Street and promoting better self-regulation. He even encouraged "rapprochement" with the government, which won him a number of enemies on the stock exchange. In *A Declaration of Policy,* a crucial letter sent to partners and managers in 1940, the two men outline their strategy for taking Wall Street to Main Street and answer concerns raised by Otto Kahn almost 30 years earlier.

A Declaration of Policy
Charles E. Merrill and E. A. Pierce

To Partners and Managers:

We are glad to be able, at last, to write you in some detail about this new firm of ours.

We think you will want to know more about what led to the consolidation of the three companies—E. A. Pierce & Co., Cassatt & Co., Incorporated, and Merrill, Lynch & Co., Inc.—and you will want to know where we go from here.

The first part of the story is simple. It deals with problems with which we are unfortunately all too familiar—problems of general business depression from which our industry has not even begun to recover. In the security business, as in others, the collapse shook our houses beneath us.

SECURITY BUSINESS PERFORMS
AN ESSENTIAL SERVICE

During the past few years we have been trying to readjust ourselves. Some of us have been a little slow in realizing that the readjustment has to be permanent, and a few doubt the possibilities of any successful readjustment. Nevertheless, we are convinced that the buying and selling of stocks, bonds, and other evidences of liens and ownerships, is a fundamental business which performs an essential service.

That there is no lack of opportunity for us is demonstrated by the fact that even last year the volume of stocks and bonds bought and sold was more than thirteen billion dollars. Essentially the job before us involves adapting our operations so that expenses will be in ratio to existing minimum standards of gross income; and then increasing the gross income by adapting our policies to meet the standards and requirements of our customers and public opinion. The sooner we recognize that the temper of living may never again be identical with what it was twelve or fifteen years ago, the sooner we shall gear ourselves for success under present and future conditions.

ALL MUST JOIN TO REESTABLISH FAITH

We've got a job to do—we in the security business—a job of reestablishing faith in the security market as a place for sound investment. This job ought to be done by everybody in the business, and we think in time will be. But we are not going to wait for someone else to start it. We're no smarter, or better, than our competitors, and we have no thought whatever of driving anyone out of business. But we do recognize certain fundamental facts that have to be coped with by our business in its relations with the public, and we're going to make a beginning.

We will be delighted to have the cooperation of anyone and everyone else who sees the road ahead as we think we see it. There will be no secrets in our plans or operations. What is true of our needs, we consider to be equally true of others having a direct or indirect stake in the business—our competitors, banks, insurance companies, etc. So it will be our purpose to cooperate with everyone who wants to bend his energies and direct his thinking toward the big job of saving the security business as a whole, and saving ourselves in the process.

We've got a job to do — we in the security business — a job of reestablishing faith in the security market as a place for sound investment.

LET'S ELIMINATE UNNECESSARY FRILLS

As we see it, our firm has two important things to do:

One is to get our location expenses under control. Let's get rid of any and all frills which do not make a direct contribution to the fundamental requirements of our customers. For instance, 85% of our customers do most of their business with us over the telephone. They do not need or want elaborate offices. They want simplicity, competent man power, and good, impartial service.

Which brings us to our second objective. We have developed what we consider a sound program of policies, to be put into effect when this merger becomes a reality at the end of this week.

OUR SUCCESS DEPENDS ON SERVICE TO PUBLIC

These policies rest on a conviction — not always uppermost in our minds, we'll grant you — that in order to win success we business men have to put the public's interest first. The customer may not always be right, but he has rights, and upon our recognition of his rights and our desire to satisfy them, rests our chance to succeed.

It's not banal poppycock to say today that we've got to succeed through the service we can render the investing public. And it's only looking facts in the face to say that a legitimate, honest service is the only justification for success.

We think the public is still ready and willing to invest in securities, through brokers and the exchanges. We have been having some surveys made which, along with the surveys made by the New York Stock Exchange, have turned up some disturbing—and encouraging—facts.

The customer may not always be right, but he has rights, and upon our recognition of his rights and our desire to satisfy them, rests our chance to succeed.

Disturbing is the large percentage of potential investors and speculators in securities who are suspicious of the motives and operations of the security business and the people engaged therein. You and we know the reasons for this lack of confidence and we know that it won't be eliminated until we convince the public that our house is now in order.

CONFIDENCE, IN THE MAIN, IS ON THE INCREASE

Encouraging is the even larger percentage of people who now generally express confidence in our business, but also have definite ideas about how we should continue to operate it to retain that confidence.

Our plan is based on our appraisal of what our firms ought to do to meet this situation. If we do the best we can, and if we have properly adjudged what the investing public wants, our plan will succeed.

Here are the ideas which we have developed, and have incorporated in a statement of policy which starts out by saying:

> Policies and services of Merrill Lynch, E. A. Pierce & Cassatt were formulated in a spirit of enlightened self-interest. While based on the conviction that they constitute an important advance in both facilities and protection for the investor and speculator, they represent primarily the kind of a brokerage service that we believe will have the greatest chance for enduring success. It is our opinion, as well, that the customer is entitled to this modernized form of brokerage service.

Financial Stability as the Keystone

The first specific matter set forth in this statement has to do with financial stability, the keystone of our entire operation. We consider that since the firm carries free credit balances of customers, acts as custodian of their securities, functions as pledgee and finances margin transactions, it incurs in those financial relationships a responsibility to its clients which involves not only the maintenance of a high degree of financial stability at all times, but the added duty of supplying the trading public a clear picture of the firm's condition.

To meet the first, the firm will at all times maintain a working capital position well in excess of the requirements of the New York Stock Exchange.

The second objective will be attained by the issuance of a complete financial statement, in a form designed for maximum clarity and understanding.

Now in the matter of departmental policy: we operate a brokerage business in securities and commodities, and also underwrite and distribute securities.

But these are two distinct businesses, with entirely separate functions. No conditions will be permitted which might create conflicts affecting the interests of our several types of customers.

To Help Our Customers Appraise the Possibility of Bias

In practically all transactions for account of customers the firm will act only as a commission broker. However, in transactions involving securities in which the firm acts as principal dealer, the customer will be notified in advance.

When supplying informative analytical printed reports concerning a security in which the firm is not acting as principal, the firm intends to indicate in such reports the extent of the aggregate direct and indirect ownership of such security as of the date of the report by the firm and its general partners. Such information will be given as follows: if the aggregate value of such holdings is less than $50,000, it will be described as a "small interest"; if between $50,000 and $100,000, it will be described as a "substantial interest"; if over $100,000, it will be described as a "large interest." The purpose of such disclosure is to help the customer estimate the possibility and extent of bias on the part of the firm in its presentation of facts relating to a particular security.

This has been a general objective of brokers during recent years, but we intend to test this specific practical application as a part of our plans for the year 1940.

Pledge Aid for Still Further Protection

You may be interested in knowing how your senior partners feel about the SEC. We'll tell you. We are in full accord with the fundamental purpose of the Securities and Exchange laws—to give the investor adequate information, and to prohibit manipulation and fraud—and we pledge to our customers a complete cooperation with all future efforts designed to strengthen further these fundamental purposes.

No regulations or policies, however, can pretend to guarantee profits nor insure against loss. But we believe our customers can confidently use the Exchanges for investment and speculation with assurance that there are no stacked cards.

OUR RESEARCH DEPARTMENT WILL STICK TO FACTS—CLEARLY PRESENTED

Now as to the question of advising the customer on his investments: we don't believe we can run a brokerage firm and be a good investment counsel at the same time. All that we will have to sell is service and facts. Therefore, we are going to do a little research work on our research department. We don't think there has been anything the matter with our research work, but we want to see that it makes the fullest possible use of all available data, puts that data into the clearest possible form, and then lets the facts speak for themselves. In other words, we are going to provide facts, ungarnished with advice. Advice is going to be out—unless it is specifically asked for, and then only with the approval of one of our partners or managers.

RUMORS AND "HOT TIPS" ARE TABOO

Let's take a look at our registered representatives, or customers' men. They are going to represent an important phase of our new job, principally because we think we are going to make it possible for them to operate on a different and sounder basis than in the past. One of the troubles in our business has been a potential conflict in interest between the customer and the customer's man, created by compensation practices which we believe were wrong. We're going to minimize, perhaps even eliminate, that potential conflict of interest.

Between ourselves, we think the best name for these men is service representatives, because it best expresses what we would like them to be in our organization. We think that by serving the customer's interest exclusive of all other considerations, the service representatives will really be doing the best job of serving their own interest, as well as that of the firm. To accomplish this purpose, they will assist their customers in getting all desired factual data; they will offer no advice as to the purchase or sale of securities or commodities except under restrictions we mentioned a few paragraphs back; they will circulate no rumors, "confidential suggestions," or "hot tips" designed to influence purchases or sales.

CUSTOMERS TO SAY WHAT SERVICE THEY WANT

Our customers themselves will determine the extent to which they want service. They will be asked to fill out a questionnaire stating exactly the type of service they desire. Representatives will then confine their activities strictly within the limits so outlined.

In order to make this policy genuinely workable, we propose to relate the salaries of our representatives primarily to the quality of service rendered to our clients. Their value will be judged largely by the degree of success with which they satisfy customers, and thus attract more customers. This, in our opinion, also represents the only sound way for our representatives to increase their earning power.

This whole policy means that we believe our best chance for increasing our business lies in constructively building the whole business, rather than by permitting conditions which indirectly create pressures to increase the trading of present customers.

We propose to relate the salaries of our representatives primarily to the quality of service rendered to our clients.

In order that partners and managers may contribute as much as possible to the operation of this new impartial service, we plan to release them to a large extent from routine duties, so that their services may be at the disposal of any trader, large or small, who may require their expert knowledge or skilled assistance.

ON PANIC DAYS OUR REGULAR CUSTOMERS COME FIRST

It is when transactions jump from an average day to several million shares a day that your broker's facilities must meet the test of emergency. And it is on these days that the customer requires top service to protect or establish his position.

We therefore offer the following unconditional guarantee of service in emergencies: no new accounts will be opened in any day when the volume of trading at any time indicates that the facilities of the firm may be over-taxed.

Although Merrill Lynch, E. A. Pierce & Cassatt has created one of the fastest and most accurate transmission systems for the execution of orders, we recognize that mistakes or delays can still happen. Where errors are due directly to the firm's personnel, or to any other factor under our control, we shall of course make the proper adjustments. In all other cases, effort will be made to expedite settlement through the regular processes established by the New York Stock Exchange. We trust that occasions for such adjustments will be infrequent. The matter is mentioned here only because where man and equipment are involved, there is always a chance of error.

We believe we have a sound program, but it is not enough to develop and execute a sound program. The people must know about it. That's why we are going to so some advertising.

SECURITY BUSINESS IMPORTANT
TO OUR WHOLE PEOPLE

In closing, we'd like to express our unshakable confidence in the future of our country, in the basic soundness of our type of economy—capitalism—and in the essential place that the security business has in that economy. We consider that the security business contributes more than most people realize to the development and the welfare of our whole people. It brings together those who need funds for industrial development and those who have funds to invest. It provides money for businesses to build new factories, buy new machines, finance new production, create and maintain employment.

The security business provides money for government to support public institutions and develop civic projects. It puts savings to work, gives literally millions of people a part-interest in business, and thus contributes to our economic progress.

It is estimated that between six and ten million Americans own bonds, between nine and eleven million own stocks. Fifty million of us own life insurance policies, a large portion of whose assets are invested in securities as a protection to the insured. More than thirteen million of us have savings in mutual savings banks, and twenty-six million have deposits in national and state banks and trust companies, where their money is invested in securities to bring them interest. Hundreds of private schools and colleges, hospitals, and other institutions are supported by security endowments and funds invested in securities.

Our Job Is to Make American Economy Work

Without the security market our whole system would collapse, or be radically altered along the lines of some of the European governments. We don't think we are prejudiced in our opinion that the American system of economy is as good as any yet devised by man—and we mean from the standpoint of the people as a whole, not just the privileged few.

It's our job to make that system work, to continue to improve it along lines already established by the government and by our own voluntary efforts. It's our job to see the other fellow's point of view and to reconcile our interests with his. It's our job to move forward with whatever capacities we may have—moral, mental, financial—to the end that our country may progress and that we ourselves may earn the rewards of intelligent effort, honestly applied.

We think that together we can contribute something worthwhile to our personal and the public welfare.

MICHAEL H. STEINHARDT

Michael Steinhardt is recognized as one of the premier investors of his time. At the time of his announced retirement in 1995, the average annual return for his funds was about 24 percent. Another way to look at it: A dollar invested with him at inception was worth $462 in 1995 versus $17 for the same investment in the Standard & Poor's 500 stocks. Raised in Brooklyn, where his father was a jeweler, Steinhardt first became interested in stocks when he was given some shares as a bar mitzvah present. Not long after, he started stopping by the local Merrill Lynch branch to check his investments and to use that capital to make more purchases. After graduating high school at 16, Steinhardt went to the University of Pennsylvania's Wharton School, where he completed his undergraduate program in three years. From there he went to his favorite place: Wall Street.

At age 26, he founded his own firm with two friends and $7.7 million in capital. From his years on the street, Steinhardt has blunt advice for part-time investors: "It's essential they be aware that they are at a competitive disadvantage—in terms of education, experience, and quality of information." It's not a game, he said. Consider his attitude: "I'm very committed and tense, and I'm not a good loser." And the evidence was on his desk: a number of computers and telephones (at one time he had direct connections to 75 trading rooms). To ease the pressure, Steinhardt took a year off in 1978 "to experience other areas of life."

Fortunately, operating hedge funds has given him more freedom to be creative with investments because they are less regulated than mutual funds. Also, because hedge funds are limited partnerships of 99 partners who fork over a minimum of $1 million to get in the game, not only does he have a seriously committed investor to work for, but he can indulge in shorting and other tricks of the trade that mutual fund managers cannot. In a given year, his portfolio might turn over 17 times versus about 1 for a standard equity mutual fund. The formula behind his actions is divulged in *Investing, Hedge-Fund Style,* in which Steinhardt readily admits that hedge funds have been associated with the "go-go type."

Investing, Hedge-fund Style
Michael H. Steinhardt

Steinhardt Partners began in the euphoric period of the late 1960s, reflecting in some sense the speculative nature of those times. It was one of many "hedge funds"—an emotionally charged term at that time. The term was used to describe go-go type, speculative entities, mostly employing a partnership structure that typically dealt in speculative stocks and had the flexibility to use leverage and execute short sales. In some respects, we, at that time, typified the character of such entities. I am somewhat embarrassed to say that the single stock in which we have made the most money (to this day) was a company that went bankrupt within several years after our ownership of it—King Resources.

Over the years, most hedge funds have either disappeared, diminished in size, or adopted the more traditional forms of investment management. But although there have been fairly substantial changes in the personnel at Steinhardt Partners over the years, and our investment style at any point in time is often reflective of the "game in town," there has been and continues to be a consistency in the broad investment approach, as well as the basic structure of the firm. Those characteristics that I think are distinct to our type of investment management are outlined below. There are nine areas that I think are important.

SIZE

In striving for a superior investment result, I believe that, as a generality, there is a clear diseconomy of scale. In some respects this is obvious. The more dollars you manage beyond a certain point, the more difficult it is to achieve a substantial variance from market averages. More importantly, I find there is simply a mental limitation as to the number of truly quality ideas one can come up with in any time frame. Whatever diseconomy of scale there is tends to show up most obviously in periods when one's judgment is wrong. Sometimes it seems that when you're right, the sky's the limit in terms of size. But when you are wrong in your market exposure or individual stock selection, your ability to adjust positions and market portfolios is distinctly related to the size in which you deal. This holds true not only for liquidity but, more importantly, for mental flexibility.

Obviously, there is no ideal size: one's style is a key factor. I would think an amount perhaps less than double what we presently manage would begin to restrict our ability distinctly. I guess the moral of the story is *don't be wrong*.

FLEXIBILITY

Our firm is structured so that we can be both long stocks and short stocks. We can use options and futures. We can use leverage in stocks to the extent of the Federal Reserve Board margin requirements. We trade fixed-income securities and we may use leverage. (Our performance in the first nine months of fiscal 1982 was almost entirely due to a leveraged position in intermediate Treasury notes.) In addition, we can concentrate our security holdings to a substantial degree and are relatively insensitive to the thought of diversification.

The flexibility inherent in our structure can create enormous variance in our performance relative to market averages. It places great emphasis on judgment and frees one's mind from the normal encumbrances that often exist in institutional money management. It probably makes one grow a little older, a little sooner, too.

RISK

We use a somewhat superficial measure in determining our overall exposure, which we call our "risk factor." This is simply the relationship between the total dollars on our long side and the total dollars on our short side in relation to our capital. While a typical institution can vary its market exposure between 100 per cent and zero, our risk factor can, at least in theory, vary from plus 200 per cent to minus 200 per cent (in view of current Federal Reserve margin requirements).

This approach to risk measurement does not deal with individual stock volatility or stock selections *per se*. But it does create a much broader framework for dealing with market exposure. We have at various times been "net short," which means having more dollars on the short side than the long side. I view our approach as *conservative* relative to most institutions whose market exposure is relatively or even extremely inflexible. Over the 15 years of the firm's existence, our exposure on average has been less than 50 per cent of capital; put another way, less than 50 per cent of the firm's capital has been net long exposed to the market on average.

SELLING SHORT

Selling short conjures up all sorts of pejorative implications; it sometimes feels unpatriotic. It is psychologically unnerving and takes a greater degree of discipline than that needed in buying stocks. The cliché about being able to make only 100 per cent on the short side, while the sky's the limit on the long side, sometimes lurks in the background.

The criteria for a good short sale are in some sense the reverse of the criteria for a good buy—deteriorating fundamentals, substantial premium to book, high multiple, low yield. Having said all that, I must admit that the short side of the firm's portfolio often looks like "Who's Who in Corporate America." We pay great attention to relative price action and, therefore, often find ourselves shorting the strongest stocks—the institutional favorites. At the least, this approach is not conducive to a tranquil lifestyle.

TURNOVER AND TRADING

In terms of relative turnover, ours is simply "off the page." We manage about $185 million and, although we do not pay high commission rates, we have generated approximately $15 million a year in commissions. At times, in attempting to justify what seems like frenetic activity, I've thought about a theory of circularity: If you're a major brokerage client, you receive the best research call, the greatest liquidity and the largest underwriting allotments; thus there is a greater comfort in responding to nuance, in making judgments based upon incomplete data—which is in a real sense what this business is about.

Selling short . . . is psychologically unnerving and takes a greater degree of discipline than that needed in buying stocks.

Moreover, via active trading you achieve a feel for the market that cannot be attained in any other way. Along these lines, our traders exercise substantial discretion and, since I've often been on the desk myself, I like to think some intellectual quality, relative to the competition.

When all is said and done, I admit to some uncertainty about the utility of all this activity. Somehow, I think it is a relevant part of the process—at least for us.

RESEARCH AND LONG-TERM INVESTING

Internally, we currently have three people who devote their full efforts to industry and individual stock research. They are highly knowledgeable on a variety of industries and spend considerable time visiting managements and attending seminars in an effort to become truly intellectually competitive. Over a one-year period we deal with 70 to 80 brokerage firms, most of which provide us with some sort of research service.

The great thrust of our efforts is to obtain a long-term understanding of what's happening in both a micro and macro sense. Sometimes this translates into longer-term holdings and concentration in various stocks and industry groups. Often, however, the results of this work are used in making transactions that are of short-term duration. This may occur when a long-term development has an exaggerated short-term impact, or when for market timing considerations we adjust our portfolio to reflect a changed view on market direction.

MARKET TIMING AND STOCK SELECTION

I suspect that over the years we have had substantially fewer "doubles and triples" in our stock portfolio than other investment entities that have had but a fraction of our historical rate of gain. Perhaps because of our emphasis upon market timing, our relative stock selection has probably been no better than average. On the other hand, there has been a terrific relationship between our largest size positions and their success, perhaps reflecting our ability to relate our own level of confidence to ultimate market performance.

There is no doubt that great emphasis is placed on market timing. Here there is no magic formula. Like our competitors, we pay a great deal of attention to broader economic variables, including interest rates. At this time, we have a large long position in intermediate bonds while being net short in the stock market. We believe this creates a natural hedge, but we really hope to make money from both ends of the portfolio. This may seem simplistic, but I think that substantially lower interest rates are a necessary precondition for an important stock market gain. Much of our portfolio rationale flows from that concept, and we translate it both in broader terms as well as in individual stock selections, long and short. We tend to be long higher-quality, high-yielding stocks now, and we are short "growth" type stocks that are, or we think will be, suffering from cyclical downturn. We tend to trade very actively on the short side, with the view that an 800 or so Dow will prove a major buying area in the not-too-distant future, and therefore one should be nimble.

COMPENSATION

With some minor variations on the theme, compensation to the general partners of the firm, and to a great degree to the important employees of the firm, is based exclusively on the firm's investment performance in each year. Basically, we receive 20 per cent of the net profits. If there are no profits, the general partners are paid nothing—no salary, no fee, nothing. This is on an absolute basis; even if being flat for the year is a good relative result, there is no compensation.

It's hard to judge how, if at all, this compensation structure impacts the longer-term performance of the firm. It does, however, tend to create an intensity and commitment that I believe to be very positive. For better or worse, it further reinforces the short-term focus, particularly because of the annual measurement.

CONGRUENCE WITH INVESTOR INTEREST

Perhaps most importantly, the compensation structure gives everyone—those working at the firm, those investing with the firm and those dealing with the firm in the brokerage area, a single-mindedness that I think is a terrific virtue. There are no cosmetics. The numbers both on individual transactions and annual performance must speak for themselves.

No decision-maker in the firm invests in equities on his own, except through the funds. The capital of the general partners is handled precisely the same as that of the limited partners or investors. There is no regular marketing effort, for the rewards and the growth of assets are achieved via performance. When it works, all this leads to a wonderful and exciting environment.

The goal is simple—the greatest capital growth consistent with risk. This goal is our single-minded continuing objective. We have benefited from considerable investor loyalty and, for me over these 15 years, this has added a real sense of personal satisfaction.

LAURA PEDERSEN

Laura Pedersen went to Wall Street at 17; at 20 she was the youngest person, to that point, to have her own seat on the American Stock Exchange (her employer rented it for her because she wasn't old enough to own it); and before turning 24, she made $1.5 million. Growing up outside of Buffalo, Pedersen was a born money-maker: at 6 she sold tomatoes from her mother's garden, played poker, and bet on horses; at 10 she asked for Pepsi-Cola stock for a birthday gift; at 14 she visited New York City and toured the AMEX. After a dull first semester at the University of Michigan, she dropped out. "If I'd wanted to be a movie star," she reflected, "I suppose I'd have headed west, to Hollywood; as I only sought to make a fortune, I flew east, to Wall Street."

Pedersen started as a clerk in January 1984, making $120 a week. She went through several companies before landing with Spear Leeds Kellogg/Investors Company as a clerk for the traders. When the traders left for cigarette breaks, she started filling in as a pinch hitter. It was a world full of obscenity and nasty gestures, and as Pedersen said, "For the four years, three months, and thirteen days I traded—initially as a pinch hitter, then as a credentialed specialist—I did everything my parents told me never to do." Over that four-year-plus span, she made a respectable $5.3 million in profits for her company. In the October 1987 crash, she made $100,000 the day the bubble burst, but the next week she lost about $1.6 million.

Pedersen, with a variety of throat, ear, and eye problems as a result of her work, ended up seeing a doctor, who urged her to quit. She did at age 24. Through those years, Pedersen kept a diary, which she turned into a book, *Play Money*. In it, she recalls such wild events as the time there was a fire but no one would leave the floor for fear of losing money. There were no regrets. "My reason for writing *Play Money*," she said, "is that I wanted to record what I perceived to be the final gasps of a tradecraft that has been rendered almost superfluous by high technology." In *The Last Frontier*, she paints a vivid picture of what it was like to be a trader and describes how to survive in the dog-eat-dog pit.

The Last Frontier

Laura Pedersen

Ⅰf there is such a thing as a dog-eat-dog workplace, the options trading pit comes pretty close. When the trading is in full swing, one of my friends used to say, "The only rule of thumb is to stick it in the other guy's eye before he can stick it in yours."

But the days of the trading floor may be numbered: The entire concept is bound to become an anachronism once the markets become fully automated early in the twenty-first century. Electronic trading has already revolutionized the Cincinnati Stock Exchange, embracing approximately five hundred stocks listed in the U.S., and overseas, with electronic trading, the antiseptic London and Hong Kong stock exchanges now exude as much excitement as a grocery store, even during the busiest trading days.

If there is such a thing as a dog-eat-dog work-place, the options trading pit comes pretty close.

Over the next five years, both the New York Stock Exchange and a consortium led by the American Stock Exchange and Chicago Board of Options Exchange expect to swing into twenty-four-hour-a-day worldwide electronic trading. Already the New York Stock Exchange has launched a program that would effectively bypass its members with an electronic system matching buyers and sellers, a function that has been performed by the specialists for most of the past two hundred years. The mere confirmation, in September of 1990, of these plans for around-the-clock trading sent shivers of fear down the backs of thousands of floor brokers and traders who could clearly see the handwriting on the wall. Many already feel obsolete as they see their paychecks—reduced by the industry-wide imposition of negotiated commissions—further eaten into by the automated execution systems. Today, a clerk in the Little Rock, Arkansas, office of Merrill Lynch need only push a button to buy ten thousand shares of stock or twenty options direct from the specialist halfway across the country, completely bypassing the floor broker. Will the trader be far behind?

For the time being, the traders are still safe and the floor remains one of the few places on earth—a last frontier—where it is still possible for a high-school dropout to start as a runner, quickly rise to clerk, make as much as a hundred thousand dollars a year and learn to trade, and by the time he's twenty-five end up owning a multimillion-dollar specialist firm.

Not everyone can become a specialist, though many try. For one, it takes a great deal of hands-on trading experience. For another, it takes a lot out of a person, physically and mentally as well. According to Exchange statisticians, the average forty-one-year-old specialist brings to the job twelve and a half years of floor-trading experience and another four and a half spent elsewhere in the securities industry.

The introduction of index options trading, however, has tended to accelerate the learning process. I was told I would learn as much in six intensive months of hot-and-heavy clerking in the pit as I would in twelve years as a broker on the trading floor. They were right.

Index options trading caught on and multiplied in volume more quickly than anyone at the Exchange had anticipated. Stock indexes were designed to protect investors trading large portfolios. Thus, mutual-fund managers controlling large blocks of stock use index contract "sell" positions as insurance against declining stock prices, much as farmers use cotton futures to protect themselves against falling cotton prices. Conversely, investors planning to buy stock in the future can lock in a price by taking an index contract "buy" position. One reason for the unexpected success of the indexes was the emergence of a new breed of speculators who were willing to be either buyers or sellers, depending on whether they thought the stocks in an index would rise or fall in value.

Just like other stocks and options, the index options were given to the specialist firms to run. All it takes to start up one of these firms are two or more traders, operators of specific stocks or options with proven track records, and a lot of capital. Compared to the big full-service firms that provide their clients with all sorts of amenities, such as research, mailing of monthly statements, and investment seminars, the specialist firms are bare-bones, minimal operations. All they do is trade, and selectively at that.

Under the rules, regulations, and bylaws of the Exchange, the specialist firms are mandated "to conduct fair and orderly markets" and to "be the buyer and seller of last resort" in their allocated product(s). Ours was XMI, the Major Market Index. Even if we had wanted to, we couldn't have taken on any other products, so big did XMI become during the time I was at the AMEX. As it was, the Exchange had to rebuild the XMI pit several times to accommodate the soaring volume; by the time I left, XMI occupied most of the northwest quadrant of the main trading floor.

Because their *entire* business takes place on the floor or in the pits, and their staffs have no dealings with investors other than the order-bearing brokers, the specialist firms have no need to maintain offices away from the Exchange. That's why the investing public seldom hears of them. (The only reason we kept offices at 115 Broadway, as well as at the Exchange, was that Spear Leeds & Kellogg, which owned almost fifty percent of our firm, had its headquarters there.)

Most specialist firms tend to be very small, fiercely independent, turf-protective, and quite profitable. They do virtually nothing to build a public identity off the trading floor, but are well known inside the securities industry, as are the equities or options assigned to them by the Exchange.

The specialist's role originated long ago, with the explosion of stock trading during the post–Civil War speculative frenzy. Prior to 1869, the vice-president of the Curb Exchange would read aloud to the throng of brokers gathered around him the entire list of New York Stock Exchange stocks being traded that day, reeling off current bids (the highest price anyone was willing to pay at that moment) and asked price (the lowest at which anyone was willing to sell). This he did three times during trading hours. Lacking today's electronic tote boards and fast-moving "tapes," a broker with orders to fill might have had to wait for hours for a particular stock's name to be called. It was one thing if the broker had been ordered to buy at the going price (market order), but during a period of volatility, many investors unwilling to risk sharp price changes in the time between placement and execution of an order imposed upper and lower limits on their buy-sell orders. With more and more new issues to trade, no broker had the time to hang around, instead handing such "limit orders" to a new breed of sub-broker—soon to be referred to as "the specialist." To make it worth both their while, the floor broker would split his commissions with the specialist. Naturally, as new stocks were introduced, the role of specialist grew in importance—and power—and soon assumed the role of a market maker. Once the Exchange moved indoors in 1921, instead of mingling at curbside the specialists began congregating at set locations, or "trading posts," forcing the trading partners to come to them.

Today's specialists actually have to wear four different hats in order to accomplish their market-making functions—

often at the same time, so frenzied have things become: *broker, dealer, auctioneer,* and *referee.*

As a *broker* the specialist holds orders that can't be executed at the price stipulated by the customer until an opportunity arises.

The specialist must, according to Exchange rules, act as a *dealer* in his allocated stocks and options. In doing this he must risk the firm's capital by buying and selling for his own account whenever there is a temporary imbalance between buy and sell orders. To close the gap between bids and offers, the specialist, trading for his own account, may have to offer to buy at a higher price than anyone else is accepting, and sell at a price lower than anyone else is offering.

As an *auctioneer,* when the bell rings the specialist establishes an opening price for the stocks or options. If a reopening is necessary because of a trading halt, the specialist presides and manages order imbalances while setting the new prices.

Specialists are involved in every trade, even if they do not participate financially. That's how they operate as *referees* or, on busy days, as traffic cops. Somebody has to separate the brokers, representing public and institutional orders, from the traders, who establish positions for their personal accounts. Priorities are usually set on a first come–first serve basis—actually, first *yell*—first *heard*. It's up to the specialist to monitor the cacophony and determine who was first and who *claimed* to have been first. Though specialists are not required, under Exchange rules, to risk life and limb by breaking up brawls, they are empowered to levy fines ranging from five hundred to one thousand dollars—assuming a floor official approves.

Operating a specialist firm on the trading floor can be very profitable because you're ideally situated to react to fast-breaking news, often at the moment it happens. The tradeoff is that by your pledge to "make markets" and risk the firm's capital, you can be wiped out in a single afternoon, as indeed a number of specialist firms were during the October 1987 crash. They were done in by the market's unexpected free-fall, unable in time to clear out their tremendous inventory of stocks and options or meet their margin calls.

Telephones seem to be the most vulnerable to fits of pique: Not a day went by when at least five of them weren't ripped off the walls or hurled across a trading post.

So stressful is the environment in which these traders operate that, on the busiest days, it is not uncommon to see traders tear up their position cards or pick up the keyboard to their Quotron (computers displaying real-time market data) and smash it into the terminal screen. I saw one guy pick up the entire unit and hurl it to the floor.

Telephones seem to be the most vulnerable to fits of pique: Not a day went by when at least five of them weren't ripped off the walls or hurled across a trading post. Things got so bad that it was rumored that New York Telephone, fed up with having to constantly replace phones, finally demanded that the Exchange buy them by the gross and do its own installation work. The Exchange now has its own army of installers out on the floor, doing triage in much the same way Army medics roam the battlefield after the fighting.

Imagine turning over the set design for the war room of the starship *USS Enterprise* to an undisciplined fourteen-year-old owner of the world's largest Erector set, whose father has cornered the market in video monitors, and you can begin to picture our working environment. An octagonal pen, off to the side of the main trading floor, the pit is actually an enclosed series of raised, rubber-matted tiers and platforms bisected by several passageways leading to the main floor of the Exchange and hopelessly cluttered with computer keyboards, monitors, time clocks, order racks, banks of telephones, half-filled Styrofoam coffee containers, hundreds of unopened foil packs of ketchup and plastic envelopes of soy sauce, empty soda cans, coils of insulated wire, Plexiglas boxes resembling hamster cages, stacks of note pads — and, standing largely unused near the exit, huge garbage cans and a couple of push brooms.

Wherever you went, you'd run into big metal pipes and girders bristling with odd-size video-display screens and terminals — our "data banks." The screens ranged in size from a six-inch personal-size monitor to the kind of tote boards found in most high-school or college gymnasiums. The first impression of a visiting friend of mine was, "Gee, just like the TV display wall at Sears!" There were so many video monitors stacked seemingly willy-nilly that, unless you were looking down from the balcony that runs along the side of the main AMEX trading room, it was impossible to see what was going on inside the pit. I suppose it could be argued that the Exchange's governors wanted it that way, but that presupposes they'd actually hired a space designer.

Actually, the pit *evolved* from a glamorized trading post and, like kudzu vine, ran amuck, consuming more and more real estate as XMI volume shot up. Changes came about through necessity. In the beginning the pit was littered with twenty or so fruit crates and cardboard boxes, courtesy of Greenwich Gourmet Deli, on which short traders and clerks used to stand in order to read broker badge numbers when it came time to record the trades. Built to transport fruit across the country, these boxes could not sustain the weight of people jumping up and down and so usually didn't last the day. It could be embarrassing for the clerks to stand atop a box, signal frantically, and find themselves suddenly sinking from sight as, one after another, the boxes collapsed. That sight must also have offended the governors' sense of decorum, as one morning a space-design consultant showed up with a clipboard to ask us all sorts of questions on our work habits. Not long afterward, the cardboard boxes disappeared. In their place, the house carpenters built and installed a number of wooden boxes covered with industrial "no-slip" black-rubber matting. We all fought over the new boxes like tigers foraging for their cubs—our clerks. They needed to be kept happy. Turns out this was the least of our problems.

Like a Broadway theater, there was the "stage"—in our case, a high platform on which the specialists stood, looking across a chasm at the hordes of traders who were stationed atop a series of graduated tiers. In between, in the orchestra section, was a long passageway, ostensibly reserved for the waves of brokers who, during trading hours, moved in and out of the pit like spawning salmon. At least that was the way it was supposed to work, on paper. It never did. Chaos is not the sort of thing that lends itself to space allocation.

One thing that went wrong almost from the start was that the carpenters were designing this thing from blueprints instead of from observation. Had they bothered to see us in action, understood human greed, they'd have seen instantly that what mattered more than unobstructed vision—sight lines between traders and specialists—was (a) the proximity between the two groups, and (b) the need to be in voice contact with the specialists, to catch the hand signals, eye movements, and so forth. The problem was that the higher the traders and specialists were placed, the greater the distance. The communications gap became a chasm in which a lot of hand-to-hand combat took place. To keep the brokers from being overrun by the surge of frenzied traders, it became necessary to install a long metal railing, similar to the one found in every zoo around the polar bear cages. Actually, the analogy isn't that farfetched. Before the railing was built, the poor brokers found themselves quite literally bulldozed up the other side of the pit by a swarm of angry traders, pinning us specialists against the makeshift wall behind us, and leaving us no choice but to use our feet to violently shove these bodies back down. There were days it looked like that famous castle-siege scene in any one of half-a-dozen Hollywood epics. Thanks to all those discarded ketchup packets, we even had the "bloodstains," to show our battle worthiness.

Efforts at noise abatement proved equally futile. The "walls" of the enclosure were wrapped in thick industrial carpeting to muffle the ungodly combination of noises that emerged from there. On top of the roaring of three hundred or so maniacal traders, there was the noise of the beeping monitors, the overhead public-address system, and thirty phones incessantly ringing off the hook. All at once.

Even before the opening bell, well in advance of trading, the players would jockey for position in the pit so as to be the first to be recognized by the specialists, standing slightly above them on the podium overlooking the floor of the pit.

The best way for X to get a front-row position was to finagle Y out of the pit. This was often accomplished by the simple expedient of arranging for Y to be paged out front — usually by X's clerk standing two feet away, using a wall phone. The minute Y left, X would slip into the vacated spot and stay there, not budging an inch. By the time an infuriated Y returned to the pit, he would find it impossible to worm his way back in.

Given that sort of competitive environment, mistakes were bound to occur that could test the best of friendships.

One particularly active day, my clerk jotted down that I had bought "*fifteen* options contracts at the price of thirteen and a half," while the opposing trader yelled back that he'd sold me "*fifty* contracts at thirteen and a half."

The difference between saying fifteen and hearing fifty led to a $47,250 misunderstanding that had to come out of one of our pockets the following day. What made it particularly awkward was that the aggrieved trader was a rather good-looking guy I'd had a date with the evening before, one of those rare occasions when my restricted life-style allowed me a night out. Because the transaction reporter standing next to me during the trade also swore to having heard me say "fifteen," my opponent had a tough time proving the error to be mine.

Either of us could have sought a ruling by a floor referee or gone to formal arbitration, which would have put a crimp in our budding romance. Moreover, arbitration is not a viable alternative for settling such trading arguments, because it can take hours and cost both traders precious floor time, often a sacrifice of more money than the amount being disputed.

So, instead, we grudgingly agreed to split the loss. The pit had been too loud for anyone to hear correctly. My adversary left with his copy of the rejected trade notice, but not before calling me a "first-class bitch." At least he still thought of me as first class. But not enough to resume dating me. In fact, he told me afterward that whenever he looked at me, all he could think of was losing $23,625.

Considering the overwhelming number of young men compared to the handful of women on the floor, it's surprising how very little of the old hanky-panky went on during my time on the trading floor. I suspect the guys were either too busy making big bucks or too tired to do anything but flirt.

I admit to having my share of admirers, most of whom proved eminently forgettable. A nice exception was my friend Roger Fenn from Merrill Lynch, a real gentle giant who took a protective interest in me and kept my podium stocked with candy bars. On the way back from an AMEX marketing presentation one day, on impulse, he bought all fifty balloons from a street vendor for twenty-five dollars and handed them to me. Then he left to do some errands. As I walked down the street, people approached me and asked if they were for sale. Naturally, I said "Of course," and sold them all, at two bucks apiece. One of the women in the marketing department had seen Roger buy them for me and was shocked at my callousness. "How can you do that to Roger?" she said, voicing her disapproval. "Okay, okay," I said, "I'll tell him." I did more than that. I handed him fifty dollars — half the profits. He beamed. "Atta girl!" After all, a trader is a trader.

PART VI

Lessons from Notorious Characters

Part VI presents a series of essays by or about notorious Wall Street characters. Why? Because something valuable can be learned from their (mis)deeds. Stock manipulator Daniel Drew, for example, shares what he learned from his shenanigans: "Operators can swear everlasting vengeance on each other one day, and be thick as molasses before sundown the next." T. Boone Pickens, who has been called a corporate raider, a greenmailer, and a piranha, among other names, provides an insightful lesson on what it means to be an active shareholder. In diagnosing what economic circumstances gave rise to Michael Milken and the junk bond craze, James Grant, founder of *Grant's Interest Rate Observer*, explains why debt is a fair-weather friend. Sometimes, those who know how to stretch or even break the rules teach the most memorable lessons.

One of the more notorious characters of Wall Street, Daniel Drew was a complex man who never hesitated to enter into a dubious money-making scheme, but also founded a major theological seminary and taught Sunday School himself. Drew grew up on a farm in rural Carmel, New York. School was a luxury (and not an option), so he made extra money for the family by working for circuses that had their winter quarters nearby; no doubt he learned a few tricks from the hucksters that would prove profitable later in life. His father died in 1812, and Drew, only 14, joined the army as a substitute, collecting $100 in the process. Eventually, he would peddle that money into more than $16 million.

His first line of business was buying cattle on credit and then driving them into places like New York City, where he sold them to the butchers. Even then, he pulled a trick or two, according to Henry Clews, who noted: "By the way, the significant term of 'watering stock' originated in the practice of Uncle Daniel giving his cattle salt in order to create a thirst in them that would cause them to imbibe large quantities of water, and thus appear bigger and fatter when brought to market." As an aside, he started acting as a banker for the other drovers, and that was the beginning of his involvement with Wall Street. In 1836, he formed a brokerage house, Drew, Robinson and Company.

Drew became an expert at making money in falling markets, and was known to incite a panic or two. One writer of the time said: "Drew is a most robust architect of panics. . . . Well too does he deserve the title of 'merry old gentleman' of Wall Street. In his most earnest operations he never seems to lose sight of 'the fun of the thing.' " In *Daniel Drew on Wall Street*, written in Drew's voice by Bouck White, one of his merry adventures with Jay Gould and Jim Fisk is described along with the lessons learned. White, who wrote *The Book of Daniel Drew*, claimed that he found a trunk full of Drew's notes and used them as a source for Drew's "autobiography." Whether this was true or not, one historian determined that "the basic facts and the flavor of the narrative were indisputably authentic."

Daniel Drew on Wall Street
Bouck White

I sometimes wish I had stayed in the steamboat business and let Wall Street alone. I'd have made money in a more steady way and without the risk. Steamboats are not so liable to ups and downs as stocks are. And at this time I was earning from my steamboats alone enough money to have made me in time a man of comfortable means.

But the trouble with business of that kind is, there are so many little things to look after, which keep you on the go well-nigh all the time. Because the profits from a business line are made up of a lot of small profits; and each detail is liable to leak money unless you look out.

I sometimes wish I had stayed in the steamboat business and let Wall Street alone.

For instance, there was the one item of the bar, on my steamboats. Going into the bar one day on the steamboat *Drew,* who should I see there but the Captain of the boat taking a drink. I was going to be mad at first, and stood watching him in order to think what I should do. He stood very cool, finished his glass, put it down, and then paid the bar-tender a quarter. When I saw that, I wasn't so mad.

"Do the employees on the boat pay every time they get anything from the bar?" I asked.

"Always," said he; "at least I do. In fact, Mr. Drew, I find it a very good way to keep in check a natural propensity of mine which might otherwise grow into something inconve-nient." I was glad to know that he always paid; but the inci-dent merely shows the many leaks that could occur in a business as big as this steamboat business of mine, if a fellow were to follow it up as a life pursuit.

I like Wall Street because you stand a chance of making money there so much faster than you can in the slow-poke ways of regular business.

Then, also, there is the bother which small business mat-ters bring you. I had a lawsuit hanging over my head for years over the sale of the steamboat, *Francis Skiddy.* It belonged to the line which went from New York to Troy. I sold it to the People's Line. In reality I was buyer and seller too. Because I owned a controlling interest in both lines, and so could make the seller sell, and the buyer buy. Well, some of the smaller *Skiddy* stock-holders got mad at the transac-tion and sued me for damages. Because on the last trip of that boat, just before she was going to be delivered to the People's Line, she ran on a rock off of Statt's Landing, and ripped a hole in her bottom sixteen feet long and three planks wide. This, of course, lowered now by a good deal the selling value of the boat. And yet gave me the thing I wanted out of her, the engine. This was still undamaged, and could now be transferred into another boat, and at a reasonable figure. I had been wanting the *Skiddy* engine for this other boat a long time back. I gave out that her running on the rocks just at this time when the sale was about to be made, was an accident which I hadn't had anything to do with. But her stock-holders made a big fuss. They went into court and sued me for sixty thousand dollars. The thing dragged and dragged, and now finally the court has made me pay it. It merely shows the vexations of spirit that come when you are in a business line.

I like Wall Street because you stand a chance of making money there so much faster than you can in the slow-poke ways of regular business. One turn of two or three points in shares will, if you are on the right side and have put out a big enough line, net you as much money in six days as an ordinary business would in six months. By this time I had got so that I knew all the ins and outs of Wall Street. There are trade secrets in every calling. The newcomer is always at a discount compared to the old veteran. I found that many times now I could turn this expert knowledge of mine to account. One morning, I remember, I was riding down to the Street in the carriage of a young stock operator who had taken me in with him, to save paying fare in the Broadway stage. He knew that I was on the inside of some of the big stock-market operations, and he thought he might get some inside tips. I had looked for something of the sort to occur. It's a caution the way outsiders hang around people who are on the inside. The flies get at you when you're covered with honey. Whilst we were driving down Broadway he pumped and pumped; but I was as dumb as a heifer. I made believe there were big things just then under way which we, who were on the inside, didn't want other people to get onto.

Well, when we reached the Street, and he had got the carriage stopped in front of my office, I opened the door and stepped out. In doing so, I contrived to bump my hat against the top of the doorway. It was a black felt hat. (I like black felt for a hat. It's so durable. You can wear one several years before it begins to show signs of wear.) My hat fell off, and some pieces of paper fell out. On those pieces of paper I had written what seemed to be orders to my brokers: "Buy 500

Erie, at 68." "Buy 1,000 at 67." "Buy 2,000 Erie at the market." "Buy 3,000 Erie at 67½," and such-like. Of course, as they spread over the floor of the carriage, he or any one else couldn't help but see what they were, and read them. I made believe I was awfully put out to have the secret given away like that. I made a scramble as though to gather them up before any one should see them; then I said good-bye and went into my office.

I calculated he would most likely act on the hint. And he did. He drove rapidly to his office. He told his crowd of the discovery he had made. "A big Bulling movement in Erie is on! The old man" (that's what they sometimes called me) "is buying Erie! A campaign is under way. Boys, we must get in on this!" So he bought a block of five thousand shares of Erie. The rest of his crowd followed him. Their combined buying forced Erie up point after point.

An operator, if he is onto the tricks of the trade and has natural ingenuity besides, can make business in a sick market.

That was what I had been looking for. I had been wanting for some time back to find a buyer for some of my surplus stock. Now it was coming my way fine. I immediately dumped onto the market all the Erie it would stand. I succeeded in disposing of a large share of my holdings at the top figure. Then of course the market broke. It sagged four points in the next two days. My broker friend and his crowd were badly caught. He came to me with a face as long as your arm; said how he had been led to believe that there was going to be an upward movement in Erie; he had bought heavily; and now it had all gone to smash. "Uncle, what in the world shall I do?"

I told him he could do anything he pleased. And I couldn't keep from chuckling at the fine way I had got him to gobble the bait. In fact I always did like a joke. So much so that they got to calling me the "Merry Old Gentleman of Wall Street." They had other names for me, too; such as, "the Speculative Director," "the Big Bear," "the Old Man of the Street" and so on. Some of these names I didn't like. But "the Merry Old Gentleman"—I kind of liked that. I believe in being merry when you can. A good chuckle, when you've got a fellow in a tight box and you watch him squirm this way and that, does more good than a dose of medicine.

As to this particular Erie deal, by thus making a market for my shares, I cleaned up a fine profit. That merely shows how an operator, if he is onto the tricks of the trade and has natural ingenuity besides, can make business in a sick market, where a newcomer would have to sit and twiddle his thumbs.

I have always had a natural bent for stock-market dickers. I suppose it's because I have been sort of humble in my manner. That puts people off their guard. (I never was proud, anyhow. People used to say: You couldn't tell from Dan Drew's clothing but what he was a butcher in a Third Avenue shop. But I let them talk. You can't tell a horse by his harness. And I have always thought a man should have more in his pocket than on his back.) I have found a spirit of humility very helpful. It makes the man you're dealing with think he is winding you around his finger; whereas you are the one who is doing the winding.

A good chuckle, when you've got a fellow in a tight box and you watch him squirm this way and that, does more good than a dose of medicine.

That's how I got the best of a lawyer friend of mine once. He was a young fellow. I had him do some legal work for me. He did it. Then he sent in a bill. It seemed an almighty big fee to ask for just a few months' work. I paid it. But I made up my mind I'd get it back. And I did. I was talking with him not long after. I turned the conversation to Wall Street matters.

"Sonny," said I, "you won that lawsuit for me, and I've taken a kind of liking to you. I want to help you. We fellows on the inside sometimes know what's going to happen in stock-market affairs before other people. It's my advice to you to take some of your spare cash, all the money you can lay your hands on, in fact, and buy Erie stock."

He held off. He said that his business was law and not the stock-market. He believed that a shoemaker should stick to his lasts. Fair words made him look to his purse. And such-like.

"Now, son," said I, "do as I say. I knew your father. And because of that friendship, I feel a kind of interest in you. I want to see you get a start. You buy Erie. Buy all you can of it, at the present market price. Trust me, you'll never be sorry." He thought for a while. He said he guessed he'd try the thing for once.

That was what I'd been waiting for. I went out and immediately gave orders to my brokers to sell all the Erie they could. Soon the ticker told me that my brokers were finding a buyer for the Erie they were offering. I thought I could give a pretty shrewd guess as to who was the buyer. I supplied him with all he would take. By the time the market broke, I had saddled him with enough Erie at a good high figure to sluice from his pocket into mine all of that fee which he had scooped out of me just a few weeks before. I now called the account even.

For a spell after settling up with the Commodore at the close of the Erie War, I got out of Wall Street. I was by this time over my scriptural allowance of three score years and ten. I thought I had earned a rest. I figured that I had made my wad, and now should begin to enjoy it.

> Let worldly minds the world pursue;
>   It has no charms for me.
> Once I admired its trifles, too,
>   But grace has set me free.

I seemed to myself to be now in a quiet harbour, like that fine big bay that dents in from the Hudson River at Fishkill. I could look out from that safe retreat onto the human vessels that were tossing in the billows outside. "From every stormy wind that blows"—that has always been a favourite hymn of mine. And that other tune, too:

> Oh, Beulah Land, Sweet Beulah Land,
> Where on the highest mount I stand;
> I look away across the sea,
> Where mansions are prepared for me,
> And view the shining glorious shore,
> My heaven, my home forever more.

But after two or three months of nothing to do, I kind of got tired of resting. I saw Gould and Fisk making money in Erie hand over fist, and I hankered to get back. I wanted to stick a finger in that pudding, so to speak. They had taken Bill Tweed and Pete Sweeney into the Board of Directors. This was giving them such a fine pull with the law courts and the New York City authorities that they could do most anything they wanted to, and not be troubled with suits or legal technicalities. Tweed became a director of the railroad, "to get square with Erie," as he put it. For he was still nettled over those old losses in Erie speckilations which he said I had caused him, and now he vowed he was going to get it back—was going to take it out of the road, no matter what it cost her. When I had got out of Erie at the time of our settlement with Vanderbilt, I figured that in taking my pay in cash and leaving Fisk and Gould the road, I had got the best end of the bargain. I was chuckling to myself to think how I had

343

taken the horse, so to speak, and had left them holding onto the halter. But Jay's words were proving true. And although Erie seemed a badly waterlogged craft, there was a lot of service left in her yet. Therefore I wanted to get back on board, so to speak.

At the time of that settlement, a little feeling had arisen between me and the other two, Jay and Jimmy. But personal feelings don't count in Wall Street. Operators can swear everlasting vengeance on each other one day, and be thick as molasses before sundown the next. In financial circles, it's the money that counts. No matter how mad you may be at a fellow, if you need his money you make up with him easy as anything. Erie was still a money-maker. So I wanted to get on the inside once more. If I could have another turn or two at the milking stool, so to speak, I felt I'd be willing to retire from active business altogether. Accordingly, before the summer was over, I was calling on Gould and Fisk, and they were coming to see me, just as though we hadn't had any differences at all. Before I knew it, I was back in the thick of things, and busy as a pup.

We now set out on a Bear campaign—we three, Gould, Fisk and I. Being backed by Tweed and his political crowd, it promised big returns. But it required a lot of nerve. In fact, before it was through, it raised more excitement than I had bargained for. It was the Lock-up of greenbacks.

Personal feelings don't count in Wall Street. . . . No matter how mad you may be at a fellow, if you need his money you make up with him easy as anything.

It seemed a foolhardy thing to do—go short of stocks just at that particular time. Because it was the fall of the year. The Government reports showed that bumper crops were to be harvested in nearly all parts of the country. A big traffic from the West to the seaboard was promised. The election of General Grant as president was almost a settled thing; and if he was elected, the policy of the Government would be an immediate resumption of specie payment. Money was easy as an old shoe. When money is easy, stocks go up. Because at such times people have got the means to margin large holdings and so are hopeful and Bullish. It was about the last time in the world, one would have said, to begin a Bear campaign. But that's really just the time in which to begin it. Because the way to make money in Wall Street, if you are an insider, is to calculate on what the common people are going to do, and then go and do just the opposite. When everybody is Bullish, that is just the time when you can make the most money as a Bear, if you work it right. And we of our little clique thought we could work it right.

When money is easy the public buys stocks, and so the prices go up. The way to do, we calculated, would be to make money tight. Then people would sell, prices would go down, and we could cover our short contracts at a fine low figure. In this work of making money tight we were helped by one fact. The Government, in order to resume specie payments, had adopted a policy of contracting the amount of greenbacks in circulation. It was refusing to reissue greenback notes after it had once got them back into its vaults.

---

*The way to make money in Wall Street . . .
is to calculate on what the common people
are going to do, and then go and do just the
opposite.*

But that wasn't enough to tighten the currency to the point where it would serve our ends. So we set about working it ourselves. For this purpose we made a pool of money to the amount of fourteen millions. Fisk and Gould provided ten millions, and I agreed to put in four millions.

The banks, as everybody knows, are required by law to keep as reserve twenty-five per cent. of their deposits. This is in order to take care of their depositors. When their cash on hand is over and above this twenty-five per cent. margin, bankers loan money free and easy. As soon as their cash begins to creep down to the twenty-five per cent. limit—which can almost be called the dead line—bankers begin to get the cold shivers; they tighten their rates, and if the need is urgent enough, call in their outstanding loans. Knowing this we made our plans accordingly. We would put all of our cash into the form of deposits in the banks. Against these deposits we would write checks and get the banks to certify them. The banks would have to tie up enough funds to take care of these certifications. With the certified checks as collateral we would borrow greenbacks—and then withdraw them suddenly from circulation.

When our arrangements were complete, we went onto the stock market and sold shares heavily short. People thought we were fools, because of all the signs pointing to a big revival of trade. Soon these contracts of ours matured. We held a council. We decided that the time had come to explode our bomb. So all of a sudden we called upon the banks for our greenbacks. I remember well the scared look that came over the face of one banker when I made the demand. At first he didn't understand.

"Oh, yes," said he, after I had made my request; "you wish to withdraw your deposits from our bank? Of course, we can accommodate you. We shall take measures to get your account straightened up in the next few days."

"The next few days won't do," said I; "we must have it right away."

"Right away!" he said. "What do you mean?"

"I mean," said I, "within the next fifteen minutes."

He began to turn white. "Do you understand that a sudden demand of this kind was altogether unlooked for, and will occasion a great deal of needless hardship? A wait on your part of only a very short time would permit us to straighten out the whole affair without injustice to our other depositors and clients."

"I'm not in business," I said, "for the benefit of your other depositors and clients. I've got to look out for number one."

"So I perceive," he said; "and I suspect that you are willing to look out for that person quite regardless of other 'number ones' that are scattered somewhat thickly through human society. However, we will probably have to do your bidding. I will see what help we can get from some of the other banks."

As soon as he began to communicate with the other banks, his alarm increased. Because he found that their funds were being called on in the same way as his own (we were calling in the greenbacks from our chain of banks all to once). Then he got to work in good earnest. Because our fourteen millions (through the working of that law of a twenty-five per cent. reserve), meant a contracting of the currency to four times that amount, or fifty-six millions in all, besides the certifications. He called a hasty council of the officers of the bank. He ordered them to make up my greenbacks into a bundle, for me to take out to the carriage which I had brought along with me for that purpose. I started to thank him, but he seemed too busy to notice me. Messengers were being sent out on the double-quick to all the brokers who were customers of the bank, notifying them they were to return their borrowings to the bank at once.

As each of these brokers found his loans being suddenly called by the banks, he sent word in turn to his clients that they must put up the money themselves to carry their holdings of stock. Because the public in buying shares don't pay for them outright; they only pay a margin, say of ten per cent. The broker, therefore, has to put up the other ninety per cent., which he borrows from the banks, and charges his customers the interest.

The customers immediately sent back word to the brokers: "We haven't anywheres near the cash to pay for our stocks outright. Borrow from the banks, even though you have to pay ten per cent. interest."

"But we can't get money at ten per cent.," answered the brokers.

"Then pay fifteen," said the customers.

"But we can't get it at fifteen," came the answer. "The rates for money have gone up to 160 per cent. There's a terrible tightening. No one was looking for it. We've got to have the cash, or we can't carry your stocks a moment longer."

"Then let the stocks go," came back the last answer; "throw them on the market, and do it before anybody else begins."

You can imagine, when a thousand people begin to sell, what a slump takes place. The money market is the key to the stock market. They who control the money rate control also the stock rate. Stocks began to tumble right and left. Many stop-loss orders were uncovered. Prices sagged point after point—thirty points in all. And every point meant one dollar in our pockets for every share we were dealing in.

People everywhere began to curse us. The air round about us three men was fire and sulphur. Men couldn't get money to carry on their business. Merchant princes, who had inherited the business from their fathers through several generations, lost it now in a night. This was the time of the year when ordinarily money would flow out to the South and West to pay the farmers for the crops which they had been working all spring and summer to bring to harvest. But now that money couldn't flow, and so these farmers in a dozen states also began to hurl their curses at us. Many of them had been counting on the money from their crops to pay off mortgages. Some were driven from their homes, and their houses sold.

In fact, the curses got so loud after a while that I kind of got scared. I hadn't thought the thing would kick up such a rumpus. It almost looked as though our lives weren't safe. They might burn down my house over my head, or stab me on a street corner. So I got out of the thing. My shirt fits close, but my skin fits closer. I told Gould and Fisk that I wasn't going to be with them in this lock-up deal any longer—my life was too precious. If they chose to be dare-devils and stand out against a whole country rising up in wrath against them, they could do it. But for my part I was going to make my peace with my fellow men. So I released the money I was hoarding, and was glad to be out of the thing at last.

Yes, Richard Whitney did jail time. Yes, he stole from his friends. And yes, he was once a very articulate and well-respected symbol of Wall Street, who attempted to restore order after the 1929 crash. Considered an aristocrat, Whitney attended an elite private school and then went to Harvard. After graduating, he worked briefly for Kidder, Peabody & Company before buying his own seat on the New York Stock Exchange and founding Richard Whitney & Co in 1917. While well-respected, it was the 1929 crash that thrust him into the lime-light. "Whitney first achieved important public attention," wrote one historian, "during the October 1929 crash, when he appeared on the floor to rally support for the market."

Of Black Tuesday, Whitney recalled: "The ticker ran hours behind; it was impossible to place orders promptly because of congestion on both telephone lines and the pneumatic tube, the wooden boxes which ordinarily hold orders were replaced by tall waste-paper baskets, and in some instances all the parties to a transaction could not be identified." The image of Whitney buying a large block of U.S. Steel stock to rally the troops did indeed make an impression—he was elected president of the exchange in 1930, and subsequently became its most important spokesman in the face of growing criticism.

About that same time, Whitney, who had invested heavily in a failing business, found himself in financial trouble. To cover his losses, Whitney swindled his customers, partners, and friends of more than $5 million, at times using money borrowed from one friend to pay off another. When an audit conclusively proved he was dipping into his customers' accounts, Whitney admitted his crimes. He promised to return all funds, but insisted there be no charges filed against him. "After all," he said, "I'm Richard Whit-ney. I mean the Stock Exchange to millions of people. The Exchange can't afford to let me go under." His plea fell on deaf ears—Whitney was indicted for grand larceny in 1938 and was sentenced to 5 to 10 years in Sing Sing. The irony and lessons of his 1933 essay, *In Defense of the Stock Exchange,* cannot be lost as Whitney calls for discipline and order.

In Defense of the Stock Exchange
Richard Whitney

I t is one of the paradoxes of modern life that so many of its institutions are misunderstood almost in proportion to their real usefulness to society. Undoubtedly this is the case with stock exchanges. Many people see in the stock market only its momentary speculative surface, and never look beneath this restless froth and foam into the great economic tides which flow through it. To such a shortsighted view, stock exchanges take on the appearance of mere gambling casinos, where reckless wagers may be placed upon the meaningless fluctuations of prices. It seems needless to remark that if this were really the truth, the sooner all stock exchanges were abolished the better.

The confusion concerning the nature and functions of security markets is always greatest during depressions, when the shrinkage of earning power in industry inevitably impairs credit and depresses security and commodity prices. Investors and speculators alike experience severe losses, and very humanly wish to find a scapegoat for what in many cases are their own errors of judgment. One cannot easily attack the abstract law of supply and demand. It is always far easier to assail the stock exchanges. Such recurrent waves of fallacious opinion should not be taken too seriously. After all, short of a complete revolution in our whole economic system, we will always need stock exchanges, and with the return of normal business and its reflection in rising security prices, agitation against them speedily disappears. It is, however, unfortunate that such prejudices should gain currency at times of real financial strain, when every effort should be made to restore sound conditions, instead of being wasted in combatting foolish economic fallacies and false panaceas. Correct diagnosis must always remain the first necessary step in effecting genuine cures.

How Stock Exchanges Arose

Stock exchanges have evolved gradually during the course of several centuries, and to understand their present-day functions it is necessary to consider their past history. As their name implies, they are organizations by means of which money can be exchanged for securities, or securities for money. Until the seventeenth century there were no real stock exchanges in our sense of the term, because there were no bond or share issues. But when government financing came to be done by the creation of national debts and the issuance of government bonds, rather than by the private financial operations of the sovereign ruler, security investment began and there at once developed a need for a market where this new form of property could readily be priced, purchased and sold.

Similarly, so long as business enterprise remained a small-scale affair, business firms needed little capital and rarely organized as stock companies; hence, there were no company bonds or shares and no need of a market for them. But with the coming of the industrial revolution, steam power was for the first time harnessed to transportation and industrial production, business enterprises came to need extensive capital, stock companies were in consequence rapidly formed, and the frequent issue of corporate securities began. The new company bonds and shares thus created in turn needed a market where they could easily be bought and sold. These same conditions have arisen in all modern countries, earlier in some and later in others. But everywhere the effect was the same — the imperative need of a regular and dependable market for both government and company securities.

NECESSITY OF DISCIPLINE

The form which such security markets ultimately assumed has also been roughly alike in all modern countries, and has followed a very similar course of natural evolution. The earliest security markets, both here and in Europe, sprang up in the already existing markets for wholesale materials and merchandise. In London, the first stockbrokers gathered in the Royal exchange, which had been erected primarily as a facility for merchants. In New York the original stockbrokers appeared in the mercantile auctions held on the wharves at the foot of Wall street, and in the adjacent coffeehouses frequented by merchants. As the volume of security transactions increased, however, a second stage of evolution occurred, in which the stockbrokers and security dealers organized separate markets in the streets. In London, they thronged in Exchange alley, in Paris in the Rue Quincampoix, and in New York in lower Wall street under the traditional buttonwood tree. The New York stock exchange met as a curb market in this way from 1792 to 1817, and in our own times the New York curb exchange held its meetings in lower Broad street until it went under a roof in 1921.

Stock exchange discipline and self-regulation are based squarely upon the power to expel, suspend or fine its members. Everywhere experience has shown that it is impossible in practice to regulate and control a market in the city streets, because brokers who employ improper tactics cannot be expelled, and dealings in improper security issues cannot be prevented. Accordingly, in every important financial center, the early curb markets have gradually moved indoors, adopted regulation for the business of their members, and enforced these rules by their power to deny admittance to such members as broke their rules. Upon this solid basis, elaborate but enforceable codes of conduct for stock exchange members have everywhere evolved.

This imposition of order and discipline upon the stock market, brought about by the organization of stock exchanges, constitutes one of their most important functions, and any comprehensive description of its many ramifications would make a fair-sized volume by itself. A particularly comprehensive code of rules has been gradually built up by the New York stock exchange, with which securities applying for admission to dealings on the exchange floor must comply; the listing requirements of the New York stock exchange are the most intensive and searching in the world, in their insistence upon compulsory publicity and other features designed to inform and protect the investing public. Admission to membership in the stock exchange is not merely a matter of purchasing a "seat," for the applicant must be formally elected, and if his record is in any way questionable, he will not be admitted. The methods which stock exchange members and their firms employ in their business are also subject to comprehensive and at the same time detailed regulations of the stock exchange constitution and rules. The governing committee of the exchange can prescribe severe penalties for actions by its members which could scarcely be successfully prosecuted in a public court of law.

From the economic standpoint, the basic function of stock exchanges consists in rendering securities more readily negotiable than they otherwise could be. How necessary this service is, should be obvious to anyone who will reflect what thrift and investment really involve. The fundamental reason why we shortsighted human beings are nevertheless willing to deny ourselves the enjoyment of present wants and satisfactions in order to save our money and invest it in securities, is because we all desire a reserve of funds to fall back on in emergencies. But if the securities in which savings are invested in this way cannot be readily sold whenever their owner wishes, one of the most important advantages of thrift has been nullified.

BASIC FUNCTION

By organizing the security market, by maintaining elaborate wire systems to all parts of the country and likewise an almost instantaneous ticker system for dispatching and printing current quotations, the New York stock exchange is able to attract bids and offers for its listed issues from all parts of the nation and even from beyond its borders. Without this organization and these facilities which it maintains, the actual negotiability of listed securities would prove as uncertain and undependable as that for issues not admitted to the exchanges but dealt in "over the counter."

Always highly important, this factor of negotiability has been of vital significance during the most trying periods of the depression. At times when no other form of property was in fact readily salable, security holders could always avail themselves of the security market to obtain cash. The task of thus holding the stock exchange open and keeping it functioning has not always been an easy one, yet curiously enough the stock exchange authorities have sometimes been bitterly assailed by shortsighted persons at the very time when the free and open securities market, which they were maintaining under great difficulties, stood almost alone in the path of a wholesale moratorium of credit.

Another function of the stock exchange which is frequently misunderstood has to do with the prices established on its floor. Sometimes, when the trend of security prices does not please particular groups or individuals, they are apt to take the stock exchange itself to task for it. This is thoroughly illogical, for the stock exchange itself neither buys nor sells securities, and does not fix prices. The actual function of the stock exchange consists in maintaining a free and open market under strict rules and with convenient facilities, in which everyone can readily buy and sell. Prices in the stock market in consequence reflect the forces of supply and demand arising from the buying and selling orders of the whole public.

NEW CAPITAL FOR INDUSTRY

Another important function of the stock exchange less seldom appreciated is the stimulus which its ready marketing machinery affords to the flow of new capital into industry. The stock market is not simply a passive meeting place where supply and demand come together—it is a dynamic mechanism whereby securities can be seasoned and gradually distributed to investors. In many cases an entirely new security issue will fail to attract conservative investors, who like to see a long and well-tested record of earning power behind the securities they purchase. The existence of an organized security market enables just this desired "seasoning" process to be carried on, and thus for new securities to pass gradually into investors' strongboxes. New issues can in turn be underwritten because there is this undertow of absorption of the older issues by investors. Upon these processes, the financing of large-scale industry and trade in turn depends.

With these and other equally basic functions of the stock market few have any quarrel. The principal point of criticism of the stock exchange is that its facilities are so commonly employed for "speculation." Yet a closer analysis of "speculation" itself will readily reveal the fact that it cannot be abolished, because it is needed to sustain risks inevitable and inherent in security ownership. If the stock market were available only to investors, it could not function continuously and therefore could not render securities truly and surely negotiable. What is more, new securities could be issued only with the greatest difficulty, since ordinarily it is the speculator who absorbs so large a part of them until they become "seasoned" and made attractive to investors. Economists have in fact long compared the economic function of speculation with that of insurance, because both provide methods for the absorption of risk. In the security market, the investor can avoid or shift his risks only because of the presence and activities of the speculator. The investor can purchase "seasoned" issues because the speculator has been willing to hold them until they were "seasoned." When his securities begin to show deterioration, the investor can sell them largely because the speculator will take them off his hands, with the risks they entail. If these risks of ownership could not be shifted in this way to speculators at the will of the investor, the latter would be forced to absorb them himself, and investment itself would of necessity become speculative.

After the great fluctuations in security prices which have occurred all over the world in the last decade, it is natural that everyone should be anxious to see greater price stability in the stock market, and many superficially plausible schemes for artificially "stabilizing" the security market have been proposed. One trouble with such plans is that they fail to penetrate to the real bed rock of the situation. The only way to stabilize security prices is to stabilize industrial earning power. So long as earning power fluctuates, the prices of securities which depend upon it are bound to fluctuate. Artificial stabilization schemes for the stock market, granted that they were really workable, could only succeed in manipulating security prices in order to have them tell falsehoods concerning the security values which they should truthfully reflect. Any such perversions of security prices, however well meant, would entail the danger of creating a disparity between prices and values that could be corrected only by unusually violent and sudden price fluctuations.

T. BOONE PICKENS, JR.
1928–

T. Boone Pickens earned a reputation as a raider for taking large investment positions in a number of oil companies. Along the way, he has been called many other things, including a greenmailer, a communist, and a piranha. Pickens' disillusionment with corporate America came early in his career. After studying geology at Oklahoma State University, Pickens' first job was with Philips Petroleum in 1951 as an oil-well site geologist. Disappointed with the company's bureaucracy, he quit at age 26. For the next couple of years, he lived out of his station wagon as he drove around Texas, prospecting land to drill and raising financing to do it. In 1956, with two partners and $2,500, Pickens founded the company that would become Mesa Petroleum and would evolve into the largest independently owned oil and gas company in the United States.

Pickens, who had expanded his drilling efforts into Canada and the North Sea, was looking for a quantum leap in value, and a takeover was just the thing. His first target was Cities Service, an oil company that was number 38 on the Fortune 500 list in 1982. Over a couple of years Pickens bought enough Cities stock to make a serious offer, but then Gulf and Occidental Petroleum entered the picture and thwarted his takeover attempt. Regardless, Pickens pocketed a cool $32 million. And he set his sights on Gulf.

In 1983, the oil industry was hurting, and Pickens was desperate to either raise some cash or successfully take over another company with plenty of resources. He chose to target Gulf, building up a 13.2 percent stake. The battle got ugly, with Gulf hiring detectives to dig up dirt on him. In 1984, Gulf accepted a friendly offer from Socal; the combined companies renamed themselves Chevron. Pickens' profit: $218 million. Whether Pickens was truly interested in enhancing the value of these companies through better management, as he claimed, or was simply looking to make a buck, is still up for debate. However, in *Professions of a Short-Termer,* he defends his position and attacks executives concerned only with keeping their jobs and not with what's best for the shareholders.

Professions of a Short-Termer
T. Boone Pickens, Jr.

It is no coincidence that the two largest acquisitions in history had essentially the same ingredients. In each case, management had compiled a miserable long-term operating record. Equally important, a disenchanted shareholder stepped forward to serve as a catalyst for change.

In 1983 Gordon Getty and the trusts for which he had fiduciary responsibility represented the largest single block of Getty Oil stock. Dissatisfied with the meager returns received by the company's shareholders and the continuing depletion of oil and gas reserves, he orchestrated the $10 billion acquisition of Getty Oil by Texaco in early 1984.

I represented an investor group that became Gulf Oil's largest shareholder. Rather than consider the group's proposals to enhance shareholder value, Gulf ran into the arms of Chevron for $13 billion.

Before they lost their independence, Getty Oil and Gulf were case studies in unsuccessful long-term planning. Unable to find as much new oil and gas as they produced, they had entered a state of gradual liquidation. During the five years ending in 1983, Gulf depleted the equivalent of 400 million barrels of oil, or 22% of its domestic reserve base. Getty Oil lost 250 million barrels, or 14% of its domestic reserve base, during the same period. The two companies' costs of adding new domestic reserves averaged more than $14 per barrel, higher than for all but one of their competitors.

Like other major oil companies, Getty Oil and Gulf plowed a substantial portion of the excess cash flow generated by OPEC oil price increases into marginal investments and disappointing diversifications. Gulf poured its money into unprofitable refineries, uranium, and coal. Getty bought a portion of the ESPN cable network, which Texaco later unloaded.

The common stock of Gulf and Getty Oil sold at a fraction of the value of their underlying assets. In short, they had no viable long-term strategies, and their shareholders were paying the price.

Yet public perceptions of these two megadeals were much different. No one called Gordon Getty a raider, a pirate, or a predator, although his insurrection ended Getty Oil's independence.

I was called all those things and more.

The reason for the name-calling? Unlike Getty, who had inherited his holdings long ago, we in the Gulf Investors Group had bought our shares in late 1983. We were short-term shareholders with short-term objectives. Or so our critics claimed.

AN APPEALING THEORY . . .

I raise the contrast between the Getty Oil and the Gulf cases because it underscores a fundamental issue affecting the future accountability of corporate America. After decades of near sovereign autonomy, the professional managers of many large, publicly held corporations are finding themselves on the firing line. They are being asked to justify lackluster performance and questionable strategies. They are being called on to address the chronic undervaluation of their securities.

In some cases, their indifference or antipathy gives rise to hostile tender offers or activist shareholders' proxy fights.

As often as not, these besieged managers decry their detractors as short-termers. Consider the following comments:

> The vast majority of unfriendly acquisitions reflect strategies for short-term gain at the expense of long-term values. (Raymond Plank, chairman, Apache Corporation, and founder, Stakeholders in America)

> Today, equity is valued in the marketplace in relationship to its current, or immediate past, or immediate future earnings. . . . This translates to a tremendous pressure on every corporation that is owned by these people for short-term performance. (Andrew C. Sigler, chairman and CEO, Champion International, and spokesman, Business Roundtable)

> Can you run America with a fairly large percentage of your investors being casino gamblers? That's the problem you've got with all of your managers of your pension funds and foundation funds. . . . You know they trade on a tenth of a point. They'll sell and buy your stock twice in one day. They have no wait, no holding periods, no taxes to pay . . . it's entirely fast buck. (Fred Hartley, chairman, Unocal Corporation)

> It's not just the oil companies. A majority of the *Fortune* '500' companies are susceptible. . . . If this persists, American industry will move into a short-term strategy of decision making. With a short-term strategy, who's going to do the research for tomorrow? (Charles Kittrell, executive vice president, Phillips Petroleum Company)

These sentiments appear throughout corporate America. In 1985 the Conference Board surveyed the attitudes of nearly 300 chief executive officers in the United States and abroad. On the question of accountability, the respondents acknowledged their responsibility to the owners of their companies. Yet the Conference Board's report noted that allegiance to shareholders is waning:

> In the United States particularly, shareholders, as such, do not command the esteem they used to. . . . The changing structure of equity holdings evokes a bit of cynicism among some CEOs about shareholders. A U.S. CEO complains: "A year from now, 70% of my stockholders will have changed. On that basis, I put my customers, and my employees, way ahead of them."

In recent months comments like these have become the rallying cry of entrenched managements. Many CEOs and their lobbying organizations have seized on a new philosophical rationale for insulating themselves from the expectations of owners and explaining away the undervaluation of their securities.

This new argument against shareholder activism has come to be known as the short-term theory. It is based on the premise that achieving value for shareholders within a reasonable time frame is incompatible with pursuing future growth. When confronted with a perceived threat to their sovereignty, managers have learned to portray themselves as long-term visionaries and their dissident stockholders as short-term opportunists.

Increasing acceptance of the short-term theory has freed executives to scorn any shareholders they choose to identify as short-termers. Executives aim their contempt not only at the initiators of takeover attempts but at the arbitrageurs and the institutional investors who frequently trade in and out of stocks.

Armed with this argument, growing numbers of corporations are erecting potent new takeover defenses. These corporations are subdividing shareholders into categories based solely on seniority. Those that management determines have been on the shareowners' roster a sufficient length of time are accorded increased voting rights, preferential treatment, and much more respect. Those who have climbed on board more recently are seated at the back of the bus or disenfranchised altogether.

When confronted with a perceived threat to their sovereignty, managers have learned to portray themselves as long-term visionaries and their dissident stockholders as short-term opportunists.

An example of this indentured shareholder concept is the creation of dual classes of stock, with one class bestowing "super" voting rights on its holders. Another is the adoption of waiting periods before new shareholders are entitled to vote on an equal basis with other shareholders. One variation on the separate-and-unequal theme is the selective self-tender. This tactic, recently employed against Mesa by Unocal, excludes a specified shareholder from participating in a corporate stock repurchase. Like other discriminatory defensive tactics, the tactic allows companies, on the basis of their perceived objectives, to deny full rights of ownership to selected shareholders.

Although they take different forms, these strategies to differentiate classes of owners are alike in one respect: they effectively cast aside the traditional tenet of stockholder equality and give managements the ability to categorize, divide, and conquer.

. . . THAT'S PURE HOKUM

On a rational level, the short-term theory attracts support because it seems plausible to those not closely involved with takeover activity. On an emotional level, the theory appears to embrace basic American values such as patience, perseverance, and faith in future rewards.

In reality, the short-term theory is pure hokum. Any observer who believes in even a modicum of market efficiency should be able to see through the smoke.

There is a virtual vacuum of empirical evidence to indicate that sound planning for tomorrow depresses today's stock prices and increases vulnerability to takeovers. In fact, recent research indicates that the opposite relationship may exist.

In a 1985 study Gregg Jarrell and Kenneth Lehn of the Securities and Exchange Commission compared the relative levels of research and development expenditures among 324 companies representing a cross-section of 19 research-intensive industries. The SEC economists found no evidence that increasing stock ownership of performance-oriented institutional investors has coerced managements to forgo long-term expenditures such as those for R&D. As average institutional ownership of the 324 companies grew from 1980 to 1983, average ratios of R&D expenditures to corporate revenues also rose.

In 217 companies that had been targets of takeover attempts, average R&D expenditures were measurably lower than for other rivals in their industries. It's interesting that institutional investors owned an average of only 19% of the takeover targets but an average of nearly 34% of the non-target businesses.

"The evidence strongly refutes the proposition that the stock market values only short-term earnings, and not expected future earnings," the SEC economists concluded. "A logical inference to be drawn from this evidence is that it is futile for corporate managers to try to forestall a hostile takeover by pumping up short-term earnings at the expense of investing in long-term projects with positive net present values."

Preliminary findings from another 1985 study, undertaken on behalf of the Investor Responsibility Research Center (IRRC), indicate that the objects of unfriendly takeover attempts do not have superior financial characteristics. Yale University researcher John Pound determined that target companies have neither higher levels of cash flow and capital expenditures than nontarget companies nor superior returns on equity and rates of earnings growth. The targets in Pound's sample also tend to have as much or more debt on their balance sheets, a finding in conflict with the contention that "stronger" companies are often targets of acquisition offers.

In a separate study also commissioned by the IRRC, Pound corroborates the SEC's earlier finding that a high level of institutional ownership does not appear to increase vulnerability to takeovers. He found that institutional ownership averaged only 22% among 100 companies that were takeover targets from 1981 through 1984, whereas for the market as a whole it averaged 35%.

The findings of the SEC and the IRRC researchers illustrate the fallacy of the short-term theory. To those who understand the fundamentals of stock market valuation, the inherent contradiction of this theory has been obvious all along.

The market price of any common stock represents the investing public's collective judgment of the value of underlying assets and the anticipated results of corporate strategies. If investors have good reason to believe that current strategies will yield superior returns, they will gladly pay a premium to participate. If they are convinced that current strategies will yield inferior returns, they will undervalue the stock. The securities of a corporation expected to generate average returns will be priced in the market at a level approximating the underlying asset value.

In projecting a company's performance, only a fool would ignore its past. In many cases, undervaluation reflects the market's recognition that previous long-term planning has not panned out. Without apparent change in corporate strategies or industry economics, the future is unlikely to appear much brighter.

In the oil industry, the undervaluation of many companies stems largely from corporate strategies that have yielded dismal returns on recent investments. For years, many oil companies poured funds into marginal exploration programs, underutilized refineries, and unsuccessful diversification efforts. These investments continued despite ominous economic signals such as excess supply, diminished demand, declining prices, and low inflation.

A 1985 study by Bernard J. Picchi, a petroleum analyst with the investment firm of Salomon Brothers, documented the subpar returns achieved by 30 large oil companies on their exploration expenditures. From 1982 through 1984, Picchi reported, the companies' expenditures on exploration far exceeded the discounted present value of their added oil and gas reserves. His findings indicate that every dollar invested yielded new oil and gas reserves with a present value of only $.80.

"Very few companies really have very much to crow about," Picchi told a group of drilling contractors in November 1985. "Most firms' exploration expenditures, in my estimation, have achieved such poor rates of return as to constitute a waste of the shareholders' assets."

Despite clear indications of declining industry fundamentals, America's major oil companies spent approximately $105 billion on exploration and development from 1982 through 1984. Extrapolating from Picchi's findings, we see that the major oil companies lost as much as $200 billion in present value during this period.

What many managements seem to be demanding is more time to keep making the same mistakes.

The oil companies' ill-conceived attempts to diversify have compounded their problems. In the late 1970s and early 1980s, the majors rushed headlong to acquire companies engaged in unfamiliar undertakings. Exxon bought Reliance Electric. Mobil bought Montgomery Ward. Atlantic Richfield and Standard of Ohio bought into the minerals business at the top of the cycle. Gulf invested in uranium, and Getty became a broadcaster. The list goes on.

Many of these acquisitions have caused huge writedowns in recent months, and some have been sold at substantial losses. The assets the majors are writing down and selling off today are the legacy of their long-term strategies of five years ago.

Judging from the experience of the oil industry, it is questionable how much more long-term planning America's shareholders can stand. What many managements seem to be demanding is more time to keep making the same mistakes.

IN DEFENSE OF OWNERS — ALL OF THEM

If the confidence of America's investing public is to be maintained in the years ahead, the short-term theory must be exposed for what it really is: a weak argument advanced by weak managements. Companies are not punished for taking the long view; they are applauded. Investors are not impressed by efforts to embellish the near term; they question the impact on future returns.

Perhaps proponents of the short-term theory have lost sight of the commitment they or their predecessors made when their companies went public. Corporations issue stock to the public to acquire capital for financing future growth. The market provides those funds with the expectation that management will strive to achieve competitive returns. Management's failure to do so invites undervaluation and, ultimately, acquisition offers.

In many cases, the professional managers of mature or declining corporations seem to feel little affinity for shareholders. It may have been decades since their companies last went to the equity markets for capital. Today's stockholders may bear little resemblance to the investors who helped bankroll company growth. Why should shareholders' interests take precedence over relationships with employees, customers, and other corporate constituencies?

If the confidence of America's investing public is to be maintained in the years ahead, the short-term theory must be exposed for what it really is: a weak argument advanced by weak managements.

Because shareholders own the companies. In any public corporation they bear the ultimate financial risk for management's actions. The exposure is no less for the investors who bought their stock 5 days ago than for those who inherited their stock 50 years earlier. There is no initial grace period during which new shareholders are shielded from the effects of corporate blunders. No money-back guarantee protects the recently arrived from unexpected earnings declines. When it comes to allocating risk, length of ownership is not a factor.

The same standards should apply to the rights of ownership. Companies that invite public investors to participate in their glory years should not selectively ignore them once growth slows and performance turns sluggish. Their decision to go public encumbers them with a continuing obligation to serve the interests not only of the initial equity owners but of their successors as well. After all, short-termers would not exist if it weren't for long-termers who were ready to sell. If managements fail to earn competitive returns, they must stand equally accountable to all owners, not just to those who have suffered the longest.

Finally, I encourage investors, managers, and policy-makers to think twice before endorsing antitakeover devices based on unequal treatment of investors. These strategies not only fail to advance any corporate purpose other than management tenure, but they also undermine a basic democratic tradition. America's publicly owned corporations should not selectively abrogate the one-person, one-vote principle inherent in any representative form of governance.

As I observe an increasing number of corporate executives embrace the short-term theory, I am reminded of remarks made by Gulf's chairman James E. Lee. In early 1984 I met with Lee to discuss Gulf's future. Another major oil company, which Chevron subsequently outbid, had offered to pay $70 per share to acquire Gulf.

As Gulf's operating decline became apparent, the price of its stock receded from an oil boom high of $54 in 1980 to about $37 in the fall of 1983. The stock was trading at roughly a third of the intrinsic value of Gulf's assets, estimated by analysts at about $114 per share.

Still, Lee wanted to talk long term.

"Boone, you're our largest shareholder. Would you be willing to give me two or three years more?" he asked.

"Why would you want two or three more years?" I replied.

"Because I think we can get the stock up to $60 or $65 by then."

"Jimmy, why would we want to wait two or three years to get the price up to $60 or $65 when you have an offer on the table for $70?"

"Boone, I was afraid you would say that."

As an unrepentant short-termer, I offer a final suggestion to the 47 million other shareholders who have placed their funds at risk in America's public corporations: beware the manager who proclaims to the world he is a long-termer, beginning today.

JAMES GRANT

The founder and publisher of the highly respected *Grant's Interest Rate Observer* is anything but a notorious character, although his subject certainly is. Grant has dedicated himself not only to predicting interest rate movements, but to interpreting the Wall Street scene through a skeptical eye. After serving in the Navy during the Vietnam War, he fell into journalism. Grant was working as a staff writer for *Barron's* until the summer of 1983, when he left to start his twice-monthly publication. The first issue was published in November of that year. Since then he has started two other newsletters, *Grant's Asia Observer* and *Grant's Municipal Bond Observer*. His offices are (ironically) in a converted boardroom of a bankrupt Wall Street bank.

Of his approach, Grant wrote: "Our editorial approach was to ask the deceptively simple question, 'What's next in financial markets' . . . *Grant's* developed a niche in truth-telling, which sometimes amounted to nothing more than quoting the hair-raising legal language of the bond prospectuses. . . ." An over-bearish attitude, however, has sometimes caused him to miss the mark. For example, in early 1991 he wrote what he called "first-rate pieces" on why the stock market wouldn't go up. But it did, for the next seven years. In admitting his erroneous ways, Grant concludes, "There is little or no permanent truth in financial markets." Another insight to failure: "Extensive experience has taught me that there are many ways to be wrong about markets: through shortsightedness, of course, but also through excessive farsightedness; through pride, ignorance, bad luck, impatience, imagination, or sophistry."

While Grant was criticized for being overly pessimistic, he did anticipate the downfall of characters like Michael Milken and Donald Trump (although they have since rehabilitated themselves). He also predicted the spectacular rise in real estate prices of the late 1980s and Japan's economic collapse in the 1990s. But it was the junk bond era of the 1980s that provided plenty of fodder for his witty writing. *Michael Milken, Meet Sewell Avery* is in that vein, as he puts the junk bond craze into historical perspective and explains why debt is a fair-weather friend.

Michael Milken, Meet Sewell Avery

James Grant

Trammell Crow, the king of the surviving Dallas real estate developers and a charter Forbes Four Hundred member, is credited with a number of pithy business sayings. Builders are leveraged and optimistic fellows, and some of Crow's remarks are inspirational, e.g., "The way to wealth is debt." However, recent goings-on in the credit markets may force a revision in that epigram. The updated version may read, less pithily, "The way to wealth in a bull market is debt. The way to oblivion in a bear market is also debt, and nobody rings a bell."

Debt is the original fair-weather friend. It is with you on the upside, and against you on the downside. So long has the financial sun been shining that it seems—especially to the bulls on Wall Street—as if the skies will never darken. But if you can acknowledge the possibility of even one inclement business season, you will want to reflect on the leveraged American condition, and on many of the private American fortunes that constitute the Forbes Four Hundred. You will want to consider that debt may become just as unpopular one day as it now is popular. You may want to anticipate how a forward-thinking investor might profit from such a turn in events.

When the legendary showman P. T. Barnum stretched to buy his American Museum more than a century ago, a friend asked him how he intended to pay for it. "Brass," he replied gaily, "for silver and gold have I none."

"The way to wealth in a bull market is debt. The way to oblivion in a bear market is also debt, and nobody rings a bell."

This is an account of the new brass age in American finance — where we are now, how we got here and where we are going.

Financially speaking, the story of the 20th century has been the mellowing of the American lender. At the turn of the century, it was hard to get a loan. In 1989, if you have a mailbox into which a credit card can be dropped, it is almost impossible not to get one. Consumers, governments and businesses have borrowed as never before. It is the decade of the five-year Yugo loan, the leveraged-buyout loan, the unsecured bridge loan, the teaser-rate adjustable-rate mortgage loan, the rescheduled Brazilian or Mexican loan, the Sotheby's art-quality loan and the liposuction and breast-enlargement loan. It is the decade of retractable facsimile bonds, subordinated primary capital perpetual floating rate notes and collateralized fixed-rate multi-tranche tap notes. All in all, the 1980s are to debt what the 1960s were to sex.

Debt is more than a financial medium — more, even, than the de facto legal tender of the great bull market. Debt is an industry in itself, like auto parts. What is so notable about the gilded career of billionaire Michael R. Milken is that it happened at all. Its timing was a stroke of luck. In the 1950s, when the intense young Milken was almost certainly not wasting his time watching Lassie on television, interest rates were low, tax rates were high and the stock market (by our lights) was moderately valued. In retrospect, it was the perfect time to launch a junk bond enterprise, except for one important catch. The shadow of the Great Depression still fell across American finance. As recently as the mid-1950s, Citibank put more of its depositors' money into Treasury securities than it did into loans.

During Christmas week 1955, a panel of distinguished economists convened in New York to assess the disquieting state of American credit. The scholars observed that three-year auto loans had begun to proliferate (in the 1920s, the average maturity was one year) and that mortgage loans were available on suspiciously lenient terms. Geoffrey Moore, a leading authority on the business cycle, found parallels between the credit expansion of the mid-1950s and that of the 1920s, and he suggested that caution was the order of the day.

What is so notable about the gilded career of billionaire Michael R. Milken is that it happened at all. Its timing was a stroke of luck.

What was not then apparent was that the postwar relaxation of lending standards had only just begun. The process would continue for decades, and would reach extremes unimagined in the 1920s. You can make the case that this liberalization began with A. P. Giannini, founder of the Bank of Italy in turn-of-the-century San Francisco. Giannini had the radical notion that the workingman would actually repay a loan. His idea was visionary, and his bank—renamed BankAmerica—was once the largest in the country.

The founding of the Federal Reserve System in 1913, the advent of the General Motors Acceptance Corporation in 1919, and the ballooning of margin debt in the Coolidge bull market were the financial milestones of the 1910s and 1920s.

Nobody was in a mood for liberalization in the 1930s, and it will be noted that no Milken look-alike made his mark on American finance in the 1940s, 1950s or 1960s. What the creditors of those years knew is that heavy borrowing was a technique favored by people like Charles E. Mitchell, chairman of National City Bank, who wound up explaining themselves before congressional investigating committees.

Milken didn't know that, or wisely ignored it if he did. As he was entering business in the early 1970s, a generation of Depression-scarred lenders was exiting. Their mental baggage—the trauma of the 1930s debt liquidation—was not his, and he rediscovered the forbidden fruit of extreme financial leverage.

The 1980s are to debt what the 1960s were to sex.

What he knew about debt is that it magnifies financial results. It hefts prosperity up by its bootstraps and makes it something larger than it would otherwise be. It facilitates the sale of houses, cars and businesses to buyers who otherwise couldn't afford them. It nullifies the old idea, propounded by John Kenneth Galbraith, that entrenched corporate managements may safely live the life of Riley behind a wall of equity. It produces stupendous fees and underwriting commissions for investment bankers.

In Milken's case, it produced one of the greatest fortunes in Wall Street history. It simultaneously smiled on the decade's big debtors, including such Four Hundred members as Nelson Peltz (of Triangle Industries fame), cellular mogul Craig McCaw and leveraged buyout guy Henry Kravis.

What Milken may not have reckoned with is that success breeds success. Good ideas become bad ideas through a competitive process of "Can you top this?" So completely have the old antidebt prejudices been erased that extraordinary transactions have begun to seem commonplace, and astonishing numbers have lost their power to amaze. Old fogies, having complained about an imminent day of reckoning for the past 30 years, are no longer taken seriously, and the debt keeps on being piled higher and higher. It is a fact, for example, that fewer than 9,000 Americans filed for personal bankruptcy in 1946 but that more than 9,000 filed each week in 1988. It is okay to borrow and no mortal sin to welsh.

It is a fact that, in this business expansion, the nation's ratio of corporate cash flow to interest expense has fallen to the lowest level in the postwar period—lower, even, than in the trough of the 1973 recession. It is a fact that William J. Stoecker, a bearded former welder with a line of blarney about the Rust Belt renaissance, succeeded in borrowing millions without the conventional preliminary step of presenting his lenders with a set of aduited financials.

Good ideas become bad ideas through a competitive process of "Can you top this?"

Nor did anyone seem to think it odd when Duff & Phelps, the Chicago-based bond-rating service, underwent a management buyout early this year and issued its own junk bonds. When the deal closed, long-term debt ballooned to $112 million from $34 million. Net worth fell to minus $10.8 million from positive $3.6 million. Fees and expenses in connection with the buyout ran to almost $13 million, which was more than the equity contribution of the management investors.

More notable than the numbers was the symbolism. D&P was founded in the Depression to analyze the securities of the then-shipwrecked public utility holding companies. Its stock in trade was the like of Middle West Utilities, part of the Samuel Insull empire, which failed in 1932. Insull, no mere financial manipulator but a utilities builder par excellence, ran aground on the rocks of leverage. He borrowed heavily in 1930, which, of course, was the wrong time to do almost anything except turn over and go back to bed. Anyway, D&P's foray into the junk bond market constitutes yet another vivid reminder that the ghost of the Great Depression had been laid to rest.

If you lived in the stifling credit environment of the 1930s or 1940s, you may be moved to cheer, "High time." No doubt, bankers in that inhibited era were as unreasonably fearful as the current crop is unreasonably bold. But even so, you must wonder if a good thing hasn't been pushed too far.

It is impossible to date the beginning of the change in lending attitudes, but sentiment has radically turned. In 1989 borrowers may browse through 40-year mortgage loans, 6-year car loans and zero coupon junk bond loans. What is so revealing of the crowd psychology of lenders is that some of today's risky corporate-finance techniques may have made sense a decade ago, when they just weren't done. At the time, common stocks were cheap and real rates of interest were low or negative, but leveraged buyouts were viewed with distrust. In the late 1970s—in retrospect, an ideal time to take a company private with borrowed money—the pioneers of the leveraged buyout movement were doing deals of $350 million or less. In the late 1980s, a time of punitively high real rates and not-cheap stock prices, RJR Nabisco was acquired for $25 billion.

Buried in a recent *Wall Street Journal* was an innocuous-sounding feature on one of the decade's trendiest banks. "Having taken an unprecedented role in Alfred Checchi's pending $3.65 billion purchase of NWA Inc.," the story led off, "Bankers Trust New York Corp. has assumed a new high-risk profile in the lucrative merchant banking field. Its main unit, Bankers Trust Co., not only is arranging $3.35 billion of senior debt for the bid but also acted as a financial adviser to Mr. Checchi. The bank's parent is taking an $80 million chunk of equity in the parent of Northwest Airlines, by far the biggest equity investment in the company's $475 million pool of equity investment."

Here was an onion of oddity. Layer number one: Someone proposed to recapitalize an airline. Layer number two: That someone found a partner in a commercial bank. Layer number three: This commercial bank, impersonating Henry Kravis, resolved to become an equity player.

The Northwest story created no more shock than the Duff & Phelps story did. What was so striking about the *Journal* item was what was left unsaid.

A telltale sign of a mania is that people and institutions readily do things they wouldn't do — in fact, wouldn't be caught dead doing — in ordinary times.

A decade ago, Forstmann Little & Co. and Kohlberg Kravis Roberts & Co. had some conservative ideas about which companies might, and which might not, be appropriately leveraged. The ideal LBPO candidate was one that produced steady and predictable cash flow. It was insulated from the business cycle. It was unregulated and unburdened by heavy capital spending requirements. It preferably had nothing to do with labor unions. In just about every detail, in fact, it was the polar opposite of NWA.

A telltale sign of a mania is that people and institutions readily do things they wouldn't do—in fact, wouldn't be caught dead doing—in ordinary times. Do you remember the picture of the late Sewell Avery being carried out of his office in 1944, sedan-chair style, for disobeying a government order? This was the same Avery who led U.S. Gypsum Co., a producer of wallboard and other building materials, from 1905 to 1951, and was chairman of Montgomery Ward & Co. Avery's regime spanned thick and thin, and he excelled in the thin. A bear's a bear—he was prepared for the Depression, but not for the great postwar prosperity.

At Montgomery Ward, he piled up cash just when he should have been expanding to compete with Sears, Roebuck & Co. And it is a cinch that he would not have believed, much less relished, the events of 1988. Desert Partners L.P., assisted by Merrill Lynch, mounted a bid for USG Corp., which USG repelled with a leveraged recapitalization. It is a sign of the times that this transaction—the leveraging of a cyclical company—provoked no general amazement.

In boom-time corporate finance, it is hard to distinguish the balance sheet of a bankrupt company from that of a newly leveraged one. Both are likely to show high indebtedness, low (or negative) net worth and modest working capital. USG unveiled its absolutely up-to-the-minute finances last year. Long-term debt was $3 billion, and net worth was minus $1.6 billion. The numbers made a provocative contrast not only to the 1987, investment-grade USG but also to the 1933 company, with the mossback Avery presiding. In that Depression year, equity comprised 98% of capital and current assets were 14.5 times greater than current liabilities. In comparison with the Depression-era Gypsum, the contemporary company, blessed by the greatest business expansion in postwar annals, looks as though it has been hit by a bus.

Are we crazy, or were they? Are we overleveraged, or were they underleveraged? Was Avery the crank, or is Milken? Is there ever such a thing as a new era, and, if so, could this be one?

In boom-time corporate finance, it is hard to distinguish the balance sheet of a bankrupt company from that of a newly leveraged one.

The partial answer to the last question is "yes." There are new eras all the time. In living memory, there have been new eras in politics, medicine, middleweight boxing and computer technology. In financial affairs, however, new eras are few and far between, because markets are driven by crowds. Have you ever seen just one bold banker? One timid banker? Like the Washington press corps, lenders are suggestible people. They see what others see and do what others do.

A valuable study of the psychology of the credit markets was performed by Ilse Mintz of the National Bureau of Economic Research in 1950. In the 1920s, a favorite investment was the high-yielding debt of South American governments. By 1935, defaults in those bonds were endemic, and the defaults occurred in a logical pattern. Securities issued early in the 1920s did relatively well. Those issued late in the decade—a time of seemingly limitless blue skies—fared badly. For foreign government bonds sold in the 1925–29 period default rates ran as high as 50%. In banking, success begets success, and confidence spawns confidence.

"After years of watching their big-city cousins amass huge equity and mezzanine-debt portfolios in leveraged buyouts and other corporate restructurings, regional banks are chasing the risky but potentially lucrative investments," *American Banker* recently reported. "Regionals Seeking Share of LBO Jackpot," was the suggestive headline. The story reported on the results of a recent poll of corporate-finance officers at 21 regional banks. Seventeen of these worthies expressed a "newfound willingness to buy subordinated debt or equity," *American Banker* said. A year and a half earlier, the story continued, "only two said their banks would dip below the secure senior debt level, despite the low returns."

If men and women were angels, of course, the trend would work in reverse. Lenders would be bold at the bottom and worried at the top. By the same token, investors would buy at the bottom and sell at the top, and it would be, although dull, a more lucrative world.

"The more intense the craze, the higher the type of intellect that succumbs to it," said a banker in the 1930s; and nobody who has lived through the 1980s can doubt the wisdom of that remark. The nature of tidal market events is that they carry further than almost anyone can imagine. They either make you believe in them, or they make you poor. By 1989 this Darwinian process had weeded out doubters, bears and conservatives by the score, while enriching numerous members of the burgeoning American debt industry, and larding the Forbes Four Hundred with big-time debtors. It caused the standards of prudent corporate lending to be loosened and conditioned a small army of junk bond investors not to believe the plain English in debt prospectuses.

When, at long last, Integrated Resources Inc., the property syndicator and financial services company, hit the wall this summer, it was a lesson in blind faith and inevitability. For years, Integrated—an issuer and buyer of speculative-grade debt through the offices of Drexel Burnham Lambert Inc.—told anybody who cared to listen that its numbers didn't work. "The company believes that it will continue to require additional funds from sources other than operations in order to finance its operations," said a 1986 quarterly report. In fact, its operating income had peaked as long ago as 1984. Its cash flow was chronically negative. Its capitalization—heavily weighted to long-term debt, preferred stock and commercial paper—was swollen. Then, on an ordinary Wednesday in June, it ran out of borrowed money.

"In retrospect, it was a fragile capital structure," remarked President and Chief Operating Officer Arthur H. Goldberg to the *New York Times*, after that structure fell to pieces. That it took so long to come unstuck is one of those curiosities that have made the 1980s such an interesting decade. It only stands to reason that a few weeks before Integrated's collapse, the company was rumored to be a takeover candidate at $21 a share (the stock duly closed above $15).

In markets, everything has its season, and borrowed money is no more likely to prove a permanent sure thing than one-decision stocks, portfolio insurance or bags of silver coins. The habits of a long prosperity have bred the conviction that asset values always appreciate: They don't. Well-intended academics have contended that a well-diversified portfolio of high-yield bonds will always outperform a portfolio of government bonds: It won't. Five years of easy money have popularized the balmy idea that you can always get a loan: As Integrated Resources unexpectedly showed, sometimes you can't.

As Milken understood, easy access to credit facilitates the marginal transaction. It makes possible the sale of the nth product to the nth buyer. It enlarges the gross national product, expands the debt industry and creates the rationale for a future relaxation of lending standards.

But when the cycle turns, the process must swing into reverse. Marginal transactions, financed by debt, must be unwound through foreclosure or bankruptcy. Asset values, propped up by debt, must fall, and thereby reduce other asset values in a chain reaction—in a generalized process similar to what is now happening to Arizona real estate. The staple idea of junk bond finance—that corporate assets can always be sold, or debt advantageously refinanced—must be discredited.

As Milken understood, easy access to credit facilitates the marginal transaction.

On form, the reaction will be too severe. Lenders will become too conservative, and respected financial leaders will try to show that two plus two makes three. Junk bond prices will go down too far, and the debt industry will be tarred and feathered.

The composition of the Forbes Four Hundred will undergo sudden change. A pair of wings in the boom debt will prove a ton of bricks in the slump. The new rich will be the people with cash and courage. There will be fewer debtors and more creditors on the Forbes list, fewer Peltzes and Crows, and more Rockefellers (the purpose of a bear market, as someone once said, is to restore wealth to its rightful owners). Investment-grade balance sheets will become newly fashionable. And—one more prophecy—someone will build a monument to Sewell Avery.

On that day, buy junk bonds.

PART VII

Crash and Learn

In the opening essay, Frank Vanderlip, a premier banker of the early 1900s, states that panics make for a "swift education." Vanderlip goes on to describe their 1907 savior, J. P. Morgan, as a man whose "words were literally fired from the remarkable, cannon-like cigars that he smoked habitually." As with most crashes, reforms quickly followed, with the 1907 panic leading to the creation of the Federal Reserve System in 1913. The devastating impact of the 1929 crash, which destroyed the lives of both the poor and the rich, is summed up by renowned journalist Edwin Lefèvre, who wrote, "a worldwide earthquake doesn't ask for personal references." For J. Paul Getty, panics are a time to buy, as was the case in 1962. However, he says, you must still do your homework and not expect just any depressed stock to "get hot." Most of the authors agree: The key to surviving market crashes is to avoid delusion. Look around. Is speculation rampant, as it was in 1929? Are monetary problems hurting the economy, as they were in 1987? The greatest investment lessons can be learned from past mistakes.

FRANK A. VANDERLIP
1864–1937

By the end of World War I, Frank Vanderlip was considered the most aggressive financier in the United States. His ambition had roots in his poverty-stricken youth: He grew up on an Illinois farm; his father died when he was 12; and he took a job in a machine shop, making 75 cents a day. At the shop, he encountered a new phenomenon—electricity—and vowed he would go to college to study engineering. And he did for a year, attending the University of Illinois, after which he applied to Thomas Edison for a job, but was rejected. Eventually, Vanderlip took a reporting job with the local paper. At 25, he became the financial editor of the Chicago Tribune and started taking business classes at the University of Chicago.

Vanderlip's big break came when a mentor was appointed Secretary of the Treasury and invited him to become his personal assistant in Washington. Before long, Vanderlip was made Assistant Secretary, and he won recognition by being instrumental in acquiring financing for the Spanish War. In 1901 he was recruited by National City Bank, the largest in the country, and he became its president in 1909. His employer, the venerable Mr. Stillman, taught him, he said, as "a parent mongoose teaches its young." Caution was foremost, but he also learned "that a man is never so rich he can afford to have an enemy; enemies must be placated; competition must never become so keen as to wound the dignity of a rival; and, above all, I was to avoid having too many banking eggs in one basket."

Such advice would pay off as Vanderlip became the director of a railroad, butted heads with the temperamental robber baron E. H. Harriman, and built himself an alliance with J. P. Morgan. Vanderlip's own remarkable accension was not lost on him and he kept life in perspective. A reporter once asked him, "What has been the hardest step of all your career?" He answered, "To get out of my overalls." The panic of 1907 must have been another; Vanderlip described it as "madness." In the following selection, *The Haunting Specter,* he describes what happens when a leaking ship doesn't have a stern captain.

The Haunting Specter
(1907)

Frank A. Vanderlip

The specters that haunt a banker when his world goes mad are terrible. I can tell you because I remember 1907.

A "run" is always appropriate material for the nightmare of a banker. Just fancy yourself as a banker—and discovering outside your plate glass façade an ever-lengthening column of men and women, all having bankbooks and checks clutched in their hands. Fancy those who would be best known to you, the ones with the biggest balances, pushing to the head of the line—there to bargain excitedly with the depositors holding the places nearest the wickets of the paying tellers. Even that won't give you a hint of what a banker's dread is like unless you heighten the effect with a swarm of hoarse-throated newsboys, each with his cry pitched to an hysterical scream; and then give the hideous concert an overtone of sound from the scuffling feet of a mob.

Although the depositors never gathered as a mob outside our bank, I knew the flavor of terror just from contemplating the possibility. We had the biggest and strongest bank in the country, but obviously we could not hope to be in a position, ever, to pay their cash to all of our depositors if they should demand it simultaneously. Bigness does not save an elephant staked on an ant-hill. Bigness will not save a bank if a run endures long enough. In that year, 1907, the size of the National City Bank was regarded as phenomenal in America, and more than impressive in London, Paris, Berlin and St. Petersburg. We had in our own vaults as our lawful reserves more than $40,000,000—and three-quarters of that sum was in gold. On our books were sums representing millions due us from other banks; we had paper that represented nearly $120,000,000 of loans and discounts; we had many other millions in the form of Government bonds; every day we held possession of pieces of paper representing millions of dollars which were expressed on our books as "exchanges for clearing house." In August, 1907, we were a fabulous organism.

Our total resources were:

$231,455,057.07

But, of course, our liabilities were:

$231,455,057.07

If it was a big, strong beast, it was a gentle one, and I was one of its mahouts, charged with responsibility for its well-being, its continued existence, its further growth. You can bet I worried as the nation became infected with fear-madness.

Although the depositors never gathered as a mob outside our bank, I knew the flavor of terror just from contemplating the possibility.

The Roosevelt in the White House at that time was Theodore, and his policies and behavior were thoroughly obnoxious to the orthodox financial group. They called him a demagogue, and he, for his part, threatened dire things. Once he threatened to take over the coal-mines as a way to settle a strike. He said he would use the Army to do it. As a matter of fact, most of the things that Theodore Roosevelt wanted to do were good for the country; but some of his schemes were dangerous.

However, his antagonism to railroads and railroad financiers was intense; that antagonism extended to practically all of the very large corporations. Even without his enmity, the railroads would have been having a hard time. Their facilities were unequal to the task of moving the freight on the first continent ever to have a single nation spread clear across it. James J. Hill had shocked the country by declaring that twelve and a half billion dollars would have to be spent within ten years if the railroads were to be put in shape to do the work that was demanded of them. Industries quite generally found themselves in unsatisfactory position, and so were dismissing many of their employees. At the same time all of the unemployed were finding themselves in competition for such jobs as there were, with myriads of immigrants. In the ten months ending in October, 1,150,000 strangers had reached our shores, and all had come to seek their fortunes in America. In the very month that the panic began, 111,000 immigrants were landed. In view of what was happening, that one fact represented a ghastly piece of bad management on the part of the Government. But this was not all: the copper industry had received a severe shock—a drop in the price of copper. In six months copper had declined from twenty-six cents to twelve cents a pound. Amalgamated Copper cut its dividend in half, and certain speculators in the stocks of copper companies found themselves in a financial vise.

The Knickerbocker Trust Company had been financing some of those copper speculations. It had improperly loaned some of its money to Charles W. Morse; something for which John T. Barney, the president, was held responsible later. This, of course, was a hidden weakness in the structure. What started a fatal run on the Knickerbocker Trust was an entirely different matter.

In our individualistic banking system of that time, the trust companies, operating under too-tolerant state laws, were engaged in some unsound banking practices. These created an annoying element of unfair competition for the more strictly controlled National Banks. In that period none of the rapidly growing trust companies was a member of the Clearing House Association. Some of the stronger trust companies made shift to use the facilities of the clearing house by having special arrangements with one or another of the banks which were members. In such a case, a bank would send a trust company's daily accumulation of checks for collection to the clearing house, just as if those checks were a part of the bank's own business. This parasitical device, akin to the habitual borrowing by an improvident neighbor of one's lawn-mower, finally tried the patience of the National Bank of Commerce, which had been performing this service for the Knickerbocker Trust Company. In a curt announcement, the public read that the National Bank of Commerce had declined any longer to clear the checks of the Knickerbocker. The depositors of the Knickerbocker believed they read in this statement something of deeper significance. They began to pour into the trust company, determined to withdraw their deposits. The Knickerbocker did not have much cash. Trust companies were not required to keep cash reserves against their deposits at a ratio at all comparable with that required of the National Banks in the central reserve cities, New York, Chicago and St. Louis, which had to have in their vaults, always, cash equal to 25 per cent of their demand deposits. Lacking cash, the Knickerbocker quickly had to close its doors.

Immediately, an already timorous public grew suspicious of most of the other trust companies, and lines of depositors began to form in front of their doors. Extra editions of the newspapers, falling prices registered in the stock-market, wild rumors, these things contributed force to the wave of emotion that engulfed the banking system.

Almost every caller was some one needing to be soothed. One acquaintance who came to my desk was a man with black eyebrows so mobile from excitement they seemed likely, any moment, to scamper up his forehead and vanish into his hair. He was Julian Street, the young author, and he was clutching in a trousers' pocket something unprecedented in the pockets of all other authors I had ever known. Street had fifty yellow $1,000 bills. He explained possession credibly; the money was part of his wife's inheritance and, after an adventure, he had just retrieved it from one of the trust companies.

On that first morning of the panic Street had taken fright as had every one else; you could catch the infection of terror over the telephone from the tone of a voice. A short while before a considerable part of his wife's fortune had been turned into cash. Pending reinvestment, it was on deposit with one of the trust companies; but even the strongest trust companies had become suspect. As he came down-town everywhere Street saw men and women dashing about in the manner of ants when their hill is trod on. He determined to get the money and bring it to me.

When he presented his certificate of deposit at the trust company he was invited into a conference with a vice-president. This man attempted to reason with Street; he said the company was as strong as the country itself and that it was foolish for Mr. Street to incur the risk of robbery or loss by some other means. But Street was firm, and so another official added his arguments and when he could not change the client's mind, the president himself joined the group. For nearly three hours those men argued and cajoled. Probably their pride was involved, but all that they said simply frightened Street more, until he was the personification of the 1907 panic.

"The country is in terrible shape," he said, "if you three men can spend hours making such a to-do about an account of this size."

"But for your own good, Mr. Street . . ."

"Cash!" roared Street. "I want the cash. Read what it says on this certificate: payment on demand. I demand the cash."

"Not so loud, please, Mr. Street, because we are simply trying to keep you from a foolish action. What can you do with the money?"

"None of your business. I want that cash."

"Well, if you insist, let us give you a certified check."

"Cash," repeated Street shrilly, "or I go out and give the story to the newspapers."

They surrendered then and gave him his bundle of thousand-dollar bills. As I received that welcome money from him and gave my hurried assurance it would be quite safe in the City Bank, neither of us had a clairvoyant hint of a future in which his son and my daughter would marry and make us grandfather-partners in a completely adorable little girl; indeed, two adorable little girls.

Madness, of course, is the word for the sudden, unreasonable, overpowering fright that communicates itself through all the human herd at such a time as that to which I refer. From too much usage, the word "panic" has ceased to have its proper cutting-edge as a tool for the mind. It has degenerated into a mere time symbol in our vocabularies, a sort of asterisk, marking the calendar of our memory opposite such years as 1873, 1893, and 1907. Yet, a banking panic, such as occurred in 1907, is actually akin to that which happens when a leaking ship's company is mastered by fear, instead of a stern captain, and rushes for the small boats, forgetful of all obligations except the brutish one of self-preservation. This swift contagion comes, when it does, as quickly as you can say the word: "panic!"

Oh, but we had a stern captain in 1907; it was during those days of strain that I discovered for myself what an admirable intelligence gleamed through the fierce eyes of J. Pierpont Morgan. He was our captain; he was literally the nation's captain. His leadership was something that was taken for granted when the banking mechanism was floundering in difficulties. The most important men responded to his call, eagerly, and usually were quick to do his bidding. Mr. Morgan could be savage when he was out of patience, and, when he was crossed, unrelenting.

One of the first moves that Mr. Morgan made, in an effort to quell the panic, was to summon the presidents of all the trust companies. Astonishingly enough, they never before had been brought together.

A banking panic . . . is actually akin to that which happens when a leaking ship's company is mastered by fear, instead of a stern captain . . .

Well, Mr. Morgan, with his back to the fireplace, watched those men as they gathered in response to his call. In sharp contrast to the linkage of the bank presidents, through their Clearing House Association, and in other connections, was the complete lack of organization among the trust companies. In an angry undertone, Mr. Morgan complained to Mr. Stillman that on this morning he had actually had to introduce to one another the presidents of some of the biggest trust companies. As was true of all bankers, Mr. Morgan had been going without sleep—hurrying from meeting to meeting; at the Morgan offices, at his home, at the Waldorf, or in one or another of the banks. His nerves were raw that morning. He was using every fiber of his intelligence to encompass the problem of a nation. Moreover, he had, I think, a sound banker's contempt for the slovenly banking operations of some of those who were then gathering at his bidding.

Old Governor Morton moved about clasping and unclasping inky-veined hands under the tails of his Prince Albert. As was his custom, he was wearing on his egg-bald skull a wig, one of a series of three that he owned, graded as to length of hair, and which he wore in succession. That old man—he was 83 in 1907—had been Minister to France, he had been Vice-President of the United States when Benjamin Harrison was President, he had been Governor of

New York; for eight years he had been the president of the Morton Trust Company. Presently he planted himself before Mr. Morgan, mouth partially opened as if he were carefully trying to select words for an important utterance.

The big weakness was in the lack of coordination in the banking system as a whole. . . .

"John," he said at last, "how old are you?"

Mr. Morgan's scowl would have blighted an oak. "Too old to waste my time talking to you," he growled as he strode away.

That particular morning Mr. Morgan had time only to urge upon the trust company presidents a need for united action. Hastily the New York Clearing House Association amended its by-laws so as to permit the admission of any trust company which agreed to keep a 15 per cent cash reserve. But it was clear to all of us, I think, that the big weakness was in the lack of coordination in the banking system as a whole. . . .

Those weeks in October and November were a period of swift education for most bankers, and I was certainly an eager student. I was learning that the banking reforms which I had long been preaching would have to be expressed in the form of some sort of a central banking organization. We would have to invent a wholesale banking mechanism that would relieve our economic system from the intolerable strains to which periodically it was being subjected. I was learning also that banking is not a field for weaklings. If I was strong, I had need of all my strength and my own physical reserves were being drawn upon in the same way that we were having to take assets out of the bank's vaults. I ate when I could, and slept, if at all, in the home of Mr. Stillman; at this time he had a house in Seventy-second Street.

In response to some prescient warning of the trouble to come, Mr. Stillman had returned to the United States before the panic began in earnest. Be sure that I welcomed him. If any man possessed power to look into the future, that man was Mr. Stillman. His mind was ceaselessly trying to fit together the things that he knew, so as to give him a better understanding of what was coming. It was not precisely like having a crystal ball to have access to Mr. Stillman's intelligence, but it was, I think, the next thing to it. Often the proposal that Mr. Stillman uttered quietly was the thing that Mr. Morgan executed; but Mr. Stillman was above the struggle, rather than in it.

Banking is not a field for weaklings. . . .

One of the early features of the panic had been the discrediting of individuals who had come to occupy important positions in the banking structure. Among them were Charles W. Morse, Edward R. Thomas, and Orlando F. Thomas. These men who had acquired important banking interests by daring operations were forced to retire from all banking positions. Public opinion was aroused against Morse in particular, and his resignations created vacancies on the boards of a number of banks. In some cases entire boards of directors were forced out of office. There was, as a result, just that much more work to be done by those experienced bankers in whom confidence continued.

I remember one incident in a small, private room of one of the up-town banks. It was quite late at night. Seven or eight of us who represented the strongest institutions in the city had gathered to determine if we would be justified in using some of the doubly-precious cash of our banks to enable a weaker one to open its doors on the following morning. Mr. Morgan had come to this meeting.

Mr. Morgan's utterances usually came with a force that suggested his words were literally fired from the remarkable, cannon-like cigars that he smoked habitually. He was a connoisseur of wines and in tobacco, too, his taste was aware of equally subtle gradations. He smoked only the tobacco of certain favored crop years. It was Havana tobacco, but it was rolled in shapes never sold in any cigar store. Morgan cigars had the form of a Hercules club, bulging thickly at the outer end, and they were absolutely poisonous for all but the most experienced smokers. I know I smoked myself giddy the first time I lighted one that he had thrust into my hand. Thereafter, until I had become inured to strong tobacco, I would always put his gift cigars in my pocket, and so keep my mind free for the calm consideration of whatever financial matter we might be under the necessity of discussing. On this night to which I refer, Mr. Morgan was listening as a report was made on the contents of the portfolio of the bank we were considering. That astonishing brain of his would take into itself a welter of facts and then, after consideration, he would speak, and we who listened would know that we were hearing wisdom. Suddenly I saw that the hand holding his cigar had relaxed on the table; his head had sunk forward until his chin was cushioned on his cravat. His breathing had become audible. The weary old man had fallen asleep.

One of the early features of the panic had been the discrediting of individuals who had come to occupy important positions in the banking structure.

Some one there, with a touch on the arm, silenced the one who was talking; another reached forward and lifted from the relaxed fingers, as one might take a rattle from a baby, the big cigar that was scorching the varnish of the table. Then we sat quietly, saying nothing whatever. One who went for a drink of water walked on tiptoes. The only sound that could be heard was the breathing of Mr. Morgan. It seems to me now that it was a long while before he awakened. When he did consciousness returned abruptly; in a second he was wide awake and our conference was resumed with no reference being made to Mr. Morgan's nap.

We were not always so gentle in those harsh days. I recall as if it were an act in a melodrama a day in November, when a group of us gathered for a meeting in a private office in the Trust Company of America Building. We were the directors of the Norfolk & Southern Railway. The road was in difficulties, as were most railroad corporations. The problem could be expressed always in one way: cash. We were there to go through the legal formalities necessary to authorize the issuance of a mortgage for $25,000,000. The shareholders had given their approval.

Among those present was Oakleigh Thorne, president of the Trust Company of America. He was as restless as a cat detained from its basket of mewing kittens; downstairs were many things demanding his attention. Who could say what bad news there might be coughing out of the stock-ticker? At any minute that menacing line of depositors might begin again to extend itself into the street to grow monstrously until it would be giving off a wave of hysteria, having repercussions all over the country.

As the lawyer lifted papers from his bag in preparation for the reading of the mortgage, there was a little talk of the latest gossip out of the Knickerbocker Trust Company mess. Most of us there knew, and had an affection for, John T. Barney who had been its president. Some were inclined to blame Charles W. Morse or F. Augustus Heintze for Barney's difficulties. Then the lawyer began his *pro forma* reading.

While he was in the midst of its dull phrases a telephone bell rang and, as Oakleigh Thorne answered it, the lawyer stopped reading.

"Barney has committed suicide," said Thorne. "Shot himself with a pistol."

No one commented. The lawyer went on reading. That was not callousness. We simply had no time to express our feelings. At that moment the battle was on; we were in it.

As author of the investment classic *Reminiscences of a Stock Operator,* among many other great books and articles, Edwin Lefèvre provided significant insight into the human nature of the investor. Lefèvre's life began far from Wall Street; he was born in Panama, where his father was stationed for business reasons. Although he graduated from Lehigh University in 1890 with a degree in engineering and mining, he embarked on a journalism career with the *New York Sun.* Unfortunately, his job entailed the tedious compiling of the daily commodities quotes for everything from eggs to petroleum. Finally, he convinced his editor to let him write a story on the banana industry. After it was published, he forged a lavish fan letter that convinced his editor to make him a full-time writer.

Lefèvre wrote exclusively for *The Saturday Evening Post* in the 1920s and 1930s, and during those years he became renowned for his Wall Street insights. For example, of bull markets he wrote: "They run their course because human nature does not change. Before they end they are apt to degenerate into a frenzied carnival of gambling. . . ." And take an example from 1932: "Reckless fools lose first because they deserved to lose, and careful wise men lose later because a world-wide earthquake doesn't ask for personal references." Never having dabbled in stocks, Lefèvre's primary means for obtaining the investor's perspective was through interviews. His son once recalled how his father could spend a mere 10 minutes with a subject and know all there was to know.

The 1929 crash and its aftermath provided plenty of material. In contemplating whether it would ever again be safe to invest, he wrote: "1. Never! 2. Always! Never for the crowd. . . . Always for the reasonable man; for it all depends upon what you call 'safe,' in a world peopled by fallible human beings." In *Vanished Billions,* Lefèvre brings out some of those fallible traits, such as the investor's unwillingness to acknowledge warning signs that the bull has run its course. He leaves the reader wondering if delusional mankind has learned anything from the horror of 1929.

Vanished Billions
(1929)
Edwin Lefèvre

It would have meant money and comfort to millions of Americans if they had followed advice given three thousand years ago: "In the day of prosperity be joyful, but in the day of adversity consider!" Translated from the King James version into stock-market jargon, it is: "In a bear market be sure you do what you didn't do in the bull market!" When you deal with states of mind you learn that men have always been what they are today, ticker or no ticker.

The reason why the stock market must necessarily remain the same is that speculators don't change; they can't. They could see no top early in 1929 and they could see no bottom late in 1931. Shrewd business men who wouldn't sell absurdly overpriced securities would not buy, two years later, underpriced stocks and bonds. The same blindness to actual values was there, only that while the heavy black bandage was greed in the bull market, it was fear in the bear market. Reckless fools lost first because they deserved to lose, and careful wise men lost later because a world-wide earthquake doesn't ask for personal references. Nevertheless, there is a general belief that the wise rich escaped punishment—as usual. You incessantly hear about the huge losses of the unlucky multitude, though there has not been any destruction of actual wealth or tangible property, as happens in war.

The financial reviews at the end of the year that dwelt on the extent of the losses did not remind the losers that the first to go were the dream dollars. Everybody who looked for easy money in 1928 or 1929 lost both dreams and cash in 1929 or 1930. In 1931 nobody was spared.

Reckless fools lost first because they deserved to lose, and careful wise men lost later because a world-wide earthquake doesn't ask for personal references.

FOR THE OTHER FELLOW ONLY

The powerful millionaires accumulated minus signs then, when owners and former owners of stocks and bonds consisted of poor, poorer and paupers. Poverty, like riches, is relative. A poor man finds this hard to believe because he thinks in superlatives: Himself and his hardships. The great social equalizer is the common need to live on less than a man has been accustomed to spending; and everybody has had to do that lately. Nevertheless, delusions persist: The delusion that the world, so wonderful during the boom, is going to pot via the lost-money route; that the way to recover from hard times is to keep on hoping that somebody else will do something about it, preferably the politicians or the bankers; that cities, states and Uncle Sam can put off giving the taxpayers their money's worth as long as they try to offset deficits by increasing the taxes of the rich. This last is as great a delusion as the human mind can hold, its chief purpose being to win votes and to increase the burdens of the ultimate consumer—the deluded poor. You can pass a law that will make rich men poor, but you cannot enact one that will make poor men rich. But they tell you that the rich, having suffered less than the poor in the past, must suffer more in the future! Reduce wages, but don't touch mine! Sell your goods cheaper, but don't ask me to come down in my prices! I am playing safe by hoarding my money, but you must spend more than ever, to make work for the unemployed.

The behavior of the stock market of late months has had only a post-mortem interest for millions of once-courageous Americans. The delusion of the bulls in 1928 and 1929, costly as it proved, was not so destructive to society as the later delusion that bargains are not bargains because of the possibility that prices may go still lower. Not one American in a million, as this article is being written, asks himself the intelligent trader's question: *How much can I lose?* He does not wish to lose at all, and experience proves that it is the inveterate sure-thing player who eventually buys gold bricks.

You can pass a law that will make rich men poor, but you cannot enact one that will make poor men rich.

WHEN THE DOLLAR DEPARTS

I propose to tell men who were never rich, except for a brief moment on paper, how men who were always rich have ceased to be rich. Men of experience, ability, courage and capital, who never had to take heavy losses before, have taken more than their share of the universal wallop. Read on; for now it may be told.

It is natural that the worst financial collapse in the world's history should set a high record for money losses. The average man prefers to hear in detail how, why and when money is lost, rather than to listen to old proverbs about the evanescence of riches, but about the only point on which all commentators on the world depression agree is that many millions of people have lost many millions of dollars. Of course, the same people lost many other things as well, for the revenge that easy money takes on its temporary possessor is that, when it leaves him, after a boom, it carries away skin as well as securities, vanity as well as values. Some part of the loser always manages to adhere to the departing dollar—a fact well known to the maimed victims. Two years ago the vast army of greed-stricken Americans, male and female, who lost billions when the bull market ended were called silly asses for thinking they could get something for nothing—fools who deserved to lose because they violated the fundamental principles of the ancient art of making money the moment they tried to play the other man's game. Now we see that if poor fools lost in 1929, the wise rich lost in 1931. Nobody escaped. It was a lesson for everybody to learn—and we have learned it.

From the peak in 1929 to the low of December of the same year, the shrinkage in the market value of stocks dealt in on the New York Stock Exchange amounted to more than $26,000,000,000. From the peak of the boom to the low of 1931, the shrinkage in the same stocks amounted to nearly $60,000,000,000. From the high of 1930 to the low of 1931, it was about $45,000,000,000. The shrinkage in 1929 from peak to bottom in listed bonds, in which poor fools didn't gamble, was less than $1,000,000,000, but from September, 1930, to December, 1931, the difference exceeded $10,000,000,000. In bonds, remember! In other words, from the height of the speculative madness to the time when the poor pikers were eliminated, the total loss was only about $27,000,000,000 in both stocks and bonds on the New York Stock Exchange. But from the spring of 1930 to the end of 1931, or after the little fellow had been wiped out, the loss exceeded $55,000,000,000. From the top of the boom to December, 1931, the net shrinkage was nearly $66,000,000,000.

WALL STREET, THE INDIAN GIVER

These statistics make no more impression on the average mind than the figures of the distance to Betelgeuse. They are too great to grasp. And at that, these unassimilable sums represent only a part of the total depreciation. If we were to include the losses in the value of unlisted stocks and of all kinds of bonds and real estate and commercial and banking failures, it would be found that the aggregate realizable assets of the American people have temporarily shrunk beyond calculation. After considering these figures, I am convinced that the most remarkable thing about it all is that we could take such a loss and still live—buy and sell and vote. Less than 3 per cent of the American people pay an income tax to Uncle Sam, and 90 per cent of the entire tax is paid by less than one-quarter of 1 per cent of the population. The 1930 tax figures showed that the sturdy old 3 per cent of the population suffered a loss in income running into the hundreds of millions; and, of course, the 1931 income will show still greater losses. The boom that turned so many average Americans into stock-market millionaires in 1928 and 1929 was an Indian giver. It gave, and then proceeded to take away far more than it had given.

But it has been discovered that the losses of millions by millions have more than a conversational value: They automatically become the universal and unassailable alibi. Ask any doctor, banker, landlord, credit manager or any seller of anything. All will testify that they get the same answer from customers: "I lost every cent I had in the world in the stock market and I haven't had a chance to get any of it back. I will pay as soon as I can. . . . No, I can't pay you a part of it."

If the creditor happens to be obstinate and an optimist, he gets mass-production excuses and some autobiography. The chapters may be three or ten, but the last one is always: "Well, I didn't know enough to be satisfied with a good profit. I didn't think there was any top to them. I was a fool."

Times when a postscript is deemed necessary, it is always: "It serves me right."

Millions of these stock-market losers seem incapable of forgetting their Waterloo. The blunders of '29 hide the vista of possible successes in '32. It is a bad state of mind for a nation to fall into, especially when it is demonstrable that what the multitude, in their ignorance, did in 1929, the élite, in their wisdom, did in 1930 and 1931. The minus microbe plays no favorites. Neither native ability nor business experience, neither unusual sagacity nor ample capital can keep men from losing money at losing time.

Some thousands of years ago a wise man said: "There is a time to get and a time to lose." And don't forget that Solomon, in his day, was considered quite a getter.

Millions of these stock-market losers seem incapable of forgetting their Waterloo. The blunders of '29 hide the vista of possible successes . . .

The average man is apt to endow the multi-millionaire with infallible judgment in business matters. That probably is the reason why we hear so much about the present non-spending of the presumably rich. Perfectly decent families are insulted, vocally and in print, for not buying more of everything. What is a tragedy if you are idle, prudence if you are on part time and thrift if you are underpaid, becomes murder in the first degree in the rich man who could instantly end the depression by buying four overcoats or ten hats and considerately wearing them out in a week.

There is no question that the poor are poorer, but the rich certainly are not richer. The man who had nothing has doubled one of his zeros, but the average millionaire has lost three of them. One of the richest men in the world, according to an intimate friend, dropped eight zeros—preceded by a seven or eight. The rich somehow always manage to beat the poor at everything, even in money losses.

An old-fashioned banker who philosophizes on the slightest provocation said to me the other day: "Humanity progresses through the recognition of its mistakes. It is reasonable to assume that this lesson will prove to be less expensive than we now think it."

"Why must we assume that we are learning it?" I asked.

J. PAUL GETTY
1892–1976

When the Great Depression hit in the 1930s, J. Paul Getty realized that he could make more money buying oil companies than by drilling for oil. So, while oil stocks plummeted, Getty turned from being a wildcatter to a lone wolf, hunting for victims. He looked for companies trading below book value, but with valuable assets. His first investments in other oil companies, however, lost another $1 million. The stakes were high. "My stock purchases were financed by every dollar I possessed," he said, "and every cent of credit I could obtain. Had I lost the campaign . . . I would have been left personally penniless and very much in debt." Getty's biggest target was Tide Water, an oil company controlled by Rockefeller's Standard Oil—only Getty didn't know that when he first started buying its shares. After several years of sparring, Getty gained control through a backdoor maneuver by buying into a company that controlled a large block of Tide Water stock.

A financial genius, the richest man in the world once paid only $500 in income tax. Looking for loopholes at every opportunity was a trait Getty learned from his father, a Minneapolis lawyer who in 1904 brought his family to Oklahoma, a state not yet admitted to the Union. The elder Getty witnessed the oil rigs going up and knew there was money to be made as a wildcatter. An 11-year-old Getty followed his father through the fields and started keeping a diary, noting all aspects of the oil business. This experience proved to be his best education—college years at Berkeley and Oxford were wasted, he said.

The family later moved to California. Getty left abruptly in 1933 for fear of earthquakes, causing his wife to comment that he was "not really and truly a bold man except for investments." Of course, she wasn't around long either; Getty was married five times. Although he was a womanizer, he never forgot his top priority: "When I'm thinking about oil, I'm not thinking about girls." The same could be said for his other investments. In *The Wall Street Investor,* Getty reflects on the 1962 crash, draws on his experience from the Great Depression, and explains the importance of banking on trends, not tremors.

The Wall Street Investor
(1962)

J. Paul Getty

On Monday, May 28, 1962, prices on the New York Stock Exchange crumbled rapidly before an avalanche of sell orders. The Dow-Jones industrial average plunged nearly 35 points to register its biggest one-day drop in over 32 years. Crashing through the 600 level for the first time since 1960, it hit a day's low of 576.93.

By the end of the day, many big-board stocks were selling at prices from 30 to 80 percent below their 1962 highs. Shares traded on the American exchange and over-the-counter markets followed suit and also went into nosedives. Headline writers were quick to respond to the developments being reported by the lagging ticker:

BLACK MONDAY PANIC ON WALL STREET

INVESTORS LOSE BILLIONS AS MARKET BREAKS

NATION FEARS NEW 1929 DEBACLE

Such were the scare heads that appeared on the front pages of the nation's newspapers after the New York Stock Exchange closed for the day. By the time later editions came off the press, experts and analysts, economists and pundits were offering their explanations, hindsight diagnoses and spur-of-the-moment prognostications. As is often the case in

405

such situations, some of the second-guessers and crystal-ball gazers tried to gloss over the implications of the collapse, while others appeared to take an almost sadistic delight in prophesying even worse things to come.

Two days later, several newspaper and wire-service correspondents descended on me. They wanted to know my opinions and reactions and asked what I was doing because of the break in stock prices. I told them quite frankly that, while I sympathized wholeheartedly with anyone who had lost money because of market developments, I saw little if any reason for alarm and absolutely none for panic.

The over-all current business picture was favorable and, what was even more important, gave promise of getting better in the future. There was nothing basically wrong with the American economy nor the vast majority of companies whose stocks were listed on the New York Stock Exchange. In my view, some stocks had been grossly overpriced. Irrational buying had driven their prices to totally unrealistic levels. The May 28 break was an inevitable consequence.

I said that I felt the stock market was in a much healthier and certainly in a much more realistic position because of the long-needed adjustment of prices. As for what I was doing, the answer was simple. I was buying stocks.

Stock certificates are deeds of ownership in business enterprises and not betting slips.

"I'd be foolish *not* to buy," I explained to a young correspondent who looked as though he thought I'd taken leave of my senses by buying when everyone else seemed to be selling. "Most seasoned investors are doubtless doing much the same thing," I went on, feeling somewhat like a schoolmaster conducting a short course in the First Principles of Investment. "They're snapping up the fine stock bargains available as a result of the emotionally inspired selling wave."

Since the petroleum industry is the one I know best, I bought oil stocks. By the end of the New York Stock Exchange trading day on May 29, my brokers had purchased several tens of thousands of shares for my account. I hasten to emphasize that I bought the stocks for *investment* and not for speculation. I fully intend holding on to them, for I believe they will continue to increase in value over the years to come.

It has long been the custom for journalists and financial writers to interview successful businessmen and investors whenever there is an "unusual" stock market development. The opinions, information and advice gathered from these sources are then published, ostensibly for the guidance of less sophisticated investors. For as long as I can remember, veteran businessmen and investors—I among them—have been warning about the dangers of irrational stock speculation and hammering away at the theme that stock certificates are deeds of ownership in business enterprises and *not* betting slips.

Get-rich-quick schemes just don't work. If they did, then everyone on the face of the earth would be a millionaire. This holds as true for stock market dealings as it does for any other form of business activity.

Don't misunderstand me. It is possible to make money— and a great deal of money—in the stock market. But it can't be done overnight or by haphazard buying and selling. The big profits go to the intelligent, careful and patient investor, not to the reckless and overeager speculator. Conversely, it is the speculator who suffers the losses when the market takes a sudden downturn. The seasoned investor buys his stocks when they are priced low, holds them for the long-pull rise and takes in-between dips and slumps in his stride.

"Buy when stock prices are low—the lower the better— and hold onto your securities," a highly successful financier advised me years ago, when I first started buying stocks. "Bank on the trends and don't worry about the tremors. Keep your mind on the long-term cycles and ignore the sporadic ups and downs . . ."

Get-rich-quick schemes just don't work. If they did, then everyone on the face of the earth would be a millionaire.

Great numbers of people who purchase stocks seem unable to grasp these simple principles. They do not buy when prices are low. They are fearful of bargains. They wait until a stock goes up—and up—and then buy because they feel they are thus getting in on a sure thing. Very often, they buy too late—just before a stock has reached one of its peaks. Then they get caught and suffer losses when the price breaks even a few points. . . .

History shows that the overall trend of stock prices— like the overall trends of living costs, wages and almost everything else—is up. Naturally there have been and always will be dips, slumps, recessions and even depressions, but these are invariably followed by recoveries which carry most stock prices to new highs. Assuming that a stock and the company behind it are sound, an investor can hardly lose if he buys shares at the bottom and holds them until the inevitable upward cycle gets well under way.

Withal, the wise investor realizes that it is no longer possible to consider the stock market as a whole. Today's stock market is far too vast and complex for anyone to make sweeping generalized predictions about the course the market as such will follow.

It is necessary to view the present-day stock market in terms of groups of stocks, but it is not enough merely to classify them as, say, industrials or aircrafts, and so on. This is an era of constant and revolutionary scientific and technological changes and advances. Not only individual firms, but also entire industries must be judged as to their ability to keep pace with the needs of the future. The investor has to be certain that neither the products of the company in which he invests nor the particular industry itself will become obsolete in a few years.

In the early part of the century, farsighted individuals realized that automobiles had more of a future than buckboards, that automobile-tire manufacturers' stocks were better investment bets than the stocks of firms that manufactured wagon wheels.

The trolley-car industry was a good bet—until trolley cars began to be supplanted by buses. Airplane makers who insisted on producing nothing but canvas-covered planes after the day of the all-metal airplane dawned had little future. Today, the manufacturer of jet or turboprop transport planes is much more likely to be in business and make money than one, say, who insisted on turning out trimotored, piston-engined transports.

It is indeed surprising that so many investors fail to recognize business situations only slightly less obvious than these dated or farfetched examples. They will buy stocks in faltering or dying firms and industries and ignore tempting opportunities to buy into companies and industries that cannot help but burgeon as time goes on.

It follows that the investor must know as much as he possibly can about the corporation in which he buys stock. The following are some of the questions for which he should get satisfactory answers before he invests his money:

1. What is the company's history: Is it a solid and reputable firm, and does it have able, efficient and seasoned management?
2. Is the company producing or dealing in goods or services for which there will be a continuing demand in the foreseeable future?

3. Is the company in a field that is not dangerously overcrowded, and is it in a good competitive position?

4. Are company policies and operations farsighted and aggressive without calling for unjustified and dangerous overexpansion?

5. Will the corporate balance sheet stand up under the close scrutiny of a critical and impartial auditor?

6. Does the corporation have a satisfactory earnings record?

7. Have reasonable dividends been paid regularly to stockholders? If dividend payments were missed, were there good and sufficient reasons?

8. Is the company well within safe limits insofar as both long- and short-term borrowing are concerned?

9. Has the price of the stock moved up and down over the past few years without violently wide and apparently inexplicable fluctuations?

10. Does the per-share value of the company's net realizable assets exceed the stock exchange value of a common stock share at the time the investor contemplates buying?

Many stock buyers have failed to ask these questions. In some cases, they bought the stocks of companies that had not shown a profit for some time. But the issues would "get hot," as speculators are wont to say, and multiply several times over their issue price within a matter of weeks or even days. Then, someone would realize that the heat was being generated solely by irrational buying—and the prices would plummet.

I repeat that I personally believe that selected—and I want again to emphasize the word *selected*—common stocks are excellent investments. There are innumerable fine buys on the market today. Among them are many stocks issued by companies with net realizable assets two, three, four and even more times greater than the stock exchange value of their issued shares.

What does this mean to the investor? Well, for example, let's suppose that the mythical XYZ Corporation has realizable assets with a net value of $20,000,000. At the same time, it has 1,000,000 shares of common stock outstanding and the stock is selling at $10 per share. The arithmetic is simple. The $20,000,000 net value of the company's realizable assets is double the total $10,000,000 value of its outstanding common shares. Thus, anyone buying a share of the XYZ Corporation's common stock at $10 is buying $20 worth of actual, hard assets.

Such situations are not nearly so unusual as one might imagine—and the shrewd, seasoned investor takes the time and trouble to seek them out. Occasionally—though admittedly such instances are rare—especially astute investors discover companies that have undistributed surpluses equal to a sizable percentage of the market value of the outstanding common stock. Anyone buying stock in such a company is actually buying an amount of money equal to a goodly portion of his investment, as well as a share in the corporation's other assets.

I might point out, however, that the exact opposite may be true, and that the investor will still be safe. An individual does not necessarily have to buy stocks in a company whose vaults are bulging with cash in order to make a sound investment. There are many times when an entirely healthy company will be very short of cash.

Another valuable investment secret is that the owners of sound securities should never panic and unload their holdings when prices skid. Countless individuals have panicked during slumps, selling out when their stocks fell a few points, only to find that before long the prices were once more on their way up.

The professional or experienced semiprofessional investor has little in common with speculators who hopefully play the market when prices are spiraling up. The veteran investor objectively looks for bargains in growth stocks — which he buys and holds, and from which he generally reaps handsome profits over a period of years. He banks on the climate — and makes all necessary allowances and takes all precautions so that he can ride out any stock market storms.

There is still a lingering misconception that the small or amateur investor is at the mercy of the big investors and the Wall Street financiers. This might have been the case in the dim, distant and unlamented days of Jay Gould, but nothing could be further from the truth today. No ruthless, rapacious Wall Street tycoon can rig the market or corner the stocks of an entire industry these days. For one thing, stock market transactions are closely regulated by such highly efficient and potent watchdog organizations and agencies as the Federal Securities and Exchange Commission — the SEC. For another, the common stocks of most large corporations are owned by thousands and tens of thousands of individuals, organizations, mutual fund groups and so on. "Big" investors seldom own more than a comparatively small percentage of a large corporation's common stock.

If anything, it is the professional investor who is at the mercy of the speculator and the amateur — at least in the sense that the latter categories of stock buyers and sellers set the pattern for the market.

The professional investor purchases stocks on what might be termed a scientific, or at least a cerebral, basis. He analyzes facts and figures objectively and with great care and does his buying for purposes of long-term investment. He is, in effect, banking that the stocks he buys will increase appreciably in value over the next few or several years.

It is the emotional nonprofessional investor who sends the price of a stock up or down in sharp, sporadic and more or less short-lived spurts. A politician's speech, an ivory-tower pundit's pronouncements or prophecies, a newspaper item or a whispered rumor — such things are enough to trigger wildly enthusiastic buying sprees or hysterical orgies of panicky selling by thousands of self-styled investors. The professional investor has no choice but to sit by quietly while the mob has its day, until the enthusiasm or the panic of the speculators and nonprofessionals have been spent.

The seasoned investor does not allow temporary fluctuations in stock-market prices to influence his decisions to any great extent. Usually, he waits until prices return to approximately the levels at which he wants to buy or sell. He is not impatient, nor is he even in a very great hurry, for he is an investor—not a gambler nor a speculator.

It is the emotional nonprofessional investor who sends the price of a stock up or down in sharp, sporadic and more or less short-lived spurts.

People often ask me what specific advice I would give to individuals who have various amounts—$1000, $10,000, $100,000 or even more—to invest in common stocks. My answers are always the same. Whether I had $100 or $1,000,000 to invest, I would consider buying *only* such common stocks as are listed on a major stock exchange. I would apply the rules and tests I've enumerated and select the soundest and most promising growth stocks. And, I might add, I would certainly ignore the advice of promoters and theorists who peddle harebrained formulas or "secret" methods for making huge and quick profits on the stock market. There has been a spate of *How to Get Rich Overnight* books in recent years. Seasoned financiers and investors laugh at them—or rather, they feel only pity for the gullible individuals who follow the "advice" contained in such tomes. The May, 1962 Wall Street collapse pulled down many of these "blinkered" speculators, so its history should be worth examining.

In order to achieve any understanding of that collapse, it is helpful to first quickly trace the course of the market over

413

the preceding 12 years. The easiest way to do this is by following the Dow-Jones industrial average.

At the 1950 low, the Dow-Jones industrial average stood
at 161.60. It climbed to 293.79 by the end of 1952, dropped
to 255.49 in mid-1953, then climbed steadily to 521.04 in
1956, from which level it drifted down to around 420 at the
end of 1957.

From 420 in 1957, the Dow-Jones average rose to well
over 650 in 1959, made some up-and-down zigzags and hit a
late-1960 low of 566.05. From that base, it shot up to a then
all-time peak of 734.91 on December 13, 1961.

As the market moved upward through 1961, some Wall
Street veterans dusted off the oft-quoted pre-1929 crash saying that the stock market was discounting not only the
future, but the hereafter as well.

Many years ago, the per-share price *vs.* per-share earnings ratio was widely—though unofficially—adopted as a
reliable rule-of-thumb indicator of stock values. "Ten times
earnings" was long considered the maximum permissible
price one could pay for a stock and still reasonably expect to
make a profit.

Then, in the late 1920s, GM–Du Pont's John J. Raskob—
whose outlook was judged quite bullish—ventured the opinion that certain stocks might be worth as much as 15 times
their per-share earnings. After the 1929 crash, ratios were, of
course, very much lower and, even as late as 1950, the price-
earnings ratios of the stocks listed in the Dow-Jones industrial index averaged out to about 6:1.

Views on the price-earnings ratio underwent considerable revision in recent years. Some knowledgeable investors
allowed that in a rapidly burgeoning economy, stocks of
especially healthy companies might reasonably sell for as
much as 20 times their per-share earnings. Other professional investors argued persuasively that when healthy companies had tangible assets with net, per-share replacement or
liquidation values in excess of per-share prices, the importance of the price-earnings ratio would logically dwindle.

But few seasoned investors approved such situations as developed in 1960–1962, when frenzied buying drove prices so high that some issues were selling for more than 100 times their per-share earnings. In more than a few instances during the 1960–1962 period, staggering prices were paid for the stocks of companies that had only negligible assets, questionable potentials — and that hadn't shown much in the way of profits for a considerable time.

It has been suggested that the boom that began in 1960 was caused by people buying stocks as a hedge against inflation. If this is true, the insane inflation of certain common-stock prices was an extremely odd way to go about it. But the hedge theory appears even less valid when one remembers that buyers consistently ignored many fine stocks that, by any standards of measurement, were *under*priced and concentrated on certain issues, continuing to buy them after their prices had soared out of sight. All evidence inclines the observer to believe that the great mass of nonprofessional buyers was obeying a sort of herd instinct, following the crowd to snap up the popular issues without much regard for facts. Many people were doing their investment thinking — if it can properly be called that — with their emotions rather than with their heads. They looked for lightning-fast growth in stocks that were already priced higher than the limits of any genuine value levels to which they could conceivably grow in the foreseeable future.

It is an old Wall Street saw that the stock market will always find a reason for whatever it does — after having done it. Innumerable theories have been advanced to explain why the market broke on May 28, 1962. The blame has been placed on everything from "selling waves by foreign speculators" to the Kennedy Administration's reaction to the aborted steel industry price increase — in fact, on everything but the most obvious reasons.

The factors that bring on financial panics are many and varied. For example, in 1869, the cause was an attempted corner on gold. In 1873 and 1907, bank failures started the trouble. In 1929, the stock market was vastly overpriced, and the general state of American business and the rate of America's economic expansion were such as to justify little or none of the stock buying that carried prices to the towering peaks from which they inevitably had to fall.

Despite all the efforts that have been expended to draw a close parallel between the 1929 crash and the 1962 price break, the two have practically nothing in common.

True, some segments of the stock market were grossly overpriced in 1960–1962; far too many stocks were priced far too high. But the nation's business outlook was generally good in 1962 and the economy was expanding at a merry clip. There were no hidden, deep-down structural flaws in the economy such as there had been in 1929.

There were other great differences. In 1929, stock speculation was done mainly on borrowed money; shares were purchased on the most slender of margins. Thus, when prices collapsed, credit collapsed, too.

Then, of course, there is the most important difference of all, the one the calamity howlers conveniently forgot. May 28, 1962, was not a crash. It was an adjustment—albeit a somewhat violent one.

As I've said, some stocks were selling for more than 100 times their earnings during the height of the 1960–1962 boom. Now, it would be rather difficult for a company to expand enough to justify stock prices that were 100 times the company's per-share earnings. Even assuming that every penny of the company's earnings were paid out in dividends to common-stockholders, the stockholders would still be receiving only a one-percent return on their investment. But if all earnings were distributed in dividends, there would be no money left for the company to spend on expansion. That, of course, would effectively eliminate any possibility of capital growth. Yet, even with these glaringly self-evident truths staring them in the face, people bought overpriced stocks.

Such were the difficult situations that developed—and that caused the stock market to fall. Experienced investors should have been able to read the warning signals loud and clear long before the May 28 break took place.

As I stated previously, the Dow-Jones industrial average shot to its all-time high of 734.91 on December 13, 1961. The downward movement began immediately afterward and continued through December 1961 and January 1962. There was a brief recovery that continued until March, when the Dow-Jones average edged up over 720, but the graph line shows the recovery was an uncertain, faltering one. The downward trend was resumed in March—and the graph line from then on makes a steep descent that is broken by only a few spasmodic upward jogs.

The May 28, 1962, price break had its beginnings in December 1961. The downward adjustment was evidently needed and unavoidable. That it culminated in the sharp price plunge of May 28 was due to the emotional reaction— verging on panic—shown by inexperienced investors who were unable to realize that what was happening *had* to happen and, what was worse, who understood almost nothing of what was going on around them. To paraphrase Abraham Lincoln, *all* stock market investors cannot fool themselves *all* of the time. The awakening had to come—and it did.

The anatomy of a stock market boom-and-bust such as the country experienced in 1962 is not too difficult to analyze. The seeds of any bust are inherent in any boom that outstrips the pace of whatever solid factors gave it its impetus in the first place.

An old and rather corny comedy line has it that the only part of an automobile that cannot be made foolproof by a safety device is the nut that holds the wheel. By much the same token, there are no safeguards that can protect the emotional investor from himself.

Having bid the market up irrationally, these emotional investors became terrified and unloaded their holdings just as irrationally. Unfortunately, an emotionally inspired selling wave snowballs and carries with it the prices of all issues, even those that should be going up rather than down.

GEORGE SOROS
1930–

Hungarian-born George Soros learned all his survival instincts from his father during the German occupation in World War II. Because they were Jewish, his father obtained false papers and found places to hide. This was a man to respect; he had been captured by the Russians during World War I and subsequently had escaped from prison. Soros' takeaway: "Obeying the law became a dangerous addiction; flaunting it was the way to survive." And he himself admits to not accepting rules imposed by others and has been accused of exceeding the limits of fair play in trading both stock and currencies.

Stifled by the post–World War II communist regime, Soros left for Great Britain in 1947 and studied at the London School of Economics. After a travelling salesman stint, he found a job with a financial institution. While Soros gained some arbitrage experience, he was mostly restricted to boring clerical work, didn't excel, and left with the company's blessing. His sights were on New York, but he couldn't get a working visa because he was too young to be a specialist in anything, a requirement for entering the United States. So he "flaunted" the laws and secured an affidavit stating that arbitrage experts had to be young because they died young; the government let him in.

Eventually, Soros set up his own hedge fund. His investing techniques ran the gamut from hard-core research to gut instinct. Soros once said, ". . . I suffered from backache. I used the onset of acute pain as a signal that there was something wrong in my portfolio." That was some back pain—$10,000 invested with Soros in 1969 was worth $2.8 million plus in 1988. Soros has been characterized as having three investment techniques: "1. Start small. If things work out, build up a larger position. . . . 2. The market is dumb, so don't try to be omniscient. . . . 3. A speculator has to define the first level of risk that he dares assume." As for what can go wrong, Soros provides some insight by diagnosing the 1987 crash in *After Black Monday.* One of his points: The management of monetary policy is a critical global issue in preventing stock market crashes and recessions.

After Black Monday
(1987)

George Soros

T he stock market crash of
1987 was an event of historical significance for the world
economy. The crashes of 1893, 1907, and 1929 were comparable, but the 1929 plunge is the most widely known and in
many ways the most relevant. In drawing the comparison,
however, care must be taken not to confuse the crash itself
with its aftermath.

In the crash of October 1929, prices on the New York
Stock Exchange fell by about 36 per cent, as measured by
the Dow Jones industrial average; this figure is almost identical with the loss that occurred in October 1987. After the
1929 fall, stocks recovered nearly 50 per cent of their losses
and then declined by another 80 per cent in the long-drawn-
out bear market from 1930 to 1932. It is that bear market,
associated with the Great Depression, that preys on the public imagination. Precisely because it is so well remembered,
history is not likely to repeat itself. The U.S. government's
immediate reaction to the 1987 crash already has borne out
this contention. After 1929 the monetary authorities made a
momentous mistake by supplying too little liquidity, thus
failing to counter a drop in the money supply. The danger
now is that the pressures of avoiding a recession, especially
strong in a presidential election year, will lead the authorities

419

to supply too much liquidity and thereby further undermine the dollar's value.

Technically, the crash of 1987 bears an uncanny resemblance to the crash of 1929. The principal difference is that in 1929 the first selling climax was followed in a few days by a second one that carried the market to a lower low. In 1987 the second climax was avoided; and even if the market were to reach new lows in the future, the pattern would be different.

The crash of 1987 came just as unexpectedly as the crash of 1929. The worldwide stock boom was seen generally as unsound and unsustainable, but few people correctly predicted the sudden turn of events. I was as badly caught as the next person. I was convinced that the crash would start in Japan. That turned out to be an expensive mistake.

The most compelling similarity between the crash of 1929 and the crash of 1987—one not sufficiently appreciated by policymakers and the public—is that both incidents revealed a historic ongoing transfer of financial and economic power in the world economy. In 1929 the United States was superseding Great Britain as the world's predominant economic force. In 1987 the power was flowing from the United States to the Asian economic superpower, Japan. The crash of 1987 will be remembered as a signal event in that process as well as a harbinger of change in the international financial order because it offered dramatic evidence of the growing inadequacy of a global financial system based on an unstable and depreciating reserve currency, the U.S. dollar.

In retrospect, it is easy to reconstruct the sequence of events that led to the crash. The stock boom was fed by a growing supply of dollars; a reduction in liquidity then established the preconditions for a crash. In this respect, too, 1987 resembles 1929: It will be recalled that the 1929 crash was preceded by a rise in interest rates on short-term borrowing for stock transactions.

Exactly how the reduction in liquidity came about in 1987 is a thornier question. A definitive answer will have to await a great deal of research. But it is clear that the crucial role was played by international efforts to shore up the exchange value of the dollar—specifically through the Louvre Accord, which was initialed in February 1987 by finance ministers of the leading industrial countries called the Group of Seven— Britain, Canada, France, Italy, Japan, the United States, and West Germany. In the months following the Louvre Accord, the dollar was defended by sterilized intervention in financial markets—that is, domestic interest rates were left unaffected. When the Group of Seven's central banks found that they had to purchase more dollars than they had an appetite for, they changed tactics. After then Japanese Prime Minister Yasuhiro Nakasone's April 1987 visit to Washington, they allowed interest-rate differentials between the United States and other countries to widen until the private sector abroad became willing to hold dollars. In effect the banks privatized the intervention.

What is still unclear is whether it was the sterilized or the unsterilized intervention that actually caused the drop in liquidity. Sterilized intervention transferred large amounts of dollars to the coffers of central banks abroad, and the Federal Reserve Board may have inadvertently failed to inject equivalent amounts into the U.S. domestic money market. Alternatively, it may be that the monetary authorities in Japan and West Germany were afraid of the inflationary implications of unsterilized intervention, and their attempt to rein in their domestic money supplies led to the worldwide rise in interest rates.

I favor the latter explanation, although I cannot rule out the possibility that the former also contributed to the liquidity squeeze. The West Germans harbor a strong anti-inflationary bias. The Japanese are more pragmatic; they did, in fact, allow their interest rates to fall after Nakasone's return to Tokyo. But when the Japanese found that an easy money policy was merely reinforcing the unhealthy speculation in financial assets, including land, they had second thoughts. The government tried to slow the growth of the

Japanese domestic money supply and bank lending, but speculation already was out of control. Even after the Bank of Japan started to tighten its monetary grip, bond market prices continued to soar. As a consequence, the yield on the bellwether Coupon #89 bond issue fell to a historic low: 2.6 per cent in May before the bond market crashed.

The September 1987 collapse of the Japanese bond market was the first in a sequence of events that will enter the annals of history as the crash of 1987. Investors speculated heavily in September bond futures, but they could not liquidate their positions. Hedging against these losses led to a collapse of prices for December futures. The yield on the Coupon #89 issue climbed above 6 per cent before the bond market bottomed out. It appeared at first that the collapse would carry into the stock market, which was even more overvalued than the bond market. But, in fact, speculative money moved from bonds to stocks in a vain attempt to recoup the losses. As a result, the Japanese stock market reached minor new highs in October.

The consequences for the rest of the world were more grievous. The government bond market in the United States had grown dependent on Japanese buying. When the Japanese began to sell U.S. government bonds, even in relatively small quantities, the bond market suffered a sinking spell that went beyond any change justified by economic fundamentals. Undoubtedly the U.S. economy was stronger than had been expected, but the strength came in industrial production rather than in consumer demand. Commodity prices were rising, encouraging inventory accumulation and raising inflationary expectations. The fear of inflation was more a rationalization for the decline in bonds than its root cause. Nevertheless, it served to reinforce the bond market's fall.

The weakness in bonds widened the disparity between bond and stock prices that had been developing since the end of 1986. Such a disparity can persist indefinitely, as it did in the 1960s, but as it widens it creates the preconditions for an eventual reversal. The actual timing of the reversal depends on a confluence of other events. This time political considerations played a major role: Reagan had lost his political luster, and the 1988 elections were approaching. When downward pressure on the dollar was renewed, the stock market's internal instabilities converted a decline into a rout.

Analysts generally regard the stock market as the passive reflection of investors' expectations. But in fact, it is an active force in shaping them.

The first crack came when a widely followed Wall Street guru, the technical market analyst Robert Prechter, issued a bearish signal before the October 6 market opening. The market responded with a resounding fall of 90 points. This signaled underlying weakness in the market, but similar incidents had occurred in 1986 without catastrophic results. The situation deteriorated further this time when the dollar also started to weaken. On Tuesday, October 13, Alan Greenspan, chairman of the Federal Reserve Board, announced that the trade balance was showing an "extraordinary" structural improvement. So the figures published on Wednesday, October 14, which showed an improvement in the trade deficit only half as much as expected, proved all the more disappointing. The dollar experienced severe selling pressure.

Pursuing unsterilized intervention would have required an increase in interest rates—one that would need to be all the larger because of the earlier increases in Japan and West Germany. U.S. authorities were not willing to undertake such a tightening; and by Thursday, October 15, as the stock market continued to decline, Treasury Secretary James Baker was reported to be pressing Bonn to lower West German interest rates or else face a further fall in the dollar. The stock market decline continued to accelerate amid reports that the House Ways and Means Committee was planning to limit the tax deductibility of risky "junk" bonds issued in leveraged buy-outs of companies. Although the provision was abandoned the next day, October 16, stocks that had been bid up in the expectation of takeovers or leveraged buy-outs declined sufficiently to force the liquidation of margin accounts by professional arbitrage traders.

Then came the sensational lead article in the Sunday, October 18, issue of the *New York Times*. Treasury Department officials reportedly were advocating openly a lower dollar and blaming the West Germans in advance for the stock market collapse that these remarks helped precipitate. Some selling pressure on "Black Monday," October 19, was inevitable because of the instabilities accumulating in the stock market; but the *Times* article had a dramatic effect, exacerbating the built-in instabilities. The result was the largest single-day decline in history: The Dow Jones industrial average dropped 508 points, or 22.6 per cent of its value.

Analysts generally regard the stock market as the passive reflection of investors' expectations. But in fact, it is an active force in shaping them. Investors' expectations are presumed to be rational, but it is impossible to be rational in the face of genuine uncertainty. The greater the uncertainty, the more investors are likely to take their cue from the stock market. In turn, the more their investment decisions chase market trends, the more volatile the market becomes. The reliance on market trends has been carried to its logical conclusion in portfolio insurance programs. Portfolio insurance and other trend-reinforcing devices such as stock and index options in theory allow individual participants to limit their risk at the cost of aggravating the instability of the system. In practice, when too many people use such devices, the system breaks down. On October 19, such a breakdown occurred. The market became disorganized and panic set in.

PART VIII

Beyond Your Average Blue Chip

While the average do-it-yourself investor won't dabble in futures trading or short selling, if you're in a hedge fund, you ought to know about these more sophisticated practices. The authors in Part VIII explain the skills needed for trading in instruments beyond buying stocks. At the same time, much of the advice is useful in any investing arena. Consider part of Leo Melamed's third rule for options trading: "[F]ollow a predetermined trading plan; a set of rules or established guidelines that you believe are valid . . ." Stanley Kroll, a legendary commodities trader, gives some prime examples of why futures trading is part science and part art. For Martin Zweig, best known for his top ranked Zweig Forecast newsletter, selling short is a pretty simple affair because he finds it easier to dig up the negative information on a company than the positive. But why is Donald Trump included? Because there are alternatives to the stock market when it comes to investing. Whether it be stocks and bonds or real estate, as Trump concludes, "The dollar always talks in the end."

As one of the most powerful figures in finance, Leo Melamed revolutionized futures trading on the Chicago Mercantile Exchange. However, like fellow financial genius George Soros, Melamed first had to undertake a remarkable journey that involved eluding the Nazis and the Russians to come to the United States. In 1939 he and his family escaped from Poland to Lithuania, but once there, they needed a transit visa to continue. "Even my philosophic father," Melamed said, "couldn't explain how a person's life was reduced to waiting in line for a slip of paper that could mean the difference between living and dying." On the train ride through Siberia, young Melamed learned his first lesson in strategy—keeping cool and focused under fire— for, to his amazement, his father proceeded to play an intense game of chess, apparently oblivious to the chaos around him.

In 1950 he entered the University of Illinois, where he began as a premed student then switched to prelaw. After he graduated, he entered law school, and while he hated the rigorous study, he admitted: "It made me think, and think with precision." While a law student Melamed applied for a job as a "runner" at what he thought was the law firm of Merrill, Lynch, Pierce, Fenner & Bean. At their office, the oblivious Melamed filled out the application, was interviewed briefly, and got the job. When he found himself on the floor of the Chicago Mercantile Exchange, he reflected: "I was Alice stepping through the Looking Glass into a world of not just one Mad Hatter, but hundreds."

Pretty soon he was "in love" with the Merc and convinced his father to loan him $3,000 to buy a seat and trade for himself. In those days there was still plenty of manipulation, with the cornering of everything from eggs to onions; so, when Melamed was eventually elected to the Merc's board of governors in 1967 and was elected chairman in 1969, he focused on reforms and better self-government. Upon reflection, he wrote: "We were . . . pioneers, we told ourselves, fueled by ingenuity and guts, and dedicated to preserving the spirit of the frontier." In *The Art of Futures Trading,* he discerns between frontier myths and everyday reality when it comes to the skills needed for futures trading.

The Art of Futures Trading
Leo Melamed

To many, futures trading is a blessing.
To many, it is a curse.
To the majority, it is an enigma.

Why this divergence of opinion? Why this love–hate relationship? Perhaps because futures trading today represents one of the last frontiers of the business world. A frontier where the courageous trader must rely solely on his own ingenuity and common sense, where he must be brave and willing to meet formidable personal challenges, where the challenges demand intelligence, fortitude, character, and adventuresome spirit, and where the reward justifies the risks.

Personal futures trading is one of the last remaining spheres where an individual can still pyramid a sizable fortune from a modest investment. Little wonder so many try, though so many fail. Little wonder many of those who fail blame the challenge rather than their own inadequacies. Little wonder those who succeed become obsessed with the adventure. And little wonder so few know about it, for as with any frontier, the unknown is awesome, complicated, and frightening. And as with most things of consequence, the challenge is formidable and fraught with risk.

For these reasons, many myths have developed about trading futures: You must be on the in; you have to be lucky; it's only for the pros; you have to be a gambler; there's no rhyme or reason to it. These myths are false. Often these myths are used as excuses and alibis by those who have failed at futures trading for a variety of reasons, some of them rather personal. Perhaps they lacked the ability to concentrate or did not possess sufficient analytical skills; perhaps they lacked a well-adjusted personality, a mature temperament, or business discipline. Others fail because they lack adequate capital; but capital, although important, is not usually the central reason individuals fail at trading.

Futures trading today represents one of the last frontiers of the business world.

Take the element of luck. Futures trading is one of the few areas where luck is of minimal importance. While luck never hurts (and on occasion — as in all things — it can play an important role) luck, in general, is not a factor. Luck can go both ways and usually evens out. And good luck can also have an adverse effect. For example, a trader who is lucky in his early trading experience either has learned nothing or has learned the opposite of what he should. In the long run, an early streak of good luck will do him in.

In the final analysis, success at trading futures is determined by the person's ability to decipher and analyze salient facts and statistics in order to reach a logical opinion about the intermediate or ultimate price of a given product. In short, it depends on the ability to correctly measure supply and demand.

If that sounds simple, it isn't! It is a most difficult task. Implicit in the challenge are some exacting requirements: knowing the significant economic components that can affect the price of a given product; keeping abreast of current facts and statistics; comprehending these facts and their effects on supply and demand; correctly prorating the importance of the various components as they apply to a given price structure — a ratio that changes from year to year, sometimes from week to week, as well as from commodity to commodity; understanding the different price idiosyncrasies of different commodities; adjusting for all unknown variables; and finally, having the courage to apply your conclusions to the market.

Futures trading is one of the few areas where luck is of minimal importance.

It is this last requirement—the courage to apply your conclusions to the market—that proves to be the Waterloo for most futures traders. It is the point where your personality meets its most formidable challenge and you learn the type of trader you really are. Indeed, a trader's psychological makeup is the most critical component in his success in futures trading.

While special education and professional training will help, they are not mandatory. Tips or inside information are of small consequence. What is necessary is an orderly thought process, a businesslike approach, a well-balanced personality, a willingness to study the significant factors, and a working knowledge of the past history. And, of course, patience. The trader needs patience to learn from trading experiences, patience to learn from past mistakes, and patience for confidence and trading ability to grow. These are not simple requisites, and yet they are not impossible or so complicated as to warrant the taboos or prohibitions that so many have placed on this challenging field.

The rules of odds or probabilities—the normal tools of a good gambler—are not required for futures trading and can be a distinct disadvantage. Successful professional futures traders, as a rule, are not gamblers in the classic sense; most of the time, when gamblers try their skill at futures, they lose. The reasons for this are quite simple. Futures prices are dictated by the laws of economics, whereas successful gambling is a consequence of the rules of chance. These two regimes are light years apart. Rules of chance, over the long haul, cannot be applied successfully to trading. A good bet based on odds in other areas of life may be the worst possible trade in futures. A bad chance based on probabilities may in fact be a terrific futures position. For instance, in a bear market of long duration, pure odds will favor a rally; unfortunately, if an oversupply continues to dictate lower prices, those who buy the market on the basis of probabilities will lose money.

I have often heard the statement, "I had to liquidate my long position because the market was up ten days in a row." Those traders are applying the rule of probabilities to trading. While that may sometimes turn out to be a correct decision, it is far from the right reason. The long position may have been a better position on the eleventh day than it was on the first; maybe, on the eleventh day the world finally recognized what the trader's instincts had told him ten days before. Thus, the rule of probabilities cannot be the controlling factor for a market decision.

Successful futures traders are good businessmen and good money managers. Though traders risk their capital, those who are successful follow conservative and disciplined business practices. Thus, money management is every bit as important as being correct in the market. Unfortunately, this principle has somehow been lost by the public, and futures exchanges are instead often likened to gambling casinos.

I am often asked how much money is needed to begin trading. It is not really a question about the *amount* of capital required, rather it is a question of the *type* of capital. While I would not recommend it, you can begin trading futures with as little as a couple of thousand dollars—the minimum margin requirement—if a brokerage firm will accept your account.* The amount of capital available to begin trading

---

* The rules pertaining to the amount of capital required for futures trading have changed considerably since this essay was written in 1969. Inflation, the type of products available, and volatility of prices have affected the amount of margin capital required.

will determine the trader's latitude in the learning process. With a small amount, he has little room for error. With a larger sum, he has more time to learn. More important than the amount of money is that it not be *necessary* money. The trader should not speculate with capital needed for daily subsistence; that is, the money required for food and shelter, for school or clothing, or for any of the other normal demands of life. The capital recommended for futures trading is "risk capital": money that, if lost, would not materially affect the trader's living standards. While this precondition excludes a great many from futures trading, it still leaves the possibility open to a good many others.

Successful professional futures traders, as a rule, are not gamblers in the classic sense; most of the time, when gamblers try their skill at futures, they lose.

Will a large sum of risk capital provide a better chance at success than a small sum? Yes, to the degree that it will provide more room to learn. However, more capital may produce a false sense of security, which in the long run will impair your ability to succeed. Whether you begin with a large or small pool of risk capital, you must adjust the size of your futures position accordingly: With a small sum, you should begin trading on a very small scale; conversely, with a large sum, you may want to begin with larger positions. In either case you must pace yourself so that there will be some risk capital remaining after you have learned to trade. It will do you little good to face all the dangers and learn all the lessons if, after you graduate, you have no cash left to put your knowledge to work.

Since it takes years of study and firsthand application to become thoroughly familiar with all the principles, rules, variations, and exceptions involved for successful futures trading, it would be impossible to discuss these in depth. However, the following are three of the most salient principles.

First, spend time educating yourself about the product you plan to trade; that is, the various statistics and other factors that affect the supply–demand equation and therefore the price of the product. Implicit in this requirement is the corollary that you cannot rely solely on another's opinion. For example, if you use a broker, never take his word as gospel. While you should listen to what he has to say because he is an expert, you would be foolish to rely solely on his information or interpretation of the facts. This will also require that you fully understand the broker's jargon and reasoning, which again requires some personal education.

The second most important principle is not to overtrade. This cannot be defined in terms of money or in terms of the number of trades per week, month, or year. It will depend on your proximity to the market — how closely you can monitor price movement, the amount of time spent studying the product, and the objectives of your trading plan. Overtrading will overexpose you to risk and danger, as well as to unnecessary commissions. Consequently, you must accept that you cannot participate in every market move, nor should you want to. The most successful trader who is not daily on the trading floor of the exchange will pick his spots carefully. Futures prices have trends as well as seasonal movements. Concentrate on these rather than the daily fluctuations, which are best left to the professionals. A successful trader who chooses his moves judiciously needs to be correct only 30 to 40 percent of the time. On the other hand, a non-member trader attempting to trade daily must maintain a profitable track record 60 to 70 percent of the time to come out ahead.

The third principle is to follow a predetermined trading plan; a set of rules or established guidelines that you believe are valid, that have withstood the test of time, and that will guide your decisions. There is not one special formula or one set of trading rules. There are many. If you are not a professional trader, it will require a great deal of study to determine which rules make the most sense to you and best fit your temperament and your primary vocation. Whichever they are, once you choose your trading rules, adhere to them. This will require discipline and will test your emotional qualities. Unless you abide by a set of sound trading practices, you will be subject to the whim of every market idiosyncracy and fall easy prey to the stresses of a given moment. As an extension of this principle, I would caution you not to allow successful speculation to go to your head and cause you to discard your rules. Conversely, if at first you are unsuccessful or suffer a series of defeats, do not despair and discard a sound set of trading principles.

A successful trader who chooses his moves judiciously needs to be correct only 30 to 40 percent of the time.

Futures markets represent financial democracy. They offer an open marketplace for investment and speculation where everyone has a right to an opinion. Some opinions are more qualified than others. How qualified you become depends on you alone. This frontier is still open to a multitude of Americans who have the heart and spirit to learn what it takes. It is one field where the victorious have the satisfaction of knowing they have no one to thank for success except their own intellect, fortitude, and capability. And the reward can certainly justify the effort and risk involved.

Stanley Kroll, one of the most respected commodities traders, staked his success on steely patience. In his desk drawer, Kroll kept a quote from Edwin Lefèvre's book, *Reminiscences of a Stock Operator*. It reads, in part, "After spending many years in Wall Street and after making and losing millions of dollars, I want to tell you this: It never was my thinking that made the big money for me. It was always my sitting. Got that? My sitting tight." That was Kroll's key to success—no matter what, he held onto his convictions and didn't panic. If he got jumpy, he'd take a vacation to Europe or an extended trip on his boat, just to stay away from the market and not jump the gun.

Kroll started his career with Merrill Lynch in the late 1950s. In the early years he never accumulated much capital, but he had plenty of theories, so he decided to put them to the test and cofounded Kroll, Dallon and Company in 1967. After a successful run, he retired in 1975 for five years. His next surprise move was in 1985, when he set up office in a 54-foot yacht, furnished with communications equipment so he could trade from anywhere. Not only was commuting time reduced to a few seconds, but he loved the solitude. "After all," he wrote, "what could be more peaceful and conducive to clear thinking than a comfortable boat tied up (most of the time) to some very stout piers and pilings?"

For Kroll, that concentration involved following every trade in the commodities in which he was interested. His office staff wasn't allowed to talk to him during trading hours, and any communication was via gestures. Kroll's buying and selling decisions were based purely on movements in the market, nothing else, because he believed too many so-called facts were unreliable. "Take cocoa, for instance," Kroll said. "It's almost all grown in Ghana and Nigeria. The information that comes out of two countries is issued by their cocoa marketing boards, which are what they sound like—instruments for getting the best price they can for their cocoa growers—about as impartial and factual a source of information as Tass." In *How to Win Big and Lose Small*, Kroll explains why commodities trading is part science and part art.

How to Win Big and Lose Small
Stanley Kroll

Someone once said the surest way to make a small fortune in futures trading is to start with a large fortune. Unfortunately, there is considerable truth in that bit of cynical logic.

Clearly, the losses outnumber the winners, and by a large margin. So what is it that keeps us in the "game"?

For me, it is the knowledge, confirmed by experience, that the futures market is still the best way for an investor to enjoy the potential of being able to play a relatively small stake into a substantial fortune.

We should focus, however, on the fact that we are speculators and not gamblers. We study each market situation—past and projected price action—concentrating on either the technical or fundamental factors, or possibly a balance of both. Then we formulate a strategy that should include contingencies for both winning and losing positions. And all this should be done before entering the market.

THE 'BIG SCORE'

Furthermore—and this should be paramount—we do not trade for the action, the excitement or to entertain friends with wild and woolly stories. We accept the accompanying risks for one reason only—to make a big score . . . a home run . . . lots and lots of money!

In order to enter and stay within the coveted "winner's circle," the speculator must be practical and objective, pragmatic and disciplined and, above all, independent and confident in his analysis and market strategy. One of my most valuable maxims comes from Jesse Livermore, and it bears serious reflection: "There is only one side of the market . . . the right side." Period.

We do not trade for the action, the excitement or to entertain friends with wild and woolly stories. We accept the accompanying risks for one reason only—to make a big score . . . a home run . . . lots and lots of money!

Futures trading is part science (technical) and part art (instinctive). This includes a sound and viable investment strategy and a practical sense of money management.

Some years ago, when I was operating my own clearing firm, two friends and I got together to formulate a strategy for trading in cocoa. The market was then around 12¢, and the bottom line of our analysis projected a bull move to the 22¢ area over the intermediate term. Simple enough, right?

We all started buying the next day around the 12¢ level and over the next few months, our analysis proved quite accurate. The market did advance to the low 20s. And I made some money on the move, although not as much as I should have. Cocoa has always been my nemesis and it continues to be.

But during the same period of time, my two friends lost some $200,000 in their cocoa operations. Why? Their market strategy was perverse, their trade timing terrible and their self-confidence (it is imperative that you have confidence in your work) was shaky, at best.

Even though they started buying around 12¢ and sold their final long contract around 23¢, nearly everything they did in between was costly. Their buying pyramids were inverted (two, then five, then 10, etc.). They tended to buy rallies but then sell quickly on weakness (also shorting on further weakness). It was a near-total disaster, despite their initial analysis (which they adhered to in principal during the entire campaign) being uncannily accurate.

There are a number of what I call "speculator's laments" that I have observed—from firsthand experience, I must admit. The speculator watches as the market goes according to his analysis. Then, as soon as he has entered, c-r-a-s-h . . . and it completely reverses.

Here is another universal one: She's always buying on strength and then selling on weakness, inevitably resulting in small profits and big losses.

COURTING DISASTER

Taking big losses has to be the number one method of courting disaster and I, too, am constantly fighting this tendency—and not with consistent success, either.

A couple of years ago, after silver had topped out at the $50 level and was on the way down, one of my clients called and in a hushed and confidential tone advised me not to buy my silver yet. He said he was in touch with the big boys and would be told when they are buying and at that point he would buy for himself and advise me to buy.

Well on the face of it that sounded fine. After all wouldn't everyone want to buy when "the big boys" (whoever *they* are) were buying?

I didn't hear from this gentleman for some months after that. But one day he suddenly appeared in my office, furtively shut the door and, in a conspiratorial whisper, advised me that this was the time. "They" were beginning their buying operations, and he bought five contracts at the market for himself, advising me to buy as well for the big move.

Needless to say, I found this approach to trade timing extremely resistible and opted to sit out.

To summarize the incident, after meeting umpteen margin calls, my friend finally sold out his position for a loss of some $90,000—equal to a mere $18,000 per contract. It reinforced for me one of the simplest adages of trading: You cut your losses and let your profits run.

My good friend and mentor, Joe Klein, perhaps the best all-around floor trader to enter any commodity pit in the last 50 years, taught me this same concept in a different way. According to Klein, you keep what shows you a profit and close out what shows you a loss.

A number of years ago, while I was formulating and structuring trading strategies, I did a detailed survey of my clients' trading results. The conclusion was hardly surprising. It was generally dismal. Then I restructured my survey, projecting what the results might have been had all losses been limited to a given percentage of the respective margins, say 45%. In every case, the results were impressively better and, for illustration, I cite three typical cases as examples [see table].

A New England metals fabricator invested $105,000 in a trading account and, after nine months, had lost its original capital plus an additional $30,000. A recap of their trades reveals there were 35 total trades, of which 12 were profitable and the rest losing trades. The average size of the profits was $1,799, while the average loss was $6,844.

Terrible, isn't it. But if this corporation had limited its losses to just 45% of margin for each position, it would have lost just $9,232, instead of the $135,000 it did lose. The average size of its loss would have been $1,340 instead of $6,844. Some difference.

Why You Should Cut Your Losses and Let Your Profits Run

	Metals fabricator	*European bank*	*Small private pool*
Amount invested	$105,000	$100,000	$18,000
Percent profitable trades	34%	21%	65%
Gained	—	—	$112,000
Lost	$135,000	$54,500	—
Average loss	$6,844	$4,156	$515
Loss if limited to 45% margin	$9,232	$6,719	—
Average loss if limited to 45% margin	$1,340	$634	—

And here is the trading record of a highly sophisticated European bank whose commodity department used to send me its orders for execution on our exchanges. Starting capital was $100,000. After 13 months, it had been reduced to $45,500, at which time the bank discharged its local trader and quit speculative trading.

COULD'VE STAYED IN

During those 13 months, three of the 14 total trades were profitable, the rest resulting in losses. The average profit was $255, while the average loss was $4,156. Had the bank limited its losses to 45% of margins, its overall loss would have been just $6,719 (or $634 average loss), and it probably would have continued operating until it caught some good moves and gotten back into the black.

It is enlightening to compare these two traders' results with those of another of my clients, a small private trading fund that started with $18,000 and, after 18 months, had appreciated its capital to $130,000. Of the total 230 trades, 150 were profitable and the rest losses. The average profit was $1,020, while the average loss was $515.

The three recaps tell the story. The first two traders tended to trade against the major trends and made no serious attempt to limit losses on adverse positions. On the contrary, profitable positions were quickly closed out, while losses were held for even bigger losses.

The third account, on the other hand, was obviously disciplined to trade with the prevailing trends and followed a strict policy of minimizing losses and allowing profits to run (average profit was twice the average loss).

KEEP LOSSES LOW

To trade successfully, you'll need adequate trading capital, but that's quite relative. I would think you could start with as little as $12,000 to $15,000, assuming you trade intelligently. That means small positions, low frequency of activity and accuracy in your trade timing.

Keeping losses low is much more important than being able to start with a large sum because the careless trader with the large account very quickly becomes the careless trader with the small account.

This was brought vividly into focus for me some months ago when I was visited by a man who had bought a computerized trading system with which I had been involved.

He understood how to use the program and the micro-computer, and he was starting his account at his broker with $25,000. He asked for suggestions concerning his starting portfolio, and I counseled him to start with just five or six markets and trade just one contract of each.

As a simple rule of thumb, I suggested that, when the profit on any position equals 75% of margin, he double up on the position and, when the loss equals 75%, he liquidate it. He agreed to follow the strategy and left.

About four months later, he phoned me with a sad story that he had already lost some 80% of his capital, and did I have any suggestions? This came as a total surprise to me, because I had been using this system and had been doing reasonably well with it during that time.

The careless trader with the large account very quickly becomes the careless trader with the small account.

I asked him to send me copies of his monthly statements for the period. After a cursory examination, the answer was obvious. His initial soybean position was 20,000 bu. He put on three Commodity Exchange silver contracts, three on sugar and so forth. He was grossly overtrading, and he completely overlooked our agreed-upon strategy of limiting losses to margin. It was a disaster, but this is a very unforgiving market.

One aspect of futures trading that is very different from even five or 10 years ago is the growth and dependency on microcomputers and computer programs. It seems that just about every account executive and speculator has a top-secret system, and all are claimed to produce consistent winners. I think we have gone too far in our dependency on this kind of technical trading, especially in tick-by-tick on-line charts.

Can you imagine? A five-minute tick bar chart! Some trader recently phoned me and wanted to talk about the developing head-and-shoulders bottom in beans.

"What head and shoulders?" I asked. It turned out he was looking at a 90-minute "bottom formation" during the course of a powerful long-term bear market. Well, he may have been impressed with this "bottom formation," but the market wasn't. And it took not more than another hour for it to make a shambles of his five-minute tick "bottom." It also cost him a few thousand.

FITTING THE CONTEXT

There is a useful and constructive application for these short-term "games," but only when they are viewed within a larger context. If you have taken a longer-term view of the market oriented toward trend, you can use the short-term signals as a timing aid to get into or out of a position based on a prevailing trend.

If your basic view of a particular market is down, you can use the short-term signal to time your sell order or maybe even to exit your short position. But you shouldn't use it to get onto the long side against a prevailing market trend. You just don't want to be long in a powerful bear market simply because a 90-minute segment of your five-minute tick chart shows what looks like a fragmented bullish formation.

Let's focus on the moving average approach to trade timing because it seems currently to be the most useful and viable method of trend-following for longer-term position trading.

It is becoming increasingly difficult to trade profitably with just a simplistic kind of moving average—buying when line A advances up through line B or selling when the opposite occurs. Markets are too volatile, and strong traders can instinctively influence short-term price fluctuations to move markets through resting stoporder points in either direction.

But some excellent work in moving average analysis today focuses on the slope of the moving average or the rate of change. If you're looking for an area of technical analysis to concentrate on, this could be it.

Over the years, we have seen some ambitious research in optimized crossover analysis, especially by Dave Barker and Frank Hochheimer. For example, one analyst studying the markets from 1970 to 1979 found that the optimum crossover combination for corn was 12 days vs. 48 days and for copper, 17 days vs. 32 days.

Most of the time, markets are in relative equilibrium or in more of a broad sideways formation than a distinct trending formation.

Another analyst, using the period 1975–80, found the optimum combination for corn to be 14 days vs. 67 days and for copper four days vs. 20 days.

This kind of approach could work well for very long-term position trading, but its shortcoming is its inherent slowness. And it gives up a significant part of each major move before it flips.

I would like to challenge technically oriented traders and researchers with this thought: Since most long-term position traders are trend-followers, we are constantly trying to make discernible trends out of all markets. As a result, we are invariably buying upside "breakouts" and then selling downside "breakouts" and, I regret to say, losing money on most of these trades.

The simple and inescapable truth is that most of the time, markets are in relative equilibrium or in more of a broad sideways formation than a distinct trending formation. So buying strength and selling weakness turns out to be a costly exercise.

Instead, I think a dual trading approach should have the most merit. During the period in which a market is locked within a broad trading range, we would want to play an anti-trending game — buying toward the lower range of the sideways formation and selling toward the upper range.

But once the market breaks out of this broad trading range, we would want to abandon this anti-trend approach and to follow the direction of the breakout. Here, we would be buying strength and selling weakness.

This is simple in concept but complex in execution. First, it must be specified what is meant by a "trading range." How is it defined — by time period or by price containment within a specified range? And how does one specify the precise buying and selling ranges within the sideways formation?

GETTING ABOARD EARLY

The next problem is recognizing early when the market has changed from a sideways to a trending affair. The accompanying challenge is to get aboard the newly developing trend early in the move, but not too early, where the minibreakout could still be nothing more than a random and temporary foray out of the sideways range.

I would counsel you to fasten your seat belt and put on your crash helmet.

Other considerations would include a means of limiting losses on adverse trades. I would suggest that it be pegged to some percentage of the respective margin, say 50% to 75%. But if the position turns out to have been exited prematurely (and this is not always easy to discern), you must have some built-in means for entering the market again. It is truly written that the commission paid to get back aboard is the cheapest part of any speculative transaction.

Furthermore, I think this system should have some inclusive method of pyramiding, but only on favorable moving markets. No matter how efficient or accurate your trading system may be, I do not believe you can realize its full potential without such a pyramiding feature.

I am mindful that there are undoubtedly people who are already working with or toward such a system, and I believe that those who can put these conditions and features into a practical and viable trading system should be the big winners in the coming campaigns. . . .

I would counsel you to fasten your seat belt and put on your crash helmet.

BENJAMIN GRAHAM
1894–1976

Benjamin Graham is considered the father of modern securities analysis; his most famous protégé is Warren Buffett. It was a poverty-stricken upbringing in New York City, where he had to use brains rather than brawn to survive the streets, that cemented Graham's persona. The years of poverty, Graham said, "had developed in my character a serious concern for money, a willingness to work hard for small sums, and an extreme conservatism in all my spending habits." After graduating from Columbia University, Graham was offered teaching positions in three of its departments: literature, mathematics, and philosophy. However, he had his family to support (his father died when he was nine), so he took a position with a Wall Street firm as an apprentice in the bond department.

Graham's academic orientation, which made him "searching, reflective, and critical," proved an asset. In addition, he said, "I was able to add to these qualities two others which generally do not accompany the theoretical bent: first, a good instinct for what was important in a problem or a situation and the ability to avoid wasting time on inessentials; and second, a drive towards the practical, towards getting things done, towards finding solutions, and especially towards devising new approaches and techniques." When offered a promotion to bond salesman, Graham declined, and instead suggested that he would be more valuable in statistical or risk analysis.

After nine years on Wall Street, Graham formed his own company. It was a heady time, of which he said, "I was too ready to accept materialistic success as the aim and goal of life and to forget about idealistic achievements." The glorious break from abject poverty would explain the momentary frivolous outlook; however, there was a definite alter ego to the "Dean of Wall Street," who had a penchant for blondes and married three times. According to Buffett, Graham wanted "to do something creative, something foolish, and something generous everyday." Graham's conservative side is on display in *The Art of Hedging*, in which he explains how investors can protect themselves through various hedging techniques.

The Art of Hedging
Benjamin Graham

W ebster defines "to hedge" as "to protect oneself from loss by betting on both sides." Hedging as a commercial operation is practiced quite generally among flour millers and cotton spinners. While the details thereof might appear rather complicated, in essence it consists of selling "futures" short at the time the staple is purchased, so as to guard against fluctuations in price during the period of manufacture.

In the securities market a form of hedging very common on foreign Stock Exchanges is the use of puts or calls against long or short stock respectively. If a man purchases one hundred shares of U. S. Steel at 106, for instance, he might limit his possible loss by buying also a put good for thirty days at 102. This means that however low the stock may break, he has the right to sell it at any time within the next month at 102, so that his maximum loss under the worst possible conditions would be $400 plus the cost of the put (and commissions). This arrangement is often preferable to a stop loss order, because it guards against loss through a temporary fluction. Should Steel drop to 101½ and then rally to 115 during the month, the man with a stop loss order at 102 would have been forced out at his limit, while a put would have carried him safely through to a large ultimate profit.

The purpose of this article is not, however, to discuss either hedging in commodities or the use of privileges in trading, although both might well deserve extended treatment. We intend to discuss a similar class of market operations, which is little understood or appreciated even by professionals, and which nevertheless affords the opportunity of excellent profits with very moderate risk.

HEDGING BETWEEN BONDS AND STOCKS

What we have in mind is the simultaneous purchase of one security and sale of another, because the first is relatively cheaper than the second. Where the security bought sells lower than the one sold, there must be good reason for believing that the price of the two will come closer together, — and conversely for the opposite circumstance.

Without further tarrying on the general theory involved, let us hasten to a concrete example. On November 2, last, let us say, we purchase $10,000 of Lackawanna Steel convertible 5 per cent bonds, due 1950, and at the same time sell short 100 shares of Lackawanna Steel stock at 100. Should Lackawanna continue its headlong advance, we might be forced to convert our bonds into stock, in order to make delivery of the shares we sold. In this case our operation would have proved unsuccessful—we should have lost $25 and commissions. But if the stock declines it is evident that the bonds will not suffer as severely, because their investment rating alone assures them of a certain minimum value. In actual fact, at this writing the stock is down to 83, while the bonds hold firm around 94. We could therefore undo our little operation by selling the bonds for $9,400 and buying back our stock for $8,300. This would show a net credit of $1,100, from which expenses and the original difference of $25 are to be deducted, still leaving a net profit of over $1,000.

Here then was a venture which under the most unfavorable conditions could have shown a maximum loss of only $56.50, but contained by no means remote possibilities of a thousand dollar profit. Not a bad chance, was it? Add further that it required little capital (as the money really tied up was negligible), and that the carrying charge was insignificant since the bond interest almost offset the dividends on the stock. How much safer this is than the ordinary market commitment is apparent when we consider that the man who bought the 100 Lackawanna at par is out $1,700, if he still holds it; while on the other hand if Republic had been sold short when *it* reached par, the speculator would soon afterwards have faced a forty point loss.

The arbitrageur always expects to exchange the security he buys for the one he sells; the hedger will only do so if he must, and usually suffers a small loss thereby.

This is a good opportunity to point out the technical difference between hedging, as described above, and arbitraging. An arbitrage is supposed to assure a definite profit within a fairly definite time. If, for instance, it had been possible (as no doubt it was for the bond specialist) to buy Lack Steel convert. 5s at par, and simultaneously sell the stock at 100¼, such an operation would have constituted a real arbitrage. For the bonds could have immediately been converted and the new stock delivered, with a $25 profit.

The arbitrageur always expects to exchange the security he buys for the one he sells; the hedger will only do so if he must, and usually suffers a small loss thereby. His profit is found in selling out what he buys and buying in what he sells at a more favorable difference, or "spread," then at the beginning of the operation. The arbitrageur may of course delay converting in the hope of undoing his operation to better advantage in the market. He then becomes a hedger, but with an assured minimum profit instead of merely a miximum loss.

Even experienced "hedge artists" often forego the chance of excellent profits because they wait in vain for the possibility of loss to be reduced to too small a figure.

The relation of these two operations is very prettily shown by the Southern Pacific situation last October. At that time any one could have sold a large quantity of stock and replaced it by the convertible 5 per cent bonds at apparently ¼ point cheaper. In reality, however, the adjustment of accrued dividend and interest on conversion would have made the bonds about ¼ point higher than the stock. The supply of bonds was forthcoming from specialists who had been able to sell stock on rallies, above the corresponding price of the five per cent bonds, and who were about to present the bonds for conversion. They of course were glad enough to obtain an extra ¼ point profit by buying the stock and selling the bonds instead of converting. As it turned out, the trader who took over the bonds on this basis would have fared better than the original owner, because on the subsequent break he could have bought back the stock and sold his bonds at a five points difference. This would have meant about 4½ points "easy money" for a shrewd hedger.

Even experienced "hedge artists" often forego the chance of excellent profits because they wait in vain for the possibility of loss to be reduced to too small a figure. For example, in the ill-fated boom of Allied Packers stock last October, it sold at 66, while the convertible 6 per cent bonds were quoted at 91. Each $1,000 bond was convertible at any time for thirteen shares of stock, so if bought at 91 they constituted a call on the stock at $70 per share. The purchase of eight bonds at that time, together with the sale of 100 shares of stock at 66, would have subsequently shown no less than $3,200 profit, for the stock sold down to 26 with the bonds at 82. On the other hand, no matter how much higher the stock might have gone, the loss on this deal was absolutely limited to $400—the difference between 66 and 70. In this case, however, the temptation was to buy the bonds, and to wait for the stock to go a little higher before selling. Alas! the wait would have been in vain.

PREFERRED STOCKS

Convertible preferred stocks present the same opportunities for hedging operations as do the bonds. A current example is Gilliland Oil preferred, which is exchangeable at any time for twice as many shares of common. On January 15, the preferred could have been bought at 100 and the common sold at 49. The maximum loss, in case of a great advance of the common, would have been two points per share of preferred, which in fact would have been made up by the $2 dividend coming off the latter on February 2. As it happened, two days later the common was down to 43, while the preferred was actually higher at 101. Thus on a hundred shares of preferred and two hundred common, there was a chance for $1,300 gross profit in two days, with negligible risk.

If someone with a little nerve had sold Pierce Arrow at 99 against a purchase of the preferred at 110, his courage would have been well rewarded. Yet his very greatest loss could not have exceeded eleven points, since the preferred is exchangeable for common, share for share—and in addition had the advantage of an 8 per cent dividend against nothing on the common. There is today a difference of about thirty-five points between the two issues, so that this not especially risky operation would now show a profit of well over twenty points.

Rights to subscribe to new stock can sometimes be made the basis of profitable hedging operations, especially when the stock is selling close to the subscription price. In such cases the rights can be bought and the stock sold against them, with the idea that should the shares fall below the subscription figure the rights can then be discarded and the stock bought in at a profit. Unfortunately for such schemes, inside manipulation usually keep up the price of the issue until the rights expire, in order to stimulate subscriptions. The severe declines, as in the case of Sinclair Oil and Pan American Petroleum, usually come a little after the expiration of the rights—that is, too late for value to the hedger. Studebaker and Saxon Motors are recent instances of the stock falling below the offering price of the new stock before the last day for subscribing.

THE "STRADDLE"

Perhaps the best way to operate with rights is to straddle,— that is to play the market for both an advance and a break. This can be done by selling only half the stock corresponding to the rights purchased. It is very important here that the price of the rights be very low, and they still have a substantial period to run. A good current example is that of Simms Petroleum. On January 15, when the news of salt water in the Homer Field was published, this stock declined to 47, and the rights to 1. The latter entitled the holder to obtain one new share of Simms for each two rights, on payment of $47.50, the privilege expiring February 2. Since the oil stocks were then in a highly speculative position, Simms Petroleum held possibilities of either a big further slump or a radical recovery within the next two weeks. It appeared a good idea, therefore, to purchase say 400 Simms rights at 1, and sell only 100 shares of the stock against them at 47. The trader would then have been in a position to make profit from a wide move in either direction. Had the stock fallen to 40, for example, he could have covered his 100 shares with a gain of $650, and thrown away his rights, which cost him $400—leaving him still over $200 to the good. On a recovery to 55, however (which subsequently happened) he would have used 200 of his rights to replace his short stock, and disposed of the other 200 rights at a nice profit. The reader can easily calculate that in this case he would have made $300, less commissions.

Operations of this kind, involving rights, are very similar to the use of puts and calls for hedging purposes alluded to at the beginning of this article. Rights to subscribe are neither more nor less than calls issued by the company. But practically speaking, these rights usually carry a more attractive option, in proportion to their cost, than does the ordinary 30-day privilege.

Perhaps the best way to operate with rights is to straddle, —that is to play the market for both an advance and a break.

In the types of hedging heretofore considered the trader is always in a position to obtain the security he has sold, at a fixed price—either through conversion or by subscription. Yet one is often justified in selling one security against purchase of another, with no other safeguard than the definite knowledge that the two prices are far out of line.

On December 29 last, B. R. T. certificates of deposit sold at 5, while the undeposited stock was quoted above 10. It was true that the deposit agreement made withdrawal unusually difficult, but this was an entirely inadequate reason for the free stock selling at twice the price of the certificates. The two represented exactly the same property rights, and further there was enough stock in the control of the committee to enable it most probably to force the undeposited shares to accept their reorganization plan, when finally adopted. Hence the investor was running very little risk in buying 200 B. R. T.

certificates at 5 and selling 100 shares of free stock against them at 10¼. Temporarily the spread might have widened perhaps, but ultimately the two prices were bound to approach each other. The latter happened very quickly in effect, as a few days later the certificates had advanced to 7 while the stock remained at 10¼. Today the trader could sell his certificates at 10 with a gain of $1,000, and cover his stock at 13¼—a loss of only $300—showing an excellent net profit on a very modest commitment.

At the present time, when the outlook is so clouded with uncertainty, the trader might well turn his attention for a while to the unspectacular, but safely profitable, business of hedging.

A very similar opportunity was presented last November, when Interborough-Metropolitan 4½s broke to 13¾, while the preferred stock was selling at 12½. Considering the priority of lien "enjoyed" by the bonds, a spread of only 1¼ points between the two issues was ridiculously small. This has now widened to six points (which is still insufficient), but which nevertheless would allow a handsome profit to the man who bought the bonds and sold the stock at 13¾ and 12½ respectively. At the present time one or two of the Missouri, Kansas & Texas bond issues—the St. Louis Division 4s, for example,—can be bought only a few points above the 4 per cent non-cumulative referred stock: while in view of the large accruals of interest and their prior lien, they should of right be selling at a much wider spread.

DISCREPANCIES ARE COMMON

Discrepancies of this kind occur in almost endless variety and most of them can be availed of to advantage. But in many cases the outside trader cannot conveniently go short of the overvalued security, because of the difficulty of borrowing for an indefinite period and the interest problem. Nevertheless those who are holding the issue which is selling too high have every reason in the world for switching into the cheaper security. In the very first article of the present writer to appear in THE MAGAZINE OF WALL STREET (in September, 1917), he pointed out that there was no adequate reason for the ten point spread then existing between Japanese 4½s, "plain" and "German Stamped." The man who exchanged from the former into the latter would now be ahead exactly ten points, since the Stock Exchange has abolished the stamp discrimination entirely as to these bonds, so that they all have exactly the same value.

The latter point is made in order to indicate that the three operations of switching, arbitraging and hedging all have very much in common, and that we may easily pass from one to another. They are all based upon exact information and analysis, and their success is usually entirely independent of market movements. At the present time, when the outlook is so clouded with uncertainty, the trader might well turn his attention for a while to the unspectacular, but safely profitable, business of hedging.

MARTIN E. ZWEIG
1942–

Martin Zweig, who cofounded Avatar Associates and manages several of his firm's mutual funds, is best known for his top-ranked *Zweig Forecast,* a newsletter for do-it-yourself investors. As a kid growing up in Cleveland, he first became interested in statistics while following the Indians baseball team. As a first grader, he became acquainted with the fickleness of the stock market—the year was 1948, and the day after Harry S. Truman won his stunning upset, the market plunged 3.8 percent. Apparently, the brokers preferred the Republican candidate, Dewey. His education continued: At 13 he received a gift of six shares of General Motors stock, and he started reading the financial pages to keep track.

In 1960 Zweig went to the University of Pennsylvania's Wharton School of Business. As a freshman he hoped to learn about investments, but the closest he got was a rather dry economics course. However, he learned: "If you master the lessons of economics and the laws of supply and demand it's bound to be beneficial in business or the stock market." Another lesson came when he and some friends thought about starting their own investment group—the drawback in getting started was in working more or less by committee. "I've never heard of a great investor who operated by committee" he said.

After a short stint as a broker at Bache & Co., Zweig attended the University of Miami for an MBA and then went to Michigan State for a Ph.D. in finance. In researching his dissertation he learned how to track investor sentiment. "In accumulating data for my dissertation, I unearthed some figures from the Securities and Exchange Commission going back to World War II and found that when options investors got too optimistic—buying lots of calls and shunning puts—the stock market was generally heading for trouble. The reverse was also true." After making a couple of correct predictions, Zweig launched his newsletter in 1971. He formed the Zweig Total Return Fund in 1986, and has formed several more funds since. A strategy he feels is misunderstood is short selling, which he espouses in *Selling Short—It's Not Un-American.*

Selling Short—
It's Not Un-American
Martin E. Zweig

No discussion about making money in the stock market would be complete without some attention to short selling, a subject that many traders do not truly understand. The idea in short selling is simple— you're betting that a certain stock will go down. So you sell it now and hope you can buy it back later at a lower price. When you think about it, *this is similar to any transaction where you try to buy at a lower price than you sell. The only difference in this case is just that you're selling first.*

Technically, when you sell short you borrow the securities from a brokerage house and sell them in the market. You owe the broker these securities. For collateral, you deposit a certain amount of required cash with that broker. Since he knows that there's enough money to repurchase the securities if necessary, there is no time limit. Don't be concerned about that old saying, "He who sells what isn't his'n must buy it back or go to prison." But, sooner or later, all shorts are covered or bought back.

There are at least two good reasons for selling short. If you think it's a bear market or that a particular stock is on the skids, you can garner good profits by selling short. You may also want to sell short to hedge your portfolio. Let's say you have a $100,000 portfolio. You think the market will weaken over the next six months but you don't want to disturb some long-term holdings, perhaps for tax reasons. What you can do is sell short other stocks as a hedge. For example, you own some General Motors on which you're hoping for a long-term gain. In the short run, you might want to sell short Ford to protect yourself. So for either speculating or hedging, short selling can be very useful.

Somehow it just doesn't seem like apple pie and the flag to sell short. People perceive it as a bet against the country and that's just wrong.

I personally like to sell short and frequently feel more comfortable on the short side of the market than on the long. But short selling has a bad rap. The average person has a tremendous hang-up about selling short. I don't know why but it exists. In no particular order, here are some of the perceived negatives about short selling, none of which is true.

The first misconception is that short selling is un-American. Somehow it just doesn't seem like apple pie and the flag to sell short. People perceive it as a bet against the country and that's just wrong. If you sell short General Motors or AT&T, you're not betting against the United States. All you're saying is that at times these stocks may be overvalued. If the stock is worth $50 and it's selling for $70 or $80, there's a good chance it may recede to $50 or even $40, especially if it's a bear market. There's nothing unethical about that appraisal. It's just reality—the stock may go down.

Sometimes you may sell a stock short when you feel that the company will go bankrupt. That's not un-American either. thousands and thousands of bankruptcies each year Your selling short is not going to cause any company to go under. All you're doing is wagering in the stock market that a firm is in trouble. Even if it doesn't go bust, it may have poor earnings, and the stock may decline. *If you profit from your judgment, it's not different in principle from profiting on the long side when you anticipate that a company's earnings will increase.*

Also, selling short is a very common business practice outside the stock market. They just don't call it selling short. For example, you go to a car dealer to buy a Chevrolet and you want it with fancy red paint, a stereo, and an automatic seatwarmer. You order all these extras and the dealer says, "I don't have such a car in stock, so I'll have to order it for you." You say, "Okay, that's fine. Order it." He says, "I'll have the car in a month. Pay me a deposit now. We'll order the car and deliver it to you." You agree. What's happened is that the dealer has sold short a car. He has actually sold you something before he's bought it from the factory.

The second rap on selling short is the belief that your profits are limited and your losses unlimited—and that is absolute nonsense. For example, there is a misconception that if you were to sell short a $50 stock, the most you could earn is $50, or 100% on your investment, if the company were to go bankrupt. Conversely, people believe that if you guess wrong there is no theoretical limit to how much you can lose. The stock could go to 1000, in which case you're out twentyfold on your money. Such thinking is faulty to say the least.

In the first place, when you sell short you put up collateral with a broker, which can be in the form of Treasury bills if you want to continue earning interest on the money. The minimum collateral is 50% of the transaction. So, if you were to sell short 100 shares of a $50 stock, that's $5,000, and you'd have to put up at least $2,500 in collateral.

To simplify it, let's say you put up the whole amount. You place $5,000 in T-bills with a broker. If that stock were to go up, he would eventually call you for more money. By the time the stock rose to $80, you would have a $3,000 loss.

Your equity would be down to $2,000. Before that point, the broker would have requested more collateral. If you didn't put it up, he would cover the sale by buying the stock and you would be out.

The only way you can lose an infinite amount is to keep advancing more and more money, which is like pyramiding your loss. *Remember the golden rule, "The trend is your friend. Don't fight the tape."* If you have a loss like that, get out. Nobody's holding a gun to your head for more money. Only a fool would keep putting up money on a losing short sale like that.

On the brighter side, your profit potential in a short sale is not limited to 100% profit. It is virtually unlimited. For example, you short 100 shares at $50 and the stock falls to $25. That's a $2,500 profit for you. If you started with $5,000 in equity, your total equity in the account is now $7,500. At this point the stock is trading at $25, which is $2,500 per 100 shares. To maintain 100% equity behind your position, you only need $2,500 in the account.

You then pyramid (without using margin as such), selling short an additional 200 shares. You now have 300 shares short, which would require the $7,500 backing. If that stock were to go to zero, you'd make an additional $7,500 in profit. So your total profit would be $10,000 on a $5,000 investment, which is 200 percent.

But it doesn't have to stop there. Suppose the stock then drops from $25 to $10. Now you have 300 shares of a $10 stock. The total capital you need in the account without margin is $3,000. Remember, you have $7,500 in capital. On the drop from $25 to $10 you've made 15 points, or $1,500 per hundred shares, which is $4,500 in profit added to your $7,500 equity. That gives you $12,000 of equity when the stock is at 10. You're only short 300 shares. You could then short another 900 shares at $10 without putting up any more money or without using margin.

Let's say you did that. Now, at $10 you're short 1,200 shares. What you're doing is following the tape. You're shorting more as the stock drops. Now suppose the company goes bankrupt. The stock falls from $10 to zero. You've made $12,000 on the drop, but you had an additional $12,000 in the account when the stock was $10. So your total ending equity is $24,000 when the stock is at zero. Since you started at $5,000, you have made almost a fivefold profit. If you want to, you can pyramid a lot more on the way down than in the example. You could short more at $5 or at any other price. So your profit on the downside is virtually unlimited.

Remember, if the stock goes down and you don't short any more, you have excess equity in the account. If a $50 stock falls to $25, you've got $7,500 of equity in the account. Since you need only $2,500, you could take out the extra $5,000 and earn interest on it or do something else with it.

On the other hand, if you are on the long side and the stock goes from $50 to $100, you can't pull any money out unless you go on margin. Therefore, on the upside you are always pyramiding, because you have to let your money ride all the time. On the short side, to be fully invested you actually have to keep shorting more and more as the stock goes down. People don't think of that for some reason.

Another plus about short selling is that not many people do it. So you have the field relatively to yourself

---

Many investors believe it's risky to short more on the way down. It really isn't if you know what you're doing. If the company is going to go broke, it doesn't really matter where you short. You'd make just as much money shorting at $5 as you could at $25. Stocks that are already down from $100 to $10 are still pretty good shorts if the stock is going lower. If the stock eventually dips to $2, you can make 80% by shorting at 10, even without pyramiding. If you short it at

$100, you'd make 98%. Returns of 80% and 98% are not all that different.

That's one reason I find shorting very reasonable. If you're willing to let your money ride, you can make far more than 100% without even using margin. Your loss is not unlimited. The only way it becomes unlimited is if you're crazy enough to throw more money away in a losing cause. Yes, short selling has a bad rap.

There is a third negative on short selling that *is* real. After the crash in 1929, the government had to blame somebody. The cause did not rest with the short sellers, but they were a vulnerable target. Attributing the market collapse to the fact that some people sold short, the government decided to make short selling more difficult. That's why they imposed an uptick requirement. That means that if you're going to sell short, you have to sell at a price higher than the previous price for listed stocks. That makes it a little harder to get off the short sale, but it doesn't preclude it.

Additionally, the tax people discriminate against short selling. Even if you hold the short position for more than six months you can never get a long-term capital gain on it. No matter how long you hold the short sale, it will always be considered a shortterm gain or loss. However, the alternative might be worse, such as bear market losses or a bear market without your participating on the downside.

Another plus about short selling is that not many people do it. So you have the field relatively to yourself as opposed to participating on the long side.

I also find that negative research on a company is usually superior to positive research. An extensive study covering several years of market activity disclosed that following buy recommendations of brokerage houses was really no better than choosing at random. In other words, on buy recommendations you could do just as well by throwing darts at the stock market page. Sell recommendations are a different story. About three-quarters of them underperformed the market. That is, they went down more than the market.

Partly because sell recommendations are so rare, they tend to be better.

Based on personal experience, it's easier to ferret out negative information. If a company has taken advantage of permissible accounting rules and has overstated earnings, that will catch up with it eventually. Or if a company has a fundamental problem, such as inventory accumulation in the face of declining orders, that will surface sooner or later. Since it's already in the works, the bad news will get out and the stock will probably decline. If you're betting on the long side, frequently you're depending on a prediction that may not work out.

I am not recommending that the average investor engage in short selling. I consider it a supplemental strategy for the really sophisticated investor.

For example, XYZ has a terrific product and forecasters estimate that sales and earnings should grow 20% a year for the next five years. All too often, unexpected competition appears or the economy turns down, and the earnings don't climb as anticipated. It's harder for a story on the long side to work out as well as one on the short side. Once the bad news is in the can, it's there and you can't get rid of it. Eventually the stock should get hit. That's why I think playing the short side is easier than the long side. Of course, short selling in the wrong market can kill you. You don't want to sell short in a bull market unless you are hedging something.

I happen to feel comfortable with short selling, a practice I think is terribly misunderstood, and have written this chapter to clear up some of the misconceptions about this investment strategy. *However, at this point I am not recommending that the average investor engage in short selling. I consider it a supplemental strategy for the really sophisticated investor.*

DONALD J. TRUMP
1946–

Donald Trump has been called every name in the book, has been fodder for the tabloids, and has almost lost his real estate and casino empire; however, through it all, he has kept his flamboyant zest for investing. His formula for real estate investment was simple: Trump laid "claim to prime location with a minimal early investment, parlayed political advantages and a locally downturned economy into a series of government concessions, and then used both the location and the concessions as a lure for an institutional partner that could help deliver the financing he otherwise could not obtain." Those political advantages were back-room alliances forged by his dad, who had already made a sizable fortune in real estate.

Raised in Queens, Trump enjoyed a privileged upbringing until his father tired of his pranks and sent him to a military school. Interestingly, the once and future freewheeling Trump excelled and was selected commander of the honor guard. After two years at Fordham University, he transferred to Wharton, and then joined his father's business, where he managed thousands of apartments, from maintenance to rent collection. Trump declared that he would be bigger than New York real estate baron Harry Helmsley in five years.

Trump's ambitions took him to Atlantic City; gambling had been legalized in New Jersey in 1976. He built his first casino, the Trump Plaza in 1984, followed by the Trump Taj Mahal and the Trump Marina. But then a recession hit, and Trump almost lost his empire in 1990. His latest casino, the Taj Mahal, wasn't generating the revenue expected, and Trump, already strapped with excessive debt, couldn't meet his payments. At the same time, he and Ivana were getting divorced and she was pressing for big bucks. An eleventh-hour restructuring saved him. He admitted that he had felt invincible, gotten lazy, and taken his eye off the ball. One comeback tip: Play golf; he found it relaxing and a way to generate ideas. A less universal tip: Always have a prenuptial agreement. As for strategic investing advice, such as not trying to hit a home run on every at-bat, he provides it in *Trump Cards: The Elements of the Deal.*

Trump Cards: The Elements
of the Deal
Donald J. Trump

My style of deal-making is quite simple and straightforward. I aim very high, and then I just keep pushing and pushing and pushing to get what I'm after. Sometimes I settle for less than I sought, but in most cases I still end up with what I want.

More than anything else, I think deal-making is an ability you're born with. It's in the genes. I don't say that egotistically. It's not about being brilliant. It does take a certain intelligence, but mostly it's about instincts. You can take the smartest kid at Wharton, the one who gets straight A's and has a 170 IQ, and if he doesn't have the instincts, he'll never be a successful entrepreneur.

Moreover, most people who do have the instincts will never recognize that they do, because they don't have the courage or the good fortune to discover their potential. Somewhere out there are a few men with more innate talent at golf than Jack Nicklaus, or women with greater ability at tennis than Chris Evert or Martina Navratilova, but they will never lift a club or swing a racket and therefore will never find out how great they could have been. Instead, they'll be content to sit and watch stars perform on television.

When I look back at the deals I've made—and the ones I've lost or let pass—I see certain common elements. But unlike the real estate evangelists you see all over television these days, I can't promise you that by following the precepts I'm about to offer you'll become a millionaire overnight. Unfortunately, life rarely works that way, and most people who try to get rich quick end up going broke instead. As for those among you who do have the genes, who do have the instincts, and who could be highly successful, well, I still hope you won't follow my advice. Because that would just make it a much tougher world for me.

Deal-making is an ability you're born with. It's in the genes. . . . It's not about being brilliant.

THINK BIG

I like thinking big. I always have. To me it's very simple: if you're going to be thinking anyway, you might as well think big. Most people think small, because most people are afraid of success, afraid of making decisions, afraid of winning. And that gives people like me a great advantage.

My father built low-income and middle-income buildings in Brooklyn and Queens, but even then, I gravitated to the best location. When I was working in Queens, I always wanted Forest Hills. And as I grew older, and perhaps wiser, I realized that Forest Hills was great, but Forest Hills isn't Fifth Avenue. And so I began to look toward Manhattan, because at a very early age, I had a true sense of what I wanted to do.

I wasn't satisfied just to earn a good living. I was looking to make a statement. I was out to build something monumental—something worth a big effort. Plenty of other people could buy and sell little brownstones, or build cookie-cutter red-brick buildings. What attracted me was the challenge of

466

building a spectacular development on almost one hundred acres by the river on the West Side of Manhattan, or creating a huge new hotel next to Grand Central Station at Park Avenue and 42nd Street.

The same sort of challenge is what attracted me to Atlantic City. It's nice to build a successful hotel. It's a lot better to build a hotel attached to a huge casino that can earn fifty times what you'd ever earn renting hotel rooms. You're talking a whole different order of magnitude.

One of the keys to thinking big is total focus. I think of it almost as a controlled neurosis, which is a quality I've noticed in many highly successful entrepreneurs. They're obsessive, they're driven, they're single-minded and some-times they're almost maniacal, but it's all channeled into their work. Where other people are paralyzed by neurosis, the people I'm talking about are actually helped by it.

It's nice to build a successful hotel. It's a lot better to build a hotel attached to a huge casino that can earn fifty times what you'd ever earn renting hotel rooms.

I don't say this trait leads to a happier life, or a better life, but it's great when it comes to getting what you want. This is particularly true in New York real estate, where you are dealing with some of the sharpest, toughest, and most vicious people in the world. I happen to love to go up against these guys, and I love to beat them.

PROTECT THE DOWNSIDE AND THE UPSIDE WILL TAKE CARE OF ITSELF

People think I'm a gambler. I've never gambled in my life. To me, a gambler is someone who plays slot machines. I prefer to own slot machines. It's a very good business being the house.

It's been said that I believe in the power of positive thinking. In fact, I believe in the power of negative thinking. I happen to be very conservative in business. I always go into the deal anticipating the worst. If you plan for the worst—if you can live with the worst—the good will always take care of itself. The only time in my life I didn't follow that rule was with the USFL. I bought a losing team in a losing league on a long shot. It almost worked, through our antitrust suit, but when it didn't, I had no fallback. The point is that you can't be too greedy. If you go for a home run on every pitch, you're also going to strike out a lot. I try never to leave myself too exposed, even if it means sometimes settling for a triple, a double, or even, on rare occasions, a single.

People think I'm a gambler. I've never gambled in my life. To me, a gambler is someone who plays slot machines. I prefer to own slot machines.

One of the best examples I can give is my experience in Atlantic City. Several years ago, I managed to piece together an incredible site on the Boardwalk. The individual deals I made for parcels were contingent on my being able to put together the whole site. Until I achieved that, I didn't have to put up very much money at all.

Once I assembled the site, I didn't rush to start construction. That meant I had to pay the carrying charges for a longer period, but before I spent hundreds of millions of dollars and several years on construction, I wanted to make sure I got my gaming license. I lost time, but I also kept my exposure much lower.

When I got my licensing on the Boardwalk site, Holiday Inns came along and offered to be my partner. Some people said, "You don't need them. Why give up fifty percent of your profits?" But Holiday Inns also offered to pay back the money I already had in the deal, to finance all the construction, and to guarantee me against losses for five years. My choice was whether to keep all the risk myself, and own 100 percent of the casino, or settle for a 50 percent stake without putting up a dime. It was an easy decision.

Barron Hilton, by contrast, took a bolder approach when he built his casino in Atlantic City. In order to get opened as quickly as possible, he filed for a license and began construction on a $400 million facility at the same time. But then, two months before the hotel was scheduled to open, Hilton was denied a license. He ended up selling to me at the last minute, under a lot of pressure, and without a lot of other options. I renamed the facility Trump's Castle and it is now one of the most successful hotel-casinos anywhere in the world.

MAXIMIZE YOUR OPTIONS

I also protect myself by being flexible. I never get too attached to one deal or one approach. For starters, I keep a lot of balls in the air, because most deals fall out, no matter how promising they seem at first. In addition, once I've made a deal, I always come up with at least a half dozen approaches to making it work, because anything can happen, even to the best-laid plans.

For example, if I hadn't gotten the approvals I wanted for Trump Tower, I could always have built an office tower and done just fine. If I'd been turned down for licensing in Atlantic City, I could have sold the site I'd assembled to another casino operator, at a good profit.

Perhaps the best example I can give is the first deal I made in Manhattan. I got an option to purchase the Penn Central railyards at West 34th Street. My original proposal was to build middle-income housing on the site, with government financing. Unfortunately, the city began to have financial problems, and money for public housing suddenly dried up. I didn't spend a lot of time feeling sorry for myself. Instead, I switched to my second option and began promoting the site as ideal for a convention center. It took two years of pushing and promoting, but ultimately the city did designate my site for the convention center—and that's where it was built.

Of course, if they hadn't chosen my site, I would have come up with a third approach.

KNOW YOUR MARKET

Some people have a sense of the market and some people don't. Steven Spielberg has it. Lee Iacocca of Chrysler has it, and so does Judith Krantz in her way. Woody Allen has it, for the audience he cares about reaching, and so does Sylvester Stallone, at the other end of the spectrum. Some people criticize Stallone, but you've got to give him credit. I mean, here's a man who is just forty-one years old, and he's already created two of the all-time-great characters, Rocky and Rambo. To me he's a diamond-in-the-rough type, a genius purely by instinct. He knows what the public wants and he delivers it.

I like to think I have that instinct. That's why I don't hire a lot of number-crunchers, and I don't trust fancy marketing surveys. I do my own surveys and draw my own conclusions. I'm a great believer in asking everyone for an opinion before I make a decision. It's a natural reflex. If I'm thinking of buying a piece of property, I'll ask the people who live nearby about the area—what they think of the schools and the crime and the shops. When I'm in another city and I take a cab, I'll always make it a point to ask the cabdriver questions. I ask and I ask and I ask, until I begin to get a gut feeling about something. And that's when I make a decision.

I have learned much more from conducting my own random surveys than I could ever have learned from the greatest of consulting firms. They send a crew of people down from Boston, rent a room in New York, and charge you $100,000 for a lengthy study. In the end, it has no conclusion and takes so long to complete that if the deal you were considering was a good one, it will be long gone.

I don't hire a lot of number-crunchers, and I don't trust fancy marketing surveys. I do my own surveys and draw my own conclusions.

The other people I don't take too seriously are the critics—except when they stand in the way of my projects. In my opinion, they mostly write to impress each other, and they're just as swayed by fashions as anyone else. One week it's spare glass towers they are praising to the skies. The next week, they've rediscovered old, and they're celebrating detail and ornamentation. What very few of them have is any feeling for what the public wants. Which is why, if these critics ever tried to become developers, they'd be terrible failures.

Trump Tower is a building the critics were skeptical about before it was built, but which the public obviously liked. I'm not talking about the sort of person who inherited money 175 years ago and lives on 84th Street and Park Avenue. I'm talking about the wealthy Italian with the beautiful wife and the red Ferrari. Those people—the audience I was after—came to Trump Tower in droves.

The funny thing about Trump Tower is that we ended up getting great architectural reviews. The critics didn't want to review it well because it stood for a lot of things they didn't

471

like at the time. But in the end, it was such a gorgeous building that they had no choice but to say so. I always follow my own instincts, but I'm not going to kid you: it's also nice to get good reviews.

USE YOUR LEVERAGE

The worst thing you can possibly do in a deal is seem desperate to make it. That makes the other guy smell blood, and then you're dead. The best thing you can do is deal from strength, and leverage is the biggest strength you can have. Leverage is having something the other guys wants. Or better yet, needs. Or best of all, simply can't do without.

Unfortunately, that isn't always the case, which is why leverage often requires imagination, and salesmanship. In other words, you have to convince the other guy it's in his interest to make the deal.

The worst thing you can possibly do in a deal is seem desperate to make it. That makes the other guy smell blood, and then you're dead.

Back in 1974, in an effort to get the city to approve my deal to buy the Commodore Hotel on East 42nd Street, I convinced its owners to go public with the fact that they were planning to close down the hotel. After they made the announcement, I wasn't shy about pointing out to everyone in the city what a disaster a boarded-up hotel would be for the Grand Central area, and for the entire city.

When the board of Holiday Inns was considering whether to enter into a partnership with me in Atlantic City, they were attracted to my site because they believed my construction was farther along than that of any other potential

472

partner. In reality, I wasn't that far along, but I did everything I could, short of going to work at the site myself, to assure them that my casino was practically finished. My leverage came from confirming an impression they were already predisposed to believe.

When I bought the West Side railyards, I didn't name the project Television City by accident, and I didn't choose the name because I think it's pretty. I did it to make a point. Keeping the television networks in New York—and NBC in particular—is something the city very much wants to do. Losing a network to New Jersey would be a psychological and economic disaster.

Leverage: don't make deals without it.

ENHANCE YOUR LOCATION

Perhaps the most misunderstood concept in all of real estate is that the key to success is location, location, location. Usually, that's said by people who don't know what they're talking about. First of all, you don't necessarily need the best location. What you need is the best deal. Just as you can create leverage, you can enhance a location, through promotion and through psychology.

When you have 57th Street and Fifth Avenue as your location, as I did with Trump Tower, you need less promotion. But even there, I took it a step further, by promoting Trump Tower as something almost larger than life. By contrast, Museum Tower, two blocks away and built above the Museum of Modern Art, wasn't marketed well, never achieved an "aura," and didn't command nearly the prices we did at Trump Tower.

Location also has a lot to do with fashion. You can take a mediocre location and turn it into something considerably better just by attracting the right people. After Trump Tower I built Trump Plaza, on a site at Third Avenue and 61st

Street that I was able to purchase very inexpensively. The truth is that Third Avenue simply didn't compare with Fifth Avenue as a location. But Trump Tower had given a value to the Trump name, and I built a very striking building on Third Avenue. Suddenly we were able to command premium prices from very wealthy and successful people who might have chosen Trump Tower if the best apartments hadn't been sold out. Today Third Avenue is a very prestigious place to live, and Trump Plaza is a great success.

My point is that the real money isn't made in real estate by spending the top dollar to buy the best location. You can get killed doing that, just as you can get killed buying a bad location, even for a low price. What you should never do is pay too much, even if that means walking away from a very good site. Which is all a more sophisticated way of looking at location.

GET THE WORD OUT

You can have the most wonderful product in the world, but if people don't know about it, it's not going to be worth much. There are singers in the world with voices as good as Frank Sinatra's, but they're singing in their garages because no one has ever heard of them. You need to generate interest, and you need to create excitement. One way is to hire public relations people and pay them a lot of money to sell whatever you've got. But to me, that's like hiring outside consultants to study a market. It's never as good as doing it yourself.

One thing I've learned about the press is that they're always hungry for a good story, and the more sensational the better. It's in the nature of the job, and I understand that. The point is that if you are a little different, or a little outrageous, or if you do things that are bold or controversial, the press is going to write about you. I've always done things a little differently, I don't mind controversy, and my deals tend to be somewhat ambitious. Also, I achieved a lot when I was very young, and I chose to live in a certain style. The result is that the press has always wanted to write about me.

I'm not saying that they necessarily like me. Sometimes they write positively, and sometimes they write negatively. But from a pure business point of view, the benefits of being written about have far outweighed the drawbacks. It's really quite simple. If I take a full-page ad in the *New York Times* to publicize a project, it might cost $40,000, and in any case, people tend to be skeptical about advertising. But if the *New York Times* writes even a moderately positive one-column story about one of my deals, it doesn't cost me anything, and it's worth a lot more than $40,000.

I play to people's fantasies. People may not always think big themselves, but they can still get very excited by those who do.

The funny thing is that even a critical story, which may be hurtful personally, can be very valuable to your business. Television City is a perfect example. When I bought the land in 1985, many people, even those on the West Side, didn't realize that those one hundred acres existed. Then I announced I was going to build the world's tallest building on the site. Instantly, it became a media event: the *New York Times* put it on the front page, Dan Rather announced it on the evening news, and George Will wrote a column about it in *Newsweek*. Every architecture critic had an opinion, and so did a lot of editorial writers. Not all of them liked the idea of the world's tallest building. But the point is that we got a lot of attention, and that alone creates value.

The other thing I do when I talk with reporters is to be straight. I try not to deceive them or to be defensive, because those are precisely the ways most people get themselves into trouble with the press. Instead, when a reporter asks me a tough question, I try to frame a positive answer, even if that means shifting the ground. For example, if someone asks me what negative effects the world's tallest building might have on the West Side, I turn the tables and talk about how New Yorkers deserve the world's tallest building, and what a boost it will give the city to have that honor again. When a reporter asks why I build only for the rich, I note that the rich aren't the only ones who benefit from my buildings. I explain that I put thousands of people to work who might otherwise be collecting unemployment, and that I add to the city's tax base every time I build a new project. I also point out that buildings like Trump Tower have helped spark New York's renaissance.

The final key to the way I promote is bravado. I play to people's fantasies. People may not always think big them-selves, but they can still get very excited by those who do. That's why a little hyperbole never hurts. People want to believe that something is the biggest and the greatest and the most spectacular.

I call it truthful hyperbole. It's an innocent form of exag-geration—and a very effective form of promotion.

FIGHT BACK

Much as it pays to emphasize the positive, there are times when the only choice is confrontation. In most cases I'm very easy to get along with. I'm very good to people who are good to me. But when people treat me badly or unfairly or try to take advantage of me, my general attitude, all my life, has been to fight back very hard. The risk is that you'll make a bad situation worse, and I certainly don't recommend this approach to everyone. But my experience is that if you're fighting for something you believe in—even if it means alien-ating some people along the way—things usually work out for the best in the end.

When the city unfairly denied me, on Trump Tower, the standard tax break every developer had been getting, I fought them in six different courts. It cost me a lot of money, I was considered highly likely to lose, and people told me it was a no-win situation politically. I would have considered it worth the effort regardless of the outcome. In this case, I won—which made it even better.

When Holiday Inns, once my partners at the Trump Plaza Hotel and Casino in Atlantic City, ran a casino that consistently performed among the bottom 50 percent of casinos in town, I fought them very hard and they finally sold out their share to me. Then I began to think about trying to take over the Holiday Inns company altogether.

Even if I never went on the offensive, there are a lot of people gunning for me now. One of the problems when you become successful is that jealousy and envy inevitably follow. There are people—I categorize them as life's losers— who get their sense of accomplishment and achievement from trying to stop others. As far as I'm concerned, if they had any real ability they wouldn't be fighting me, they'd be doing something constructive themselves.

Deliver the Goods

You can't con people, at least not for long. You can create excitement, you can do wonderful promotion and get all kinds of press, and you can throw in a little hyperbole. But if you don't deliver the goods, people will eventually catch on.

I think of Jimmy Carter. After he lost the election to Ronald Reagan, Carter came to see me in my office. He told me he was seeking contributions to the Jimmy Carter Library. I asked how much he had in mind. And he said, "Donald, I would be very appreciative if you contributed five million dollars."

I was dumbfounded. I didn't even answer him.

But that experience also taught me something. Until then, I'd never understood how Jimmy Carter became president. The answer is that as poorly qualified as he was for the job, Jimmy Carter had the nerve, the guts, the balls, to ask for something extraordinary. That ability above all helped him get elected president. But then, of course, the American people caught on pretty quickly that Carter couldn't do the job, and he lost in a landslide when he ran for reelection.

Ronald Reagan is another example. He is so smooth and so effective a performer that he completely won over the American people. Only now, nearly seven years later, are people beginning to question whether there's anything beneath that smile.

I see the same thing in my business, which is full of people who talk a good game but don't deliver. When Trump Tower became successful, a lot of developers got the idea of imitating our atrium, and they ordered their architects to come up with a design. The drawings would come back, and they would start costing out the job.

What they discovered is that the bronze escalators were going to cost a million dollars extra, and the waterfall was going to cost two million dollars, and the marble was going to cost many millions more. They saw that it all added up to many millions of dollars, and all of a sudden these people with these great ambitions would decide, well, let's forget about the atrium.

The dollar always talks in the end.

Acknowledgments

Now that the *Wisdom* series has expanded to a third collection with a fourth on its way, I am more than ever indebted to Ruth Mills, my editor at John Wiley & Sons. Continued thanks to Ed Knappman, my agent, for taking care of the fine print.

I am eternally grateful to my family. Diana, my wife, and Pierson, Alex, and Julia, my children, continue to motivate me to work harder (if it's not another pair of shoes, it's something from a toy catalog). Be patient, kids—now that I've done an anthology on investing, I'm hoping to truly reap the rewards, but at the moment, the stock market is facing a great deal of uncertainty.

Thanks also to Rachel Masters for helping with research, to Dave Silberstein for throwing a few good nuggets my way, and to the folks at North Market Street Graphics, who do a great job cleaning up after me.

Notes

The biographical sketches were drawn from the following sources:

Roger W. Babson:
Babson, Roger W. *Actions and Reactions*. New York: Harper & Brothers Publishers, 1935.
Babson, Roger W. *Business Barometers and Investment*. New York: Harper & Brothers Publishers, 1952.
Fisher, Kenneth L. *100 Minds That Made the Market*. Woodside, CA: Business Classics, 1993.

Bernard M. Baruch:
Baruch, Bernard M. *Baruch: My Own Story*. New York: Henry Holt and Company, 1957.
Grant, James. *Bernard M. Baruch: The Adventures of a Wall Street Legend*. New York: Simon & Schuster, 1983.

Arnold Bernhard:
Bernhard, Arnold. *The Evaluation of Common Stocks*. New York: Simon and Schuster, 1959.
"Arnold Bernhard is Dead at 86." *The New York Times:* December 23, 1987.

Peter L. Bernstein:
"Betting on the Market" from *Frontline* interview on PBS, 1998.
The Editors of Institutional Investor. *The Way It Was: An Oral History of Finance: 1967–1987*. New York: William Morrow and Company, 1988.

John C. Bogle:
Bogle, John C. *Bogle on Mutual Funds*. Burr Ridge, IL: Irwin Professional Publishing, 1994.
Spears, Gregory. "The First Family of Frugality." *Kiplinger's Personal Finance Magazine:* September 1996.

Warren E. Buffett:
Hagstrom, Robert G. *The Warren Buffett Way: Investment Strategies of the World's Greatest Investor.* New York: John Wiley & Sons, 1995.

Philip Carret:
Train, John. *The New Money Masters.* New York: Harper & Row, 1989.
"Lessons from the Investor Whom Warren Buffett Admires Most . . . Philip Carret." *Bottom Line Personal:* November 1, 1996.
Wyatt, Edward. "Philip Carret, Money Manager, Dies at 101." *The New York Times:* May 30, 1998.

Henry Clews:
Clews, Henry. *Fifty Years in Wall Street.* New York: Irving Publishing Company, 1908
Clews, Henry. *The Wall Street Point of View.* Silver, Burdett and Company, 1900.

Abby Joseph Cohen:
Bianco, Anthony. "The Prophet of Wall Street." *Business Week:* June 1, 1998.
Current Biography: June 1998. New York: H. W. Wilson Company.

Arthur Crump:
Crump, Arthur. *The Theory of Stock Exchange Speculation.* London: Longmans, Green, Reader & Dyer, 1874.
Duguid, Charles. *The Story of the Stock Exchange: It's History and Position.* London: Grant Richards, 1901.

Charles H. Dow:
Wendt, Lloyd. *The Wall Street Journal: The Story of Dow Jones & the Nation's Business Newspaper.* New York: Rand McNally & Company, 1982.

Daniel Drew:
Clews, Henry. *Fifty Years in Wall Street.* New York: Irving Publishing Company, 1908.
Gordon, John Steele. *The Scarlet Woman of Wall Street.* New York: Weidenfeld & Nicolson, 1988.
White, Bouck. *The Book of Drew.* George H. Doran, 1910.

Philip Fisher:
Michaels, James W. "Are You Doing Things Your Rivals Haven't Yet Figured Out?" *Forbes:* September 23, 1996.
Train, John. *The Money Masters.* New York: Harper & Row, Publishers, 1980.

B. C. Forbes:

Winans, Christopher. *Malcolm Forbes: The Man Who Had Everything*. New York: St. Martin's Press, 1990.

Jones, Arthur. *Malcolm Forbes: Peripatetic Millionaire*. New York: Harper & Row, Publishers, 1977.

W. W. Fowler:

Fowler, W. W. *Ten Years in Wall Street*. Hartford, CT: Worthington, Dustin & Co., 1870.

Werner, Walter, and Steven T. Smith. *Wall Street*. New York: Columbia University Press, 1991.

Mario Gabelli:

Armour, Lawrence A. "Super Mario's Super Slump." *Fortune:* April 28, 1997.

Edgarton, Jerry. "Value-Oriented Mario Gabelli Still Invests by the Numbers." *Money:* August 1986.

Goldberg, Steven T. "Will Super Mario Gabelli Regain His Touch? Bet on It, He Says." *Kiplinger's Personal Finance Magazine:* May 1997.

Tanous, Peter J. *Investment Gurus*. New York: New York Institute of Finance, 1997.

J. Paul Getty:

Getty, J. Paul. *As I See It*. Englewood Cliffs, NJ: Prentice-Hall, 1976.

Lenzner, Robert. *The Great Getty*. New York: Crown Publishers, 1985.

Benjamin Graham:

Graham, Benjamin. *Benjamin Graham: Memoirs of the Dean of Wall Street*. New York: McGraw-Hill, 1996.

James Grant:

Grant, James. *Minding Mister Market: Ten Years on Wall Street with Grant's Interest Rate Observer*. New York: Farrar Straus Giroux, 1993.

"The Talk of the Town." *The New Yorker:* January 13, 1997.

Joseph E. Granville:

Brammer, Rhonda. "Fallen Prophet." *Barron's:* August 24, 1992.

William Peter Hamilton:

Bishop, George W., Jr. *Charles H. Dow and the Dow Theory*. New York: Appleton-Century-Crofts, Inc., 1960.

Wendt, Lloyd. *The Wall Street Journal: The Story of Dow Jones & the Nation's Business Newspaper*. New York: Rand McNally & Company, 1982.

Edward C. Johnson, II:
"Edward Johnson 2d." *The New York Times:* April 4, 1984.
Johnson, Edward C, III. "Adventures of a Contrarian." *Daedalus: Journal of the American Academy of Arts and Sciences:* Spring 1996.

Otto Kahn:
Kobler, John. *Otto the Magnificent: The Life of Otto Kahn.* New York: Charles Scribner's Sons, 1988.

Stanley Kroll:
Kroll, Stanley. "Trading from a Boat." *Futures:* August 1987.
Train, John. *The Money Masters.* New York: Harper & Row, Publishers, 1980.

Edwin Lefèvre:
Fisher, Kenneth L. *100 Minds That Made the Market.* Woodside, CA: Business Classics, 1993.
Lefèvre, Edwin. *Reminiscences of a Stock Operator.* New York: John Wiley & Sons, 1994.

Gerald M. Loeb:
Fisher, Kenneth L. *100 Minds That Made the Market.* Woodside, CA: Business Classics, 1993.
"Gerald Loeb, Broker, Sold Holdings Before '29 Crash." *The New York Times:* April 16, 1974.
Loeb, Gerald. *The Battle for Investment Survival.* New York: John Wiley & Sons, 1996.

Peter Lynch:
Current Biography Yearbook, 1994. New York: H. W. Wilson Company.
Spragins, Ellyn E. "Hard Times for the Mutual Fund King." *Newsweek:* April 10, 1995.

Leo Melamed:
Melamed, Leo, with Bob Tamarkin. *Escape to the Futures.* New York: John Wiley & Sons, 1996.

Charles E. Merrill and E. A. Pierce:
Current Biography 1956. New York: H. W. Wilson Company.
Sobel, Robert. "The People's Choice: How Charles Merrill Brought Wall Street to Main Street." *Barron's:* February 17, 1997.

Paul F. Miller, Jr.:
The Editors of Institutional Investor. *The Way It Was: An Oral History of Finance: 1967–1987.* New York: William Morrow and Company, Inc., 1988.

John Moody:

Copley, F. B. "John Moody." *American Magazine:* April 1914.

Singleton, John. "Stories of Winning and Losing in Wall Street." *The American Magazine:* June 1920.

Thomas, Dana L. *The Plungers and the Peacocks.* New York: G. P. Putnam's Sons, 1967.

Laura Pedersen:

Pedersen, Laura, with F. Peter Model. *Play Money: My Brilliant Career on Wall Street.* New York: Crown Publishing, 1991.

Owings, Julie A. "Play Money: My Brief But Brilliant Career on Wall Street" (book review). *Business Credit:* January 1992.

T. Boone Pickens, Jr.:

Pickens, T. Boone. *Boone.* Boston: Houghton Mifflin Company, 1987.

Robert R. Prechter:

Brimelow, Peter. "Skirts Up, Stocks Down." *Forbes:* January 3, 1994.

Grimes, Millard. "Whatever Happened to Robert Prechter?" *Georgia Trend:* August 1994.

Wandycz, Katazyna. "Music for Bears to Dance By." *Forbes:* November 11, 1991.

Jim Rogers:

Rogers, Jim. *Investment Biker: On the Road with Jim Rogers.* New York: Random House, 1994.

Train, John. *The New Money Masters.* New York: Harper & Row, Publishers, 1989.

Fred Schwed, Jr.:

"Fred Schwed, Jr., Writer of Humor." *The New York Times:* May 11, 1996.

Schwed, Jr., Fred. *Where Are the Customers' Yachts?* New York: John Wiley & Sons, 1995.

Edward H. H. Simmons:

Fisher, Kenneth L. *100 Minds That Made the Market.* Woodside, CA: Business Classics, 1993.

Sobel, Robert. *N.Y.S.E.: A History of the New York Stock Exchange 1935–1975.* New York: Weybright and Talley, 1975.

Simmons, E. H. H. "What the Swindler Steals Besides Money." *Collier's:* May 16, 1925.

Adam Smith (George J. W. Goodman):

Contemporary Authors, New Revision Series, vol. 31. Detroit, MI: Gale Research Co., 1981.

Smith, Adam. *The Money Game.* New York: Random House, 1967.

George Soros:
Soros, George, with Byron Wien and Krisztina Koenen. *Soros on Soros: Staying Ahead of the Curve.* New York: John Wiley & Sons, 1995.
Train, John. *The New Money Masters.* New York: Harper & Row, Publishers, 1989.

Michael H. Steinhardt:
Meyer, Marsha, and Jeanne L. Reid and Walter Updegrave. "The Best Investors of Our Time." *Money:* Fall 1987.
Moody, John. "A Farewell to Hedges." *Time:* October 23, 1995.
The Editors of Institutional Investor. *The Way It Was: An Oral History of Finance: 1967–1987.* New York: William Morrow and Company, Inc., 1988.

Sir John Templeton:
Jaffe, Thomas. "A Talk with John Templeton." *Forbes:* January 25, 1988.
Minard, Lawrence. "The Principle of Maximum Pessimism." *Forbes:* January 16, 1995.
Train, John. *The Money Masters.* New York: Harper & Row, Publishers, 1980.

Donald J. Trump:
Barrett, Wayne. *Trump: The Deals and the Downfall.* New York: Harper-Collins, 1992
Trump, Donald, with Kate Bohner. *Trump: The Art of the Comeback.* New York: Times Books, 1997.

Frank A. Vanderlip:
Forbes, B. C. *Men Who Are Making America.* New York: B. C. Forbes Publishing Co., 1917.
Vanderlip, Frank. *From Farm Boy to Financier.* D. Appleton-Century Co., 1935.

Richard Whitney:
Sobel, Robert. *N.Y.S.E.: A History of the New York Stock Exchange 1935–1975.* New York: Weybright and Talley, 1975.
"When It's a Man, Wall Street Doesn't Gamble." *The Business Week:* January 15, 1930.
Woolf, F. J. "The Man Behind the Ticker." *World's Work:* March 1931.

Ellen Douglas Williamson:
Contemporary Authors, New Revisions Series, vol. 39. Detroit, MI: Gale Research Co., 1981.
"Ellen Douglas Williamson." *New York Times:* October 2, 1984.
Williamson, Ellen Douglas. *Wall Street Made Easy.* New York: Doubleday, 1965.

Martin E. Zweig:

Donnelly, Douglas J. *The Money Monarchs: The Secrets of 10 of America's Best Investment Managers*. Burr Ridge, IL: Business One Irwin, 1994.

Zweig, Martin. *Winning on Wall Street*. New York: Warner Books, 1986.

Credits and Sources

"Three Different Stock Market Movements" by Roger W. Babson, from *Bonds and Stocks: Elements of Successful Investing.* Published by Babson Statistical Organization, Wellesley Hills, MA, 1912.

"Does a Stock Market Slump Mean a Business Slide-Off?" by Bernard M. Baruch, from *System: The Magazine of Business*, July 1926.

"The Valuation of Listed Stocks" by Arnold Bernhard, reprinted with permission from *Financial Analysts Journal*, March/April 1949. Copyright © 1949, Financial Analysts Federation, Charlottesville, VA. All rights reserved.

"Is Investing for the Long Term Theory or Just Mumbo-Jumbo?" by Peter L. Bernstein, from the *Journal of Post Keynesian Economics*, Spring 1993. Reprinted by permission of M. E. Sharpe Publishers.

"A Mandate for Fund Shareholders" from *Bogle on Mutual Funds* by John C. Bogle. Copyright © 1993 by John C. Bogle. Reprinted by permission of The McGraw-Hill Companies.

"Track Record Is Everything" by Warren E. Buffett, from *Across the Board*, October 1991. Reprinted by permission of The Conference Board.

"When Speculation Becomes Investment" from *Art of Speculation* by Philip Carret. Published by *Barron's*, 1930.

"The Study of the Stock Market" from *The Wall Street Point of View* by Henry Clews. Published by Silver, Burdett and Company, 1900.

"A Fundamental Strength" by Abby Joseph Cohen, from the *Financial Times*, December 2, 1996. Reprinted by permission of Goldman, Sachs & Company.

"The Importance of Special Knowledge" from *The Theory of Stock Exchange Speculation* by Arthur Crump. Published by Longmans, Green, Reader & Dyer, London, 1874.

"Booms and Busts" by Charles H. Dow, from *The Wall Street Journal*, April 24, 1899; June 8, 1901; and August 31, 1901.

"The People Factor" from *Common Stocks and Uncommon Profits & Other Writings* by Philip Fisher. Copyright © 1958 by Philip Fisher. Reprinted by permission of John Wiley & Sons.

"Wall Street Millionaires" from *Finance, Business and the Business of Life* by B. C. Forbes. Published in 1915.

"The Stock Exchange" from *Ten Years In Wall Street* by W. W. Fowler. Published by Worthington, Dustin & Co., Hartford, CT, 1870.

"Grand Slam Hitting" by Mario Gabelli, from *Barron's*, May 20, 1996. Reprinted by permission of *Barron's*. Copyright © 1996 by Dow Jones & Company, Inc.

"The Wall Street Investor" by J. Paul Getty copyright © by HMH Publishing Co., Inc. Reprinted from *How to Be Rich* by J. Paul Getty. Permission granted by The Berkeley Publishing Group, a member of Penguin Putnam Inc. All rights reserved.

"The Art of Hedging" by Benjamin Graham, from *The Magazine of Wall Street*, February 7, 1920.

"Michael Milken, Meet Sewell Avery" by James Grant, from *Forbes*, October 23, 1989. Reprinted by permission of *Forbes* magazine. Copyright © Forbes, Inc., 1989.

"Market Movements" from *Granville's New Key to Stock Market Profits* by Joseph E. Granville. Copyright © 1963. Reprinted with permission of Prentice Hall.

"The Dow Theory" from *The Stock Market Barometer* by William Peter Hamilton. Published by Harper and Brothers Publishers, 1922.

"Contrary Opinion in Stock Market Techniques" by Edward C. Johnson, II, from a speech delivered before the First Annual Contrary Opinion Foliage Forum, 1963. Reprinted by permission of FMR Corp.

"The New York Stock Exchange and Public Opinion" by Otto Kahn, from a speech delivered before the Association of Stock Exchange Brokers, New York, January 24, 1917.

"How to Win Big and Lose Small" by Stanley Kroll, from *Futures*, May 1984. Reprinted by permission of *Futures*.

"Vanished Billions" by Edwin Lefèvre, from *The Saturday Evening Post*, February 13, 1932.

"Importance of Correct Timing" reprinted with the permission of Simon & Schuster from *The Battle for Investment Survival* by Gerald M. Loeb. Copyright renewed © 1993 by H. Harvey Scholten.

"Stalking the Tenbagger" reprinted with the permission of Simon & Schuster from *One Up On Wall Street* by Peter Lynch. Copyright © 1989 by Peter Lynch.

Chronology

491

Author Index

Index